The Old Farmer's Almanac

Calculated on a new and improved plan for the year of our Lord

1995

Being 3rd after LEAP YEAR and (until July 4)
219th year of American Independence

FITTED FOR BOSTON AND THE NEW ENGLAND STATES, WITH SPECIAL
CORRECTIONS AND CALCULATIONS TO ANSWER FOR ALL THE UNITED STATES.

Containing, besides the large number of Astronomical Calculations
and the Farmer's Calendar for every month in the year, a variety of

NEW, USEFUL, AND ENTERTAINING MATTER.

ESTABLISHED IN 1792

by Robert B. Thomas

Age appears best in four things:
old wood to burn,
old wine to drink,
old friends to trust,
and old authors to read.

– FRANCIS BACON

COVER T.M. REGISTERED
IN U.S. PATENT OFFICE
ISSN 0078-4516
LIBRARY OF CONGRESS
CARD NO. 56-29681

Address all editorial correspondence to

THE OLD FARMER'S ALMANAC, DUBLIN, NH 03444

CONTENTS

Features

12
Consumer
Tastes & Trends
for 1995

28
The
Practical Pepper
Primer

46
Every 17 Years,
Like Clockwork

page 46

80
The Revolution That
Began on Tuesday,
October 23, 1945

page 80

(continued on page 4)

Index of Charts, Tables, Forecasts, and Departments

1 Heatwave Hybrid. Sets fruit in the hottest weather!

2 Big Girl® Hybrid VF. Perfect for slicing or wedges.

3 Supersteak Hybrid VFN. Extra-meaty 1-2 lb. fruits.

4 Super Sweet 100 Hybrid. Long season, extra sweet.

5 Early Girl Hybrid. Produces fruit early and often.

6 Delicious. Its seed grew the world's largest tomato!

7 Long-Keeper. Keeps up to five months!

8 Viva Italia Hybrid. Tastes great fresh and in sauces.

9 Gardener's Delight. An old time favorite.

10 Tumbler Hybrid. Very early, great for containers!

11 Yellow Pear. Mild and pleasing, great for salads.

12 Celebrity Hybrid. Great flavor, disease resistant.

12 Juicy Reasons to Send for Burpee's <u>FREE</u> 1995 Catalogue!

Tomatoes! Burpee's 1995 Garden Catalogue features 26 different tomato varieties! Early ones, late ones, big beauties and bite-sized gems. All packed full of garden-fresh flavor and *guaranteed* to satisfy. You will be able to choose from over 300 varieties of vegetables and over 400 varieties of flowers. Your new catalogue will arrive in early January.

☐ YES! Send me my FREE 1995 Burpee Catalogue

☐ Mr.
☐ Mrs. _____
☐ Ms.

Address _____

City _____ State _____ Zip _____

Please mail to:
Burpee, 002956 Burpee Building, Warminster, PA 18974

© 1994 W. Atlee Burpee & Co.

BURPEE®

CONTENTS

The Old Farmer's Almanac • 1995

Don't Buy a Big Tiller

For a Small Job

If your garden is an acre or more, you may want to buy a big tiller. If it's any less, you should buy a Mantis Tiller/ Cultivator.

Big tillers till and weed 20" or more wide. The Mantis tills and weeds a practical 6" to 9" wide.

Big tillers weight almost 300 lbs. The Mantis weights just 20 lbs.!

Costs Hundreds Less!

Most big tillers were designed to just till. The Mantis was designed from the beginning to precisely match a small, powerful engine to a variety of useful attachments for your yard and garden. Tiller. Cultivator. Furrower. Edger. Lawn Aerator. Lawn Dethatcher. Hedge Trimmer. Crevice Cleaner.

Most big tillers cost an arm and a leg. Despite the fact that the Mantis is a tough, durable, precision instrument...it costs a fraction of what you'll pay for a big tiller.

Two Year Warranty

All components are warranted against defects in materials or workmanship for a period of two full years. All Mantis tines are **guaranteed against breakage forever.**

- **Just 20 lbs. - but all muscle.**
- **Easily weeds an average garden in 20 minutes.**
- **Does so many jobs...from lawn care to trimming...and more!**
- **Lightweight. Easy to handle.**
- **Early order bonus (if you hurry).**
- **All tines guaranteed forever against breakage.**
- **NO-RISK One Year Trial.**

Call toll-free 1-800-366-6268 or mail coupon today!

We're Changing the Way Americans Garden.®

The Mantis Promise

Try any product that you buy directly from Mantis with NO RISK! If you're not completely satisfied, send it back to us within one year for a complete no hassle refund.

To PATRONS

First of all, our thanks to all the hundreds of you from all over the United States and Canada who wrote us this past year with questions, criticism, comments, and advice. We received more mail than ever in our history.

Following a tradition begun by our first editor, Robert B. Thomas, we tried to answer every one. But, unlike Thomas, we replied with letters or postals. During Thomas's 54 years at the helm (1792-1846), this "To Patrons" section, then titled "Acknowledgments to Patrons and Correspondents," served as the vehicle for Thomas's replies. It's difficult to imagine people today being as patient with that process. The reader who wrote Thomas in the summer of 1802, for instance, asking how to make "hop beer" and raise "white clover seed" was required to wait until the 1804 edition came out in the fall of 1803 for the answers. Like today, people wanted information — but apparently they weren't in a big hurry for it.

They also must have been thicker-skinned than we are because Thomas's replies were often pretty blunt. "M. C.'s hints are unintelligible and futile," he wrote in 1808 (he used readers' initials only). In the 1830 edition: "J. B.'s riddle is rather stale." In the next paragraph, perhaps thinking he'd been overly harsh on J. B., he added he might nonetheless use his submitted riddle the following year "should not a better one be offered."

After Thomas's death in 1846, subsequent editors took over these pages in his name. During the late 19th and early 20th centuries, several editors ignored the tradition, but the 11th editor, Robb Sagendorph, reestablished it with an added tongue-in-cheek, "can-you-top-this" style that readers obviously enjoyed. Their questions became less serious. In 1949, for instance, when a "Lulu B." asked Sagendorph "the actual number of snowflakes which fell in New England during the month of December 1947," he happily replied in kind: "Our count for that month is inaccurate inasmuch as several of the flakes which fell on the eastern side of Mount Mansfield in Vermont became mixed up with a number of others which had blown up from the ground and had thus been already counted."

There were, of course, lots of letters to do with last winter's weather. Many pointed out that our forecast for the cold, snowy January 1994 in New England and much of the Northeast was, well, let's say somewhat short of perfect. True enough. We're adding some important elements to this coming January's Northeast forecast and this time we think we'll be pretty close to the mark. We'll see. However, one of our favorite letters, from J. P. D. of Derry, New Hampshire, said our January 1994 forecast was indeed "perfect" after all! "Your forecast for January 21-24 said it would be sunny and very mild," she wrote, "so we decided on January 22nd as our wedding day. It was sunny and cold — but warmer than it had been all month. So to me it was perfect. Thank you."

S. G. of Brooklyn, New York, suggested we drop the word "Old" from our title in order to dispel the notion that *The Old Farmer's Almanac* is a publication "only for curmudgeons with wind-cracked faces and soil-filled broken fingernails." Problem is, S. G., that the word

The 1995 Edition of

THE OLD FARMER'S ALMANAC

Established in 1792 and published every year thereafter

ROBERT B. THOMAS *(1766-1846)*

FOUNDER

EDITOR *(12th since 1792)*: JUDSON D. HALE SR.

MANAGING EDITOR: SUSAN PEERY

EXECUTIVE EDITOR: TIM CLARK

ART DIRECTOR: MARGO LETOURNEAU

WEATHER PROGNOSTICATOR: DR. RICHARD HEAD

ASTRONOMER: DR. GEORGE GREENSTEIN

COPY EDITOR: LIDA STINCHFIELD

ASSOCIATE EDITORS: MARE-ANNE JARVELA,
DEBRA SANDERSON

ASSISTANT EDITORS: ANNA LARSON,
JODY SAVILLE, MARY SHELDON

ARCHIVIST: LORNA TROWBRIDGE

CONTRIBUTING EDITORS: CASTLE FREEMAN JR.,
Farmer's Calendar; FRED SCHAAF, *Astronomy;*
JAMIE KAGELEIRY

PRODUCTION DIRECTOR: JAMIE TROWBRIDGE

PRODUCTION MANAGER: PAUL BELLIVEAU

PRODUCTION ASSISTANT: CLARE INNES

SENIOR PRODUCTION ARTISTS: LUCILLE RINES,
DAVID ZIARNOWSKI

PRODUCTION ARTIST: CHRIS SIMARD

PRODUCTION SYSTEMS COORDINATOR: STEVE MUSKIE

GROUP PUBLISHER: JOHN PIERCE

PUBLISHER *(23rd since 1792)*: SHERIN WIGHT

ADMINISTRATIVE ASSISTANT: SARAH DANFORTH

MAIL ORDER MARKETING MANAGER: DEB WALSH

SPECIAL MARKETS DIRECTOR: RONDA KNOWLTON

MARKETING RESEARCH MANAGER:
MARTHA BENINTENDE

ADVERTISING PRODUCTION: RITA TROUBALOS,
Manager; STACY CHANSKY, LORI HILL

NEWSSTAND CIRCULATION:
KEMCO PUBLISHERS SERVICES

EDITORIAL, ADVERTISING, AND PUBLISHING OFFICES:
P.O. BOX 520, DUBLIN, NH 03444

PHONE: 603-563-8111 • FAX: 603-563-8252

YANKEE PUBLISHING INC., MAIN ST., DUBLIN, NH 03444

JOSEPH B. MEAGHER, *President;* JUDSON D. HALE SR.,
Senior Vice President; BRIAN PIANI, *Vice President* and *Chief
Financial Officer;* JODY BUGBEE, BROOKS FISHER, JAMES
H. FISHMAN, JOHN PIERCE, and JOE TIMKO, *Vice Presidents.*
The Old Farmer's Almanac cannot accept responsibility for
unsolicited manuscripts and will not return any manuscripts
that do not include a stamped and addressed return envelope.

"Old" has been part of the copyrighted title since 1858, and besides, although everything in the Almanac is brand-new each year, it nonetheless is the oldest continuously published periodical on the North American continent.

J. L. C. of Arroyo Grande, California, wrote to say she was about to have an operation and did we know the best time to spay female dogs so that they don't gain weight afterward, and do our animal Moon-phase charts for such things work on people? Oh, dear. Well, maybe the best answer is to refer to a letter from D. P. H. of Colorado Springs who, after admonishing us to not recommend (as we did last year) using cheap shampoo on dogs, said that "dogs ain't people ain't dogs."

M. C. of Dorchester, Massachusetts, asked the name of the first U.S. president born in the United States (Martin Van Buren). And T. C. M. of Chicago, Illinois, suggested the 7,500 pounds of paper punched out of the Almanac's "hanging hole" each year be used "for gerbil nest bedding." Nice idea, T. C. M.

A good number of all these sorts of letters received last year — and every year — are addressed to Robert B. Thomas, who has, of course, been resting peacefully in the cemetery at Sterling, Massachusetts, for almost 150 years. No matter. He'd be pleased. He'd like knowing his relationship with his readers, begun on these pages 203 years ago, grows stronger with each passing annual edition. So from him, and us all . . . thanks, everyone.   *J. D. H.* (June 1994)

However, it is by our works and not our words that we would be judged. These, we hope will sustain us in the humble though proud station we have so long held in the name of,

Your ob'd servant,

Rob't. B. Thomas.

CONSUMER
Tastes & Trends
FOR 1995

by Jamie Kageleiry

GOOD NEWS

Generosity Is in Style

☞ Since 1959, the year the Trust for Philanthropy started tracking **charitable giving** in America, the total money given each year has risen. Even during the eighties, the supposed "decade of greed," giving grew faster than the economy. In 1992, the last year tabulated, Americans gave $124.3 billion to charity (and only 11.5 percent of it came from foundations and corporations). That's about $450 from every man, woman, and child in the country.

Bowling Scores Are Expected to Rise

☞ . . . thanks to a better bowling ball. Science has dedicated its efforts to producing a **high-tech** bowling ball, called a "reactive" ball. A resin additive allows for better reaction on lanes, which means the ball "grabs" the wood lane and "hooks" harder into the

pins, and that means more strikes for bowlers.

The Land of the Fat-Free

☞ In 1960 North Americans were eating **diets** that were 40 percent fat. That number has fallen to 34 percent, and cholesterol levels have fallen along with fat intake.

Where to Go for Help

☞ Rochester, New York, was found to be the "most helpful" of 36 large American cities in a study conducted by the magazine *American Demographics.*

In Rochester, apparently, more people **helped strangers** (researchers) who dropped pens, asked directions, and pretended they were blind while crossing the street.

BAD NEWS

☞ The weight of the average young American (between the ages of 25 and 30) has **risen** ten pounds since 1986. Given the drop in cholesterol levels and total fat intake, this finding has surprised researchers.

YOU'RE NOT PARANOID IF . . .

☞ Does it ever seem as if all the good weather is midweek and all the bad weather gangs up on the weekend? Don't feel paranoid: Scientists now say it's true. Weekdays are warmer. By at least .04 degree Fahrenheit. Climatologists believe it's due to the increase in pollutants ("human-induced heat activity" like cars and factory smoke) in the air on weekdays.

INVITE OUR FAMILY TO YOUR HOUSE . . .

AND YOU'LL NEVER HAVE SEPTIC SYSTEM PROBLEMS AGAIN!

(You'll Save Big Bucks, Too!)

Vigilant's family of products has been around for a long time. In fact, *we've been keeping septic systems clean since 1954!*

Our products are **safe:** for you, the environment, pets, and shrubbery. We were pioneers in helping nature clean itself. We grow specially mutated bacteria and specially designed enzymes to keep your environment clean, sanitary, and livable. You may have heard of other products on the market. But make the smart choice: *Vigilant is proud to be the manufacturer of the* **original** *and* **best** *product and the* **most complete** *septic system maintenance program.*

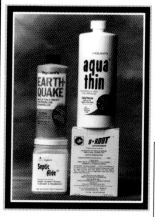

Vigilant's "family portrait"

Earthquake® ... Soil conditioner strong enough to punch through even the toughest sludge buildup. Can save you thousands of $ in drainfield replacement costs.

Septic Aide® ... Cleans septic tanks and systems automatically and safely. The original product!

Aqua Thin® ... Dries up smelly, soggy drainfields fast...and *keeps them dry!*

D-Root™ ... Root destroyer is your *best, safest,* and *cheapest* insurance against pipe damage caused by roots and root hairs.

Products also available separately at regular price. Ask for our free booklet on septic system maintenance. Other products available!

Vigilant Products ℠

VIGILANT'S ONE-YEAR SEPTIC SYSTEM MAINTENANCE PROGRAM...

Totally eliminates septic system problems! In fact, we guarantee it.* **Get with the Program!**

Includes: 2 bottles Aqua Thin, 1 bottle Earthquake, 1 container Septic Aide (optional Program with 2 lbs. D-Root)

Total Regular Price: $49.80; with 2 lbs. D-Root: $59.75
Our Usual Special Maintenance Program Offer: $44.95; with 2 lbs. D-Root: $49.95

A RED-HOT OFFER FOR YOU!
SAVE AN EXTRA $5.00!
ONE-YEAR PROGRAM: $39.95
WITH 2 LBS. D-ROOT: $44.95

To order...or for more information...call toll-free: 1-800-526-9842. In New Jersey, call collect: 201-744-8400. We welcome MasterCard and Visa.

Or order by mail: Vigilant Products Co., Inc., 24 Woodland Ave., Glen Ridge, NJ 07028. Please make check payable to Vigilant Products.

Shipping and handling (US only) : Basic kit, $6.00; with D-Root, $7.00
NJ residents: Add 6% sales tax.

*We guarantee that Vigilant's Septic System Maintenance Program will perform as indicated in our product descriptions, used as directed. You must be completely satisfied or **we will refund your full purchase price** *(proof of purchase is all we need).*

Vig OFA/HH/GC 94

What's Good for You in 1995

☞ **Mozart** — Not only is it nice to listen to, but Mozart can make you **smarter**, too. Researchers in California found that students taking tests after listening to Mozart's Sonata for Two Pianos in D Major scored eight or nine IQ points higher than after two other "listening conditions" (a relaxation tape and silence). Unfortunately, the effects lasted only about ten minutes.

☞ **Cranberry Juice** — Women have often thought so, but now it's official: Cranberry juice kills **bacteria** that cause urinary-tract infections. (Doctors, however, stress that cranberry juice is no substitute for antibiotics.)

☞ **Chocolate** — OK, well, maybe it's not exactly good for you, but it's not as bad as we used to think. For some reason (there is a God!), the highly saturated **cocoa butter** that makes chocolate chocolate spares blood vessels. And, to make matters even sweeter, studies have concluded that chocolate does not cause acne.

☞ **A Positive Attitude** — Are your teenagers acting surly and insolent? Researchers at Ohio State and the University of Arizona say that maybe you ought to take a good look at yourself, rather than just endlessly grounding your offspring. It seems that parents use more and more **negative expressions**, in arguments as well as in conversation, as their children grow from childhood to adolescence. The kids seem more bothered by the parents' negative outlook than the parents are by the children's surliness.

Some Costs of Living in 1995

☞ **$6,000** A Japanese designer fountain pen made by Pilot Pen, adorned with traditional Japanese hand-painted scenes.

☞ **$250,000** Cost for a regular citizen to be mummified in Moscow (at the lab in charge of preserving Lenin's body).

☞ **$334,600** Cost to bring up a baby born this year to age 18 for parents earning over $55,000 in 1995 (not including college).

New Answers to Old Questions

☞ Where does all the **luggage** the airlines lose end up? At the "Unclaimed Baggage Center" in Scottsboro, Alabama, where it's sold. Some people have reportedly found and bought back their own missing goods!

☞ Didn't Columbus introduce European **diseases** to the New World? Not tuberculosis. TB was found in the body of a 1,000-year-old woman in Peru, leading scientists at the National Academy of Sciences to conclude that the plague was here before the Europeans.

☞ Why can't we go **swimming** after eating? We can! Though many "old wives' tales" are true (chicken soup really does help the congestion of a cold), many aren't. Normal meals should not cause any problems for swimmers, reported *The Berkeley Wellness Letter.*

(continued on page 18)

"Warmth Technology" Makes Feet Warmer, Drier

Nearly 100 years ago, Kaufman Footwear created its distinctive Sorel pac boot – combining natural rubber bottoms and leather uppers. Later a removable liner was added to provide more insulation and warmth. Now Sorel has combined years of experience with technological advances to create the best possible insulation system for your feet: ThermoPlus 100.

This new liner system is the result of years of design refinement and testing under extreme Arctic conditions. ThermoPlus 100 boots combine a liner and insoles that will keep feet warm and dry to temperatures as low as -100 degrees F. (-74C.). The inner removable liner provides insulation, moisture absorption, and heat reflection, while a series of insoles trap body heat and actually create warmth inside the boot. The ThermoPlus 100 liner system is composed of:

• *a 1/2-inch felt liner that, in addition to providing insulation, draws perspiration away from the foot to prevent chilling. It also reflects the body's heat back into the boot for another source of warmth.*

• *a pair of insoles beneath the liner: one further absorbs perspiration and reflects body heat, while the other acts as a "furnace" inside the boot. Once warmed by the body, this insole continues to heat the foot.*

Altogether, the ThermoPlus 100 liner system provides one inch of insulation, yet remains lightweight.

The Sorel ThermoPlus 100 concept is unique to Kaufman Footwear and is the most advanced development in Warmth Technology for boots, whether for hunting, hiking, winter sports, or around the yard – wherever your feet take you in the great outdoors.

I'll send you $5.00 FREE if you don't agree my ALL NATURAL beer is better than any commercial beer you've ever tasted.

Hello, my name is Tom Lee, President of Bierhaus International, Inc.

If you're tired of paying $12-$18 a case for beer, I don't blame you.

That's why I'd like to show you an amazing *new* way to brew your own superb lager for as little as $4.56 per case. You actually SAVE up to $10 on EACH CASE OF BEER. And wait until you taste the beer. Compare it to the finest premium beers. Referring to this method of making beer, the *New York Times* stated, "..the quality of the beer may surprise many people. Wait two to four weeks and friends may be placing orders."

The secret is in an anaerobic mini-brewery that lets YOU make up to 6 gallons of ALL NATURAL BEER, using only the finest barley malt and hops. No chemicals. No preservatives. You can brew several cases of beer in about 25-30 minutes. And everything you'll need (except the bottles and a little household sugar) comes with your mini-brewery.

IS IT EASY TO MAKE?

Using the Bierhaus Mini-Brewery, you can brew beer in just 27 minutes on your kitchen stove. Let it ferment for seven days, bottle it, and you're done. Aging takes 3-5 weeks.

• No more late night trips to the carryout
• No more lugging back empty beer cases in the trunk of your car
• No more chemistry set taste.
• No more standing in line to pay $12-$18 per case of beer.

Just brew what you need when you need it... for as little as 19 cents a bottle.

WHAT ABOUT ALCOHOLIC CONTENT?

You can make a super light beer (1.8%-2% alcohol), regular strength (4.5%-5%), or a European-style lager, ranging as high as 7.5% alcohol.

CAN I MAKE DIFFERENT KINDS OF BEER?

Certainly. Just vary the ingredients and recipes according to the instructions supplied with each kit. You can make...

• LIGHT LAGER. Comparable to most Canadian premium beers and some light European lagers.

• BAVARIAN DARK LAGER. Full bodied, yet not bitter. The head is incomparable—rich and creamy.

• STOUT. Rich in body with a hearty, robust flavor. In the finest tradition of grand Irish Stouts.

• ALE. Popular with American home brewers. From England's favorite hoppy, dry "bitter" ales, to the sweeter brown ales enjoyed in fine European pubs.

IS IT LEGAL?

You can make up to 200 gallons of beer per year — tax free — and you don't need a federal license of any kind.

I realize you may still be skeptical, and I don't blame you — that's why w're offering our unheard-of **$5.00 FREE GUARANTEE.**

Try your mini-brewery. Keep it for up to 6 months. Make the beer at your leisure. If you don't agree that this is the best beer you've ever tasted in your life, we'll buy the kit back.

What's more, we'll pay the return postage (by regular UPS or Parcel Post rates) and send you an extra $5.00 for your time and trouble. No conditions. No excuses.

CUSTOMER COMMENTS

"I like your beer better than any on the market and that's the TRUTH."
—Elmer Smart, Missouri

"My friends and I had tours of duty in Europe and were looking for that "old country" flavor and body. Your Bavarian Dark has it all."—Lt. Fred Frances, Texas

"Your Continental Amber is as close to a perfect beer as I have ever consumed." —Dwayne Staner, Iowa

"I no longer wonder whether I prefer the best commercial beer or your beer which I made. NO QUESTION, YOURS IS THE BEST."
—Ed Pearson, New York

WHERE DO I GET SUPPLIES ONCE I GET THE KIT?

Just call us to reorder ingredients. Bierhaus is among the largest mail order suppliers of equipment and ingredients in the U.S.A. You can choose from over 50 different malts from countries all over the world. We also carry a wide range of brewing supplies and accessories... everything you need to brew the best beer you ever tasted.

We have sold more than 75,000 beer kits since 1978 and some of our first customers are still brewing with their original equipment. Remember, your equipment is guaranteed unconditionally for one full year from date of purchase.

Your new Bierhaus mini-brewery contains an FDA foodgrade 7½ gallon fermentation tank with lid and air lock, complete siphon unit, bottle capper and caps, bottle brush, and brewing guide—plus ingredients to make 2+ cases of beer. The ingredients will be for a rich American lager—our best selling beer. Compare it to your favorite American commercial beer.

$5.00 FREE

Serve the beer to your family and friends. If everyone doesn't agree it's far better than commercial beer, simply return the kit. I'll pay the return postage and send you a check for your full purchase price. Plus I'll send you an EXTRA $5.00 for your time and trouble.

©1994 Bierhaus International, Inc.

Bierhaus International, Inc.
3723 West 12th Street, Dept.
Erie, Pennsylvania 16505

VISA MasterCard DISCOVER

Please send me the following mini-brewery:

☐ **Basic Kit** (as described above)
$39.95 plus $7.50 s&h (UPS) continental USA only

☐ **Super Kit** (includes two fermentation tanks and double ingredients enabling you to brew up to 12 gallons— over 4 cases)
$59.95 plus $9.50 s&h (UPS) continental USA only

NAME _____
ADDRESS _____
CITY _____ STATE ___ ZIP _____
PHONE _____

☐ Check enclosed
☐ Charge to: ☐ MasterCard ☐ VISA ☐ Discover

Acct. # _____

Expires _____ (PA residents add 6% sales tax)

☎ **FOR EXTRA FAST SERVICE** Call us at **814-833-7747** from 8:30 a.m.-5:00 p.m. EST weekdays and charge to MasterCard, VISA or Discover.

The Differences Between Men and Women (in 1995)

Want to impress your significant other with **flowers**? Seventy percent of women surveyed by the American Floral Marketing Council prefer this to other gestures; only 38 percent of men say it's their favorite.

☞ Women need approximately twice as much time (almost three minutes each) in **public rest rooms** as men do (a mere 83.6 seconds). Relief is on the way in the form of "Potty Parity" bills swiftly being passed in state capitols around the country, decreeing that public arenas of a certain size must contain twice as many facilities for women as men.

☞ The differences between the way men and women are portrayed in **advertising** are narrowing. Watch for men being used as sex objects: Diet Coke already features an office full of female office workers ogling a bare-from-the-waist-up construction worker. (This is progress?)

WHY DIDN'T WE THINK OF THAT BEFORE?

☞ An inventor in Detroit has figured out the silver lining to traffic: energy. Thomas Wither has designed a windmill that will be turned by the air currents from passing traffic.

☞ Reuters reported that a teacher in England has come up with a gadget that will keep bagpipers from driving their neighbors mad. With Brian Watchman-Atkinson's device, the bagpiper plays not the actual pipes when practicing, but a "chanter," a pipe that records the melody being blown. Then the machine plays back what the piper has played, but mercifully, only he hears it (using headphones). Can this machine be adapted, say, for drums?

Food Trends

We predict that **"rustic" foods** with lots of flavor and down-to-earth heartiness will be popular; **Caribbean cuisine** will continue to be hot; and **Greek food**, involving lots of tomatoes, olives, and pungent goat cheeses (not just the souvlaki you find in your local diners) will become very popular.

☞ **Neotraditionalism** — A desire for quality is showing up in the increased demand for **gourmet coffee**, specialty cheeses, and exotic vegetables and fruits.

☞ **Adventure and variety** — An increasingly diverse population and a "world-is-getting-smaller" perception have fostered an increase in the number of households trying **ethnic alternatives**.

☞ **Clear products**, so popular last year, are **out**.

☞ **Red meat** is back in favor as people tire of "being good" all the time. **Steak houses** are booming.

☞ **Newest seafood item:** salmon pastrami (fresh salmon cured pastrami-style to give it a spicy edge).

Chain-saw art — buy it now before prices really go sky-high and before too many "wanna-be" chain-saw artists flood the market. Creations range from a full-size **moose sculpture** sold (for $4,000) at the Spinning Wheel gift shop in Waterbury Center, Vermont, to the stunts of experts such as Ray Murphy of Ellsworth, Maine. Ray carves names on wooden belt buckles while the owners wear them. (Ray told *The Wall Street Journal,* "If there's any movement in that belt buckle, you're gone.")

Hobo art is another manifestation of folksiness in art. The authentic stuff was created during the Depression by men and women on the road, who used whatever materials they could find. Original sculptures (houses, boats, etc., often decorated with buttons) made of **popsicle sticks** and matchsticks fetch up to $700 in some San Francisco antique shops. Cigar-box creations can cost even more.

ƒureƒhopping:
What's Collectible in 1995?

Old computers are being snatched up at flea markets. Original Macintoshes, IBM's first PC, old disk drives. Never mind that the technology is obsolete: These soon-to-be-**hot items** are in demand the way the old Bakelite radios were — as culturally significant icons.

Ashtrays — now that so few people are smoking, ashtrays are becoming valuable as **collectibles**. Though prices are now low ($5 to $10), expect them to rise somewhat as people grab up the old chrome, copper, glass, marble, or Bakelite ashtrays.

Hammered aluminum trays, handbags, and jewelry. During the Depression, people were forced to sell their silver, and hammered aluminum became "the poor man's silver." Aluminum was used through the 1950s. Handbags get about $75, even more if stamped with the names of designers Rodney Kent, Arthur Armour, and Wendell August.

Silverplate spoons, knives, and forks allowed the Victorian masses to have large sets of **silverware**. Machines let designers go wild on the silver plate. A fancy spoon that sold for 50¢ in the 1880s can command at least $25 at flea markets.

AGRICULTURAL NEWS

☞ The crop of the future? Plastic. Bioengineers are planning to make a plastic that will biodegrade as quickly as paper: In about six weeks, it will turn to dirt. To do this, the engineers will plant corn or potatoes and replace the gene that makes starch with a gene that makes "PHB," the crucial ingredient in the biodegradable plastic. When the corn or potatoes have grown, the "plastic" will be harvested.

It's barely a trend yet, but the newest areas of growth in the country aren't cities or suburbs, but farm regions called "exurbia." People moving in (attracted by low taxes) are starting mail-order cottage industries or are employees of light and high-tech manufacturing companies that have relocated.

Here's to Your Health in 1995

There's been a lot of talk recently about losing weight by cutting fat intake. Watch for this discussion to become more detailed in the coming year. Cutting fat alone, doctors say, is no miracle diet. For instance, the portion of calories derived from **carbohydrates** rises in response to cutting fats. This can trigger diabetes in genetically predisposed people.

☞ Researchers have recently found that low intake of some **B vitamins**, especially B_6 and folic acid, may contribute significantly to heart disease. We will soon see folic acid listed as a fortification in foods.

☞ Look for **calcium** to star on the nutrient stage this year. Sure, we know it's good for our bones, but it might also be a cancer preventative and a protection against high blood pressure, says Walter Willet of the Harvard School of Public Health.

☞ The American Heart Association says, "**Vitamin E** and monounsaturated fats such as olive oil may team up to protect against hardening of the arteries."

☞ **Morning sickness.** Up to 90 percent of all pregnant women experience its symptoms — nausea, vomiting, and dry heaves. It's a mixed blessing: Because it seems to be linked to rapidly rising hormone levels, morning sickness may be a **good sign** that the pregnancy will thrive. Women who have no signs of it are two to three times more likely to miscarry than those who do. Nutritionists advise sufferers to go ahead and eat whatever

Another Myth Bites the Dust:

☞ We've always heard that sugar and artificial sweeteners make normal children run around like crazy and make "hyperactive" children completely off-the-wall. Recent studies have found no behavioral effect on children from any sweeteners.

In Case You Were Wondering...

☞ Five percent of all people in the U.S. walk to work.

☞ Americans now have close to $4 trillion in equity in their homes.

they crave, even if it's the proverbial pickles and ice cream. Once stomachs are filled and soothed, researchers found, women can usually go on to more balanced diets.

☞ There's a boom afoot in "**adult day care**" — centers for seniors who still live at home but are in need of some daily supervision and entertainment. The number of such centers has increased from 300 to 3,000 in the last decade and should triple by the turn of the century. Another trend: an alternative to nursing homes that allows patients to stay at home. They are provided with housecleaning and nursing services and physical therapy as needed in return for signing over their Medicare and Medicaid policies to the provider.

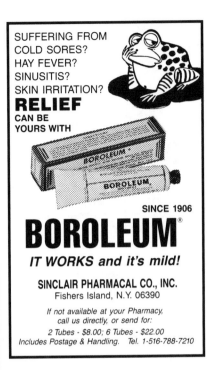
NEED A BACK ISSUE?

Most back issues of *Yankee* and *The Old Farmer's Almanac* available.
Please write to: Yankee Archives
P.O. Box 289
Dublin, NH 03444

Cultural Barometers, 1995

According to the *Fortean Times*, a magazine in London that keeps track of bizarre happenings around the world, these are truly weird times — 3.5 percent weirder than 1993, to be precise. The overall "Index of Strangeness" (which *Fortean Times* calculates by counting bizarre incidents worldwide) has risen from 3,400 to 3,520. Some of the curious incidents reported:

☞ Sixty lambs in Germany were attacked and killed by a large flock of crows.

☞ A deaf man in Sweden was cured when doctors pulled a 47-year-old bus ticket from his ear.

☞ Many of the 34 components of the index have risen sharply, including the "Strange Behavior" category, which, according to *The Wall Street Journal*, includes "people who throw birds into cars waiting at stoplights." Other sharply increasing phenomena are sightings of the Virgin Mary and of "highway ghosts." What does all this mean? The *Fortean Times* Index doesn't explain.

Demographica

In 1996, 10,000 **baby boomers** a day will turn 50. They are the first wave of the 80 million Americans born between 1946 and 1964. To whom does this matter?

☞ For one, to the makers of **hair dye**, whose products have already started flying off the shelves as boomers try to continue looking young. The year 1993 saw a 14.4 percent jump in sales.

☞ Travel-related businesses also celebrate those 10,000 daily birthdays. As more boomers head into their fifties, the population of married couples without children (or whose children have flown the nest) grows. In a reversal of a trend from the early 1990s, travel agents already report an increase in **longer vacations** (more than five days).

☞ Books about **death** are now one of the fastest-growing categories in publishing.

☞ There are 30 million **golfers** in the U.S. now. By the year 2000, there will be 20 million more.

....

Home, Sweet Home, 1995

Items or colors you may see more of in the next year:

☞ **Reclining chairs** are back in vogue, thanks to baby boomers who are deciding they'd rather have comfort zones than showplaces. It doesn't hurt, either, that the new recliners look better.

☞ **The color green** is now the most popular car color, and it is quickly gaining favor inside the home, due in part to a new environmental awareness and appreciation of nature. The other big home decor trend is called "**impoverished nobility**." This look features patchwork fabrics mixed with stripes on over-upholstered armchairs, Grandma's "treasures" dragged from the attic and mixed in with different eras. Romance is a big part of this look, and home furnishing stores are stocking up on whirring fans, velvet pillows, and curvy wicker armchairs.

Park Seed®
Flowers and Vegetables
1995

Yours
FREE!

The Big New Park Seed Catalog

"With color so real you can almost smell the beautiful flowers and taste the luscious vegetables!"

Our big, 132 page catalog is chock-full of delights for your garden . . . Artichokes to Zucchini — Ageratum to Zinnia — from the most advanced new varieties and the rare, to your long-time favorites. Here in one big color catalog you'll find over **2,100 quality products:** flower and vegetable seed, bulbs, plants and garden supplies — many available only from Park. We back each and every one with a solid guarantee of complete satisfaction.

Have more fun gardening this year with **Park High Performer® varieties** — flowers more beautiful and easier to grow, vegetables with better taste and higher yield. Park tests thousands each year to make sure you get only the best. **Send for your free copy today and let Park Help You Grow!**

Complete Satisfaction Guaranteed
"Home Garden Seed Specialists Since 1868"

The Mood

Busy, Busy, Busy

"Harried life is getting more harried," said Bradley Googins, the director of the Center for Work and Family at Boston University. Any product or service that **eases this busy-ness** will be popular. Watch, for instance, the boom in audio book sales — you can "read" while driving or doing an aerobic workout. Also, keep an eye on the popularity of **television shopping**. The change will come in the type of items offered: more upscale, trendy, high-cost, high-quality merchandise that appeals to upper-income earners who can no longer devote time to browsing through racks of clothes (or bins of CDs, which will also be offered soon).

Even **12-step programs** will be aired on TV for the benefit of hectic people in need of recovery of some sort.

Watch for a backlash from this busy-ness soon. For instance, **yoga** has become a bit of a rage. People are spending their fitness hours slowing down and stretching, breathing, relaxing.

Some Manners for the Nineties

☞ **ATM ETIQUETTE:** Although Americans prefer an average of 18 inches between themselves and the person they're speaking with, Automatic Teller Machines demand more space. Standing closer than two feet to the person at the machine makes the user uncomfortable. The best bet is to stand at the back wall of the booth and always avert your eyes from the screen someone is working on.

☞ **CELLULAR PHONE ETIQUETTE:** It is considered uncouth to say to someone who phones you on your cellular phone, "I've got to go, this is costing too much." Best bet: Give your phone number only to those for whom you're willing to pay the higher charges.

☞ **BRIDAL REGISTRY ETIQUETTE:** Fewer newlyweds need or want full place settings and matching towels. What they'd like instead is perhaps a backpack, or a tennis racket, or maybe a canoe. Registering at Eastern Mountain Sports or L.L. Bean is now considered acceptable.

STAY YOUNGER LONGER WITH GINKGO BILOBA

The GINKGO BILOBA tree is considered a "Biological Super Tree." It has amazing medicinal properties; medical researchers have isolated chemical compounds from Ginkgo that show startling effects in humans. Studies indicate that Ginkgo can help:

1. Improve blood circulation to the brain.
2. Improve peripheral blood circulation.
3. Improve one's mood and sociability.
4. Relieve arthritis and rheumatism.
5. Improve lung and bronchial congestion.
6. Eye weakness caused by poor circulation.
7. Relieve anxiety and tension.
8. Memory and reaction time.
9. Chronic ringing in the ears.
10. Alzheimer's and senility.
11. Coldness in the body.

IMPORTANT FACT: GINKGO HAS NO BAD SIDE EFFECTS.

Unsolicited Letter: *"I would like to inform you that your Ginkgo capsules have done wonders for my health. After 6 weeks of using Ginkgo I can tell you I have never felt better. All my friends say I look just great! I thank you for introducing this product to me."*

Ginkgo Biloba

Send Check to:
HEALTH CENTER FOR BETTER LIVING, INC.
6189 Taylor Rd, Naples, FL 33942

Mention KEYCODE 447 when ordering

Item #701

For Faster Ordering, Call:
(813) 566–2611
(VISA/MasterCard/COD)

ORDER TODAY AND RECEIVE FREE 72-PAGE HERBAL HEALTH CARE BOOK

1 month supply: $21.45 (100 caps)
2 month supply: $37.45 (200 caps)
(includes shipping & handling)
(All orders shipped within 24 hours)

FASHION TRENDS

Though **hemlines** will continue to be all over the place, keep your eyes on knees. More skirts and dresses will stop right there in the coming year. **Empire waistlines** are in, and the long, loose look of vests, wide-legged pants, and big, easy shirts and "**daytime pajama**" sets will continue to be popular (they're comfortable and flattering). Colors will be **neutral** (various shades of pale) through the fall, then look for a lot of black through the winter, with flashes of **bright color** — reds and neons — on accessories. Mohair will be a popular fabric. In formal wear (and some not-so-formal), dresses will be made of chiffon, micro-pleated, and may include a fair amount of ethnic detailing. This could be the **Year of the Hat** for women.

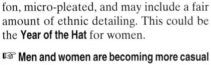

☞ **Men and women are becoming more casual** in the office — fewer "power suits" and more company-sponsored "dressing down" days.

☞ **A sign of the times:** Baby boomers are aging and bringing their more down-to-earth attitudes with them into their fifties. "Less is more" as far as makeup goes these days. And looking one's age (with occasional help in the hair color department) is becoming very chic.

☞ **Another sign of these more sensible times:** Women are running from pantyhose. Once resigned to the binding, expensive gear, women are choosing comfort with tights, or pants, or just plain bare legs.

ADIOS!

☞ **Jet Lag** — It occurs when the body's internal clock is confused by changes in the daylight cycle. Some products that will send jet lag the way of the prop plane: Circadian Travel Technologies in Bethesda, Maryland, has a computer software package that figures out when overseas fliers should be exposed to bright light in order to regulate sleep rhythms. They also sell a visor for $379 that will shine simulated sunlight into your eyes to trick your body into maintaining its own internal clock.

The Tudor Hotel in New York City has six "circadian rooms" with shades that make the room dark during the day and special clocks set to your home time zone.

☞ **Montezuma's Revenge** — This sounds too good to be true, but we should soon (within three years) be seeing an oral vaccine against diarrhea, made by the same company that plans to produce a pill to prevent ulcers, and an inhalant to immunize babies and the elderly against pneumonia.

☞ **A Busy Signal** — With voice mail, call waiting, and call forwarding, we don't often hear a busy signal anymore. Are we saying farewell to patience? Maybe a busy signal wasn't such a bad idea after all.

□□

Every explorer of the great age of discovery from Columbus on went sniffing for pepper, trying to find the fabled Spice Islands that Marco Polo had reported. The prize was enormous: The Dutch conquest of pepper-rich Sumatra made Holland one of the richest countries in the world in the 18th century. Shipowners called it prime

cargo: a commodity with concentrated value, easy to transport without spoilage. (Peppercorns last indefinitely at room temperature.)

The Dutch tried to keep a monopoly, but Yankee skippers like Captain Jonathan Carnes would not be denied. Carnes heard a rumor that pepper grew wild on the north-

west coast of Sumatra. Returning home to Salem, Massachusetts, he managed to gain command of a fast boat and head for the uncharted waters, coral reefs, and fierce pirates of the Malay archipelago. On Carnes's return to Salem in 1795, the town, as historian Samuel Eliot Morison notes, "went pepper mad." The cargo, which had cost Salem investors $18,000, including all expenses, sold for a 700-percent profit.

By 1805, only ten years later, the port of Salem, which in 1791 had shipped out only 492 pounds of pepper, was handling seven-eighths of the

entire northwest Sumatran pepper crop, more than 7.5 million pounds! "Many a Salem man's bones lie in Sumatran waters," writes Morison, "a Malay kreese between the ribs."

Black pepper, *Piper nigrum,* is a sun-dried berry, the fruit of a climbing tropical vine that lives only within 20 degrees of the equator. The vine, native to India on the Malabar coast, may have been cultivated as

early as 1000 B.C. and was later established in Sumatra, Java, and the Moluccas. The greatest bulk of the pepper trade has always been centered around the southwest coast of India, where the prized Malabar and Tellicherry black peppers are harvested. Columbus, with pepper high on his "want" list, found instead *Capsicums,* or chilies, but undaunted, called them pepper anyway, although the two are not related.

A Proper Pepper Lexicon

"Pepper is small in quantity and great in virtue." – Plato

PEPPER VARIETIES:

☞ *Piper nigrum* is the black peppercorn. It includes Malabar and Tellicherry, both from India. (Tellicherry is the largest and most pungent.) The berries are picked while green and then dried in the sun. Peppercorns from Indonesia include Lampong (Sumatra) and Sarawak (Malaysia).

White pepper is produced from the ripe red berries of the *Piper nigrum* vines, washed to

THE *Practical*

A FEW THINGS ABOUT

remove the outer layer and then dried in the sun. Most come from Indonesia and are called Muntok. White pepper is commonly used for white sauces and fish.

Green peppercorns are harvested in the green state and then packed in vinegar or brine; they are also available freeze-dried or dehydrated.

PEPPER SUBSTITUTES:
☞ Red or pink peppercorns are not true pepper but come from a weedy plant known as the Brazilian pepper tree, Christmas berry, or Florida holly. Once banned by the FDA, the ban was lifted after the French government made a case for the safety of these berries imported from the Island of Reunion under the name *baies roses* (pink berries). They are rather sweet, slightly citrous, and have little heat.

Melegueta pepper — also called Grains of Paradise — belongs to the ginger family and is used in cooking and medicine in West Africa.

Piper cubeba, the cubeb berry, grows on a shrub native to Java.

Indian long pepper, *Piper longum,* and the Java long pepper, *Piper retrofractum,* are pods about 1½ inches long, harvested while green and dried in the sun. They are hot to the taste, with the additional flavor of wintergreen, cinnamon, or clove.

Szechuan pepper is spice but not a true pepper. Used in Chinese cooking, it is hot and strong with a sometimes numbing delayed reaction.

Piper nigrum

Pepper Primer

PEPPER YOU MAY FIND USEFUL . . .

☞ One teaspoon of ground peppercorns weighs 2.1 grams and contains 5 calories, made up of 1.36 grams of carbohydrates, .023 grams of protein, .28 grams of fiber, and .07 grams of fat (no cholesterol). The same amount of pepper contains 4 IU of vitamin A and 26 milligrams of potassium, plus traces of other vitamins and minerals.

Sylvester Graham, father of the graham cracker and promoter of natural foods, warned that excessive use of pepper would cause insanity. (He also believed graham crackers to be an aphrodisiac.)

by Allene White

HOW TO USE THIS ALMANAC
Anywhere in the U.S.A.

Annually, for the interest and pleasure of our readers, *The Old Farmer's Almanac* provides a variety of astronomical data calculated for the upcoming year. The data cover a wide range of phenomena — the rising and setting times of the Sun and Moon; the declination of the Sun; the astronomical age and placement of the Moon and its monthly phases; the rising and setting times of the visible planets; solar and lunar eclipses; dates and times of meteor showers; rising and setting times of the bright stars; and a monthly summary of astronomical highlights.

THE LEFT-HAND CALENDAR PAGES
(Pages 52-78)

Much of the data is contained in the Left-Hand Calendar Pages (pages 52-78). For the enlightenment of our readers, part of a sample page is reproduced below, with an explanatory text summarizing the individual entries.

☞ **PLEASE NOTE** that all the times given in this edition of the Almanac are calculated for **Boston, Massachusetts.** However, Key Letters accompany much of the data. They are provided so that readers may correct the Boston times to those of their own localities. Several examples are given below to clarify this procedure. (**Eastern Standard Time is used throughout the Almanac.** One hour should be added for Daylight Saving Time between April 2 and October 29.)

SAMPLE LEFT-HAND CALENDAR PAGE
(from November 1994 — page 52)

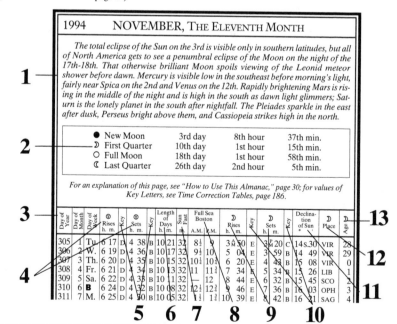

1994   NOVEMBER, THE ELEVENTH MONTH

The total eclipse of the Sun on the 3rd is visible only in southern latitudes, but all of North America gets to see a penumbral eclipse of the Moon on the night of the 17th-18th. That otherwise brilliant Moon spoils viewing of the Leonid meteor shower before dawn. Mercury is visible low in the southeast before morning's light, fairly near Spica on the 2nd and Venus on the 12th. Rapidly brightening Mars is rising in the middle of the night and is high in the south as dawn light glimmers; Saturn is the lonely planet in the south after nightfall. The Pleiades sparkle in the east after dusk, Perseus bright above them, and Cassiopeia strikes high in the north.

● New Moon	3rd day	8th hour	37th min.
☽ First Quarter	10th day	1st hour	15th min.
○ Full Moon	18th day	1st hour	58th min.
☾ Last Quarter	26th day	2nd hour	5th min.

For an explanation of this page, see "How to Use This Almanac," page 30; for values of Key Letters, see Time Correction Tables, page 186.

Day of Year	Day of Month	Day of Week	☉ Rises h. m.	Key	☉ Sets h. m.	Key	Length of Days h. m.	Sun Fast m.	Full Sea Boston A.M.	P.M.	☽ Rises h. m.	Key	☽ Sets h. m.	Key	Declination of Sun ° '	☽ Place	☽ Age
305	1	Tu.	6 17	D	4 38	B	10 21	32	8½	9	3 50	E	3 20	C	14s.30	VIR	28
306	2	W.	6 19	D	4 36	B	10 17	32	9½	10	5 04	E	3 59	B	14 49	VIR	29
307	3	Th.	6 20	D	4 35	B	10 15	32	10¼	10½	6 20	E	4 43	B	15 08	VIR	0
308	4	Fr.	6 21	D	4 34	B	10 13	32	11	11¼	7 34	E	5 34	B	15 26	LIB	1
309	5	Sa.	6 22	D	4 33	B	10 11	32	—	12	8 44	E	6 32	B	15 45	SCO	2
310	6	**B**	6 24	D	4 32	B	10 08	32	12¼	12¾	9 46	E	7 36	B	16 03	OPH	3
311	7	M.	6 25	D	4 30	B	10 05	32	1¼	1¾	10 39	E	8 42	B	16 21	SAG	4

1   2   3   4   5   6   7   8   9   10   11   12   13

1. The text heading the calendar page is a summary of the sky sightings for the month. These astronomical highlights appear on each month's calendar page.

2. The dates and times of the Moon's phases for the month. (For more details, see Glossary, page 38.)

3. The days of the year, month, and week are listed on each calendar page. The traditional ecclesiastical calendar designation for Sunday — the Dominical Letter — B for 1994, A for 1995 — is used by the Almanac. (For further explanation, see Glossary, page 38.)

4. Sunrise and sunset times (EST) for Boston for each day of the month.

5. Key Letter columns. The letters in the two columns marked "Key" are designed to correct the sunrise/sunset times given for Boston to other localities. Note that each sunrise/sunset time has its Key Letter. The values (that is, the number of minutes) of these Key Letters are given in the **Time Correction Tables**, page 186. Simply find your city, or the city nearest you, in the tables, and locate the figure in the appropriate Key Letter column. Add, or subtract, those minutes to the sunrise or sunset time given for Boston. (Because of the complexities of calculation for different locations, times may not be precise to the minute.)

Example:

To find the time of sunrise in Wichita, Kansas, on November 1, 1994:

Sunrise, Boston, with Key Letter D	6:17 A.M., EST
Value of Key Letter D for Wichita (p. 190)	+ 37 minutes
Sunrise, Wichita	6:54 A.M., CST

Use the same process for sunset. (Add one hour for Daylight Saving Time between April 2 and October 29.)

6. Length of Days. This column denotes how long the Sun will be above the horizon in Boston for each day of the month. To determine the length of any given day in your locality, follow the procedure outlined in #5 above to determine the sunrise and sunset times for your city. Then, add 12 hours to the time of sunset, subtract the time of sunrise, and you will have the length of day.

Example:

Sunset, Cleveland, Ohio, Nov. 1	5:21
Add 12 hours	+ 12:00
	17:21
Subtract sunrise, Cleveland, Nov. 1	– 6:57
Length of day, Cleveland, Nov. 1 (10 hrs., 24 min.)	10:24

– Beth Krommes

7. The Sun Fast column is designed to change sundial time into clock time in Boston. A sundial reads natural, or Sun, time, which is neither Standard nor Daylight time except by coincidence. Simply *subtract* the minutes given in the Sun Fast column to get Boston clock time, and use Key Letter C in the Time Correction Tables (page 186) to correct the time for your city. (Add one hour for Daylight Saving Time between April 2 and October 29.)

Example:

To change sundial time into clock time in Memphis, Tennessee, on November 1, 1994:

Sundial reading, Nov. 1	12:00
Subtract Sun Fast	– 32 minutes
Clock time, Boston	11:28 A.M., EST
Use Key C for Memphis (page 188)	+ 16 minutes
Clock time, Memphis	11:44 A.M., CST

8. The times of daily high tides in Boston, for morning and evening, are recorded in this column. ("8½" under "Full Sea Boston, A.M." on November 1 means that the high tide that morning will be at 8:30 — with the number of feet of high tide shown for some of the dates on the Right-Hand Calendar Pages. Where a dash is shown under Full Sea, it indicates that time of high water has occurred on or after midnight, and so is recorded on the next date). Tide corrections for some localities can be found in the **Tide Correction Tables** on page 194.

9. Moonrise and moonset times (EST) for Boston for each day of the month. (Dashes indicate that moonrise or moonset has occurred on or after midnight and so is recorded on the next date.)

10. Key Letter columns. These columns designate the letters to be used to correct the moonrise/moonset times for Boston to other localities. As explained in #5, the same procedure for calculating "Sunrise/sunset" is used *except* that an additional correction factor based on longitude (see table below) should be used. For the longitude of your city, consult the Time Correction Tables, page 186.

Longitude of city	Correction minutes
58°- 76°	0
77°- 89°	+1
90°-102°	+2
103°-115°	+3
116°-127°	+4
128°-141°	+5
142°-155°	+6

Example:

To determine the time of moonrise in Denver, Colorado, on November 1, 1994:

Moonrise, Boston, with Key Letter E (page 30)	3:50 A.M., EST
Value of Key Letter E for Denver (page 187)	+ 7 minutes
Correction for Denver longitude 104° 59'	+ 3 minutes
Moonrise, Denver	4:00 A.M., MST

Use the same procedure for moonset.

(Add one hour for Daylight Saving Time between April 2 and October 29.)

11. This column denotes the declination of the Sun (angular distance from the celestial equator) in degrees and minutes, at *noon,* EST.

12. The Moon's Place denoted in this column is its *astronomical* place, i.e., its *actual* placement in the heavens. (This should not be confused with the Moon's *astrological* place in the zodiac, as explained on page 180.) *All* **calculations in this Almanac, except for the astrological information on pages 180-183, are based on astronomy, not astrology.**

In addition to the 12 constellations of the astronomical zodiac, four other abbreviations appear in this column: Auriga (AUR), a northern constellation between Perseus and Gemini. Ophiuchus (OPH) is a constellation primarily north of the zodiac, but with a small corner between Scorpius and Sagittarius. Orion (ORI) is a constellation whose northern limit first reaches the zodiac between Taurus and Gemini. Sextans (SEX) lies south of the zodiac except for a corner that just touches it near Leo.

13. The last column lists the Moon's age, i.e., the number of days since the previous new Moon. (The lunar month is 29.53 days.)

Further astronomical data may be found on page 42, which lists the eclipses for the upcoming year, details of the principal meteor showers, and dates of the full Moon over a five-year period.

The Visible Planets (page 40) list the rising and setting times for Venus, Mars, Jupiter, and Saturn for 1995; page 44 carries the rising and setting and transit times of the Bright Stars for 1995. Both feature Key Letters, designed to convert the Boston times given to those of other localities (see #5 and #10 above).

Also, on page 192, can be found "The Twilight Zone," a chart that enables you to calculate the length of time of dawn and dark in your area.

The Right-Hand Calendar Pages

(Pages 53-79)

These pages are a combination of astronomical data; specific dates in mainly the Anglican church calendar, inclusion of which has always been traditional in American and English almanacs (though we also include some other religious dates); tide heights at Boston (the Left-Hand Calendar Pages include the daily times of high tides; the corrections for your locality are on page 194); quotations; anniversary dates; appropriate seasonal activities; and a rhyming version of the weather forecasts for New England. (Detailed forecasts for the entire country are presented on pages 118-147.)

The following details some of the entries from this year's Right-Hand Calendar Pages, together with a sample (the first part of November 1994) of a calendar page explained. Also, following the Almanac's tradition, the Chronological Cycles and Eras for 1995 are listed.

Movable Feasts and Fasts for 1995

Septuagesima Sunday	Feb. 12
Shrove Tuesday	Feb. 28
Ash Wednesday	Mar. 1
Palm Sunday	Apr. 9
Good Friday	Apr. 14
Easter Day	Apr. 16
Low Sunday	Apr. 23

Rogation Sunday	May 21
Ascension Day	May 25
Whit Sunday-Pentecost	June 4
Trinity Sunday	June 11
Corpus Christi	June 15
1st Sunday in Advent	Dec. 3

The Seasons of 1994-1995

Fall 1994	Sept. 23, 1:19 A.M., EST
Winter 1994	Dec. 21, 9:23 P.M., EST
Spring 1995	Mar. 20, 9:14 P.M., EST
Summer 1995	June 21, 3:34 P.M., EST
Fall 1995	Sept. 23, 7:13 A.M., EST
Winter 1995	Dec. 22, 3:17 A.M., EST

Chronological Cycles for 1995

Golden Number (Lunar Cycle)	1
Epact	29
Solar Cycle	16
Dominical Letter	A
Roman Indiction	3
Year of Julian Period	6708

Era	Year	Begins
Byzantine	7504	Sept. 14
Jewish (A.M.)*	5756	Sept. 24
Roman (A.U.C.)	2748	Jan. 14
Nabonassar	2744	Apr. 25
Japanese	2655	Jan. 1
Grecian (Seleucidae)	2307	Sept. 14
		(or Oct. 14)
Indian (Saka)	1917	Mar. 22
Diocletian	1712	Sept. 12
Islamic (Hegira)*	1416	May 30
Chinese (Lunar)	4693	Jan. 31
(Boar)		

Year begins at sunset

Determination of Earthquakes

☞ Note, on right-hand pages 53-79, the dates when the Moon (☾) "rides high" or "runs low." The date of the high begins the most likely five-day period of earthquakes in the Northern Hemisphere; the date of the low indicates a similar five-day period in the Southern Hemisphere. You will also find on these pages a notation for Moon on the Equator (☾ on Eq.) twice each month. At this time, in both hemispheres, is a two-day earthquake period.

NAMES AND CHARACTERS OF THE PRINCIPAL PLANETS AND ASPECTS

☞ Every now and again on these Right-Hand Calendar Pages, you will see symbols conjoined in groups to tell you what is happening in the heavens. For example, ♂ ☿ ♀ opposite November 12, 1994, (see below) means that Mercury ☿ and Venus ♀ are on that date in conjunction ♂ or apparently near each other.

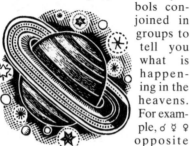

– Beth Krommes

Here are the symbols used …

☉	Sun	♂	Mars
○●☾	Moon	♇	Pluto
☿	Mercury	♃	Jupiter
♄	Saturn	♂	Conjunction, or in
♀	Venus		the same degree
♅	Uranus	☊	Ascending Node
⊕	Earth	☋	Descending Node
♆	Neptune	☍	Opposition, or
			180 degrees

EARTH AT APHELION AND PERIHELION 1995

☞ The Earth will be at Perihelion on January 4, 1995, when it will be 91,400,005 miles from the Sun. The Earth will be at Aphelion on July 3, 1995, when it will be 94,512,258 miles from the Sun.

SAMPLE RIGHT-HAND CALENDAR PAGE
(from November 1994 — page 53)

Day of the month.

Day of the week.

For detailed regional forecasts, see pages 118-147.

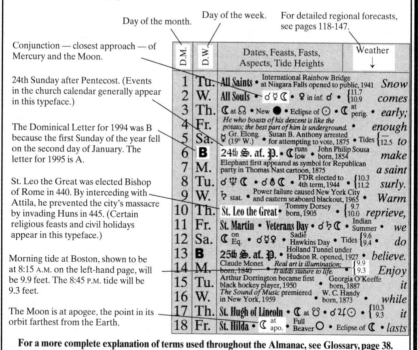

Conjunction — closest approach — of Mercury and the Moon.

24th Sunday after Pentecost. (Events in the church calendar generally appear in this typeface.)

The Dominical Letter for 1994 was B because the first Sunday of the year fell on the second day of January. The letter for 1995 is A.

St. Leo the Great was elected Bishop of Rome in 440. By interceding with Attila, he prevented the city's massacre by invading Huns in 445. (Certain religious feasts and civil holidays appear in this typeface.)

Morning tide at Boston, shown to be at 8:15 A.M. on the left-hand page, will be 9.9 feet. The 8:45 P.M. tide will be 9.3 feet.

The Moon is at apogee, the point in its orbit farthest from the Earth.

D.M.	D.W.	Dates, Feasts, Fasts, Aspects, Tide Heights	Weather ↓
1	Tu.	**All Saints** • International Rainbow Bridge at Niagara Falls opened to public, 1941	Snow
2	W.	**All Souls** • ♂ ☿ ☾ • ♀ in inf. ♂ • {11.7 / 10.9	comes
3	Th.	☾ at ☊ • New ● • Eclipse of ☉ • ☾ at perig. •	early;
4	Fr.	*He who boasts of his descent is like the potato; the best part of him is underground.* •	enough
5	Sa.	☿ Gr. Elong. (19° W.) • Susan B. Anthony arrested for attempting to vote, 1875 • Tides {12.5	to
6	B	24th S. af. P. • ☾ runs low • John Philip Sousa born, 1854	make
7	M.	Elephant first appeared as symbol for Republican party in Thomas Nast cartoon, 1875 •	a saint
8	Tu.	♂ ♆ ☾ • ♂ ♅ ☾ • FDR elected to 4th term, 1944 • {10.3 / 11.2	surly.
9	W.	♄ stat. • Power failure caused New York City and eastern seaboard blackout, 1965 •	Warm
10	Th.	**St. Leo the Great** • Tommy Dorsey born, 1905 • {9.7 / 10.0	reprieve,
11	Fr.	**St. Martin** • **Veterans Day** • ♂ ♄ ☾ • Indian Summer •	we
12	Sa.	☾ on Eq. • ♂ ☿ ♀ • Sadie Hawkins Day • Tides {9.6 / 9.4	do
13	B	25th S. af. P. • Holland Tunnel under Hudson R. opened, 1927 •	believe.
14	M.	Claude Monet born, 1840 • *Real art is illumination; it adds stature to life.* • {9.9 / 9.3	Enjoy
15	Tu.	Arthur Dorrington became first black hockey player, 1950 • Georgia O'Keeffe born, 1887	it
16	W.	*The Sound of Music* premiered in New York, 1959 • W. C. Handy born, 1873 •	while
17	Th.	**St. Hugh of Lincoln** • ☾ at ☋ • ♂ ♃ ☉ • {10.3 / 9.3	it
18	Fr.	**St. Hilda** • ☾ at apo. • Full Beaver ○ • Eclipse of ☾ •	lasts

For a more complete explanation of terms used throughout the Almanac, see Glossary, page 38.

Atlanta Housewife Investigated And Almost Arrested For Losing 73 Pounds

By Kathleen Ann Maldoney

Did you ever notice that when you're fat, people actually stare at you while you eat. It's as if they want to tap you on the shoulder and say, "If you wouldn't eat that stuff, you wouldn't be so fat!"

Hello. My name is Kate Maldoney. You don't know me from Adam. But I'm a real person. I live near Sandy Springs, Georgia. And, up until two years ago, I was the fat lady that everyone was staring at.

I was too tired to go out with my friends at night. I was even embarrassed to go out on weekends. I waddled when I walked. I sweat when I ate. I wore anything loose that would hang straight down and wouldn't cling. I couldn't even cross my legs. I wasn't just "overweight." I was fat. I was 5'4" and weighed 202 pounds.

I went to my doctor for help. But I wasn't optimistic. During the past seven years I had tried 16 *different* diets. One by one. And I failed at all of them.

My doctor listened to me very carefully and then recommended an entirely different program. This wasn't a "diet." It was a unique new weight-loss program researched by a team of bariatric physicians — specialists who treat the severely obese. The program itself was developed by Dr. James Cooper of Atlanta, Georgia.

I started the program on May 17th. Within the first four days, I only lost three pounds. So I was disappointed. But during the three weeks that followed, my weight began to drop. Rapidly. Within the next 196 days, I went from 202 pounds to 129 pounds.

The reason the program worked was simple: I was *always* eating.

I could eat *six times every day*. So I never felt deprived. Never hungry. I could snack in the afternoon. Snack before dinner. I could even snack at night while I was watching TV.

How can I eat so much and still lose weight?

The secret is not in the amount of food you eat. It's in the *prescribed combination* of foods you eat in each 24-hour period. Nutritionally dense portions of special fiber, unrefined carbohydrates, and certain proteins that generate a calorie-burning process that continues all day long ... a complete 24-hour fat-reduction cycle.

Metabolism is evened out, so fat is burned away around the clock. Not just in unhealthy spurts like many diets. That's why it lets you shed pounds so easily. Without hunger. Without nervousness.

And it's all good wholesome food. No weird stuff. You'll enjoy a variety of meats, chicken, fish, vegetables, potatoes, pasta, sauces — plus your favorite snacks. Lots of snacks.

This new program must be the best kept secret in America. Because, up until now, it's *only been available to doctors*. No one else. In fact, the Clinic-30 Program has been used by 142 doctors in the U.S. and Canada to treat more than 9,820 patients. So it's doctor-tested. And proven. This is the first time it's been available to the public.

There are other benefits too ...

• There are no amphetamines. No drugs of any kind.

• No pills. No powders. No chalky-tasting drinks to mix. Everything's at your local supermarket. No special foods to buy.

• There's no strenuous exercise program.

• You don't count calories. Just follow the program. It's easy.

• It's low in sodium, so you don't hold water.

• You eat the foods you really enjoy. Great variety. Great taste.

• You can dine out.

• There's no ketosis. No bad breath odor.

But *here's* the best part ...

Once you lose the weight, you can keep it off. Permanently! Because you're not hungry all the time.

Let's face it. We all have "eating lifestyles." Our eating habits usually include three meals a day. Plus two or three snacks. We all love snacks. Especially at night.

But most diets force us to change all that.

And that's why they fail!

The Clinic-30 Program lets you *continue your normal eating lifestyle*. You can eat six times a day. You can snack when you wish. So, when you lose the weight, you can keep it off. For good. Because no one's forcing you to change.

Here are some other patients from Georgia who entered Dr. Cooper's Clinic-30 Program with me ...

• Reverend Donald F. is a 42-year-old minister who went from 227 to 179 in just four months.

"In spite of church suppers, I've lost almost 50 pounds in four months and I'm not having a rebound gain."

• Renate M. was a G.I. bride from Germany who went from 212 to 140.2 in 8½ months.

"I believe I was a participant in every weight-reducing plan there ever was. Then, about two years ago, I started the Clinic-30 Program. And I haven't regained a pound."

And then there's me. About 4 months ago I was stopped by a policeman for not using my turning signal. When he looked at my driver's license he claimed it wasn't mine. He said it had someone else's picture on it.

After he called for a computer check, he came back to the car smiling. "You must have lost a lot of weight. This picture doesn't even look like you." I agreed. In a way, it was one of the nicest "warnings" I'd ever received.

Obviously, I'm excited about the program. This is the first time it's been available outside of a clinical setting. Dr. Cooper has asked Green Tree Press, Inc. to distribute it.

We'll be happy to send you the program to examine for 31 days. Show it to your doctor. Try it. There's *no obligation*. In fact, your check won't be cashed for 31 days. You may even postdate it 31 days in advance if you wish.

Choose a day and start the program. If you don't begin losing weight within five days — and continue losing weight — we'll promptly return your *original uncashed check*. No delays. No excuses.

Or keep it longer. Try it for six months. Even then, if you're not continuing to lose weight on a regular basis, you'll receive a full refund. Promptly. And without question. This is the fairest way we know to prove to you how well this new program works.

To order, just send your name, address and postdated check for $12.95 (plus $3.00 shipping/handling) to The Clinic-30 Program, c/o Green Tree Press, Inc., Dept. 672, 3603 West 12th Street, Erie, PA 16505.

AN IMPORTANT REMINDER

As your weight begins to drop, do not allow yourself to become too thin.

It's also very important to consult your physician before commencing any weight-loss program. Show him this program. And be sure to see him periodically if you intend to take off large amounts of weight.

HOLIDAYS AND OBSERVANCES, 1995

(*) Recommended as holidays with pay for all employees
(**) State observances only

Jan. 1 (*) New Year's Day
Jan. 16 (*) Martin Luther King Jr.'s
Birthday *(observed)*
Jan. 19 (**) Robert E. Lee's Birthday
(Ark., Fla., S.C., Tenn.)
Feb. 2 Groundhog Day
Feb. 12 (**) Abraham Lincoln's Birthday
Feb. 14 Valentine's Day
Feb. 20 (*) Presidents Day
Feb. 22 George Washington's Birthday
Feb. 28 (**) Mardi Gras *(Ala., La.)*
Mar. 2 (**) Texas Independence Day
Mar. 15 (**) Andrew Jackson Day *(Tenn.)*
Mar. 17 (**) St. Patrick's Day; Evacuation
Day *(Boston and Suffolk Co., Mass.)*
Apr. 2 (**) Pascua Florida Day
Apr. 13 (**) Thomas Jefferson's Birthday
(Ala., Okla.)
Apr. 17 (**) Patriots Day *(Fla., Me., Mass.)*
Apr. 28 Arbor Day *(except Alaska,
Ga., Kans., Va., Wyo.)*
May 1 May Day
May 8 (**) Truman Day *(Mo.)*
May 14 Mother's Day
May 20 Armed Forces Day
May 22 Victoria Day *(Canada)*
May 29 (*) Memorial Day *(observed)*;
(**) Admission Day *(Wis.)*
June 5 World Environment Day
June 11 (**) King Kamehameha I Day
(Hawaii)
June 14 Flag Day
June 17 (**) Bunker Hill Day *(Boston and
Suffolk Co., Mass.)*
June 18 Father's Day
June 20 (**) West Virginia Day

July 1 Canada Day
July 4 (*) Independence Day
July 24 (**) Pioneer Day *(Utah)*
Aug. 14 (**) Victory Day *(R.I.)*
Aug. 16 (**) Bennington Battle Day *(Vt.)*
Aug. 26 Women's Equality Day
Sept. 4 (*) Labor Day
Sept. 9 (**) Admission Day *(Calif.)*
Sept. 12 (**) Defenders Day *(Md.)*
Oct. 9 (*) Columbus Day *(observed)*;
Thanksgiving *(Canada)*; (**) Native
Americans Day *(S. Dak.)*
Oct. 18 (**) Alaska Day
Oct. 31 Halloween; (**) Nevada Day
Nov. 4 (**) Will Rogers Day *(Okla.)*
Nov. 7 Election Day
Nov. 11 (*) Veterans Day
Nov. 19 Discovery Day *(Puerto Rico)*
Nov. 23 (*) Thanksgiving Day
Nov. 26 (**) John F. Kennedy Day *(Mass.)*
Dec. 10 (**) Wyoming Day
Dec. 25 (*) Christmas Day
Dec. 26 Boxing Day *(Canada)*

RELIGIOUS OBSERVANCES

Epiphany	Jan. 6
First Day of Ramadan	Feb. 1
Ash Wednesday	Mar. 1
Palm Sunday	Apr. 9
Good Friday	Apr. 14
First Day of Passover	Apr. 15
Easter Day	Apr. 16
Orthodox Easter	Apr. 23
Islamic New Year	May 31
Whit Sunday-Pentecost	June 4
Rosh Hashanah	Sept. 25
Yom Kippur	Oct. 4
Chanukah	Dec. 18
Christmas Day	Dec. 25

HOW THE ALMANAC WEATHER FORECASTS ARE MADE

Our weather forecasts are determined both by the use of a secret formula devised by the founder of this Almanac in 1792 and by the most modern scientific calculations based on solar activity. We believe nothing in the universe occurs haphazardly; there is a cause-and-effect pattern to all phenomena, including weather. It follows, therefore, that we believe weather is predictable. It is obvious, however, that neither we nor anyone else has as yet gained sufficient insight into the mysteries of the universe to predict weather with anything resembling total accuracy.

"Discover a *Guaranteed** Way to
Boost Your Mental Energy
and
Feel More Alive Than You Have in Years!"

"I want to retain my mental and physical well-being into a ripe old age. So I started using Ginkgo Biloba about 1 1/2 years ago. Since then I have noticed a marked improvement in my mental health."
—Ann Romano, Newington, CT

Do you suffer from low energy, mental fatigue, or cold hands and feet?

Join over 20 million people who have used GINKGO BILOBA, a remarkable herbal extract that helps:

- Increase Energy
- Support Healthy Circulation
- Promote Better Memory & Mental Alertness

GUARANTEED POTENCY

**100% SATISFACTION GUARANTEED*
You take no risk in ordering. If you're not pleased with the results of Ginkgo Biloba, we'll refund 100% of your money, no questions asked.

Statements included herein by Amrion, Inc., shall not be construed to imply claims or representations that these products treat or prevent any disease, but rather are dietary supplements intended solely for nutritional support.

$9.99 ea.

ORDER GINKGO BILOBA Today and SAVE up to 45%!

TO ORDER BY CREDIT CARD, JUST CALL TOLL FREE

1-800-627-7775

M - F 6:30 a.m.- 9:00 p.m.
SAT. & SUN. 8 a.m.- 5 p.m.
(Mountain time zone)

OR MAIL IN THIS COUPON!

Rush Me: (Check a box)	Regular Price	Special Offer Price		Number Bottles		Ttl. Bottle Price	You Pay	You Save
☐ 60 capsules	$13.99	$ 9.99	x	1	=	$ 9.99	$	$ 4.00
☐ 60 capsules	$13.49	$ 9.49	x	2	=	$18.98	$	$ 9.00
☐ 60 capsules	$12.99	$ 8.99	x	4	=	$35.96	$	$20.00
☐ 120 capsules	$23.99	$14.99	x	1	=	$14.99	$	$ 9.00
☐ 120 capsules	$22.99	$13.99	x	2	=	$27.98	$	$20.00
☐ 120 capsules	$21.99	$12.99	x	4	=	$51.96	$	$44.00

ALL CAPSULES 40 mg

Colorado Residents Add 3% Tax	$
Shipping and Handling	$ FREE
TOTAL	$

Name_____
Address_____
City_____ State_____ Zip_____
Phone (_____)_____
© 1994 Amrion, Inc.   Key Code: OFA95GB

Send check or money order to:

BIOENERGY NUTRIENTS

Bioenergy Nutrients
6565 Odell Place
Boulder, CO 80301-3330

GLOSSARY

Aph. — Aphelion: Planet reaches point in its orbit farthest from the Sun.

Apo. — Apogee: Moon reaches point in its orbit farthest from the Earth.

Celestial Equator: The plane of the Earth's equator projected out into space.

Conj. — Conjunction: Time of apparent closest approach to each other of any two heavenly bodies. **Inf. — Inferior:** Conjunction in which the planet is between the Sun and the Earth. **Sup. — Superior:** Indicates that the Sun is between the planet and the Earth.

Declination: Measurement of angular distance of any celestial object perpendicularly north or south of celestial equator; analogous to terrestrial latitude. The Almanac gives the Sun's declination at noon EST.

Dominical Letter: Used for the ecclesiastical calendar and determined by the date on which the first Sunday of the year falls. If Jan. 1 is a Sunday, the Letter is A; if Jan. 2 is a Sunday, the Letter is B; and so to G when the first Sunday is Jan. 7. In leap year the Letter applies through February and then takes the Letter before.

Eclipse, Annular: An eclipse in which sunlight shows around the Moon.

Eclipse, Lunar: Opposition of the Sun and Moon with the Moon at or near node.

Eclipse, Solar: Conjunction of Sun and Moon with the Moon at or near node.

Epact: A number from 1 to 30 to harmonize the lunar year with the solar year, used for the ecclesiastical calendar. Indicates the Moon's age at the instant Jan. 1 begins at the meridian of Greenwich, England.

Eq. — Equator: A great circle of the Earth equidistant from the two poles.

Equinox, Autumnal: Sun passes from Northern to Southern Hemisphere. **Vernal:** Sun passes from Southern to Northern Hemisphere.

Evening Star: A planet that is above the horizon at sunset and less than 180 degrees east of the Sun.

Golden Number: The year in the 19-year cycle of the Moon. The Moon phases occur on the same dates every 19 years.

Greatest Elongation (Gr. El.): Greatest apparent angular distance of a planet from the Sun as seen from the Earth.

Julian Period: A period of 7,980 Julian years, being a period of agreement of solar and lunar cycles. Add 4,713 to year to find the Julian year.

Moon's Age: The number of days since the previous new Moon.

Moon's Phases: First Quarter: Right half of Moon illuminated. Full Moon: Moon reaches opposition. Last Quarter: Left half of Moon illuminated. New Moon: Sun and Moon in conjunction.

Moon Rides High or Runs Low: Day of month Moon is highest or lowest above the south point of the observer's horizon.

Morning Star: A planet that is above the horizon at sunrise and less than 180 degrees west of the Sun in right ascension.

Node: Either of the two points where the Moon's orbit intersects the ecliptic.

Occultation: Eclipse of a star or planet by the Moon or another planet.

Opposition: Time when the Sun and Moon or planet appear on opposite sides of the sky (El. 180 degrees).

Perig. — Perigee: Moon reaches point in its orbit closest to the Earth.

Perih. — Perihelion: Planet reaches point in its orbit closest to the Sun.

R.A. — Right Ascension: The coordinate on the celestial sphere analogous to longitude on the Earth.

Roman Indiction: A cycle of 15 years established Jan. 1, A.D. 313, as a fiscal term. Add 3 to the number of years in the Christian era and divide by 15. The remainder is Roman Indiction — no remainder is 15.

Solar Cycle: A period of 28 years, at the end of which the days of the month return to the same days of the week.

Solstice, Summer: Point at which the Sun is farthest north of the celestial equator. **Winter:** Point at which the Sun is farthest south of the celestial equator.

Stat. — Stationary: Halt in the apparent movement of a planet against the background of the stars just before the planet comes to opposition.

Sun Fast: Subtract times given in this column from your sundial to arrive at the correct Standard Time.

Sunrise & Sunset: Visible rising and setting of the Sun's upper limb across the unobstructed horizon of an observer whose eyes are 15 feet above ground level.

Twilight: Begins or ends when stars of the sixth magnitude appear or disappear at the zenith; or when the Sun is about 18 degrees below the horizon.

THE VISIBLE PLANETS, 1995

The times of rising or setting of the planets Venus, Mars, Jupiter, and Saturn on the 1st, 11th, and 21st of each month are given below. The approximate time of rising or setting of these planets on other days may be found with sufficient accuracy by interpolation. For an explanation of Key Letters (used in adjusting the times given here for Boston to the time in your town), see page 30 and pages 186-190. Key Letters appear as capital letters beside the time of rising or setting. (For definitions of morning and evening stars, see page 38.)

VENUS is a brilliant object in the morning sky from the beginning of the year until mid-July, when it becomes too close to the Sun for observation. The last week in September it becomes visible in the evening sky, where it stays until the end of the year. Venus is in conjunction with Jupiter on January 14 and November 19, with Saturn on April 13, with Mercury on June 19 and September 28, and with Mars on November 22.

MARS rises well before midnight, in Leo, at the beginning of the year and is at opposition on February 12, when it is visible throughout the night. Its eastward elongation gradually decreases, and from late May it is visible only in the evening until late December, when it becomes too close to the Sun for observation. Mars is in conjunction with Jupiter on November 16, with Venus on November 22, and with Mercury on December 23.

Boldface — P.M.	Lightface — A.M.	Boldface — P.M.	Lightface — A.M.
Jan. 1 .... rise 3:27 D	July 1 .... rise 3:12 A	Jan. 1........ **rise 8:28** B	July 1 .... set 10:47 C
Jan. 11....... " 3:35 D	July 11 ...... " 3:25 A	Jan. 11 .... **" 7:45** B	July 11....... " **10:20** C
Jan. 21....... " 3:46 E	July 21 ...... " 3:43 A	Jan. 21........ **" 6:55** B	July 21....... " 9:53 C
Feb. 1 .... " 3:59 E	Aug. 1....... " 4:07 A	Feb. 1......... **" 5:53** A	Aug. 1 .... " 9:23 C
Feb. 11 ...... " 4:10 E	Aug. 11..... " 4:31 A	Feb. 11....... **" 4:53** A	Aug. 11 ..... " 8:57 B
Feb. 21 ...... " 4:18 E	Aug. 21..... set **6:43** D	Feb. 21 ...... set 6:31 E	Aug. 21 ..... " 8:31 B
Mar. 1 .... " 4:21 E	Sept. 1....... " **6:32** D	Mar. 1 .... " 5:51 E	Sept. 1 .... " **8:04** B
Mar. 11 ..... " 4:22 D	Sept. 11..... " **6:20** C	Mar. 11 ..... " 5:04 E	Sept. 11 ..... " **7:40** B
Mar. 21 ..... " 4:18 D	Sept. 21..... " **6:08** C	Mar. 21 ..... " 4:19 E	Sept. 21 ..... " **7:18** B
Apr. 1........ " 4:11 D	Oct. 1 .... " **5:55** B	Apr. 1 .... " 3:35 E	Oct. 1......... " **6:57** A
Apr. 11....... " 4:01 C	Oct. 11....... " **5:44** B	Apr. 11 .... " 2:57 E	Oct. 11....... " **6:37** A
Apr. 21...... " 3:50 C	Oct. 21 ...... " **5:36** B	Apr. 21...... " 2:22 D	Oct. 21....... " **6:20** A
May 1 .... " 3:39 C	Nov. 1 .... " **5:30** A	May 1 .... " 1:49 D	Nov. 1......... " **6:03** A
May 11...... " 3:27 B	Nov. 11 ..... " **5:31** A	May 11 .... " 1:18 D	Nov. 11....... " **5:51** A
May 21...... " 3:17 B	Nov. 21 ..... " **5:38** A	May 21 ...... " 12:48 D	Nov. 21....... " **5:41** A
June 1........ " 3:09 A	Dec. 1 .... " **5:51** A	June 1 .... " 12:15 D	Dec. 1......... " **5:33** A
June 11...... " 3:05 A	Dec. 11 ..... " **6:10** A	June 11...... set **11:44** C	Dec. 11....... " **5:28** A
June 21 ..... rise 3:06 A	Dec. 21 ..... " **6:33** A	June 21...... set **11:15** C	Dec. 21....... " **5:26** A
	Dec. 31 ..... set **6:58** A		Dec. 31...... set **5:25** A

JUPITER, in Scorpius, rises well before sunrise at the beginning of the year, then moves into Ophiuchus and by early March is visible more than half the night. Its westward elongation gradually increases until, on June 1, it is at opposition and visible throughout the night. Its eastward elongation then decreases as it passes back into Scorpius in early July. By late September it can be seen only in the evening sky. Jupiter is in conjunction with Venus on January 14 and November 19 and with Mars on November 16.

SATURN can be seen in the evening sky in Aquarius (in which constellation it remains throughout the year) until mid-February, when it becomes too close to the Sun for observation; it reappears in the morning sky the second half of March. Its westward elongation gradually increases until it is at opposition on September 14, when it is visible throughout the night. Its eastward elongation then gradually decreases until mid-December, when it can be seen only in the evening sky. Saturn is in conjunction with Mercury on March 25 and with Venus on April 13.

IVPITER

Boldface — P.M.	Lightface — A.M.
Jan. 1 .... rise 4:29 E	July 1......... set 2:13 A
Jan. 11...... " 3:59 E	July 11....... " 1:30 A
Jan. 21...... " 3:29 E	July 21....... " 12:49 A
Feb. 1........ " 2:55 E	Aug. 1 .... " 12:05 A
Feb. 11 ..... " 2:22 E	Aug. 11..... set 11:22 A
Feb. 21 ..... " 1:49 E	Aug. 21...... " 10:44 A
Mar. 1....... " 1:22 E	Sept. 1....... " 10:03 A
Mar. 11 .... " 12:46 E	Sept. 11..... " 9:27 A
Mar. 21 ..... " 12:09 E	Sept. 21..... " 8:52 A
Apr. 1 ...... rise 11:23 E	Oct. 1......... " 8:18 A
Apr. 11..... " 10:42 E	Oct. 11....... " 7:44 A
Apr. 21..... " 10:01 E	Oct. 21....... " 7:12 A
May 1....... " 9:18 E	Nov. 1......... " 6:36 A
May 11..... " 8:34 E	Nov. 11...... " 6:05 A
May 21..... " 7:49 E	Nov. 21...... " 5:34 A
June 1....... set 4:23 A	Dec. 1......... " 5:04 A
June 11..... " 3:39 A	Dec. 11..... " 4:33 A
June 21 ...... set 2:56 A	Dec. 21 ..... rise 7:01 E
	Dec. 31 ..... rise 6:32 E

Boldface — P.M.	Lightface — A.M.
Jan. 1 .... set 9:06 B	July 1 .... rise 11:01 C
Jan. 11........ " 8:31 B	July 11...... " 10:22 C
Jan. 21........ " 7:57 B	July 21 ..... " 9:42 C
Feb. 1......... " 7:20 B	Aug. 1...... " 8:58 C
Feb. 11........ " 6:47 B	Aug. 11...... " 8:18 C
Feb. 21 ...... " 6:14 B	Aug. 21..... " 7:37 C
Mar. 1........ " 5:47 B	Sept. 1...... " 6:53 C
Mar. 11 .... rise 6:03 D	Sept. 11 ..... " 6:12 C
Mar. 21...... " 5:26 D	Sept. 21 ..... set 4:57 B
Apr. 1....... " 4:46 C	Oct. 1......... " 4:09 B
Apr. 11...... " 4:10 C	Oct. 11...... " 3:26 B
Apr. 21..... " 3:33 C	Oct. 21 ..... " 2:44 B
May 1 .... " 2:56 C	Nov. 1 ...... " 1:59 B
May 11 ..... " 2:19 C	Nov. 11..... " 1:18 B
May 21 ...... " 1:41 C	Nov. 21..... " 12:38 B
June 1 .... " 1:00 C	Dec. 1....... " 12:00 B
June 11...... " 12:22 C	Dec. 11..... set 11:22 B
June 21 .... rise 11:39 C	Dec. 21 ..... " 10:45 B
	Dec. 31..... set 10:09 B

MERCURY can be seen only low in the east before sunrise or low in the west after sunset. It is visible mornings between these approximate dates: February 10-April 6, June 15-July 20, and October 12-November 8. The planet is brighter at the end of each period (best viewing conditions in northern latitudes occur from mid- to late October). It is visible evenings between these approximate dates: January 1-29, April 22-May 26, August 6-September 29, and December 10-31. The planet is brighter at the beginning of each period (best viewing conditions in northern latitudes occur during the first half of May).

> *DO NOT CONFUSE 1) Venus with Jupiter in mid-January and mid-November and with Mercury in mid-July; Venus is always the brighter object. 2) Venus with Saturn in mid-April and with Mars in the second half of November and early December; Venus is always the brighter object. 3) Mercury with Saturn in late March and with Mars the second half of December; Mercury is always the brighter object. 4) Jupiter with Mars around mid-November when Jupiter is the brighter object.*

ECLIPSES FOR 1995

There will be four eclipses in 1995, two of the Sun and two of the Moon. One of the solar eclipses will not be visible from North America or Hawaii; the others will be seen in certain locations, as specified below. Lunar eclipses technically are visible from the entire night side of the Earth; solar eclipses are visible only in certain areas.

1. Partial eclipse of the Moon, April 15. The beginning of the umbral phase will be visible in the western half of North America, Alaska, and Hawaii. The end will be visible in the western United States and Canada, Baja California, Alaska, and Hawaii. The Moon enters penumbra at 5:08 A.M., EST (2:08 A.M., PST); the umbral phase begins at 6:41 A.M., EST (3:41 A.M., PST); the middle of the eclipse occurs at 7:18 A.M., EST (4:18 A.M., PST); the Moon leaves umbra at 7:56 A.M., EST (4:56 A.M., PST); the Moon leaves penumbra at 9:28 A.M., EST (6:28 A.M., PST).

2. Annular eclipse of the Sun, April 29. Only the partial phase will be visible and this only from Florida. It will begin at times ranging from noon to 1:00 P.M., EST, and will last about an hour.

3. Penumbral eclipse of the Moon, October 8. The beginning will be visible in the northwestern United States, western Canada, Alaska, and Hawaii; the end will not be visible. The Moon enters penumbra at 8:58 A.M., EST (5:58 A.M., PST); the middle occurs at 11:04 A.M., EST (8:04 A.M., PST); the Moon leaves penumbra at 1:10 P.M., EST (10:10 A.M., PST).

4. Total eclipse of the Sun, beginning on October 23 and ending in the early morning hours of October 24, will not be visible from North America or Hawaii.

FULL MOON DAYS

	1995	1996	1997	1998	1999
Jan.	16	5	23	12	1/31
Feb.	15	4	22	11	—
Mar.	16	5	23	12	2/31
Apr.	15	3	22	11	30
May	14	3	22	11	30
June	12	1/30	20	9	28
July	12	30	19	9	28
Aug.	10	28	18	7	26
Sept.	8	26	16	6	25
Oct.	8	26	15	5	24
Nov.	7	24	14	4	23
Dec.	6	24	13	3	22

PRINCIPAL METEOR SHOWERS

Shower	Best Hour (EST)	Radiant Direction*	Date of Maximum**	Approx. Peak Rate (/hr.)	Associated Comet
Quadrantid	5 A.M.	N.	Jan. 4	40-150	—
Lyrid	4 A.M.	S.	Apr. 21	10-15	1861 I
Eta Aquarid	4 A.M.	S.E.	May 4	10-40	Halley
Delta Aquarid	2 A.M.	S.	July 30	10-35	—
Perseid	4 A.M.	N.	Aug. 11-13	50-100	1862 III
Draconid	9 P.M.	N.W.	Oct. 9	10	Giacobini-Zinner
Orionid	4 A.M.	S.	Oct. 20	10-70	Halley
Taurid	midnight	S.	Nov. 9	5-15	Encke
Leonid	5 A.M.	S.	Nov. 16	5-20	1866 I
Andromedid	10 P.M.	S.	Nov. 25-27	10	Biela
Geminid	2 A.M.	S.	Dec. 13	50-80	—
Ursid	5 A.M.	N.	Dec. 22	10-15	—

* Direction from which the meteors appear to come.
** Date of actual maximum occurrence may vary by one or two days in either direction.

Comfortable, vibration-absorbing handlebars!

Now with "power steering" for easy maneuvering!

3 Models up to 5HP, 42" wide cut!

Powered wheels just roll over rugged terrain!

DISCOVER AMERICA'S #1 "OFF-LAWN" MOWER!

Make this the year you take control of overgrown property with the amazing TROY-BILT® Sickle Bar Mower!

AT LAST...now you can make your entire property more useable, accessible and beautiful! If you have over an acre of land, the TROY-BILT® Sickle Bar Mower is the perfect "Off-Lawn" mower to cut tall grass and weeds – even woody brush of any height, in any terrain.

- **Amazingly fast...** clears an acre in just 1 hour!
- **Blaze nature trails** for walking, hunting, skiing or snowmobiling.
- **Enhance the beauty** of your place by clearing ugly weeds, unsightly brush and unwanted saplings.
- **Have a safer place, too,** without fire hazards, driveway blind spots poison ivies, oaks or sumacs.

TROY-BILT®

7 year

W A R R A N T Y

BRIGHT STARS, 1995

The upper table shows the Eastern Standard Time when each star transits the meridian of Boston (i.e., lies directly above the horizon's south point there) and its altitude above that point at transit on the dates shown. The time of transit on any other date differs from that on the nearest date listed by approximately four minutes of time for each day. For a place outside Boston the local time of the star's transit is found by correcting the time at Boston by the value of Key Letter "C" for the place. (See footnote.)

Star	Constellation	Magnitude	Jan. 1	Mar. 1	May 1	July 1	Sept. 1	Nov. 1	Alt.
Altair	Aquila	0.8	**12:51**	8:59	4:59	12:59	**8:51**	**4:51**	56.3
Deneb	Cygnus	1.3	**1:41**	9:49	5:50	1:50	**9:42**	**5:42**	92.8
Fomalhaut	Psc. Austr.	1.2	**3:56**	**12:04**	8:04	4:04	12:01	**7:57**	17.8
Algol	Perseus	2.2	**8:07**	**4:15**	**12:15**	8:15	4:11	12:12	88.5
Aldebaran	Taurus	0.9	**9:34**	**5:42**	**1:42**	9:42	5:39	1:39	64.1
Rigel	Orion	0.1	**10:12**	**6:20**	**2:21**	10:21	6:17	2:17	39.4
Capella	Auriga	0.1	**10:14**	**6:22**	**2:22**	10:23	6:19	2:19	93.6
Bellatrix	Orion	1.6	**10:23**	**6:31**	**2:31**	10:32	6:28	2:28	54.0
Betelgeuse	Orion	var. 0.4	**10:53**	**7:01**	**3:01**	11:01	6:58	2:58	55.0
Sirius	Can. Maj.	−1.4	**11:43**	**7:51**	**3:51**	11:51	7:47	3:48	31.0
Procyon	Can. Min.	0.4	12:41	**8:45**	**4:45**	**12:45**	8:41	4:41	52.9
Pollux	Gemini	1.2	12:47	**8:51**	**4:51**	**12:51**	8:47	4:47	75.7
Regulus	Leo	1.4	3:10	**11:14**	**7:14**	**3:14**	11:10	7:10	59.7
Spica	Virgo	var. 1.0	6:26	2:34	**10:30**	**6:30**	**2:26**	10:27	36.6
Arcturus	Bootes	−0.1	7:17	3:25	**11:21**	**7:21**	**3:17**	11:18	66.9
Antares	Scorpius	var. 0.9	9:30	5:38	1:38	**9:34**	**5:30**	**1:30**	21.3
Vega	Lyra	0.0	11:37	7:45	3:45	**11:41**	**7:38**	**3:38**	86.4

Time of Transit (EST)
Boldface — P.M.   Lightface — A.M.

RISINGS AND SETTINGS

The times of the star's rising and setting at Boston on any date are found by applying the interval shown to the time of the star's transit on that date. Subtract the interval for its setting. The times for a place outside Boston are found by correcting the times found for Boston by the values of the Key Letters shown. (See footnote.) The directions in which the star rises and sets shown for Boston are generally useful throughout the United States. Deneb, Algol, Capella, and Vega are circumpolar stars — this means that they do not appear to rise or set, but are above the horizon.

Star	Int. hr. m.	Rising Key	Rising Dir.	Setting Key	Setting Dir.
Altair	6:36	B	EbN	E	WbN
Fomalhaut	3:59	E	SE	D	SW
Aldebaran	7:06	B	ENE	D	WNW
Rigel	5:33	D	EbS	B	WbS
Bellatrix	6:27	B	EbN	D	WbN
Betelgeuse	6:31	B	EbN	D	WbN
Sirius	5:00	D	ESE	B	WSW
Procyon	6:23	B	EbN	D	WbN
Pollux	8:01	A	NE	E	NW
Regulus	6:49	B	EbN	D	WbN
Spica	5:23	D	EbS	B	WbS
Arcturus	7:19	A	ENE	E	WNW
Antares	4:17	E	SEbE	A	SWbW

NOTE: The values of Key Letters are given in the Time Correction Tables (pages 186-190).

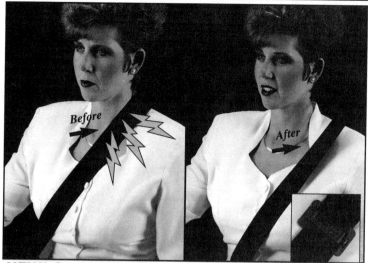

NEW! Seatbelt Adjuster - Stops Neck Chafing!

Now you can solve the problem of shoulder belts digging into your neck. Put an end to neck chafing and strangulating seat belts with this unique Seatbelt Adjuster! Keeps shoulder belt where it belongs – several inches to the side and securely over your shoulder, not digging into your neck! Easy to install – just clip adjuster onto your lap belt and slip shoulder strap through top slot. Remains in position when you unbuckle. Set includes 2 adjusters; one for driver's side and one for passenger's side. Made of sturdy black plastic – 1- 3/4" x 2-3/4" – includes complete instructions. Drive with comfort – not discomfort!

SA-210 Seatbelt Adjuster Set of 2 ONLY $5.97 + $2.00 p&h.   Send Check or M.O.

Holst, Inc. Dept. OF-95, 1118 W. Lake, Box 370, Tawas City, MI 48764

WIPES OUT FLEAS
The "ERADICATOR"™
FLEA TRAP
SPECIAL OFFER
NOT $29.95 $**8**95
NOW ONLY

Works Day and Night!

| EXTRA BONUS 3 FREE DISCS | See Coupon Offer Below |

Flea problem? You know the agony it can cause. Fleas carry diseases that put your family and pets in danger. Get rid of these perilous pests with the **"Eradicator" Flea Trap.** Fleas are lured into trap by a 4 watt bulb. They land and stick to adhesive pads inside the trap where they die. They can't get away, they're stuck DEAD! No more biting pets or laying new eggs. The **"Eradicator"** is **SAFE**, clean to use. It works where sprays, powders, all else fails. Operates silently, protects a 15 ft. area. 7 1/2 x 5", 120 V, 5 ft. electric cord. Comes with 2 non-toxic disposable adhesive pads (replace monthly). Guaranteed to work or purchase price back (less S&H). Order Today!

"ERADICATOR" WORKS SO VERY WELL!

A scientifically developed "sticky disc" lies at the base of Eradicator. This along with the 4 watt bulb becomes irresistible to fleas … draws them into the trap … and kills them dead. Can capture thousands of fleas at once. There is no better way to rid your home of these pesty, nasty fleas. Forget chemically treated pet collars or other unsuccessful methods. Avoid costly Vet, medicine, bills … Eradicator will do the job!

HOLST, Inc. Dept. OA-95
1118 W. Lake, Box 370, Tawas City, MI 48764
YES. Please rush my **ERADICATOR** FLEA TRAP(s) (Item #F233) to try out for 30 days on money back guarantee.
☐ One Flea Trap for $8.95 + $3 S&H ☐ **SAVE!** TWO Traps for only $17.50 + $4 S&H
☐ Send _____ Additional Refill Pak(s) (Item #RD230) each only $3.95 + $1 S & H.
(Each Pak contains 6 long-lasting refill discs) ☐ Check here for **FREE** Discs w/purchase.
Enclosed is $_____ (MI residents add sales tax).
CHARGE TO MY: ☐ MasterCard ☐ Visa • Make Check or M.O. payable to HOLST, Inc.

Account No. _____ Exp. Date_____

Name_____

Address_____

City_____ State _____ Zip_____

EVERY 17 YEARS,

Sometime in the spring of 1995, residents of Pennsylvania, Maryland, Virginia, West Virginia, and North Carolina will begin hearing an incredible and constant racket the likes of which they will not have heard since 1978 . . .

Their bodies a ghostly white, their eyes gleaming red, they emerge into the night in response to a summons only they can hear. Struggling up from the earth where they have been entombed for years, they claw their way onto the nearest tree trunk. And then they begin . . . to change.

Long before dawn, the metamorphosis is complete. The silent, sluglike, subterranean creatures have vanished. In their stead are some of the loudest, largest, unlikeliest insects on Earth — the aptly named *Magicicada,* or periodical cicada.

A genus unique to the United States, *Magicicada* has the longest life span in the insect world, spending up to 17 years underground before taking part in the bizarre rite of spring that transforms it from nymph to adult. (The common cicada, on the other hand, appears every year when summer is at its height, which is why it is often referred to as the "dog-day" cicada or harvest fly.)

Approximately 15 different broods of *Magicicada* — each with its own 17- or 13-year cycle — exist east of the Mississippi River. Which means that each year, somewhere, a brood is making its rare appearance. In 1995 it's showtime for Brood I, a 17-year cicada that has staked out a portion of the mid-Atlantic region.

Sometime in April and May, residents of the woodsy areas of Pennsylvania, Maryland, Virginia, West Virginia, and North Carolina (plus a small contingent in Long Island, New York) can expect to be surrounded by cicadas. There will be cicadas hanging from the trees. There will be cicadas careening overhead. There will be cicadas underfoot. And everywhere, there will be the infernal racket that an early commentator — a colonist encountering the insect in Plymouth, Massachusetts, in 1633 — described as "a constant yelling noise as made the woods ring of them and ready to deaf the hearers."

The settlers, finding themselves suddenly amid "a numerous company of flies, which were like for bigness unto wasps and bumblebees," understandably felt that a plague of Biblical proportions had been visited upon them. And subsequent generations have shared that feeling. But the periodical cicada, though bizarre in many ways, is quite benign.

Cicadas, fortunately, are *not* the ravenous locusts spoken of in the Bible, a species of grasshopper that could turn a garden into a desert in a matter of hours. The cicada is a member of the Homoptera order, which includes such relative wimps as aphids and mealybugs.

Though cicadas feed off trees, they are a sucking rather than a chewing insect;

by Deborah Papier

LIKE CLOCKWORK

they get their nourishment from the sap, which the tree can easily part with, not from the leaves. The only trees at risk from cicadas are saplings (particularly fruit bearers), whose branches can break under the weight of the eggs the female lays. To protect young trees from possible damage from cicadas, just tie cheesecloth around them — spraying is overkill.

Nor are cicadas harmful to people. Having one fly into you can give you an unpleasant jolt, but the insects do not bite or sting. And though generations of soothsayers have claimed that the "W" marking on the cicada's wings is a portent of war, that's clearly balderdash. There are always cicadas, and there are always wars.

s one would expect of a slug, the nymph

– photo: Thomas Moore, University of Michigan

A leads a fairly indolent life. But it is not entirely idle during the 13 or 17 years it spends underground. In its first seven or eight years, it grows from a hatchling about a 16th of an inch long to its full span of about two inches, shedding its skin four times. And though the nymph remains in one place for years at a time, it will bestir itself to find another food source when the root it has been feeding on is tapped out.

Clearly, too, its inner clock is running, ticking away the seasons until it is time to emerge. As the 17th spring draws near, the nymph, acting on some internal or external signal that remains a mystery, begins to burrow upward. So strong is its determination to embark on its new life that it will scrabble through pavement to get to the surface.

Once it sees daylight, the nymph might

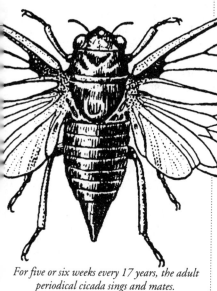

For five or six weeks every 17 years, the adult periodical cicada sings and mates.

construct a little turret at the top of its exit hole, presumably to protect it from the rain. Then it retreats several inches and waits, for weeks or even months, until the moment is right.

The adult cicada needs very little food, so it can concentrate on the really important things in life — singing and sex.

Male nymphs usually emerge first with females following a few days later. The creatures then face one more challenge: They must quickly find a rough surface to hold them while they undergo a fifth and final molt. Some nymphs never get a foothold and die. Still others are unable to split through their carapace; they also die.

But if all goes well, within an hour the nymph sheds its pale skin, develops a new dark one, unfurls its wings (transparent, save for a tracery of reddish-orange), and begins its adulthood.

Compared with its long childhood, the cicada's adulthood is brief — only about five or six weeks. But it's five or six glorious weeks. The adult cicada needs very little food, so it can concentrate on the really important things in life — singing and sex.

Cicadas begin mating within a week after attaining maturity, and the babies follow in about six weeks. The female makes a nest for her fertilized eggs by repeatedly thrusting her ovipositor into a twig, creating a pocket in the bark. She then places the eggs, one at a time,

The common or "dog-day" cicada appears every summer.

in two rows in the pocket. When she has filled up the space with about a dozen eggs, she moves out a little farther on the twig and repeats the process until she has laid as many as 600 eggs.

Under their weight of fecundity, the twigs sometimes snap off and fall to the ground. If that happens, the nymph that hatches from the egg in about six weeks is in a better position to burrow underground. But even if the twig remains on the tree, the nymph can usually land safely and get on with the business of constructing its home for the next 17 years.

pinion is divided on the musical merits of the cicada's song. In some eras in some countries, cicadas have been kept in cages, the better to regale their keepers. In other times and places, their vocalizings have been considered grounds for insecticide.

But melody or cacophony, one thing is indisputable: The cicada is LOUD. A single cicada can make itself heard a quarter of a mile away. A chorus of the insects can produce a din that will register at 100 decibels — the equivalent of a jackhammer. Like a heavy-metal musician, the cicada runs the risk of destroying its own hearing. But unlike its human counterpart, the cicada has a built-in protective mechanism: While it is singing, it collapses its eardrum, blocking out most of the noise it is making.

Only the male cicadas go in for making music (or noise), which led the Greek writer Xenarchus to quip, "Happy are cicadas' lives, for they all have silent wives." The sounds are produced by two membranes in the male's thorax, which he vibrates by lifting his abdomen. Unlike most other insects, the cicada does not wait until nightfall

Bet You Can't Eat Just One

Just the right size for popping into your mouth, with a satisfying crunch and a flavor that has been compared to a cross between a potato and an avocado, cicadas would seem to be the perfect snack food. The Native Americans were quite fond of the crispy critters, but the settlers could never be persuaded to munch along, and few people today appreciate this rare taste treat. Cicadas are easily prepared: Just dip in batter and fry in butter until golden brown. Serve with cocktail sauce.

to begin his serenade, but drones away from dawn to dusk.

Though the tonal qualities of the sounds vary from species to species, all periodical cicadas have a repertory of three works — a congregation song, a courtship serenade, and a disturbance sound the insect makes when it feels threatened.

Attention, All Cicada Watchers!

Entomologists at the Smithsonian Institution keep track of the annual hatchings of the periodical cicada, and they would love to hear from you if the insects hatch in your area. "We're interested in the 17-year cicada, black with red eyes, that hatches anytime from May to July," says researcher Richard Froeschner. Send along a dead sample cicada in a container (old film containers work fine) for verification. Write to: Richard Froeschner, Dept. of Entomology, "Cicadas," Smithsonian Institution, MRC105, Washington, DC 20560. ☐ ☐

WINDCHILL TABLE

As wind speed increases, the air temperature against your body falls. The combination of cold temperatures and high winds creates a cooling effect so severe that exposed flesh can freeze. (Inanimate objects, such as cars, do not experience windchill.)

To gauge wind speed: at 10 mph you can feel wind on your face; at 20 small branches move, and dust or snow is raised; at 30 large branches move and wires whistle; at 40 whole trees bend. *– courtesy of Mount Washington Observatory*

Wind Velocity (MPH)	Temperature (°F)												
	50	41	32	23	14	5	–4	–13	–22	–31	–40	–49	–58
	Equivalent Temperature (°F) (Equivalent in Cooling Power on Exposed Flesh under Calm Conditions)												
5	48	39	28	19	10	1	–9	–18	–27	–36	–51	–56	–65
10	41	30	18	7	–4	–15	–26	–36	–49	–60	–71	–81	–92
20	32	19	7	–6	–18	–31	–44	–58	–71	–83	–96	–108	–121
30	28	14	1	–13	–27	–40	–54	–69	–81	–96	–108	–123	–137
40	27	12	–2	–17	–31	–45	–60	–74	–89	–103	–116	–130	–144
50	25	10	–4	–18	–33	–47	–62	–76	–90	–105	–119	–134	–148
	Little Danger			Increasing Danger			Great Danger						
	Danger from Freezing of Exposed Flesh (for Properly Clothed Person)												

1994 NOVEMBER, THE ELEVENTH MONTH

The total eclipse of the Sun on the 3rd is visible only in southern latitudes, but all of North America gets to see a penumbral eclipse of the Moon on the night of the 17th-18th. That otherwise brilliant Moon spoils viewing of the Leonid meteor shower before dawn. Mercury is visible low in the southeast before morning's light, fairly near Spica on the 2nd and Venus on the 12th. Rapidly brightening Mars is rising in the middle of the night and is high in the south as dawn light glimmers; Saturn is the lonely planet in the south after nightfall. The Pleiades sparkle in the east after dusk, Perseus bright above them, and Cassiopeia strikes high in the north.

●	New Moon	3rd day	8th hour	37th min.
☽	First Quarter	10th day	1st hour	15th min.
○	Full Moon	18th day	1st hour	58th min.
☾	Last Quarter	26th day	2nd hour	5th min.

For an explanation of this page, see "How to Use This Almanac," page 30; for values of Key Letters, see Time Correction Tables, page 186.

Day of Year	Day of Month	Day of Week	☉ Rises h. m.	Key	☉ Sets h. m.	Key	Length of Days h. m.	Sun Fast m.	Full Sea Boston A.M.	Full Sea Boston P.M.	☽ Rises h. m.	Key	☽ Sets h. m.	Key	Declination of Sun °	☽ Place	☽ Age
305	1	Tu.	6 17	D	4 38	B	10 21	32	8½	9	3 A.M. 50	E	3 P.M. 20	C	14 S.30	VIR	28
306	2	W.	6 19	D	4 36	B	10 17	32	9½	10	5 04	E	3 59	B	14 49	VIR	29
307	3	Th.	6 20	D	4 35	B	10 15	32	10¼	10¾	6 20	E	4 43	B	15 08	VIR	0
308	4	Fr.	6 21	D	4 34	B	10 13	32	11	11¾	7 34	E	5 34	B	15 26	LIB	1
309	5	Sa.	6 22	D	4 33	B	10 11	32	—	12	8 44	E	6 32	B	15 45	SCO	2
310	6	**B**	6 24	D	4 32	B	10 08	32	12½	12¾	9 46	E	7 36	B	16 03	OPH	3
311	7	M.	6 25	D	4 30	B	10 05	32	1½	1¾	10 39	E	8 42	B	16 21	SAG	4
312	8	Tu.	6 26	D	4 29	A	10 03	32	2½	2¾	11 A.M. 24	E	9 50	B	16 38	SAG	5
313	9	W.	6 27	D	4 28	A	10 01	32	3½	3¾	12 P.M. 02	D	10 P.M. 56	C	16 56	CAP	6
314	10	Th.	6 29	D	4 27	A	9 58	32	4½	4¾	12 36	D	— —	–	17 13	AQU	7
315	11	Fr.	6 30	D	4 26	A	9 56	32	5½	5¾	1 06	D	12 A.M. 00	C	17 29	AQU	8
316	12	Sa.	6 31	D	4 25	A	9 54	32	6½	7	1 34	C	1 01	D	17 45	PSC	9
317	13	**B**	6 32	D	4 24	A	9 52	31	7½	7¾	2 01	C	2 02	D	18 01	PSC	10
318	14	M.	6 34	D	4 23	A	9 49	31	8¼	8¾	2 29	C	3 01	D	18 17	PSC	11
319	15	Tu.	6 35	D	4 22	A	9 47	31	9	9½	2 58	B	4 00	E	18 32	PSC	12
320	16	W.	6 36	D	4 22	A	9 46	31	9¾	10¼	3 30	B	4 58	E	18 47	PSC	13
321	17	Th.	6 37	D	4 21	A	9 44	31	10¼	10¾	4 06	B	5 55	E	19 02	ARI	14
322	18	Fr.	6 39	D	4 20	A	9 41	31	11	11½	4 45	B	6 50	E	19 16	ARI	15
323	19	Sa.	6 40	D	4 19	A	9 39	30	11½	—	5 29	B	7 43	E	19 30	TAU	16
324	20	**B**	6 41	D	4 18	A	9 37	30	12¼	12¼	6 18	B	8 33	E	19 44	TAU	17
325	21	M.	6 42	D	4 18	A	9 36	30	12¾	12¾	7 12	B	9 18	E	19 58	ORI	18
326	22	Tu.	6 43	D	4 17	A	9 34	30	1½	1½	8 08	B	9 59	E	20 11	GEM	19
327	23	W.	6 45	D	4 16	A	9 31	29	2¼	2¼	9 08	B	10 36	E	20 23	GEM	20
328	24	Th.	6 46	D	4 16	A	9 30	29	3	3	10 09	C	11 10	D	20 35	CAN	21
329	25	Fr.	6 47	D	4 15	A	9 28	29	3¾	4	11 P.M. 13	C	11 A.M. 41	D	20 47	LEO	22
330	26	Sa.	6 48	D	4 15	A	9 27	28	4½	4¾	— —	–	12 P.M. 12	D	20 58	SEX	23
331	27	**B**	6 49	E	4 14	A	9 25	28	5½	5¾	12 A.M. 19	D	12 42	D	21 09	LEO	24
332	28	M.	6 50	E	4 14	A	9 24	28	6¼	6¾	1 27	D	1 15	C	21 20	VIR	25
333	29	Tu.	6 51	E	4 13	A	9 22	28	7¼	7¾	2 38	E	1 50	C	21 31	VIR	26
334	30	W.	6 53	E	4 13	A	9 20	27	8	8¾	3 A.M. 51	E	2 P.M. 30	B	21 S.41	VIR	27

NOVEMBER hath 30 days. 1994

a wind has blown the rain away and blown
the sky away and all the leaves away,
and the trees stand. I think i too have known
autumn too long.
– *e. e. cummings*

D. M.	D. W.	Dates, Feasts, Fasts, Aspects, Tide Heights	*Weather* ↓
1	Tu.	All Saints • International Rainbow Bridge at Niagara Falls opened to public, 1941	*Snow*
2	W.	All Souls • ☌☿☾ • ♀ in inf. ☌ • {11.7 10.9	*comes*
3	Th.	☾ at ☊ • New ● • Eclipse of ☉ • ☾ at perig. •	*early;*
4	Fr.	*He who boasts of his descent is like the potato; the best part of him is underground.* •	*enough*
5	Sa.	☿ Gr. Elong. (19° W.) • Susan B. Anthony arrested for attempting to vote, 1875 • Tides {— 12.5	*to*
6	**B**	24th S. af. P. • ☾ runs low • John Philip Sousa born, 1854	*make*
7	M.	Elephant first appeared as symbol for Republican party in Thomas Nast cartoon, 1875	*a saint*
8	Tu.	☌♆☾ • ☌♅☾ • FDR elected to 4th term, 1944 • {10.3 11.2	*surly.*
9	W.	♄ stat. • Power failure caused New York City and eastern seaboard blackout, 1965 •	*Warm*
10	Th.	St. Leo the Great • Tommy Dorsey born, 1905 • {9.7 10.0	*reprieve,*
11	Fr.	St. Martin • Veterans Day • ☌♄☾ • Indian Summer •	*we*
12	Sa.	☾ on Eq. • ☌☿♀ • Sadie Hawkins Day • Tides {9.6 9.4 •	*do*
13	**B**	25th S. af. P. • Holland Tunnel under Hudson R. opened, 1927 •	*believe.*
14	M.	Claude Monet born, 1840 • *Real art is illumination; It adds stature to life.* • {9.9 9.3	*Enjoy*
15	Tu.	Arthur Dorrington became first black hockey player, 1950 • Georgia O'Keeffe born, 1887	*it*
16	W.	*The Sound of Music* premiered in New York, 1959 • W. C. Handy born, 1873 •	*while*
17	Th.	St. Hugh of Lincoln • ☾ at ☋ • ☌♃☉ • {10.3 9.3	*it*
18	Fr.	St. Hilda • ☾ at apo. • Full Beaver ○ • Eclipse of ☾ •	
19	Sa.	*If ice in November will bear a duck, There'll be nothing thereafter but sleet and muck.* •	*lasts —*
20	**B**	26th S. af. P. • ☾ rides high • ☌♇☉ •	*here*
21	M.	♀ stat. • Red Grange played last varsity game for U. of Ill. before turning pro, 1925 •	*come*
22	Tu.	St. Cecelia • President Kennedy assassinated, 1963 • Abigail Adams born, 1744	*some*
23	W.	St. Clement • First jukebox installed, San Francisco, 1889 • {8.9 9.7	*wintry*
24	Th.	Thanksgiving Day • Zachary Taylor born, 1784 • Tides {8.9 9.5	*blasts!*
25	Fr.	☌♂☾ • USS *Enterprise* aircraft carrier commissioned, 1961 • Tides {9.0 9.4	*We*
26	Sa.	*If you sleep with dogs, you'll rise with fleas.* • Windstorm (105 mph gusts) in northwest, 1949 •	*just*
27	**B**	1st S. in Advent • ☾ on Eq. • {9.5 9.4 •	*want to*
28	M.	Chanukah • Ferdinand Magellan began voyage around world, 1520 • {10.1 9.6 •	*say*
29	Tu.	Louisa May Alcott born, 1832 • Busby Berkeley born, 1895 • {10.7 9.9	*thanks to*
30	W.	St. Andrew • ☌♀☾ • Winston Churchill born, 1874	*Squanto.*

Aim above morality. Be not simply good; be good for something. – H. D. Thoreau

Farmer's Calendar

Splitting firewood is widely appreciated as exercise for the upper body and as an aid to reflection, but the work deserves to be better known as an adventure in connoisseurship in the most rarefied realm, that of the nose. We have been given our five senses to enable us to discriminate, to mark differences and similarities between things. Smell is the finest discriminator of all; learn to use your nose while you're splitting hardwood, and it will open for you a rich volume of distinctions.

Compare the heavy smell of olives that comes from a fresh-split block of red oak with the similar but far more delicate smell of white oak or with the smoky, almost musky olive smell of butternut. Beech wood is faintly sweet; paper birch has a stronger, sweeter scent; and black birch smells like bubble gum. Maple, to me, has little character besides a kind of vague vegetative smell, and ash is odorless. No doubt a finer nose than mine could make something of the last two woods, as well.

Let no one imagine wood-sniffing is a mere frippery. The potential is there for hard financial advantage. Why couldn't a really educated woodpile nose attain the kind of refinement we read the whiskey tasters of Scotland possess? They can sniff a glass of Scotch and tell you not only which district it came from, but which glen, which brook, which distiller. Since there's a good deal of money in Scotch, a lot can hang on the findings of an expert nose. Why couldn't the same apply to wood sniffing? Firewood dealers are a tough lot, almost the last of the old-time free-booting capitalists. The buyer needs all the help he can get. A sniffer who could knock ten bucks off the price of a load for an off-scent would be a valuable man.

1994 DECEMBER, The Twelfth Month

Venus climbs higher in the east before dawn, reaching its greatest brilliancy on the 9th. Golden-orange Mars now rises in the east in the late evening, brightening to rival the glorious winter stars. The Pleiades and the arrowhead formed by Aldebaran and the Hyades in Taurus lead a throng of brilliance in the southeast. At the top is Auriga with yellow Capella, at center Orion with his three-star belt and Rigel and Betelgeuse, with the two Dog Stars, Procyon and Sirius, following. We must wait until after late moonsets to see the Geminid meteors on the 13th and 14th. There is a close conjunction of Jupiter and the Moon on the 29th. Winter begins at 9:23 P.M., EST, on the 21st.

● New Moon	2nd day	18th hour	55th min.
☽ First Quarter	9th day	16th hour	8th min.
○ Full Moon	17th day	21st hour	18th min.
☾ Last Quarter	25th day	14th hour	8th min.

For an explanation of this page, see "How to Use This Almanac," page 30; for values of Key Letters, see Time Correction Tables, page 186.

Day of Year	Day of Month	Day of Week	☉ Rises h. m.	Key	☉ Sets h. m.	Key	Length of Days h. m.	Sun Fast m.	Full Sea Boston A.M.	Full Sea Boston P.M.	☽ Rises h. m.	Key	☽ Sets h. m.	Key	Declination of Sun °	Place	☽ Age
335	1	Th.	6 54	E	4 13	A	9 19	27	9	9½	5ᴍ05	E	3ᴾᴍ17	B	21s.50	LIB	28
336	2	Fr.	6 55	E	4 12	A	9 17	26	9¾	10½	6 18	E	4 11	B	21 59	LIB	0
337	3	Sa.	6 56	E	4 12	A	9 16	26	10¾	11½	7 26	E	5 13	B	22 07	OPH	1
338	4	**B**	6 57	E	4 12	A	9 15	26	11½	—	8 25	E	6 21	B	22 15	SAG	2
339	5	M.	6 58	E	4 12	A	9 14	25	12¼	12½	9 16	E	7 30	B	22 23	SAG	3
340	6	Tu.	6 59	E	4 12	A	9 13	25	1¼	1½	9 59	E	8 40	C	22 30	SAG	4
341	7	W.	7 00	E	4 12	A	9 12	24	2	2¼	10 35	D	9 47	C	22 37	AQU	5
342	8	Th.	7 01	E	4 12	A	9 11	24	3	3¼	11 07	D	10 51	D	22 44	AQU	6
343	9	Fr.	7 01	E	4 12	A	9 11	24	4	4¼	11ᴍ37	D	11ᴾᴍ53	D	22 50	AQU	7
344	10	Sa.	7 02	E	4 12	A	9 10	23	5	5¼	12ᴾᴍ05	C	— —	–	22 55	PSC	8
345	11	**B**	7 03	E	4 12	A	9 09	23	6	6¼	12 33	C	12ᴀᴍ54	D	23 00	PSC	9
346	12	M.	7 04	E	4 12	A	9 08	22	6¾	7¼	1 01	C	1 53	E	23 05	PSC	10
347	13	Tu.	7 05	E	4 12	A	9 07	22	7¾	8¼	1 32	B	2 51	E	23 09	PSC	11
348	14	W.	7 06	E	4 12	A	9 06	21	8½	9	2 06	B	3 48	E	23 13	ARI	12
349	15	Th.	7 06	E	4 12	A	9 06	21	9¼	9¾	2 44	B	4 44	E	23 16	TAU	13
350	16	Fr.	7 07	E	4 13	A	9 06	20	9¾	10½	3 27	B	5 38	E	23 19	TAU	14
351	17	Sa.	7 08	E	4 13	A	9 05	20	10½	11	4 14	B	6 29	E	23 21	TAU	15
352	18	**B**	7 08	E	4 13	A	9 05	19	11¼	11¾	5 06	B	7 16	E	23 23	ORI	16
353	19	M.	7 09	E	4 14	A	9 05	19	11¾	—	6 02	B	7 59	E	23 24	GEM	17
354	20	Tu.	7 10	E	4 14	A	9 04	18	12½	12½	7 01	C	8 38	E	23 25	GEM	18
355	21	W.	7 10	E	4 14	A	9 04	18	1	1	8 02	C	9 13	E	23 25	CAN	19
356	22	Th.	7 11	E	4 15	A	9 04	17	1¾	1¾	9 05	C	9 45	D	23 25	CAN	20
357	23	Fr.	7 11	E	4 16	A	9 05	17	2½	2½	10 09	D	10 15	D	23 25	LEO	21
358	24	Sa.	7 11	E	4 16	A	9 05	16	3¼	3½	11ᴍ14	D	10 45	D	23 24	LEO	22
359	25	**B**	7 12	E	4 17	A	9 05	16	4	4¼	— —	–	11 16	C	23 23	VIR	23
360	26	M.	7 12	E	4 17	A	9 05	15	4¾	5¼	12ᴀᴍ48	E	11ᴀᴍ48	C	23 21	VIR	24
361	27	Tu.	7 13	E	4 18	A	9 05	15	5¾	6¼	1 31	E	12ᴾᴍ24	B	23 18	VIR	25
362	28	W.	7 13	E	4 19	A	9 06	14	6¾	7¼	2 42	E	1 06	B	23 15	VIR	26
363	29	Th.	7 13	E	4 20	A	9 07	14	7¾	8¼	3 53	E	1 54	B	23 12	LIB	27
364	30	Fr.	7 13	E	4 20	A	9 07	13	8½	9¼	5 02	E	2 51	B	23 09	OPH	28
365	31	Sa.	7 13	E	4 21	A	9 08	13	9½	10¼	6ᴍ06	E	3ᴾᴍ55	B	23s.04	OPH	29

OLD FARMER'S ALMANAC

DECEMBER hath 31 days. 1994

The Darling of the world is come,
And fit it is we find a room
To welcome Him. The nobler part
Of all the house here is the heart.
– *Robert Herrick*

D. M.	D. W.	Dates, Feasts, Fasts, Aspects, Tide Heights	*Weather* ↓
1	Th.	☾ at ☊ • First drive-in gas station opened, Pittsburgh, Penn., 1913 •	*Deck*
2	Fr.	☾ at perig. • **New** ● • Henry Ford unveiled Model A, 1927 • {12.3 / 10.7	*the*
3	Sa.	☾ runs low • Oberlin College, first coed college, opened, Oberlin, Ohio, 1833 {12.5 / 10.8	*malls*
4	**B**	**2nd S. in Advent** • Rain today brings rain for a week. • {12.4 / —	*with*
5	M.	☌♆☾ • ☌♅☾ • *The Nutcracker* premiered, 1892 • {10.7 / 12.2	*plastic*
6	Tu.	St. Nicholas • Jefferson Davis died, 1889 • {10.6 / 11.7 •	*greenery,*
7	W.	*A man who does nothing never has time to do anything.* •	*stimulate*
8	Th.	Conception of Virgin Mary • Tides {10.1 / 10.4 •	*that ol'*
9	Fr.	☾ on Eq. • ☌♄☾ • ♀ Greatest Brilliancy •	*economy;*
10	Sa.	New York City's warmest winter day: 70° F, 1946 • Emily Dickinson born, 1830 •	*ice &*
11	**B**	**3rd S. in Advent** • UNICEF est., 1946 • Tides {9.5 / 8.9 •	*snow*
12	M.	George F. Grant patented golf tee, 1899 • First Bank of U.S. opened in Philadelphia, 1792	*• will*
13	Tu.	St. Lucy • ☿ in sup. ☌ • Grandma Moses died, 1961 • {9.6 / 8.7	*paint*
14	W.	☾ at ☋ • Temperature fell 79° F in 24 hours, Helena, Mont., 1924 • {9.8 / 8.7 •	*the*
15	Th.	☾ at apo. • Canadian flag adopted, 1964 • Bill of Rights passed, 1791 •	*scenery,*
16	Fr.	Boston Tea Party, 1773 • Margaret Mead born, 1901 • {10.1 / 8.9 •	*angels*
17	Sa.	☾ rides high • **Full Cold** ○ • Beware the Pogonip. • {10.2 / 9.0 •	*sing in*
18	**B**	**4th S. in Advent** • First photo of Moon, 1839 •	*four-*
19	M.	*All the world's a stage and most of us are desperately under-rehearsed.* • Tides {10.3 / — •	*part*
20	Tu.	Halcyon days. • Peter the Great reformed Russian calendar, 1699 •	*harmony.*
21	W.	St. Thomas • Winter Solstice • Pilgrims landed at Plymouth Rock, 1620 •	*May*
22	Th.	Colonial law required standard weight bread and pure flour, 1650 • Tides {9.2 / 10.0 •	*we*
23	Fr.	☌♂☾ • Colonists repealed 22-year ban on Christmas celebrations, 1681 • {9.4 / 9.8 •	*all*
24	Sa.	☾ on Eq. • Famous cold day, Kentucky: Ohio and Miss. rivers frozen, 1796	*sincerely*
25	**B**	**Christmas Day** • A green Christmas makes a fat churchyard. •	*strive*
26	M.	St. Stephen • Harry S Truman died, 1972 • Tides {10.0 / 9.4 •	*for*
27	Tu.	St. John • "Howdy Doody" show debuted, 1947 • Louis Pasteur born, 1822	*peace*
28	W.	Holy Innocents • ☌♀☾ • Tides {10.7 / 9.5 •	*on*
29	Th.	☾♃☾ • 30" + snow on ground, Mo. and Ill., 1830 • Tides {11.2 / 9.7	*earth*
30	Fr.	☾ at perig. • –32° F, Mountain City, Tenn., 1917 • Rudyard Kipling born, 1865	*in*
31	Sa.	☾ runs low • *Make the most of yourself for that is all there is of you.* • Tides {11.9 / 10.3	*'95!*

Farmer's Calendar

December 20. A big storm is coming. The forecasters are falling over one another to see who can hit the alarm bell hardest. It's early in the winter for a real snow, but indeed, outdoors it looks as though the weathermen might be right this time. The morning was palely sunny, but after lunch a gray iron sky supervened with a keen little wind out of the north. Time to get ready.

Preparing for a major storm is like preparing for war: You take thought not for what you suspect your enemy *may* do, but for what you know he *can* do. First thing, I back both cars down to the bottom of the driveway and leave them facing the road. That way the snowplow can get up the drive, and I'll be able to get out after the storm without backing downhill through deep snow, a maneuver that seldom ends well. Then I bring a couple of cartloads of fuel in from the woodshed. While I'm outside, I make sure the snow shovel is gassed, oiled, and has a new plug.

Inside I fill the bathtub. Should the storm knock out the electricity, we'll have plenty of water for washing and for operating certain articles of plumbing, the importance of which is demonstrated with real force by a three-day outage. I check the flashlights to make certain all batteries are either weak or dead. They are. I ask, as I do each year, why we don't have a kerosene lamp. I try to think where the candles are. I fail.

It's nearly dark and the snow has begun. The bare patches and the steps have turned a fuzzy gray. It's supposed to snow all night. Before I quit, I always fill the birdfeeder — my last gesture of readiness, the final perfecting touch that sets the whole place safely straight and lets me enjoy the coming storm.

Venus and Jupiter are in the east at dawn all month, but are closest together on the 14th, when more brilliant Venus (just past greatest elongation) burns three degrees north of Jupiter. All the country, except Alaska and Hawaii, gets to see the Moon move right in front of bright star Spica just before sunrise on the 23rd. Before dawn on the 27th, Venus can be seen close to the crescent Moon, which is at perigee that night. Saturn is the brightest point in the southwest at nightfall. The Quanrantid meteors fly before dawn on the 3rd and 4th. Earth is at perihelion on the 4th.

●	New Moon	1st day	5th hour	57th min.
☽	First Quarter	8th day	10th hour	47th min.
○	Full Moon	16th day	15th hour	27th min.
☾	Last Quarter	23rd day	23rd hour	59th min.
●	New Moon	30th day	17th hour	48th min.

For an explanation of this page, see "How to Use This Almanac," page 30; for values of Key Letters, see Time Correction Tables, page 186.

Day of Year	Day of Month	Day of Week	☉ Rises h. m.	Key	☉ Sets h. m.	Key	Length of Days h. m.	Sun Fast m.	Full Sea Boston A.M.	Full Sea Boston P.M.	☽ Rises h. m.	Key	☽ Sets h. m.	Key	Declination of Sun ° '	☽ Place	☽ Age
1	1	A	7 14	E	4 22	A	9 08	12	10½	11¼	7 ᴹ02	E	5 ᴹ04	B	22s.59	SAG	0
2	2	M.	7 14	E	4 23	A	9 09	12	11¼	—	7 49	E	6 15	C	22 54	SAG	1
3	3	Tu.	7 14	E	4 24	A	9 10	11	12	12¼	8 30	D	7 25	C	22 48	CAP	2
4	4	W.	7 14	E	4 25	A	9 11	11	1	1	9 05	D	8 33	D	22 42	CAP	3
5	5	Th.	7 14	E	4 26	A	9 12	11	1¾	2	9 37	D	9 39	D	22 36	AQU	4
6	6	Fr.	7 14	E	4 27	A	9 13	10	2½	2¾	10 06	C	10 41	D	22 29	PSC	5
7	7	Sa.	7 13	E	4 28	A	9 15	10	3½	3¾	10 35	C	11 ᴹ42	D	22 22	PSC	6
8	8	A	7 13	E	4 29	A	9 16	9	4¼	4¾	11 04	C	— —	–	22 14	PSC	7
9	9	M.	7 13	E	4 30	A	9 17	9	5¼	5¾	11 ᴹ34	B	12 ᴬ41	E	22 05	PSC	8
10	10	Tu.	7 13	E	4 31	A	9 18	8	6	6½	12 ᴹ07	B	1 39	E	21 56	ARI	9
11	11	W.	7 13	E	4 32	A	9 19	8	7	7½	12 43	B	2 36	E	21 47	ARI	10
12	12	Th.	7 12	E	4 33	A	9 21	8	7¾	8½	1 23	B	3 31	E	21 37	TAU	11
13	13	Fr.	7 12	E	4 34	A	9 22	7	8¾	9¼	2 09	B	4 23	E	21 27	TAU	12
14	14	Sa.	7 11	E	4 35	A	9 24	7	9½	10	2 59	B	5 12	E	21 17	AUR	13
15	15	A	7 11	E	4 36	A	9 25	6	10	10¾	3 54	B	5 57	E	21 07	GEM	14
16	16	M.	7 11	E	4 38	A	9 27	6	10¾	11¼	4 53	B	6 37	E	20 55	GEM	15
17	17	Tu.	7 10	E	4 39	A	9 29	6	11½	—	5 54	C	7 14	E	20 44	CAN	16
18	18	W.	7 10	E	4 40	A	9 30	5	12	12	6 57	C	7 48	D	20 31	CAN	17
19	19	Th.	7 09	E	4 41	A	9 32	5	12½	12¾	8 01	D	8 19	D	20 19	LEO	18
20	20	Fr.	7 08	E	4 42	A	9 34	5	1¼	1½	9 07	D	8 50	D	20 06	SEX	19
21	21	Sa.	7 08	E	4 44	A	9 36	5	2	2¼	10 13	D	9 20	C	19 53	LEO	20
22	22	A	7 07	E	4 45	A	9 38	4	2¾	3	11 ᴾ21	D	9 52	C	19 40	VIR	21
23	23	M.	7 06	D	4 46	A	9 40	4	3½	4	— —	–	10 26	B	19 26	VIR	22
24	24	Tu.	7 05	D	4 47	A	9 42	4	4¼	5	12 ᴹ29	E	11 04	B	19 12	VIR	23
25	25	W.	7 05	D	4 49	A	9 44	3	5¼	6	1 38	E	11 ᴬ48	B	18 57	LIB	24
26	26	Th.	7 04	D	4 50	A	9 46	3	6¼	7	2 46	E	12 ᴹ39	B	18 42	SCO	25
27	27	Fr.	7 03	D	4 51	A	9 48	3	7½	8	3 50	E	1 37	B	18 26	OPH	26
28	28	Sa.	7 02	D	4 53	A	9 51	3	8½	9	4 47	E	2 42	B	18 11	SAG	27
29	29	A	7 01	D	4 54	A	9 53	3	9½	10	5 38	E	3 51	B	17 55	SAG	28
30	30	M.	7 00	D	4 55	A	9 55	2	10¼	11	6 22	E	5 01	C	17 38	CAP	0
31	31	Tu.	6 59	D	4 57	A	9 58	2	11¼	11¾	7 ᴹ00	D	6 ᴹ11	C	17s.21	AQU	1

JANUARY hath 31 days. 1995

Then came old January, wrapped well
In many weeds to keep the cold away;
Yet did he quake and quiver like to quell,
And blewe his nayles to warm them if he may.
– *Edmund Spenser*

D. M.	D. W.	Dates, Feasts, Fasts, Aspects, Tide Heights	Weather ↓
1	A	New Year's Day • Circumcision • New ● • ☌☿♆	
2	M.	Georgia ratified Constitution, 1788 • 14° F, Haleakala, Hawaii, 1961 • {12.1 / — •	*Clear*
3	Tu.	☌☿♅ • ♂ stat. • March of Dimes organized, 1938 •	*and severe.*
4	W.	⊕ at perihelion • Louis Braille born, 1809 • {10.6 / 11.4 •	*Nightly*
5	Th.	☌♄☾ • Twelfth Night • George Washington Carver died, 1943	*whitely,*
6	Fr.	Epiphany • ☾ on Eq. • Carl Sandburg born, 1878 •	*warming*
7	Sa.	*Wit without discretion is a sword in the hand of a fool.* • Tides {9.9 / 9.6 •	*slightly.*
8	A	1st S. af. Epiphany • Tides {9.6 / 9.0 •	*Snowing*
9	M.	Plough Monday • First successful U.S. balloon flight, Philadelphia, 1793 •	*buckets*
10	Tu.	☾ at ☋ • Buffalo Bill Cody died, 1917 • {9.3 / 8.3 •	*north of*
11	W.	☾ at apo. • First bottled milk delivered, Brooklyn, New York, 1878 •	*Nantucket.*
12	Th.	Sunshine today foretells much wind. • John Hancock born, 1737 • {9.4 / 8.3 •	*Clear*
13	Fr.	St. Hilary • ♀ Gr. Elong. (47° W.) • ☌♆☉ •	*as a*
14	Sa.	☾ rides high • ☌♀♃ • Snowflakes seen at San Diego, 1882 {9.9 / 8.7 •	*bell,*
15	A	2nd S. af. Epiphany • Tides {10.1 / 9.0 •	*milder*
16	M.	Martin Luther King Jr.'s Birthday • Full Wolf ○ • ☌♅☉ •	
17	Tu.	*A long life may not be good enough but a good life is long enough.* • {10.4 / — •	*as*
18	W.	Jazz greats Louis Armstrong, Billie Holiday, and others performed at the Met., NYC, 1944 •	*well.*
19	Th.	☿ Gr. Elong. (19° E.) • Tin can patented, 1825 • Tides {9.6 / 10.5 •	*Like*
20	Fr.	St. Fabian • ☾ on Eq. • Tides {9.8 / 10.4 •	*Shakespeare's*
21	Sa.	St. Agnes • Smoking in public illegal for women, New York City, 1908 •	*Dane,*
22	A	3rd S. af. Epiphany • Queen Victoria died, 1901 •	*it's*
23	M.	*If you would eat eggs, take care of the hen.* • Tides {10.2 / 9.6 •	*indecisive;*
24	Tu.	☾ at ☊ • Sir Winston Churchill died, 1965 • Tides {10.3 / 9.3 •	*one*
25	W.	Conversion of Paul • ☿ stat. • *January wet, no wine you get.* •	*day*
26	Th.	Sts. Timothy & Titus • ☌♃☾ • Tides {10.6 / 9.2 •	*rain,*
27	Fr.	☾ runs low • ☌♀☾ • ☾ at perig. • National Geographic Society founded, 1888	*the*
28	Sa.	St. Thomas Aquinas • Space shuttle *Challenger* exploded, killing 7, 1986 •	*next*
29	A	4th S. af. Epiphany • ☌♆☾ •	*de-ice-ive.*
30	M.	New ● • First commercial jazz recording released, 1917 •	*Melancholy,*
31	Tu.	First successful U.S. satellite, *Explorer I*, launched, 1958 • Tides {11.6 / 10.6 •	*baby.*

Farmer's Calendar

I began to suspect that last winter would be something out of the ordinary when I got a Christmas card from the CEO of the Mobil Oil Corporation, a gentleman I didn't remember ever having met. "Greetings, and *thanks in advance for your business,*" the card said. "Do I know you?" I asked myself. Six months later — six months and about a million gallons of Mobil's best No. 2 — and I'm in no doubt. By now the CEO and I are not friends, perhaps, but no longer strangers. You could say we're partners, I guess.

Yes, '93-'94 was quite a winter. In this part of the country it broke a lot of records, particularly for cold, records some of us wouldn't have minded seeing remain intact. As I look back on the winter, it seems to me that the temperature went down below zero Fahrenheit sometime last August and stayed there well into the following May, dipping frequently to points I hadn't realized could be attained on our planet. I had always thought the negative numbers around the 7 to 8 o'clock position on my outdoor thermometer were there for show. Turns out they're not.

It was a real old-fashioned winter, everybody said — an interesting idea. The long, hard winters of old times, like their wise and honest statesmen, gallant soldiers, and matchless athletes, are a sentimental falsehood, aren't they? A trick of memory? A trick not even of memory but of shared historical fantasy? Well, maybe they aren't. Maybe the winter of '93-'94 came among us to show us that the good old days were exactly as advertised, and to make us wish them right back where they came from, in the distant past — and to stay, please.

1995 FEBRUARY, THE SECOND MONTH

Mars is at its brightest and closest and reaches opposition on the 11th, rising at sunset and taking all night to cross the south sky. This planet glows to the right of the Sickle pattern of stars that outlines Leo the Lion's mane and chest. A telescope will show the white north polar ice cap and a few dark surface areas on clear nights this month. Mars comes no closer than 63 million miles, but its radiance still nearly equals that of Sirius, the brightest star, which itself is prominent in the south at midevening. Above Sirius twinkle Procyon and the chief luminaries of Gemini: Castor and Pollux. Saturn becomes lost low in the evening twilight this month. The full Moon is an enormous ten degrees south of Mars as the two sink into the west in morning twilight on the 15th. Late on the 22nd, there is a conjunction of Jupiter and the last quarter Moon, which is at perigee. Over the three nights of the 25th to 27th, there are five conjunctions!

☽	First Quarter	7th day	7th hour	55th min.
○	Full Moon	15th day	7th hour	16th min.
☾	Last Quarter	22nd day	8th hour	5th min.

For an explanation of this page, see "How to Use This Almanac," page 30; for values of Key Letters, see Time Correction Tables, page 186.

Day of Year	Day of Month	Day of Week	☉ Rises h. m.	Key	☉ Sets h. m.	Key	Length of Days h. m.	Sun Fast m.	Full Sea Boston A.M.	Full Sea Boston P.M.	☽ Rises h. m.	Key	☽ Sets h. m.	Key	Declination of Sun °	☽ Place	☽ Age
32	1	W.	6 58	D	4 58	A	10 00	2	—	12	7 A.M. 34	D	7 P.M. 18	D	17s.04	PSC	2
33	2	Th.	6 57	D	4 59	A	10 02	2	12½	12¾	8 05	D	8 24	D	16 47	PSC	3
34	3	Fr.	6 56	D	5 00	A	10 04	2	1¼	1½	8 35	C	9 27	D	16 30	PSC	4
35	4	Sa.	6 55	D	5 02	A	10 07	2	2	2¼	9 04	C	10 28	D	16 12	PSC	5
36	5	**A**	6 54	D	5 03	A	10 09	2	2¾	3¼	9 35	B	11 P.M. 27	D	15 54	PSC	6
37	6	M.	6 53	D	5 04	A	10 11	2	3½	4	10 07	B	— —	–	15 36	ARI	7
38	7	Tu.	6 52	D	5 06	A	10 14	1	4½	5	10 42	B	12 A.M. 25	E	15 17	ARI	8
39	8	W.	6 50	D	5 07	B	10 17	1	5¼	5¾	11 A.M. 20	B	1 21	E	14 58	TAU	9
40	9	Th.	6 49	D	5 08	B	10 19	1	6¼	6¾	12 P.M. 03	B	2 14	E	14 39	TAU	10
41	10	Fr.	6 48	D	5 10	B	10 22	1	7¼	7¾	12 51	B	3 04	E	14 20	TAU	11
42	11	Sa.	6 47	D	5 11	B	10 24	1	8	8¾	1 44	B	3 50	E	14 00	GEM	12
43	12	**A**	6 45	D	5 12	B	10 27	1	8¾	9½	2 41	B	4 33	E	13 40	GEM	13
44	13	M.	6 44	D	5 13	B	10 29	1	9½	10¼	3 42	C	5 12	E	13 20	CAN	14
45	14	Tu.	6 43	D	5 15	B	10 32	1	10¼	10¾	4 45	C	5 47	E	13 00	CAN	15
46	15	W.	6 41	D	5 16	B	10 35	1	11	11½	5 50	D	6 20	D	12 40	LEO	16
47	16	Th.	6 40	D	5 17	B	10 37	1	11¾	—	6 56	D	6 52	D	12 19	SEX	17
48	17	Fr.	6 38	D	5 19	B	10 41	2	12	12¼	8 03	D	7 23	D	11 58	LEO	18
49	18	Sa.	6 37	D	5 20	B	10 43	2	12¾	1	9 12	D	7 55	C	11 37	VIR	19
50	19	**A**	6 36	D	5 21	B	10 45	2	1½	1¾	10 21	E	8 29	C	11 16	VIR	20
51	20	M.	6 34	D	5 22	B	10 48	2	2¼	2¾	11 P.M. 30	E	9 06	B	10 54	VIR	21
52	21	Tu.	6 33	D	5 24	B	10 51	2	3	3½	— —	–	9 48	B	10 33	LIB	22
53	22	W.	6 31	D	5 25	B	10 54	2	4	4½	12 A.M. 37	E	10 36	B	10 11	LIB	23
54	23	Th.	6 30	D	5 26	B	10 56	2	5	5¾	1 41	E	11 A.M. 31	B	9 49	OPH	24
55	24	Fr.	6 28	D	5 27	B	10 59	2	6	6¾	2 39	E	12 P.M. 31	B	9 27	SAG	25
56	25	Sa.	6 27	D	5 29	B	11 02	2	7¼	8	3 31	E	1 36	B	9 04	SAG	26
57	26	**A**	6 25	D	5 30	B	11 05	3	8¼	9	4 17	E	2 44	C	8 42	SAG	27
58	27	M.	6 23	D	5 31	B	11 08	3	9¼	9¾	4 56	E	3 52	C	8 19	AQU	28
59	28	Tu.	6 22	D	5 32	B	11 10	3	10	10¾	5 A.M. 31	D	5 P.M. 00	D	7s.57	AQU	29

FEBRUARY hath 28 days. 1995

All heaven and earth are still, though not in sleep,
But breathless, as we go when feeling most;
And silent, as we stand in thoughts too deep —
All heaven and earth are still.
– *George Gordon, Lord Byron*

D.M.	D.W.	Dates, Feasts, Fasts, Aspects, Tide Heights	Weather ↓
1	W.	St. Brigid • Langston Hughes born, 1902 • Tides { — 11.4	*Drippery*
2	Th.	**Candlemas** • **Purif. of Mary** • Groundhog Day • ☾ on Eq. • ☌♄☾	
3	Fr.	☿ in inf. ☌ • Income Tax Amendment ratified, 1913 • Tides { 10.5 10.6	*then*
4	Sa.	*The price of your hat isn't the measure of your brain.* • { 10.3 10.0 •	*slippery.*
5	**A**	5th S. af. Epiphany • St. Agatha • { 10.0 9.4	*•Good*
6	M.	☾ at ☋ • Midwinter Day • Ronald Reagan born, 1911 •	*time*
7	Tu.	Average wage for common labor in U.S., 54¢ per hour, 1926 • Tides { 9.3 8.3 •	*for a*
8	W.	☾ at apo. • *Skylab 4* returned to Earth after 84 days in space, 1974 •	*Florida*
9	Th.	*There is summer and there is winter; what need for hurry?* • { 9.0 7.9 •	*trippery.*
10	Fr.	☾ rides high • Gestapo authorized to arrest and imprison without trial, 1936 { 9.1 8.1 •	*I*
11	Sa.	♂ closest approach • ♂ at ☍ • Thomas Edison born, 1847 •	*cannot*
12	**A**	Septuagesima • Abraham Lincoln born, 1809 • { 9.6 8.7 •	*tell*
13	M.	*It's as difficult to win love as to wrap salt in pine needles.* • Tides { 9.9 9.1	*a lie —*
14	Tu.	St. Valentine • **Sts. Cyril & Methodius** • Arizona became 48th state, 1912 •	*the*
15	W.	☌♂☾ • ☿ stat. • **Full Snow** ○ • Susan B. Anthony born, 1820	*snow*
16	Th.	*If February gives much snow, A fine summer it doth foreshow.* • Tides { 10.7 — •	*is*
17	Fr.	☾ on Eq. • Jazz pianist Thelonious Monk died, 1982 • Tides { 10.3 10.7 •	*as*
18	Sa.	Elm Farm Ollie became first cow to fly in an airplane, 1930 • { 10.5 10.7 •	*high*
19	**A**	Sexagesima • Ohio admitted to Union as first slave-free state, 1803 • { 10.7 10.5	*•as*
20	M.	☾ at ☊ • John Glenn became first American to orbit Earth, 1962 •	*George*
21	Tu.	*Man is like palm wine; when young sweet, but without strength, but in age, strong and harsh.* •	*W.'s*
22	W.	☾ at perig. • ☌♃☾ • George Washington born, 1732 • { 10.6 9.3	*eye!*
23	Th.	Rotary Club founded in Chicago, 1905 • Heavy snow, Charleston, S.C., 1773 •	*Not a*
24	Fr.	St. Matthias • ☾ runs low • 70° F, Boston, Mass., 1985 • { 10.3 9.1	*trace*
25	Sa.	☌♆☾ • ☌♀☾ • Renoir born, 1841 • Tides { 10.4 9.3 •	*of*
26	**A**	Quinquagesima • ☌♀♆ • ☌⛢☾ •	*your*
27	M.	☌☿☾ • *He is poor who does not feel content.* • { 10.8 10.0 •	*parking*
28	Tu.	Shrove Tuesday • Baltimore & Ohio Railroad, first U.S. passenger line, chartered, 1827	*space.*

The greatest love is a mother's;
Then comes a dog's,
Then comes a sweetheart's . . .
– Polish proverb

Farmer's Calendar

It's a funny thing, though, about those same episodes of the deepest cold: As painful as they are, we seem to take a certain pride in them. The first thing on any morning when the forecast has been for extremely low temperatures, I hurry downstairs to the kitchen and look eagerly out at the thermometer. If I see -20, -25, I find I'm pleased, I'm elated, I'm somehow affirmed.

The deepest cold, then, has a kind of kick to it; it becomes an achievement. We hate such bitter cold, we even fear it, but we also find it exciting; we want it to excel itself. In effect, we're rooting for the cold. The most arctic nights are like the engagements of a local ball team: a source of frustration and affection oddly mixed. Nor are we above a certain quiet bragging on the depths to which our own thermometers sink. Every workplace, on the morning after a big freeze, becomes an arena of fierce competition as the data come in. I once worked in an office where the winter temperature derby was invariably swept by a woman who lived on the side of Stratton Mountain and showed up every morning with -30, -35. We finally had to make her spot the rest of us seven degrees — amounting to a handicap, as in golf.

For the battle of sinking thermometers I happen to be poorly equipped. I live on the east side of a hill in a house that faces east by south. It's a relatively warm spot, a fact for which I'm grateful. Sure, I'm grateful. Except on the coldest mornings when I know my -19 will not hold up for long when the reports begin to arrive from my proud neighbors who live in the cold hollow at the bottom of the hill.

1995 MARCH, THE THIRD MONTH

On the 1st, Mercury reaches its greatest elongation west of the year: 27 degrees from the Sun; look for it low in the east just before dawn. Brightening Jupiter starts rising soon after midnight, outshining all other points of light until Venus ascends in the final night hours. The Big Dipper is swinging up in the northeast, Orion and Sirius descending in the southwest. Noble Leo is high in the southeast. On the 25th there are three conjunctions (Neptune and the Moon, Uranus and the Moon, and Mercury and Saturn). Mars reverses its retrograde motion among the stars of Cancer. On the 20th the Moon is at perigee and the vernal equinox begins at 9:14 P.M., EST.

● New Moon	1st day	6th hour	49th min.
☽ First Quarter	9th day	5th hour	15th min.
○ Full Moon	16th day	20th hour	26th min.
☾ Last Quarter	23rd day	15th hour	11th min.
● New Moon	30th day	21st hour	9th min.

For an explanation of this page, see "How to Use This Almanac," page 30; for values of Key Letters, see Time Correction Tables, page 186.

Day of Year	Day of Month	Day of Week	☉ Rises h. m.	Key	☉ Sets h. m.	Key	Length of Days h. m.	Sun Fast m.	Full Sea Boston A.M.	Full Sea Boston P.M.	☽ Rises h. m.	Key	☽ Sets h. m.	Key	Declination of Sun °	☽ Place	☽ Age
60	1	W.	6 20	D	5 34	B	11 14	3	11	11½	6 A.M. 04	D	6 P.M. 05	D	7S.34	AQU	0
61	2	Th.	6 19	D	5 35	B	11 16	3	11¾	—	6 34	D	7 09	D	7 11	PSC	1
62	3	Fr.	6 17	D	5 36	B	11 19	3	12	12½	7 04	C	8 12	D	6 48	PSC	2
63	4	Sa.	6 15	D	5 37	B	11 22	4	12¾	1¼	7 34	C	9 13	E	6 25	PSC	3
64	5	**A**	6 14	D	5 38	B	11 24	4	1½	1¾	8 06	B	10 12	E	6 02	PSC	4
65	6	M.	6 12	D	5 40	B	11 28	4	2¼	2½	8 40	B	11 P.M. 09	E	5 39	ARI	5
66	7	Tu.	6 10	D	5 41	B	11 31	4	3	3½	9 17	B	— —	–	5 16	TAU	6
67	8	W.	6 09	D	5 42	B	11 33	5	3¾	4¼	9 58	B	12 A.M. 03	E	4 52	TAU	7
68	9	Th.	6 07	D	5 43	B	11 36	5	4½	5¼	10 44	B	12 55	E	4 29	TAU	8
69	10	Fr.	6 05	D	5 44	B	11 39	5	5½	6¼	11 A.M. 34	B	1 42	E	4 05	ORI	9
70	11	Sa.	6 04	D	5 46	B	11 42	5	6½	7	12 P.M. 29	B	2 26	E	3 42	GEM	10
71	12	**A**	6 02	C	5 47	B	11 45	6	7¼	8	1 27	B	3 06	E	3 18	GEM	11
72	13	M.	6 00	C	5 48	B	11 48	6	8¼	8¾	2 28	C	3 43	E	2 55	CAN	12
73	14	Tu.	5 59	C	5 49	B	11 50	6	9	9½	3 32	C	4 17	D	2 31	CAN	13
74	15	W.	5 57	C	5 50	B	11 53	6	9¾	10¼	4 38	D	4 50	D	2 07	SEX	14
75	16	Th.	5 55	C	5 51	B	11 56	7	10½	11	5 46	D	5 22	C	1 44	LEO	15
76	17	Fr.	5 53	C	5 53	B	12 00	7	11¼	11½	6 56	E	5 54	C	1 20	VIR	16
77	18	Sa.	5 52	C	5 54	B	12 02	7	—	12	8 07	E	6 28	C	0 56	VIR	17
78	19	**A**	5 50	C	5 55	B	12 05	8	12¼	12¾	9 18	E	7 05	B	0 33	VIR	18
79	20	M.	5 48	C	5 56	C	12 08	8	1	1½	10 28	E	7 47	B	0S.09	LIB	19
80	21	Tu.	5 47	C	5 57	C	12 10	8	1¾	2½	11 P.M. 34	E	8 34	B	0N.14	LIB	20
81	22	W.	5 45	C	5 58	C	12 13	8	2¾	3¼	— —	–	9 27	B	0 38	OPH	21
82	23	Th.	5 43	C	5 59	C	12 16	9	3¾	4½	12 A.M. 34	E	10 26	B	1 01	SAG	22
83	24	Fr.	5 41	C	6 01	C	12 20	9	4¾	5½	1 28	E	11 A.M. 30	B	1 25	SAG	23
84	25	Sa.	5 40	C	6 02	C	12 22	9	5¾	6½	2 15	E	12 P.M. 35	C	1 49	SAG	24
85	26	**A**	5 38	C	6 03	C	12 25	10	7	7¾	2 55	E	1 42	C	2 13	CAP	25
86	27	M.	5 36	C	6 04	C	12 28	10	8	8¾	3 31	D	2 48	C	2 36	AQU	26
87	28	Tu.	5 34	C	6 05	C	12 31	10	9	9½	4 04	D	3 53	D	3 00	AQU	27
88	29	W.	5 33	C	6 06	C	12 33	11	10	10¼	4 34	D	4 56	D	3 23	PSC	28
89	30	Th.	5 31	C	6 07	C	12 36	11	10¾	11	5 04	C	5 59	D	3 46	PSC	0
90	31	Fr.	5 29	C	6 09	C	12 40	11	11½	11¾	5 A.M. 34	C	7 P.M. 00	E	4N.09	PSC	1

MARCH hath 31 days. 1995

All Nature seems at work. Slugs leave their lair —
The bees are stirring — birds are on the wing —
And Winter, slumbering in the open air,
Wears on his smiling face a dream of Spring!
– Samuel Taylor Coleridge

D. M.	D. W.	Dates, Feasts, Fasts, Aspects, Tide Heights	Weather ↓
1	W.	Ash Wednesday • ☿ Gr. Elong. (27° W.) • New ● •	*March*
2	Th.	☾ on Eq. • ☌♀♅ • Theodore Seuss Geisel (Dr. Seuss) born, 1904 • Tides {10.9 / —	*is*
3	Fr.	*A peck of March dust and showers in May, Make corn green and fields gray.* •	*torture,*
4	Sa.	Vermont became 14th state, 1791 • Knute Rockne born, 1888 • {10.5 / 10.3 •	*March*
5	A	1st S. in Lent • ☾ at ☋ • ☌♄☉ • {10.3 / 9.8 •	*won't*
6	M.	Pure Monday • ♇ stat. • Ghana declared independent nation, 1957	*give;*
7	Tu.	St. Perpetua • Alexander Graham Bell patented telephone, 1876 • {9.7 / 8.8	*March*
8	W.	☾ at apo. • Ember Day • Oliver Wendell Holmes born, 1841 • {9.4 / 8.4 •	*cuts*
9	Th.	☾ rides high • Amerigo Vespucci born, 1451 • {9.1 / 8.1 •	*short your*
10	Fr.	Ember Day • *March will search, April will try; May will tell whether you live or die.* •	*will*
11	Sa.	Ember Day • Blizzard of 1888 began • Tides {8.9 / 8.1 •	*to live.*
12	A	2nd S. in Lent • St. Gregory • Sunday of Orthodoxy •	
13	M.	☌♂☾ • First political cartoon depicting "Uncle Sam" published, 1852 •	*March*
14	Tu.	Albert Einstein born, 1879 • Eli Whitney patented cotton gin, 1794 • {9.8 / 9.4 •	*comes*
15	W.	*Pride is said to be the last vice the good man gets clear of.* • Beware the Ides of March •	*early,*
16	Th.	☾ on Eq. • Full Sap ○ • Slow day NY Stock Exchange, only 31 shares traded, 1830	*March*
17	Fr.	St. Patrick • Camp Fire Girls founded, 1910 • Tides {10.8 / 11.0 •	*stays*
18	Sa.	Rudolf Diesel, inventor of diesel engine, born, 1858 • Tides {— / 10.9 •	*late;*
19	A	3rd S. in Lent • St. Joseph • ☾ at ☊ •	*March*
20	M.	☾ at perig. • Vernal Equinox • *Uncle Tom's Cabin* published in book form, 1852	*is*
21	Tu.	Rocking chair marathons popular throughout Quebec, 1955 • {11.4 / 10.3 •	*fingernails*
22	W.	☌♃☾ • Arthur L. Schawlow and Charles H. Townes patented the laser, 1960 •	*on*
23	Th.	☾ runs low • Patrick Henry proclaimed "Give me liberty, or give me death!" 1775	*slate.*
24	Fr.	*You can bear with your own faults, and why not a fault in your wife?* • {10.4 / 9.2 •	*Forgive*
25	Sa.	Annunciation • ☌♆☾ • ♂ stat. • ☌♅☾ • ☌☿♄ •	*me*
26	A	4th S. in Lent • Walt Whitman died, 1892 • {10.1 / 9.4 •	*if I*
27	M.	☌♀☾ • Alaska earthquake registered 8.4 on the Richter Scale, 1964 • {10.2 / 9.8 •	*seem*
28	Tu.	Circus men P. T. Barnum and James A. Bailey formed partnership, 1881	*uncharitable;*
29	W.	☾ on Eq. • ☌♄☾ • ☌☿☾ • Tides {10.4 / 10.4 •	*I find*
30	Th.	New ● • U.S. purchased Alaska from Russia, 1867 • {10.4 / 10.6 •	*March*
31	Fr.	First dance marathon held in U.S., 1923 • Tides {10.3 / 10.6 •	*unbearitable.*

Farmer's Calendar

All around the bend in the river road, cars are pulled over to the side, and on the bridge eight or ten people have gathered. They come and go all day. They're gawking at the ice. The breaking up of the frozen waters and the departure of the ice down the rivers is winter's last big show, and often it makes a mighty spectacle, a view of the underside of winter, the engine room, the groaning, grinding machinery.

The river is no more than 150 feet across at the point where it makes a bend following which the channel widens out some. There the ice, floating down from upriver, is apt to get stuck. A dam of ice begins to rise. More and more ice comes down the river, meets the dam, tries to push through it, fails, tries to climb over it, fails. The dam grows deeper, higher. It looks like a Corps of Engineers project built up of riprap blocks. These engineers are not men, though, but giants. The ice blocks are prodigious. The little ones are the size of billiard tables, king-size beds. The big ones are half-tennis-courts. They are four, five feet thick, gray in color or green, sometimes a kind of pale blue like the spring sky.

The weight of the ice sheets is unimaginable, and yet the force that moves them along seems to toss them like cards. They are flung up crazily, at all angles, on the dam. They are shot out to the sides of the channel, where they scour the river banks and mow down good-sized trees. As big as the ice blocks are, what is pushing them is bigger. They will go where they are pointed, and there is not too much that can stop them. The people watch silently, respectfully, from a safe distance.

1995 APRIL, THE FOURTH MONTH

Two eclipses this month! A small partial eclipse of the Moon will be seen in the early dawn on the 15th by viewers in the western United States. An annular eclipse of the Sun by the new Moon occurs on the 29th, but only the partial phase will be seen around midday and only in Florida. At dawn on the 13th, Venus is within a degree of much dimmer Saturn in the east. The Big Dipper is high above the North Star at nightfall, the arc of its handle pointing to Arcturus. Jupiter is the brilliant beacon rising in the late evening. Moonlight hinders views of the Lyrid meteors after midnight on the 21st and 22nd. Daylight Saving Time begins at 2:00 A.M. on the 2nd.

☽ First Quarter	8th day	0 hour	36th min.
○ Full Moon	15th day	7th hour	9th min.
☾ Last Quarter	21st day	22nd hour	19th min.
● New Moon	29th day	12th hour	37th min.

ADD 1 hour for Daylight Saving Time after 2 A.M., April 2nd.

For an explanation of this page, see "How to Use This Almanac," page 30; for values of Key Letters, see Time Correction Tables, page 186.

Day of Year	Day of Month	Day of Week	☉ Rises h. m.	Key	☉ Sets h. m.	Key	Length of Days h. m.	Sun Fast m.	Full Sea Boston A.M.	Full Sea Boston P.M.	☽ Rises h. m.	Key	☽ Sets h. m.	Key	Declination of Sun °	☽ Place	☽ Age
91	1	Sa.	5 27	B	6 10	C	12 43	11	—	12	6 A.M. 05	B	8 P.M. 00	E	4N.33	PSC	2
92	2	**A**	5 26	B	6 11	C	12 45	12	12¼	12¾	6 38	B	8 58	E	4 56	ARI	3
93	3	M.	5 24	B	6 12	C	12 48	12	1	1½	7 14	B	9 54	E	5 19	ARI	4
94	4	Tu.	5 22	B	6 13	C	12 51	12	1½	2	7 54	B	10 46	E	5 42	TAU	5
95	5	W.	5 21	B	6 14	D	12 53	13	2¼	2¾	8 38	B	11 P.M. 35	E	6 04	TAU	6
96	6	Th.	5 19	B	6 15	D	12 56	13	3	3¾	9 26	B	— —	–	6 27	AUR	7
97	7	Fr.	5 17	B	6 16	D	12 59	13	3¾	4½	10 18	B	12 A.M. 20	E	6 50	GEM	8
98	8	Sa.	5 16	B	6 18	D	13 02	13	4¾	5½	11 A.M. 14	B	1 01	E	7 12	GEM	9
99	9	**A**	5 14	B	6 19	D	13 05	14	5¾	6¼	12 P.M. 13	C	1 38	E	7 35	CAN	10
100	10	M.	5 12	B	6 20	D	13 08	14	6¾	7¼	1 14	C	2 13	D	7 57	CAN	11
101	11	Tu.	5 11	B	6 21	D	13 10	14	7½	8	2 18	D	2 46	D	8 19	LEO	12
102	12	W.	5 09	B	6 22	D	13 13	15	8½	8¾	3 25	D	3 18	D	8 41	SEX	13
103	13	Th.	5 07	B	6 23	D	13 16	15	9¼	9½	4 34	D	3 50	C	9 03	LEO	14
104	14	Fr.	5 06	B	6 24	D	13 18	15	10	10¼	5 45	E	4 23	C	9 24	VIR	15
105	15	Sa.	5 04	B	6 25	D	13 21	15	10¾	11	6 57	E	4 59	B	9 46	VIR	16
106	16	**A**	5 02	B	6 27	D	13 25	16	11½	—	8 10	E	5 40	B	10 07	VIR	17
107	17	M.	5 01	B	6 28	D	13 27	16	12	12½	9 20	E	6 26	B	10 28	LIB	18
108	18	Tu.	4 59	B	6 29	D	13 30	16	12¾	1¼	10 25	E	7 19	B	10 49	SCO	19
109	19	W.	4 58	B	6 30	D	13 32	16	1½	2¼	11 P.M. 23	E	8 18	B	11 10	OPH	20
110	20	Th.	4 56	B	6 31	D	13 35	16	2½	3¼	— —	–	9 22	B	11 31	SAG	21
111	21	Fr.	4 55	B	6 32	D	13 37	17	3½	4¼	12 A.M. 13	E	10 28	B	11 51	SAG	22
112	22	Sa.	4 53	B	6 33	D	13 40	17	4½	5¼	12 56	E	11 A.M. 35	C	12 12	CAP	23
113	23	**A**	4 52	B	6 34	D	13 42	17	5½	6¼	1 33	D	12 P.M. 41	C	12 32	AQU	24
114	24	M.	4 50	B	6 36	D	13 46	17	6¾	7½	2 06	D	1 45	D	12 52	AQU	25
115	25	Tu.	4 49	B	6 37	D	13 48	17	7¾	8¼	2 37	D	2 48	D	13 11	PSC	26
116	26	W.	4 47	B	6 38	D	13 51	18	8¾	9¼	3 07	C	3 50	D	13 31	PSC	27
117	27	Th.	4 46	B	6 39	D	13 53	18	9½	10	3 36	C	4 51	E	13 50	PSC	28
118	28	Fr.	4 44	B	6 40	D	13 56	18	10¼	10½	4 06	C	5 51	E	14 09	PSC	29
119	29	Sa.	4 43	B	6 41	D	13 58	18	11	11¼	4 38	B	6 49	E	14 28	ARI	0
120	30	**A**	4 41	B	6 42	D	14 01	18	11¾	11¾	5 A.M. 13	B	7 P.M. 46	E	14N.46	ARI	1

This is the time we dock the night
Of a whole hour of candlelight;
When song of linnet and thrush is heard —
And love stirs in the heart of a bird.
– *Katharine Tynan*

Farmer's Calendar

April 10. Went down to the train depot at Springfield and boarded the *Yankee Clipper* to Washington, D.C., a seven-hour shot. It's an interesting ride that seems to pack a great deal of geography into a small compass. You go right down the Connecticut River to New Haven. Then you make a right and go along the top of Long Island Sound toward New York. Somewhere in what may be Queens, you descend and pass under Manhattan, emerging in New Jersey. There you turn left and proceed to Philadelphia, across the river mouths emptying into Chesapeake Bay, and so into Washington, a southern city.

The best part of the trip for me is the Long Island Sound leg, say from Bridgeport to near New York. Here the train passes through the backyard of the old industrial America. It's not pretty. There would seem to be nobody home here these days. You pass every kind of factory, plant, shop, dock, most of them apparently vacant, their windows broken, their signs faded, their fences fallen down. You're riding through an industrial ruin 75 miles long, a district uniformly, relentlessly ugly.

Yet I'm reminded of the line of the poet: "And for all this, nature is never spent." A beautiful, cold, early spring day with high clouds, a keen wind, bright sun. The grimy trackside tree-of-heaven and tangled brush behind the conked-out plants are coming in green. And, most remarkable, most unexpected: swans. So help me, all along the line, in every stagnant backwater and pool, however filthy, floating placidly amongst the old tires, busted concrete, and other junk, a perfect, snow-white swan. Where do they come from?

D.M.	D.W.	Dates, Feasts, Fasts, Aspects, Tide Heights	*Weather* ↓
1	Sa.	☾ at ☊ • ♃ stat. • **All Fools** • Tides { 10.2 •	*Excuse*
2	A	**5th ☉. in Lent • Passion** • Daylight Saving Time begins, 2 A.M.	*me,*
3	M.	The Pony Express began Jesse James { 10.4 postal service, 1860 • killed, 1882 { 9.6	*ma'am,*
4	Tu.	President William Henry Harrison died of pneumonia one month after inauguration, 1841	*but*
5	W.	☾ at apo. • Pocahontas married Englishman John Rolfe, 1614 { 9.8 8.9 •	*do*
6	Th.	☾ rides high • Blue herons return to Vinal Haven, Maine • Tides { 9.5 8.5 •	*you*
7	Fr.	Love your enemy — but don't put a gun in his hand. • Walter Winchell born, 1897	*know:*
8	Sa.	Hank Aaron hit record-breaking 715th home run, 1974 • Tides { 9.0 8.3 •	*Is*
9	A	**Palm Sun.** • First tax-supported public library founded, Peterborough, N.H., 1833	*that*
10	M.	♂♂☾ • Safety pin Joseph Pulitzer { 9.1 patented, 1849 born, 1847 { 8.8	*the*
11	Tu.	President Johnson signed *The golden age never* Civil Rights Act, 1968 *was the present age.* •	*Sun?*
12	W.	☾ on Eq. • President Franklin D. Roosevelt died, 1945 { 9.7 9.9 •	*Or*
13	Th.	♂♀♄ • F. W. Woolworth Japan and Russia signed born, 1852 five-year neutrality pact, 1941	*a*
14	Fr.	**Good Friday** • ☿ at sup. ♂ • Tides { 10.5 11.2 •	*UFO?*
15	Sa.	**Passover** • **Full Pink** ○ • Eclipse ☾ •	*Focus is*
16	A	**Easter** • ☾ at ☊ • Wilbur Wright born, 1867 { 11.0 — •	*on*
17	M.	☾ at perig. • Benjamin Franklin died, 1790 { 12.0 11.0 •	*crocuses.*
18	Tu.	♂♃☾ • San Francisco Ernie Pyle earthquake, 1906 killed, 1945 •	*Winter*
19	W.	☾ runs low • U.S. abandoned the gold standard, 1933 • Tides { 11.8 10.5 •	*takes*
20	Th.	A man all wrapped up in himself makes a small package. • Tides { 11.5 10.1 •	*one*
21	Fr.	**St. Anselm** • ♂♆☾ • ♂♂☾ • Tides { 11.0 9.8 •	*parting*
22	Sa.	President George Washington Richard M. Nixon attended the circus, 1793 • died, 1994	*shot:*
23	A	**1st ☉. af. Easter • Orthodox Easter** •	*suddenly,*
24	M.	Allies liberated Dachau Robert B. Thomas concentration camp, 1945 born, 1766 •	*it's*
25	Tu.	**St. Mark** • ☾ on Eq. • ♂♄☾ • Tides { 9.8 10.0 •	*clear*
26	W.	As scarce as truth is, the supply has always been in excess of the demand. • Tides { 9.8 10.2 •	*and*
27	Th.	♂♀☾ • ♆ stat. • Ulysses S. Grant born, 1822 • { 9.8 10.4 •	*hot!*
28	Fr.	Mutiny on the Nightly din-outs began, Bounty, 1789 U.S. east coast, 1942 • { 9.8 10.5 •	*Wet,*
29	Sa.	**St. Catherine** • ☾ at ☊ • **New** ● Eclipse ☉ •	*I*
30	A	**2nd ☉. af. Easter** • Tides { 9.7 10.5 •	*wot.*

*Till April's dead
Change not a thread.*

MAY, The Fifth Month

Around 3:00 A.M., EST, on the 22nd, the rings of Saturn are presented edgewise to Earth for the first time since 1980; the planet is the untwinkling light in the southeast in the predawn hours this month, but telescopes will show the rings narrowing to a line of light, then appearing to vanish as the Earth passes through the ring plane. At dusk around the 11th, its date of greatest elongation, Mercury performs its best 1995 show, remaining visible in the west for 1½ hours or more after sunset. Jupiter rises in early evening, very near the Moon on the 15th. Dim little Pluto is at opposition on the 20th. A few Eta Aquarid meteors shoot from the southeast in the last hours of night early in the month.

☽ First Quarter	7th day	16th hour	45th min.
○ Full Moon	14th day	15th hour	49th min.
☾ Last Quarter	21st day	6th hour	36th min.
● New Moon	29th day	4th hour	28th min.

ADD 1 hour for Daylight Saving Time.

For an explanation of this page, see "How to Use This Almanac," page 30; for values of Key Letters, see Time Correction Tables, page 186.

Day of Year	Day of Month	Day of Week	☉ Rises h. m.	Key	☉ Sets h. m.	Key	Length of Days h. m.	Sun Fast m.	Full Sea Boston A.M.	Full Sea Boston P.M.	☽ Rises h. m.	Key	☽ Sets h. m.	Key	Declination of Sun °	Place	☽ Age
121	1	M.	4 40	B	6 43	D	14 03	18	—	12¼	5ₘ52	B	8ᴾₘ40	E	15N.04	TAU	2
122	2	Tu.	4 39	B	6 44	D	14 05	19	12½	1	6 34	B	9 30	E	15 22	TAU	3
123	3	W.	4 37	B	6 46	D	14 09	19	1	1¾	7 20	B	10 16	E	15 40	TAU	4
124	4	Th.	4 36	A	6 47	D	14 11	19	1¾	2½	8 11	B	10 58	E	15 58	GEM	5
125	5	Fr.	4 35	A	6 48	D	14 13	19	2½	3¼	9 05	B	11ₘ37	E	16 15	GEM	6
126	6	Sa.	4 33	A	6 49	D	14 16	19	3¼	4	10 02	B	— —	-	16 32	GEM	7
127	7	**A**	4 32	A	6 50	D	14 18	19	4¼	4¾	11ₘ01	C	12ₘ12	E	16 49	CAN	8
128	8	M.	4 31	A	6 51	D	14 20	19	5	5¾	12ₘ02	C	12 44	D	17 05	LEO	9
129	9	Tu.	4 30	A	6 52	D	14 22	19	6	6½	1 05	D	1 15	D	17 21	SEX	10
130	10	W.	4 29	A	6 53	D	14 24	19	6¾	7¼	2 11	D	1 46	D	17 37	LEO	11
131	11	Th.	4 28	A	6 54	D	14 26	19	7¾	8¼	3 20	D	2 18	C	17 53	VIR	12
132	12	Fr.	4 26	A	6 55	D	14 29	19	8¾	9	4 31	E	2 52	C	18 08	VIR	13
133	13	Sa.	4 25	A	6 56	D	14 31	19	9½	9¾	5 44	E	3 30	B	18 23	VIR	14
134	14	**A**	4 24	A	6 57	D	14 33	19	10½	10¾	6 57	E	4 13	B	18 37	LIB	15
135	15	M.	4 23	A	6 58	E	14 35	19	11¼	11½	8 07	E	5 04	B	18 51	LIB	16
136	16	Tu.	4 22	A	7 00	E	14 38	19	—	12¼	9 11	E	6 02	B	19 05	OPH	17
137	17	W.	4 21	A	7 01	E	14 40	19	12¼	1	10 06	E	7 06	B	19 19	SAG	18
138	18	Th.	4 20	A	7 02	E	14 42	19	1¼	2	10 53	E	8 14	B	19 33	SAG	19
139	19	Fr.	4 19	A	7 03	E	14 44	19	2¼	3	11ᴾₘ34	E	9 23	C	19 46	SAG	20
140	20	Sa.	4 18	A	7 04	E	14 46	19	3¼	4	— —	-	10 31	C	19 58	AQU	21
141	21	**A**	4 18	A	7 05	E	14 47	19	4¼	5	12ᴬₘ09	D	11ᴬₘ38	D	20 11	AQU	22
142	22	M.	4 17	A	7 05	E	14 48	19	5¼	6	12 41	D	12ᴾₘ42	D	20 23	PSC	23
143	23	Tu.	4 16	A	7 06	E	14 50	19	6¼	7	1 10	D	1 44	D	20 34	PSC	24
144	24	W.	4 15	A	7 07	E	14 52	19	7¼	7¾	1 40	C	2 45	D	20 45	PSC	25
145	25	Th.	4 14	A	7 08	E	14 54	19	8¼	8¾	2 09	B	3 44	E	20 56	PSC	26
146	26	Fr.	4 14	A	7 09	E	14 55	19	9¼	9½	2 40	B	4 43	E	21 07	ARI	27
147	27	Sa.	4 13	A	7 10	E	14 57	19	10	10	3 14	B	5 40	E	21 18	ARI	28
148	28	**A**	4 12	A	7 11	E	14 59	18	10¾	10¾	3 51	B	6 34	E	21 27	TAU	29
149	29	M.	4 12	A	7 12	E	15 00	18	11¼	11½	4 32	B	7 26	E	21 37	TAU	0
150	30	Tu.	4 11	A	7 13	E	15 02	18	—	12	5 17	B	8 14	E	21 46	TAU	1
151	31	W.	4 11	A	7 14	E	15 03	18	12	12½	6ᴬₘ06	B	8ᴾₘ58	E	21N.54	ORI	2

MAY hath 31 days. 1995

In May, when sea-winds pierced our solitudes,
I found the fresh Rhodora in the woods,
Spreading its leafless blooms in a damp nook,
To please the desert and the sluggish brook.
– Ralph Waldo Emerson

D. M.	D. W.	Dates, Feasts, Fasts, Aspects, Tide Heights	*Weather* ↓
1	M.	Sts. Philip & James • ☌☿☾ • Tides {— / 9.6} •	*This*
2	Tu.	St. Athanasius • ☾ at apo. • Alcatraz Prison riots began, 1946 •	*month*
3	W.	Invention of the Cross • ☾ rides high • Machiavelli born, 1469 • Tides {10.2 / 9.2} •	*just*
4	Th.	Four Kent State University students killed by National Guardsmen, 1970 • Tides {10.0 / 9.0} •	*defies*
5	Fr.	⛢ stat. • Cy Young pitched baseball's first perfect game, 1904 •	*prediction;*
6	Sa.	*A cold May is kindly, And fills the barn finely.* • Tides {9.4 / 8.7} •	*forecasts*
7	**A**	**3rd S. af. Easter** • Germany surrendered to Allies, 1945 •	*can*
8	M.	☌♂☾ • Mt. Pelée, Martinique, erupted, leaving 40,000 dead, 1902 • {9.1 / 8.9}	*sound*
9	Tu.	St. Gregory of Nazianzus • 94° F, New York City, 1979 •	*like*
10	W.	☾ on Eq. • Ethan Allen captured Fort Ticonderoga, 1775 • Tides {9.4 / 9.8} •	*fiction.*
11	Th.	☿ Gr. Elong. (22° E.) • **Three** • 6" snow, Salem, Mass., 1769 • {9.7 / 10.5} •	*Warn*
12	Fr.	Yogi Berra born, 1925 • **Chilly** • Spitting on sidewalks prohibited, NYC, 1896 •	*of*
13	Sa.	☾ at ☊ • Joe Lewis born, 1914 • **Saints** • Tides {10.4 / 11.7} •	*rain,*
14	**A**	**4th S. af. Easter** • **Full Flower** ○ • {10.7 / 12.1} •	*the*
15	M.	☾ at perig. • ☌♃☾ • 36" snow, Haverhill, N.H., 1834 •	*Sun's*
16	Tu.	☾ runs low • Food stamp program introduced, 1939 • Tides {— / 10.9} •	*aglow.*
17	W.	*We are all manufacturers: Making goods, making trouble, making excuses.* • {12.3 / 10.8} •	*Fair,*
18	Th.	☌♆☾ • Mount St. Helens erupted, 1980 • Bertrand Russell born, 1872 •	*you*
19	Fr.	St. Dunstan • ☌⛢☾ • Johns Hopkins born, 1795 • {11.6 / 10.4} •	*say?*
20	Sa.	♇ at ☍ • D. Hyde of Reading, Pa., patented fountain pen, 1830 • {11.1 / 10.1} •	*Look*
21	**A**	**Rogation S.** • *Many eyes go through the meadow, but few see the flowers.* •	*out*
22	M.	☾ on Eq. • **Victoria Day, Canada** • The Great Train Robbery, 1868 • {10.0 / 9.9}	*below!*
23	Tu.	☌♄☾ • Benjamin Franklin described his new invention, bifocal glasses, 1785 •	*Each*
24	W.	☿ stat. • Peter Minuit bought Manhattan for $24, 1626 • Tides {9.4 / 10.0} •	*defeat*
25	Th.	Ascension • St. Bede • Babe Ruth hit his 714th, and last, home run, 1935	*drains*
26	Fr.	St. Augustine of Canterbury • ☾ at ☋ •	*confidence;*
27	Sa.	☌♀☾ • Cornelius Vanderbilt born, 1794 • Tides {9.3 / 10.3} •	*save*
28	**A**	**1st S. af. Asc.** • Dionne quintuplets born, 1934 • {9.3 / 10.4}	*me a*
29	M.	Memorial Day • **New** ● • Tides {9.3 / 10.4} •	*seat*
30	Tu.	☾ rides high • ☾ at apo. • Lincoln Memorial dedicated, 1922 • {— / 9.2} •	*on the*
31	W.	Visit. of Mary • *Cast not a clout Till May be out.* • Tides {10.3 / 9.2} •	*fence.*

Farmer's Calendar

In the first days of May, along with the bloodroot, appears the red trillium *(Trillium erectum)*. It grows out of the cracks in the old stone walls and out of the moist black soil of the cool woods. It's a vigorous plant a foot or more high with three broad leaves atop its stalk and in their axis the slightly drooping flower. The red-brown flower is a plain thing. It's distinguished not by its look but by its scent, which is uniquely terrible, a kind of strong, rank smell as of dead mice.

Its powerful reek sets this flower apart and, oddly enough, seems to win it friends. There's an old saying to the effect that a well-loved child has many names, and if it's true, then this trillium must be a favorite. Books on wild plants give at least 16 different common or local names for *T. erectum.* Two of the more memorable names — stinking Benjamin and wet-dog trillium — come from the flower's outrageous smell. Others allude to the plant's supposed medicinal properties. It is thought to aid in childbirth, and the Indians used it for snakebite — hence birthroot, Indian balm, squawroot.

Another name for this flower is *wake-robin,* a name that seems to me to be an example of the highest folk poetry. What does it mean? It sounds as though it meant that this flower's blooming coincides with, and thus somehow signals, the spring arrival of the robin. But it doesn't, at least not around here; when our wake-robin comes out, the robins have been here for weeks. I think the robin who is fancifully being waked by *T. erectum* is not a bird but a boy, a man, Robin, in particular a simple country fellow, a ploughman, whose busy season on the land this flower's bloom announces.

1995   JUNE, THE SIXTH MONTH

Jupiter attains opposition to the Sun on the 1st and is biggest and brightest this month. The planet is in conjunction with the full Moon on the 12th; the latter is at perigee that evening, so look for high tides. Bright Venus passes four degrees north of Mercury on the 19th, but is low in morning twilight. Around dawn, Saturn shines above bright star Fomalhaut in the south, its rings now slightly tilted but showing us their dark southern face. Little Corvus the Crow is near Spica in the southwest, and Scorpius the Scorpion is creeping up the southeast sky. High overhead shines orange Arcturus and the six-star semicircle of Corona Borealis. The Moon is at apogee on the 26th. Summer solstice begins at 3:34 P.M., EST, on the 21st.

☽ First Quarter	6th day	5th hour	27th min.
○ Full Moon	12th day	23rd hour	4th min.
☾ Last Quarter	19th day	17th hour	2nd min.
● New Moon	27th day	19th hour	51st min.

ADD 1 hour for Daylight Saving Time.

For an explanation of this page, see "How to Use This Almanac," page 30; for values of Key Letters, see Time Correction Tables, page 186.

Day of Year	Day of Month	Day of Week	☉ Rises h. m.	Key	☉ Sets h. m.	Key	Length of Days h. m.	Sun Fast m.	Full Sea Boston A.M.	Full Sea Boston P.M.	☽ Rises h. m.	Key	☽ Sets h. m.	Key	Declination of Sun °	☽ Place	☽ Age
152	1	Th.	4 10	A	7 14	E	15 04	18	12¾	1¼	6ᴹ59	B	9ᴾᴹ37	E	22N.03	GEM	3
153	2	Fr.	4 10	A	7 15	E	15 05	18	1¼	2	7 54	B	10 13	E	22 10	GEM	4
154	3	Sa.	4 09	A	7 15	E	15 06	18	2	2¾	8 52	C	10 46	D	22 18	CAN	5
155	4	**A**	4 09	A	7 16	E	15 07	17	2¾	3½	9 52	C	11 17	D	22 25	CAN	6
156	5	M.	4 08	A	7 17	E	15 09	17	3½	4¼	10 53	D	11ᴹ47	D	22 32	LEO	7
157	6	Tu.	4 08	A	7 18	E	15 10	17	4½	5	11ᴹ56	D	— —	–	22 39	LEO	8
158	7	W.	4 08	A	7 18	E	15 10	17	5¼	5¾	1ᴹ01	D	12ᴹ17	C	22 45	VIR	9
159	8	Th.	4 08	A	7 19	E	15 11	17	6¼	6¾	2 09	E	12 49	C	22 50	VIR	10
160	9	Fr.	4 08	A	7 20	E	15 12	17	7¼	7½	3 19	E	1 23	C	22 55	VIR	11
161	10	Sa.	4 07	A	7 20	E	15 13	16	8¼	8½	4 31	E	2 03	B	23 00	LIB	12
162	11	**A**	4 07	A	7 21	E	15 14	16	9	9½	5 43	E	2 48	B	23 04	LIB	13
163	12	M.	4 07	A	7 21	E	15 14	16	10	10¼	6 50	E	3 42	B	23 08	OPH	14
164	13	Tu.	4 07	A	7 22	E	15 15	16	11	11¼	7 51	E	4 43	B	23 12	OPH	15
165	14	W.	4 07	A	7 22	E	15 15	16	11¾	—	8 44	E	5 51	B	23 16	SAG	16
166	15	Th.	4 07	A	7 23	E	15 16	15	12	12¾	9 29	E	7 03	B	23 18	SAG	17
167	16	Fr.	4 07	A	7 23	E	15 16	15	1	1¾	10 08	D	8 14	C	23 20	CAP	18
168	17	Sa.	4 07	A	7 23	E	15 16	15	2	2½	10 42	D	9 24	C	23 22	CAP	19
169	18	**A**	4 07	A	7 24	E	15 17	15	2¾	3½	11 13	D	10 31	D	23 24	AQU	20
170	19	M.	4 07	A	7 24	E	15 17	14	3¾	4½	11ᴾᴹ43	C	11ᴹ35	D	23 25	PSC	21
171	20	Tu.	4 07	A	7 24	E	15 17	14	4¾	5½	— —	–	12ᴾᴹ37	D	23 25	PSC	22
172	21	W.	4 07	A	7 24	E	15 17	14	5¾	6¼	12ᴹ13	C	1 38	E	23 25	PSC	23
173	22	Th.	4 08	A	7 25	E	15 17	14	6¾	7¼	12 44	B	2 37	E	23 25	PSC	24
174	23	Fr.	4 08	A	7 25	E	15 17	14	7¾	8	1 16	B	3 34	E	23 25	ARI	25
175	24	Sa.	4 08	A	7 25	E	15 17	13	8¾	9	1 52	B	4 30	E	23 24	ARI	26
176	25	**A**	4 08	A	7 25	E	15 17	13	9½	9½	2 31	B	5 22	E	23 23	TAU	27
177	26	M.	4 09	A	7 25	E	15 16	13	10¼	10¼	3 14	B	6 12	E	23 21	TAU	28
178	27	Tu.	4 09	A	7 25	E	15 16	13	11	11	4 02	B	6 57	E	23 18	ORI	0
179	28	W.	4 10	A	7 25	E	15 15	13	11½	11¾	4 54	B	7 38	E	23 16	GEM	1
180	29	Th.	4 10	A	7 25	E	15 15	12	—	12¼	5 49	B	8 15	E	23 13	GEM	2
181	30	Fr.	4 10	A	7 25	E	15 15	12	12¼	12¾	6ᴹ46	B	8ᴹ49	D	23N.10	CAN	3

JUNE hath 30 days. 1995

And what is so rare as a day in June?
Then, if ever, come perfect days;
Then Heaven tries earth if it be in tune,
And over it softly her warm ear lays.
– *James Russell Lowell*

D. M.	D. W.	Dates, Feasts, Fasts, Aspects, Tide Heights	Weather ↓
1	Th.	**Orthodox Ascension** • ♃ at ☍ • Marilyn Monroe born, 1928 •	*Hot*
2	Fr.	President Grover Cleveland married Frances Folsum in a White House ceremony, 1886 • {10.1 9.1	*stuff.*
3	Sa.	*June damp and warm Does the farmer no harm.* • Tides {9.9 9.1 •	*A*
4	**A**	**Whit S. • Pentecost** • Shavuot •	*torrent,*
5	M.	**St. Boniface** • ☿ in inf. ☌ • ☌ ♂ ☾ • Tides {9.5 9.2 •	*we'll*
6	Tu.	☾ on Eq. • First "drive-in" movie theater opened, Camden, N.J., 1933 •	*warrant.*
7	W.	Ember Day • Daniel Boone began Kentucky exploration, 1769 • {9.3 9.8 •	*Great*
8	Th.	United Mine Workers ended 72-day strike, 1981 • Tides {9.4 10.3 •	*days*
9	Fr.	☾ at ☊ • Ember Day • Secretariat won at 1973 Belmont, first Triple Crown since 1948	*for*
10	Sa.	Ember Day • *When people are free to do as they please, they usually imitate each other.* {9.9 11.4	*new*
11	**A**	**Trinity** • **St. Barnabas** • **Orthodox Pentecost** •	*B.A.s.*
12	M.	☌ ♃ ☾ • ☾ at perig. • **Full Strawberry** ○ • {10.5 12.2 •	*It's*
13	Tu.	☾ runs low • Thurgood Marshall became first black U.S. Supreme Court justice, 1967	*sopping,*
14	W.	**St. Basil** • **Flag Day** • Harriet Beecher Stowe born, 1811 • {10.9 —	*and*
15	Th.	**Corpus Christi** • ☌ ♆ ☾ • ☌ ♅ ☾ • Tides {12.4 10.9 •	*the*
16	Fr.	*Experience is what you get when you expected something else.* • {12.1 10.8 •	*mercury's*
17	Sa.	☿ stat. • 42° F, Chicago, Ill., 1980 • Tides {11.6 10.6 •	*dropping.*
18	**A**	**2nd S. af. P.** • **Orthodox All Saints** • {11.0 10.4	*Even*
19	M.	☾ on Eq. • ☌ ☿ ♀ • ☌ ♄ ☾ • Lou Gehrig born, 1903 • {10.4 10.2	*Eden*
20	Tu.	Great Seal of the United States adopted, 1782 • Tides {9.8 10.0 •	*needed*
21	W.	Summer Solstice • Cyrus McCormick patented his reaper, 1834 • {9.3 9.9	*weedin'.*
22	Th.	**St. Alban** • ☾ at ☋ • Tides {9.0 9.9 •	*Thunder*
23	Fr.	Before St. John's Day we pray for rain; after that we get it anyhow. •	*barrage —*
24	Sa.	**Nativ. John the Baptist** • Midsummer Day • {8.8 10.0 •	*clean*
25	**A**	**3rd S. af. P.** • Occult. ☿ by ☾ • Tides {8.8 10.1	*out*
26	M.	☾ at apo. • ☌ ♀ ☾ • Abner Doubleday born, 1819 • {8.9 10.2 •	*the*
27	Tu.	☾ rides high • **New** ● • First auto seat belt law passed, Ill., 1955 •	*garage.*
28	W.	*Even a stopped clock is right twice a day.* • Mel Brooks born, 1926 • {9.1 10.3 •	*Have*
29	Th.	**Sts. Peter & Paul** • ☿ Gr. Elong. (22° W.) • Tides {— 9.2	*a BBQ*
30	Fr.	Congress passed Pure Food and Drugs Act and Meat Inspection Act, 1906 • {10.3 9.3	*PDQ.*

The trouble with the rat race is that even if you win, you're still a rat. – Lily Tomlin

Farmer's Calendar

If we are to be invaded by alien monsters out of a 1950s creature feature, it will happen on a warm, soft summer night. Remember *Them!* (1954)? In that classic screamer the invaders were giant ants. They were frightening enough, too, but we have with us in real life a far scarier being that stalks the dark nights. The dobsonfly *(Corydalus cornutus)* is a nightmare union of dragonfly, crocodile, and helicopter. It's brown, has four narrow, transparent wings that may span four inches, a round head, and the vacant, incurious, protruding eyes of the movies' most threatening destroyers. The male dobsonfly has as well a huge pair of jaws that stick far out in front of its mouth like twin butcher's knives. It comes to night lights like a moth, flying with an ungainly whirligig action. By day it's sluggish, but if you poke it, it rears up its head like a cobra and shows you those prodigious choppers.

In fact, like many but maybe not all movie monsters, the dobsonfly is entirely harmless. It's one of the lacewings, more like a mayfly than a dragon. It takes its name from its larval form, carnivorous creatures called dobsons, which live in fresh water. That larva is a considerably more formidable animal than the fly it becomes. The encyclopedia calls it a "ferocious predator" of small aquatic life. It's a long, jointed crawler that looks like a caterpillar. Fishermen know the dobson as the hellgrammite; it's said to catch bass. Its adult form, the dobsonfly, is death on nothing, despite its menacing aspect. The main mystery about it for me is, who was the Dobson who gave his name to the larva and hence the fly? I'd like to think he was in the cast of *Them!* but the name apparently goes back to 1889.

1995 JULY, THE SEVENTH MONTH

Scorpius the Scorpion is a bright curl of stars low in the south these evenings, with its heart marked by the star Antares. Much brighter Jupiter is just above the head of the Scorpion. Dimmed Mars dots the southwest sky far to the lower right of Spica. The Summer Triangle sits on the Milky Way band halfway up the eastern sky, its three brilliant stars being Vega (on top), Altair (to the right), and Deneb (at left). The Teapot pattern of stars in Sagittarius is seen in the southeast. After midnight, late in the month, Delta Aquarid meteors fly from the southeast. Venus is lost in morning twilight this month. Earth is at aphelion at 9:00 P.M., EST, on the 3rd.

☽ First Quarter	5th day	15th hour	4th min.
○ Full Moon	12th day	5th hour	50th min.
☾ Last Quarter	19th day	6th hour	11th min.
● New Moon	27th day	10th hour	15th min.

ADD 1 hour for Daylight Saving Time.

For an explanation of this page, see "How to Use This Almanac," page 30; for values of Key Letters, see Time Correction Tables, page 186.

Day of Year	Day of Month	Day of Week	☉ Rises h. m.	Key	☉ Sets h. m.	Key	Length of Days h. m.	Sun Fast m.	Full Sea Boston A.M.	Full Sea Boston P.M.	☽ Rises h. m.	Key	☽ Sets h. m.	Key	Declination of Sun °	☽ Place	☽ Age
182	1	Sa.	4 11	A	7 25	E	15 14	12	1	1½	7ᴹ45	C	9ᴾᴹ21	D	23N.06	CAN	4
183	2	**A**	4 11	A	7 25	E	15 14	12	1½	2¼	8 45	D	9 51	D	23 02	LEO	5
184	3	M.	4 12	A	7 25	E	15 13	12	2¼	2¾	9 47	D	10 20	D	22 57	SEX	6
185	4	Tu.	4 13	A	7 25	E	15 12	11	3	3½	10 50	D	10 50	C	22 52	LEO	7
186	5	W.	4 13	A	7 24	E	15 11	11	4	4½	11ᴬ55	D	11 23	C	22 46	VIR	8
187	6	Th.	4 14	A	7 24	E	15 10	11	4¾	5¼	1ᴾᴹ02	E	11ᴾᴹ59	C	22 40	VIR	9
188	7	Fr.	4 14	A	7 23	E	15 09	11	5¾	6¼	2 11	E	—	–	22 34	VIR	10
189	8	Sa.	4 15	A	7 23	E	15 08	11	6¾	7¼	3 21	E	12ᴬᴹ40	B	22 28	LIB	11
190	9	**A**	4 16	A	7 23	E	15 07	11	7¾	8	4 29	E	1 28	B	22 21	LIB	12
191	10	M.	4 16	A	7 22	E	15 06	10	8¾	9	5 33	E	2 23	B	22 14	OPH	13
192	11	Tu.	4 17	A	7 22	E	15 05	10	9¾	10	6 30	E	3 27	B	22 06	SAG	14
193	12	W.	4 18	A	7 21	E	15 03	10	10¾	11	7 19	E	4 37	B	21 57	SAG	15
194	13	Th.	4 19	A	7 21	E	15 02	10	11½	11¾	8 02	E	5 49	C	21 49	CAP	16
195	14	Fr.	4 20	A	7 20	E	15 00	10	—	12½	8 40	D	7 02	C	21 40	AQU	17
196	15	Sa.	4 20	A	7 19	E	14 59	10	12¾	1¼	9 13	D	8 12	D	21 30	AQU	18
197	16	**A**	4 21	A	7 19	E	14 58	10	1½	2¼	9 45	C	9 20	D	21 21	PSC	19
198	17	M.	4 22	A	7 18	E	14 56	10	2½	3	10 15	C	10 25	D	21 11	PSC	20
199	18	Tu.	4 23	A	7 17	E	14 54	9	3½	4	10 46	C	11ᴬᴹ27	E	21 01	PSC	21
200	19	W.	4 24	A	7 17	E	14 53	9	4¼	4¾	11 18	C	12ᴾᴹ28	E	20 50	PSC	22
201	20	Th.	4 25	A	7 16	E	14 51	9	5¼	5¾	11ᴾᴹ53	C	1 26	E	20 39	ARI	23
202	21	Fr.	4 26	A	7 15	E	14 49	9	6¼	6½	—	–	2 23	E	20 28	ARI	24
203	22	Sa.	4 26	A	7 14	E	14 48	9	7¼	7½	12ᴬᴹ30	B	3 17	E	20 16	TAU	25
204	23	**A**	4 27	A	7 13	E	14 46	9	8¼	8¼	1 12	B	4 07	E	20 03	TAU	26
205	24	M.	4 28	A	7 12	E	14 44	9	9	9¼	1 58	B	4 54	E	19 51	TAU	27
206	25	Tu.	4 29	A	7 11	E	14 42	9	9¾	9¾	2 49	B	5 37	E	19 38	GEM	28
207	26	W.	4 30	A	7 11	E	14 41	9	10½	10½	3 43	B	6 16	E	19 25	GEM	29
208	27	Th.	4 31	A	7 10	D	14 39	9	11	11¼	4 39	B	6 51	E	19 12	CAN	0
209	28	Fr.	4 32	A	7 09	D	14 37	9	11¾	11¾	5 38	C	7 24	D	18 58	CAN	1
210	29	Sa.	4 33	A	7 07	D	14 34	9	—	12¼	6 39	C	7 55	D	18 44	LEO	2
211	30	**A**	4 34	A	7 06	D	14 32	9	12½	1	7 40	D	8 25	D	18 30	SEX	3
212	31	M.	4 35	A	7 05	D	14 30	9	1¼	1¾	8ᴬᴹ43	D	8ᴾᴹ55	C	18N.15	LEO	4

JULY hath 31 days. 1995

Deep in the greens of summer sing the lives
I've come to love. A vireo whets its bill.
The great day balances upon the leaves;
My ears can hear the bird when all is still.
– Theodore Roethke

D. M.	D. W.	Dates, Feasts, Fasts, Aspects, Tide Heights	Weather ↓
1	Sa.	Canada Day • First U.S. zoo opened, Philadelphia, Pa., 1874 • { 10.2 / 9.4 •	*Wear a*
2	A	4th S. af. P. • Thurgood Marshall born, 1908 { 10.1 / 9.5 •	*slicker*
3	M.	⊕ at aphelion • Dog Days begin. • George M. Cohan born, 1878 { 9.9 / 9.6	*or a*
4	Tu.	Independence Day • ☾ on Eq. • ☌ ♂ ☾ •	*sweater;*
5	W.	Arthur Ashe defeated Jimmy Connors at Wimbledon, 1975 • { 9.6 / 10.0 •	*perfect*
6	Th.	*A monkey dressed in silk is still a monkey.* • Tides { 9.5 / 10.3 •	*for a*
7	Fr.	☾ at ☊ • ♄ stat. • Satchel Paige born, 1906 • { 9.4 / 10.6 •	*double-*
8	Sa.	First "Ziegfeld Follies" opened in New York, 1907 • Tides { 9.5 / 11.0 •	*header.*
9	A	5th S. af. P. • ☌ ♃ ☾ • Tides { 9.6 / 11.4 •	*Like*
10	M.	☾ runs low • Hot day in East: 109° F, Md.; 100° F, N.J.; 111° F, Pa., 1936 • { 9.9 / 11.8 •	*the*
11	Tu.	☾ at perig. • *Skylab* space station left orbit and fell to earth, 1979 •	*Bible's*
12	W.	☌ ♆ ☾ • ☌ ♅ ☾ • Full Buck ○ • { 10.6 / 12.2 •	*fiery*
13	Th.	Whatever July and August do not boil, September cannot fry. •	*furnace,*
14	Fr.	Bastille Day • *Liberty is the one thing you can't have unless you give it to others.* • { — / 10.9 •	*the*
15	Sa.	St. Swithin • Manitoba joined Canada, 1870 • Tides { 11.9 / 10.9 •	*Sun*
16	A	6th S. af. P. • ☾ on Eq. • ☌ ♄ ☾ • Tides { 11.4 / 10.8 •	*is*
17	M.	♆ at ☍ • 113 died in walkway collapse, Hyatt Regency Hotel, Kansas City, Mo., 1981 •	*hot*
18	Tu.	Bob Gibson struck out his 3,000th batter, first National League pitcher to do so, 1974 • { 10.2 / 10.2	*but*
19	W.	☾ at ☋ • United Airlines Flight 232 crashed in Sioux City, Iowa, cornfield, 1989	*doesn't*
20	Th.	Plot to assassinate Hitler foiled, 1944 • Tides { 9.0 / 9.7 •	*burn us.*
21	Fr.	♅ at ☍ • Ernest Hemingway born, 1899 • Tides { 8.6 / 9.6 •	*Are*
22	Sa.	St. Mary Magdalene • Last "Ziegfeld Follies" closed after 553 performances, 1944 •	*we*
23	A	7th S. af. P. • ☾ at apo. • Tides { 8.4 / 9.7 •	*by*
24	M.	☾ rides high • Brigham Young and followers arrived at Great Salt Lake Valley, Utah, 1847 •	*our*
25	Tu.	St. James • *Till St. James' Day be come and gone, You may have hops and you may have none.*	*faith*
26	W.	St. Ann • George Bernard Shaw born, 1856 • { 9.0 / 10.2 •	*redeemed?*
27	Th.	☿ in sup. ☌ • New ● • Armistice at Panmunjon ended Korean War, 1953 •	*Or*
28	Fr.	Fourteenth Amendment ratified, 1868 • Rudy Vallee born, 1901 • Tides { 9.4 / 10.4 •	*is*
29	Sa.	Sts. Mary & Martha • NASA established, 1958 • { — / 9.6 •	*it*
30	A	8th S. af. P. • Henry Ford born, 1863 • Tides { 10.4 / 9.8 •	*SPF-*
31	M.	☾ on Eq. • Cornscateous air is everywhere. • Tides { 10.3 / 10.0 •	*15?*

Farmer's Calendar

A couple of summers ago we lost a fairly large tree to a euphemism. We were lucky. The same euphemism did a good deal of damage in the river valley. A barn was destroyed, and many trees were down. The culprit was one of the very strong, very localized summer storms that blow through here every couple of years, storms that have, in this part of the country at least, an odd kind of unreality.

Other regions are more forthright. Consider the weather in question: The sky grows darker and darker until the afternoon is as black and still as the inside of an ink bottle. Suddenly the wind begins to blow violently, a terrible thrashing, screaming wind that seems to come from all directions at once and brings sheets of rain or hail — and then abruptly stops. Trees are uprooted, roofs torn off, cars tossed about, but with an ominous capriciousness: One house will be wrecked, the one next door will be untouched.

In the Midwest, where I grew up, they know what to call these storms. They're tornadoes. But everybody knows New England doesn't have tornadoes, and so when one of these rippers occurs in Vermont, it's called a "storm front," a "line squall," or some such, in a triumph of euphemism over experience.

Maybe the storms I've tried to describe aren't true tornadoes from the point of view of science. (They lack the famous funnel cloud, for one thing.) But that's not much consolation to the fellow who lost his barn, who might well recall a bit of wisdom that was current down in Washington a few years back: If it looks like a duck, and it walks like a duck, and it quacks like a duck — it may be a duck.

1995 AUGUST, THE EIGHTH MONTH

On the 10th, Earth passes again through the ring plane of Saturn. In the south after nightfall, still prominent Jupiter is near the Moon on the 5th and moves from Scorpius back into Ophiuchus late in the month. Venus is at superior conjunction on the 20th and thus unviewable. Mars, low in the southwest after dusk, is near the crescent Moon on the 29th. Icy blue Vega beckons from overhead in miniature Lyra the Lyre. On clear, moonless evenings, the Milky Way is a soft band of radiance, brightest from high in the east to low in the south. On the nights of the 11th to 13th, the bright Moon severely hampers viewing of the Perseid meteors, but many may still be visible after midnight.

☽ First Quarter	3rd day	22nd hour	17th min.
○ Full Moon	10th day	13th hour	17th min.
☾ Last Quarter	17th day	22nd hour	4th min.
● New Moon	25th day	23rd hour	33rd min.

ADD 1 hour for Daylight Saving Time.

For an explanation of this page, see "How to Use This Almanac," page 30; for values of Key Letters, see Time Correction Tables, page 186.

Day of Year	Day of Month	Day of Week	☉ Rises h. m.	Key	☉ Sets h. m.	Key	Length of Days h. m.	Sun Fast m.	Full Sea Boston A.M.	Full Sea Boston P.M.	☽ Rises h. m.	Key	☽ Sets h. m.	Key	Declination of Sun °	☽ Place	☽ Age
213	1	Tu.	4 36	A	7 04	D	14 28	9	2	2¼	9 A.M. 47	D	9 P.M. 26	C	18N.00	VIR	5
214	2	W.	4 37	A	7 03	D	14 26	9	2¾	3	10 52	E	10 00	B	17 45	VIR	6
215	3	Th.	4 38	A	7 02	D	14 24	9	3½	4	11 A.M. 59	E	10 38	B	17 29	VIR	7
216	4	Fr.	4 39	A	7 01	D	14 22	9	4½	4¾	1 P.M. 06	E	11 P.M. 22	B	17 13	LIB	8
217	5	Sa.	4 40	A	6 59	D	14 19	10	5½	5¾	2 13	E	— —	–	16 57	LIB	9
218	6	**A**	4 41	A	6 58	D	14 17	10	6½	6¾	3 17	E	12 A.M. 12	B	16 41	OPH	10
219	7	M.	4 42	A	6 57	D	14 15	10	7½	7¾	4 15	E	1 11	B	16 24	SAG	11
220	8	Tu.	4 43	A	6 56	D	14 13	10	8½	8¾	5 08	E	2 16	B	16 07	SAG	12
221	9	W.	4 45	A	6 54	D	14 09	10	9½	9¾	5 53	E	3 25	B	15 50	SAG	13
222	10	Th.	4 46	A	6 53	D	14 07	10	10½	10¾	6 34	D	4 37	C	15 33	AQU	14
223	11	Fr.	4 47	A	6 51	D	14 04	10	11¼	11½	7 09	D	5 49	C	15 15	AQU	15
224	12	Sa.	4 48	A	6 50	D	14 02	10	—	12	7 43	D	6 59	D	14 58	AQU	16
225	13	**A**	4 49	A	6 49	D	14 00	11	12½	1	8 14	C	8 06	D	14 39	PSC	17
226	14	M.	4 50	A	6 47	D	13 57	11	1¼	1¾	8 46	C	9 11	D	14 21	PSC	18
227	15	Tu.	4 51	B	6 46	D	13 55	11	2	2½	9 18	B	10 14	E	14 02	PSC	19
228	16	W.	4 52	B	6 44	D	13 52	11	3	3¼	9 52	B	11 A.M. 15	E	13 43	ARI	20
229	17	Th.	4 53	B	6 43	D	13 50	11	3¾	4	10 29	B	12 P.M. 13	E	13 24	ARI	21
230	18	Fr.	4 54	B	6 41	D	13 47	12	4¾	5	11 10	B	1 08	E	13 05	TAU	22
231	19	Sa.	4 55	B	6 40	D	13 45	12	5½	6	11 P.M. 54	B	2 00	E	12 45	TAU	23
232	20	**A**	4 56	B	6 38	D	13 42	12	6½	6¾	— —	–	2 49	E	12 26	TAU	24
233	21	M.	4 57	B	6 37	D	13 40	12	7½	7¾	12 A.M. 43	B	3 33	E	12 06	ORI	25
234	22	Tu.	4 58	B	6 35	D	13 37	13	8½	8½	1 35	B	4 14	E	11 46	GEM	26
235	23	W.	4 59	B	6 34	D	13 35	13	9¼	9¼	2 31	B	4 51	E	11 26	GEM	27
236	24	Th.	5 00	B	6 32	D	13 32	13	10	10	3 29	B	5 25	D	11 05	CAN	28
237	25	Fr.	5 01	B	6 30	D	13 29	13	10½	10¾	4 29	C	5 57	D	10 45	LEO	0
238	26	Sa.	5 03	B	6 29	D	13 26	14	11¼	11½	5 31	C	6 28	D	10 24	SEX	1
239	27	**A**	5 04	B	6 27	D	13 23	14	11¾	—	6 34	D	6 58	D	10 03	LEO	2
240	28	M.	5 05	B	6 26	D	13 21	14	12	12½	7 39	D	7 30	C	9 42	VIR	3
241	29	Tu.	5 06	B	6 24	D	13 18	14	12¾	1	8 45	D	8 03	C	9 21	VIR	4
242	30	W.	5 07	B	6 22	D	13 15	15	1½	1¾	9 51	E	8 40	B	8 59	VIR	5
243	31	Th.	5 08	B	6 21	D	13 13	15	2¼	2¾	10 A.M. 58	E	9 P.M. 22	B	8N.38	LIB	6

AUGUST hath 31 days. 1995

Ah in the thunder air
how still the trees are!
And the lime-tree, lovely and tall, every leaf silent
hardly looses even a last breath of perfume.
– D. H. Lawrence

D. M.	D. W.	Dates, Feasts, Fasts, Aspects, Tide Heights	Weather ↓
1	Tu.	**Lammas Day** • ☌♂☾ • Herman Melville born, 1819	*Lightning*
2	W.	♃ stat. • First Lincoln penny issued, 1909 • Tides {10.0 10.3 •	*flash*
3	Th.	☾ at ☊ • Ernie Pyle born, 1900 • John T. Scopes born, 1900 • {9.7 10.4 •	*and*
4	Fr.	*If the first week in August is unusually warm, the winter will be white and long.* •	*thunder*
5	Sa.	☌♃☾ • Congress abolished flogging in the army, 1861 • {9.3 10.7	*mutter;*
6	**A**	**9th S. af. P.** • **Transfiguration** • {9.3 10.9 •	*smear*
7	M.	**Name of Jesus** • ☾ runs low • Love Canal, N.Y., declared disaster area, 1978	*on*
8	Tu.	**St. Dominic** • ☾ at perig. • ☌♆☾ • Tides {9.8 11.5 •	*gobs*
9	W.	☌♅☾ • Jesse Owens won his fourth Olympic gold medal, 1936 • {10.2 11.7 •	*of*
10	Th.	**St. Laurence** • **Full Sturgeon** ○ • 110° F, Ozark, Arkansas, 1936 •	*cocoa*
11	Fr.	**St. Clare** • ♇ stat. • Dog Days end. • Tides {10.9 11.7 •	*butter.*
12	Sa.	*The eyes are of little use if the mind be blind.* • Tides {— 11.0 •	*Folks*
13	**A**	**10th S. af. P.** • ☾ on Eq. • ☌♄☾ • {11.5 11.0 •	*from*
14	M.	V-J Day, 1945 • FDA banned use of cyclamates in food, 1970 •	*Portland*
15	Tu.	**St. Mary** • ☾ at ☋ • Julia Child born, 1912 • {10.5 10.5 •	*to New*
16	W.	Babe Ruth died, 1948 • Elvis Presley died, 1977 • Tides {9.9 10.1 •	*York'll*
17	Th.	Cat Nights begin. • Davy Crockett born, 1786 • 130° F, Amos, California, 1885 •	*do*
18	Fr.	Nineteenth Amendment, giving women right to vote, ratified, 1920 • {8.8 9.5 •	*their*
19	Sa.	*Idealism increases in direct proportion to one's distance from the problem.* • {8.4 9.3	*breathing*
20	**A**	**11th S. af. P.** • ☾ rides high • ☾ at apo. • ♀ in sup. ☌ •	
21	M.	Hawaii became 50th state, 1959 • Count Basie born, 1904 • {8.3 9.4 •	*through*
22	Tu.	da Vinci's "Mona Lisa" stolen from the Louvre in Paris, 1911 • {8.5 9.6 •	*a snorkel.*
23	W.	Fannie Farmer opened her School of Cookery, Boston, 1902 • Tides {8.8 9.9 •	*Surfers*
24	Th.	**St. Bartholomew** *St. Bartlemy's mantle wipes dry All the tears that St. Swithin can cry.*	*scowl*
25	Fr.	**New** ● • National Park Service established, 1916 • Tides {9.5 10.3 •	*and*
26	Sa.	Geraldine Ferraro born, 1935 • Krakatoa volcano erupted, 1883 • {9.8 10.5 •	*pupils*
27	**A**	**12th S. af. P.** • ☾ on Eq. • Tides {10.1 — •	*pout:*
28	M.	**St. Augustine of Hippo** • ☌☿☾ • {10.5 10.4 •	*Summer*
29	Tu.	☌♂☾ • Oliver Wendell Holmes born, 1809 • Tides {10.5 10.6 •	*is*
30	W.	☾ at ☊ • The Beatles performed last concert together, 1966 •	*a-going*
31	Th.	First giant squid captured alive, near Bergen, Norway, 1982 • Tides {10.1 10.7 •	*out.*

Farmer's Calendar

Lacking science, animals seem to have a kind of physical, or cellular, intelligence that ought to be as miraculous to us as our human learning might be to them. We have instruments and measurements: They have senses — many more and better, perhaps, than five. We have logic; they have repose. We know; they act. Our different ways of living in the same world are well demonstrated by the different ways in which we accept the seasons.

People take the seasons as they come, one at a time. They understand the seasons, foresee them, plan for them. Animals — or anyway the ones we're pleased to call the higher animals — seem in some way to live in all the seasons at once, all the time. Or at least they experience the seasons as overlapping to a far greater degree than we do. I'm thinking of a particular cat, a well-grown black male named Puss. Like most cats, Puss likes to get around. All spring and summer he checks in each morning to eat, then immediately runs back outdoors.

Sometime in August, though, Puss makes a slight adjustment in his routine. Now, in the morning after breakfast, instead of heading right back out, he goes upstairs to one of the beds and sleeps for two hours. Then he's off again. At this time, you understand, we're not far past midsummer: It's hot, green, dusty. The days are long, the nights full of fun. And yet Puss forgoes a measure of it all for the sake of a nap. I think some deep sense warns him of the distant approach of winter, a matter of which he knows nothing. In the middle of the endless summer, and for reasons no reason knows, he's preparing his complex life for another world.

1995 SEPTEMBER, THE NINTH MONTH

The autumnal equinox is at 7:13 A.M., EST, on the 23rd. The full Moon on the 8th occurs just a little closer to the equinox than that of October 8th and thus earns the title of Harvest Moon. Saturn reaches opposition on the 14th, though not much brighter than Fomalhaut, the star below it. The reason for its diminished luster is the fact that its rings are turned nearly sideways to us and don't add much radiance. Jupiter now sets by late evening and is near the Moon on the 1st. Cygnus the Swan soars overhead at midevening, its tail marked by bright star Deneb, its wings spread across the Milky Way band. Capricornus the Sea Goat looks like a dim boat in the south, and the Great Square of Pegasus is prominent in the eastern sky.

☽ First Quarter	2nd day	4th hour	4th min.
○ Full Moon	8th day	22nd hour	38th min.
☾ Last Quarter	16th day	16th hour	10th min.
● New Moon	24th day	11th hour	56th min.

ADD 1 hour for Daylight Saving Time.

For an explanation of this page, see "How to Use This Almanac," page 30; for values of Key Letters, see Time Correction Tables, page 186.

Day of Year	Day of Month	Day of Week	☉ Rises h. m.	Key	☉ Sets h. m.	Key	Length of Days h. m.	Sun Fast m.	Full Sea Boston A.M.	Full Sea Boston P.M.	☽ Rises h. m.	Key	☽ Sets h. m.	Key	Declination of Sun °	☽ Place	☽ Age
244	1	Fr.	5 09	B	6 19	D	13 10	15	$3\frac{1}{4}$	$3\frac{1}{2}$	12 P.M. 04	E	10 P.M. 09	B	8 N.16	LIB	7
245	2	Sa.	5 10	B	6 17	D	13 07	16	4	$4\frac{1}{2}$	1 08	E	11 P.M. 03	B	7 54	OPH	8
246	3	**A**	5 11	B	6 15	D	13 04	16	$5\frac{1}{4}$	$5\frac{1}{2}$	2 07	E	— —	–	7 32	OPH	9
247	4	M.	5 12	B	6 14	D	13 02	16	$6\frac{1}{4}$	$6\frac{1}{2}$	3 00	E	12 A.M. 04	B	7 10	SAG	10
248	5	Tu.	5 13	B	6 12	D	12 59	17	$7\frac{1}{4}$	$7\frac{1}{2}$	3 47	E	1 10	B	6 48	SAG	11
249	6	W.	5 14	B	6 10	D	12 56	17	$8\frac{1}{4}$	$8\frac{3}{4}$	4 28	D	2 19	B	6 26	CAP	12
250	7	Th.	5 15	B	6 09	D	12 54	17	$9\frac{1}{4}$	$9\frac{1}{2}$	5 05	D	3 29	C	6 03	AQU	13
251	8	Fr.	5 16	B	6 07	D	12 51	18	10	$10\frac{1}{2}$	5 39	D	4 38	D	5 41	AQU	14
252	9	Sa.	5 17	B	6 05	C	12 48	18	11	$11\frac{1}{4}$	6 12	C	5 46	D	5 18	PSC	15
253	10	**A**	5 18	B	6 03	C	12 45	18	$11\frac{3}{4}$	—	6 44	C	6 53	D	4 55	PSC	16
254	11	M.	5 19	B	6 02	C	12 43	19	12	$12\frac{1}{2}$	7 16	C	7 57	E	4 33	PSC	17
255	12	Tu.	5 20	B	6 00	C	12 40	19	$12\frac{3}{4}$	$1\frac{1}{4}$	7 50	B	9 00	E	4 10	PSC	18
256	13	W.	5 22	B	5 58	C	12 36	19	$1\frac{1}{2}$	$1\frac{3}{4}$	8 26	B	10 00	E	3 47	ARI	19
257	14	Th.	5 23	B	5 56	C	12 33	20	$2\frac{1}{4}$	$2\frac{1}{2}$	9 06	B	10 57	E	3 24	TAU	20
258	15	Fr.	5 24	B	5 55	C	12 31	20	$3\frac{1}{4}$	$3\frac{1}{2}$	9 49	B	11 A.M. 51	E	3 01	TAU	21
259	16	Sa.	5 25	B	5 53	C	12 28	20	4	$4\frac{1}{4}$	10 36	B	12 P.M. 41	E	2 38	TAU	22
260	17	**A**	5 26	B	5 51	C	12 25	21	5	$5\frac{1}{4}$	11 P.M. 26	B	1 27	E	2 15	ORI	23
261	18	M.	5 27	B	5 49	C	12 22	21	6	$6\frac{1}{4}$	— —	–	2 09	E	1 51	GEM	24
262	19	Tu.	5 28	B	5 48	C	12 20	22	$6\frac{3}{4}$	7	12 A.M. 20	B	2 48	E	1 28	GEM	25
263	20	W.	5 29	C	5 46	C	12 17	22	$7\frac{3}{4}$	8	1 17	B	3 23	D	1 05	CAN	26
264	21	Th.	5 30	C	5 44	C	12 14	22	$8\frac{1}{2}$	$8\frac{3}{4}$	2 16	C	3 56	D	0 42	CAN	27
265	22	Fr.	5 31	C	5 42	C	12 11	23	$9\frac{1}{4}$	$9\frac{1}{2}$	3 18	C	4 27	D	0 N.18	LEO	28
266	23	Sa.	5 32	C	5 40	C	12 08	23	10	$10\frac{1}{4}$	4 21	D	4 58	D	0 S.04	SEX	29
267	24	**A**	5 33	C	5 39	C	12 06	23	$10\frac{1}{2}$	11	5 26	D	5 30	C	0 28	VIR	0
268	25	M.	5 34	C	5 37	C	12 03	24	$11\frac{1}{4}$	$11\frac{3}{4}$	6 32	E	6 04	B	0 51	VIR	1
269	26	Tu.	5 35	C	5 35	C	12 00	24	—	12	7 40	E	6 40	B	1 15	VIR	2
270	27	W.	5 36	C	5 33	C	11 57	24	$12\frac{1}{4}$	$12\frac{3}{4}$	8 48	E	7 21	B	1 38	VIR	3
271	28	Th.	5 38	C	5 32	B	11 54	25	$1\frac{1}{4}$	$1\frac{1}{2}$	9 56	E	8 07	B	2 01	LIB	4
272	29	Fr.	5 39	C	5 30	B	11 51	25	2	$2\frac{1}{4}$	11 A.M. 01	E	9 00	B	2 25	SCO	5
273	30	Sa.	5 40	C	5 28	B	11 48	25	3	$3\frac{1}{4}$	12 P.M. 02	E	9 P.M. 58	B	2 S.48	OPH	6

SEPTEMBER hath 30 days. 1995

The sun's away
  And the bird estranged;
The wind has dropped,
  And the sky's deranged;
Summer has stopped. – *Robert Browning*

D. M.	D. W.	Dates, Feasts, Fasts, Aspects, Tide Heights	Weather ↓
1	Fr.	☌♃☾ • 110° F, Los Angeles, California, 1955 • {9.8 / 10.7 •	*Temporary*
2	Sa.	Japan formally surrendered aboard battleship *Missouri,* 1945 • Tides {9.5 / 10.6	*truce —*
3	**A**	**13th S. af. P.** • ☾ runs low • Vince Lombardi died, 1970 • {9.3 / 10.6	*a*
4	M.	**Labor Day** • ☾ at perig. • Tides {9.3 / 10.6 •	*hurricane*
5	Tu.	☌♆☾ • ☌♅☾ • Sam Houston elected President of Republic of Texas, 1836 •	*is*
6	W.	*Time is a dressmaker specializing in alterations.* • President McKinley shot, 1901 •	*on*
7	Th.	Margaret Gorman of Washington, D.C., crowned first Miss America, 1921 • Tides {10.3 / 11.2 •	*the*
8	Fr.	**Full Harvest** ○ • ☿ Gr. Elong. (27° E.) • Tides {10.7 / 11.3 •	*loose!*
9	Sa.	☾ on Eq. • ☌♄☾ • Colonel Harland Sanders born, 1890 • {10.9 / 11.2	*The*
10	**A**	**14th S. af. P.** • First drunk driving conviction, London, 1897 •	*apples*
11	M.	*You cannot shake hands with a clenched fist.* • Nikita Khruschev died, 1971 •	*come*
12	Tu.	☾ at ☋ • John F. Kennedy married Jacqueline L. Bouvier, 1953 • Tides {10.6 / 10.7 •	*a-*
13	W.	World's record high temperature, 136.4° F in the shade, Libya, 1922 •	*tumbling*
14	Th.	**Holy Cross** • ♄ at ☍ • Severe freeze New England, 1911 •	*down —*
15	Fr.	This day said to be fair in six years out of seven. • Tides {9.1 / 9.6 •	*Macs,*
16	Sa.	Henry Steinway sold his first American-made piano, 1853 • {8.7 / 9.3 •	*Delicious,*
17	**A**	**15th S. af. P.** • ☾ rides high • ☾ at apo. • {8.4 / 9.1 •	*and*
18	M.	*September blow soft till the fruit's in the loft. November take flail, let ships no more sail.* •	*Macoun.*
19	Tu.	President James Garfield died, 1881 • Tides {8.4 / 9.2 •	*Warmth*
20	W.	Ember Day • Billy Jean King defeated Bobby Riggs in $100,000 tennis match, 1973 • {8.7 / 9.5	*gives*
21	Th.	**St. Matthew** • Editorial "Yes, Virginia, there is a Santa Claus," *New York Sun,* 1897 •	*way*
22	Fr.	☿ stat. • Ember Day • *Fiddler on the Roof* premiered, New York, 1964 • {9.5 / 10.1	*to*
23	Sa.	☾ on Eq. • Autumnal Equinox • Ember Day • {10.0 / 10.3 •	*sudden*
24	**A**	**16th S. af. P.** • **New** ● • Tides {10.4 / 10.6 •	*chills,*
25	M.	**Rosh Hashanah** • ☌☿☾ • Barbara Walters born, 1931 •	*and*
26	Tu.	☾ at ☊ • John Chapman (Johnny Appleseed) born, 1774 • {— / 11.1 •	*there's*
27	W.	☌♂☾ • Samuel Adams born, 1722 • Tides {10.7 / 11.3 •	*glory*
28	Th.	☌☿♀ • *Advice is seldom welcome; and those who want it the most always like it the least.* •	*on*
29	Fr.	**St. Michael** • ☌♃☾ • ☾ at perig. • Tides {10.3 / 11.2 •	*the*
30	Sa.	**St. Jerome** • ☾ runs low • *Porgy and Bess* premiered, Boston, 1935 {9.9 / 10.9	*hills.*

Education is when you read the fine print.
Experience is what you get if you don't. – Pete Seeger

Farmer's Calendar

What tools do you really need to garden with? Well, gardening is digging; you need a spade. You need something to use on the weeds. You need a knife. Three tools: Reduced to its simplest, gardening surely requires little more. Of course, many specialized tools are helpful. They speed and improve a number of gardening jobs. Therefore, various hoes, rakes, forks, shears, and so on become more or less necessary to most, maybe all, gardeners. Nevertheless, when you have got your essential three tools and a couple more, you enter a realm in which the tools take on a curious, exotic, overevolved look, like the frail offspring of a languishing aristocracy.

I'm thinking of one tool in particular that I inherited some years ago. It's for trimming the grass around your flower borders. At least that's what I think it's for. I can't be certain, for the tool in fact does practically nothing. It's a pair of old-fashioned flat-bladed hedge shears set on tiny wheels and attached to a shaft that ends in a trigger-grip like the one on a caulking gun. The whole affair is the size of a golf club. You're evidently meant to roll this contraption around your border, working the grip and clipping away at the grass. But unless your lawn is as smooth as a billiard table, those tiny wheels won't roll over it, and the trigger is a sorry affair that does no more than make the blades of the shears nod to each other in passing. In a real garden, and in terms of its intended function, this object has about as much use as the idiot son of the Graf von Nacht und Nebel. Even it need not go idle on my place, though. I put it in the pea patch to scare the deer.

1995 OCTOBER, The Tenth Month

*This is the second month of the year with two eclipses! However, only the begin-
ning phase of the penumbral lunar eclipse on the 8th will be visible in the northwestern
United States and Canada, Hawaii and Alaska; the total solar eclipse on the 23rd-
24th will not be visible to us. Mercury has its best dawn showing of the year on the
20th; look for it low in the east before sunrise. High in the east at midevening is the
hazy glow of the great Andromeda Galaxy. The Big Dipper skims along the northern horizon. A crescent Moon will not hinder viewing of the Orionid meteor shower
before dawn on the 20th and 21st. Daylight Saving Time ends at 2:00 A.M. on the 29th.*

☽ First Quarter	1st day	9th hour	36th min.
○ Full Moon	8th day	10th hour	53rd min.
☾ Last Quarter	16th day	11th hour	27th min.
● New Moon	23rd day	23rd hour	37th min.
☽ First Quarter	30th day	16th hour	18th min.

ADD 1 hour for Daylight Saving Time until 2 A.M., October 29th.

*For an explanation of this page, see "How to Use This Almanac," page 30; for values of
Key Letters, see Time Correction Tables, page 186.*

Day of Year	Day of Month	Day of Week	☉ Rises h. m.	Key	☉ Sets h. m.	Key	Length of Days h. m.	Sun Fast m.	Full Sea Boston A.M.	Full Sea Boston P.M.	☽ Rises h. m.	Key	☽ Sets h. m.	Key	Declination of Sun °	☽ Place	☽ Age
274	1	**A**	5 41	C	5 26	B	11 45	26	3¾	4¼	12 ᴹ 56	E	11 ᴾ 02	B	3s.11	SAG	7
275	2	M.	5 42	C	5 25	B	11 43	26	5	5¼	1 44	E	— —	–	3 34	SAG	8
276	3	Tu.	5 43	C	5 23	B	11 40	26	6	6¼	2 26	E	12 ᴬ 08	C	3 58	CAP	9
277	4	W.	5 44	C	5 21	B	11 37	27	7	7½	3 04	D	1 16	C	4 21	AQU	10
278	5	Th.	5 45	C	5 19	B	11 34	27	8	8½	3 38	D	2 24	C	4 44	PSC	11
279	6	Fr.	5 46	C	5 18	B	11 32	27	9	9¼	4 10	D	3 31	D	5 07	PSC	12
280	7	Sa.	5 47	C	5 16	B	11 29	28	9¾	10¼	4 42	C	4 37	D	5 30	PSC	13
281	8	**A**	5 49	C	5 14	B	11 25	28	10½	11	5 14	C	5 41	E	5 53	PSC	14
282	9	M.	5 50	C	5 13	B	11 23	28	11¼	11¾	5 47	C	6 45	E	6 16	PSC	15
283	10	Tu.	5 51	C	5 11	B	11 20	28	—	12	6 23	B	7 46	E	6 38	ARI	16
284	11	W.	5 52	C	5 09	B	11 17	29	12½	12½	7 01	B	8 45	E	7 01	ARI	17
285	12	Th.	5 53	C	5 08	B	11 15	29	1	1¼	7 43	B	9 41	E	7 24	TAU	18
286	13	Fr.	5 54	C	5 06	B	11 12	29	1¾	2	8 29	B	10 33	E	7 46	TAU	19
287	14	Sa.	5 55	D	5 04	B	11 09	29	2¾	2¾	9 18	B	11 ᴬ 21	E	8 08	AUR	20
288	15	**A**	5 57	D	5 03	B	11 06	30	3½	3¾	10 10	B	12 ᴾ 04	E	8 31	GEM	21
289	16	M.	5 58	D	5 01	B	11 03	30	4¼	4½	11 ᴹ 05	B	12 44	E	8 53	GEM	22
290	17	Tu.	5 59	D	5 00	B	11 01	30	5¼	5½	— —	–	1 20	E	9 15	CAN	23
291	18	W.	6 00	D	4 58	B	10 58	30	6¼	6½	12 ᴬ 02	C	1 53	D	9 36	CAN	24
292	19	Th.	6 01	D	4 57	B	10 56	30	7	7¼	1 02	C	2 25	D	9 58	LEO	25
293	20	Fr.	6 02	D	4 55	B	10 53	31	7¾	8¼	2 03	D	2 56	D	10 20	SEX	26
294	21	Sa.	6 04	D	4 54	B	10 50	31	8½	9	3 07	D	3 27	C	10 41	LEO	27
295	22	**A**	6 05	D	4 52	B	10 47	31	9¼	9¾	4 13	D	4 00	C	11 02	VIR	28
296	23	M.	6 06	D	4 51	B	10 45	31	10	10½	5 21	E	4 35	B	11 23	VIR	0
297	24	Tu.	6 07	D	4 49	B	10 42	31	10¾	11¼	6 31	E	5 15	B	11 44	VIR	1
298	25	W.	6 08	D	4 48	B	10 40	31	11½	—	7 41	E	6 01	B	12 05	LIB	2
299	26	Th.	6 10	D	4 46	B	10 36	32	12	12¼	8 50	E	6 53	B	12 26	LIB	3
300	27	Fr.	6 11	D	4 45	B	10 34	32	12¾	1	9 54	E	7 51	B	12 47	OPH	4
301	28	Sa.	6 12	D	4 43	B	10 31	32	1¾	2	10 52	E	8 54	B	13 07	SAG	5
302	29	**A**	6 13	D	4 42	B	10 29	32	2¾	3	11 ᴹ 42	E	10 01	B	13 27	SAG	6
303	30	M.	6 15	D	4 41	B	10 26	32	3¾	4	12 ᴾ 27	E	11 ᴾ 09	C	13 47	SAG	7
304	31	Tu.	6 16	D	4 39	B	10 23	32	4¾	5	1 ᴹ 05	D	— —	–	14s.06	AQU	8

OCTOBER hath 31 days. 1995

Hail, old October, bright and chill,
First freedman from the summer sun!
Spice high the bowl, and drink your fill!
Thank heaven, at last the summer's done!
– *Thomas Constable*

D. M.	D. W.	Dates, Feasts, Fasts, Aspects, Tide Heights	Weather ↓
1	**A**	17th S. af. P. • St. Remigius • {9.6 10.6 •	*Am I*
2	M.	☌ ♆ ☾ • ☌ ♅ ☾ • Tides {9.5 10.4 •	*delirious?*
3	Tu.	East and West Germany reunited, 1990 • 96° F, San Francisco, 1917 •	*Or*
4	W.	St. Francis of Assisi • Yom Kippur • ♆ stat. • ☿ in inf. ☌ •	
5	Th.	Chief Joseph and Nez Perce Indians surrendered at Bear's Paw, 1877 • Tides {10.1 10.6 •	*are*
6	Fr.	☾ on Eq. • ♅ stat. • ☌ ♄ ☾ • Tides {10.5 10.7 •	*the*
7	Sa.	Georgia Tech. defeated Cumberland U. at football, 222-0, 1916 • {10.8 10.7	*Red Sox*
8	**A**	18th S. af. P. • Full Hunter's ○ • Eclipse ☾ •	*in*
9	M.	Columbus Day • Succoth • Thanksgiving Day (Canada) • ☾ at ☋ •	*the*
10	Tu.	Spiro T. Agnew resigned as U.S. vice-president, 1973 • Tides {— 10.9 •	*Serious?*
11	W.	Pope John XXIII opened Second Vatican Council, Rome, 1962 • H. J. Heinz born, 1844 •	*Maple*
12	Th.	*In October dung your field, And your land its wealth shall yield.* • {9.7 10.4 •	*days and*
13	Fr.	☿ stat. • B'nai B'rith International organized, New York, 1843 • {9.4 10.0 •	*cider*
14	Sa.	☾ rides high • ☾ at apo. • 24" rain in 24 hours, Fort Lauderdale, Fla., 1965	*nights;*
15	**A**	19th S. af. P. • Mata Hari executed, 1917 • {8.7 9.3 •	*frost*
16	M.	First U.S. birth control clinic opened, New York, 1916 • Eugene O'Neill born, 1888 •	*in the*
17	Tu.	St. Ignatius of Antioch • Arthur Miller born, 1915 • {8.4 9.0 •	*valleys,*
18	W.	St. Luke • St. Luke's little summer. • Tides {8.6 9.1 •	*snow*
19	Th.	*Riches consist not in the extent of possessions but in the fewness of wants.* • {8.9 9.3 •	*on the*
20	Fr.	☿ Gr. Elong. (18° W.) • Moscow soccer disaster, 340 fans killed, 1982 • {9.4 9.6	*heights.*
21	Sa.	☾ on Eq. • 82° F, Boston, Mass., 1920 • Tides {9.9 9.9 •	*Winter's*
22	**A**	20th S. af. P. • ☌ ☿ ☾ • Tides {10.5 10.3 •	*hollow*
23	M.	☾ at ☊ • Eclipse ⊙ • New ● • {11.0 10.5 •	*eyes*
24	Tu.	Anna Edson Taylor went over Niagara Falls in a barrel, 1901 • *Experience is good if not bought too dear.*	*will*
25	W.	St. Crispin • ☌ ♀ ☾ • Chinese communist forces invaded Tibet, 1950 •	*peer*
26	Th.	☌ ♂ ☾ • ☾ at perig. • Erie Canal opened, 1825 • {10.7 11.9 •	*from*
27	Fr.	☌ ♃ ☾ • New York subway opened, 1904 • Emily Post born, 1872 •	*under*
28	Sa.	Sts. Simon & Jude • ☾ runs low • Daylight Saving Time ends, 2 A.M. tomorrow •	
29	**A**	21st S. af. P. • ☌ ♆ ☾ • {10.1 11.1 •	*autumn's*
30	M.	☌ ♅ ☾ • John Adams born, 1735 • Ezra Pound born, 1885 • {9.9 10.7 •	*bright*
31	Tu.	All Hallows Eve • Mount Rushmore National Memorial completed, 1941 •	*veneer.*

Farmer's Calendar

The automobile, that good and bad machine, might have been invented for dwellers in the hill country in autumn when the leaves are at their height. Whatever its depredations on the landscape in other respects, the auto is the best way for those who live and work among them to see the fall colors. That's because a drive along the lanes and over the hills gives you a view of the countryside that is constantly changing, constantly renewed.

If you live in the northern forestlands where the fall colors are best, it's easy to overlook them. The roadsides, brooks, and hills are too familiar; you see them every day, every hour. The landscape disappears. Across the valley from my house is the side of a mountain. I've lived with it for 20 years, but I don't suppose I've really looked at it more than a dozen times. To adapt Sherlock Holmes's famous admonition to Dr. Watson, I've seen, but I've failed to observe. To observe you need to have your customary sights and perceptions shaken up, turned around.

That's where your car comes in. You need to get out and around. You needn't go far, just take a spin around the neighborhood, enough to give you some new angles, some different paths. Pace is also important. You need to see the landscape passing before you at a fair clip so the colors take on a kind of cinematic energy. You also need to see the leaves at varying distances: Now you're enveloped in colors as though you lived inside a kaleidoscope, now the colors withdraw to a far hillside. It's from a car that you can best get the shifting, self-renewing sense of the autumn leaves that full enjoyment of them may require if they're your home.

1995   NOVEMBER, THE ELEVENTH MONTH

This month three planets play catch-up, then are themselves all joined by the Moon for a Thanksgiving night gathering — very low in the southwest at dusk, but glorious. First, Mars passes north of Antares on the 2nd, followed by Venus on the 10th. Next, Mars goes just one degree south of Jupiter on the 16th, and Venus nudges nearly as close past Jupiter on the 19th. Venus's pursuit of Mars ends at dusk on the 22nd,when it stands a breathtaking 0.2 degree south of the planet. Finally, after sunset on the 23rd, a slender, crescent Moon (at perigee) hangs near Jupiter and not far from the Venus-Mars duo. On the 24th, the Moon is low and in conjunction with Venus and Mars. Viewing of the Leonid meteors on the 17th-18th is hampered by a thick crescent Moon.

○ Full Moon	7th day	2nd hour	21st min.
☾ Last Quarter	15th day	6th hour	41st min.
● New Moon	22nd day	10th hour	44th min.
☽ First Quarter	29th day	1st hour	29th min.

For an explanation of this page, see "How to Use This Almanac," page 30; for values of Key Letters, see Time Correction Tables, page 186.

Day of Year	Day of Month	Day of Week	☉ Rises h. m.	Key	☉ Sets h. m.	Key	Length of Days h. m.	Sun Fast m.	Full Sea Boston A.M.	P.M.	☽ Rises h. m.	Key	☽ Sets h. m.	Key	Declination of Sun °	Place	Age
305	1	W.	6 17	D	4 38	B	10 21	32	5¾	6¼	1ᴹ40	D	12ᴬ16	C	14s.25	AQU	9
306	2	Th.	6 18	D	4 37	B	10 19	32	6¾	7¼	2 12	D	1 22	D	14 44	AQU	10
307	3	Fr.	6 20	D	4 36	B	10 16	32	7¾	8¼	2 43	C	2 27	D	15 03	PSC	11
308	4	Sa.	6 21	D	4 34	B	10 13	32	8¾	9	3 14	C	3 31	D	15 22	PSC	12
309	5	A	6 22	D	4 33	B	10 11	32	9½	10	3 47	B	4 33	E	15 40	PSC	13
310	6	M.	6 23	D	4 32	B	10 09	32	10¼	10¾	4 21	B	5 35	E	15 58	ARI	14
311	7	Tu.	6 25	D	4 31	B	10 06	32	10¾	11¼	4 58	B	6 34	E	16 16	ARI	15
312	8	W.	6 26	D	4 30	A	10 04	32	11½	—	5 38	B	7 31	E	16 34	TAU	16
313	9	Th.	6 27	D	4 29	A	10 02	32	12	12¼	6 22	B	8 25	E	16 51	TAU	17
314	10	Fr.	6 28	D	4 27	A	9 59	32	12¾	12¾	7 10	B	9 15	E	17 08	TAU	18
315	11	Sa.	6 30	D	4 26	A	9 56	32	1½	1½	8 01	B	10 00	E	17 25	ORI	19
316	12	A	6 31	D	4 25	A	9 54	32	2¼	2¼	8 55	B	10 41	E	17 41	GEM	20
317	13	M.	6 32	D	4 24	A	9 52	31	3	3	9 51	B	11 18	E	17 57	GEM	21
318	14	Tu.	6 33	D	4 23	A	9 50	31	3¾	4	10 48	C	11ᴹ52	D	18 13	CAN	22
319	15	W.	6 35	D	4 23	A	9 48	31	4½	4¾	11ᴹ48	C	12ᴹ23	D	18 28	LEO	23
320	16	Th.	6 36	D	4 22	A	9 46	31	5½	5¾	— —	–	12 54	D	18 44	SEX	24
321	17	Fr.	6 37	D	4 21	A	9 44	31	6¼	6½	12ᴬ49	D	1 24	D	18 58	LEO	25
322	18	Sa.	6 38	D	4 20	A	9 42	31	7	7½	1 52	D	1 55	C	19 13	VIR	26
323	19	A	6 39	D	4 19	A	9 40	30	7¾	8¼	2 58	E	2 29	C	19 27	VIR	27
324	20	M.	6 41	D	4 19	A	9 38	30	8¾	9¼	4 07	E	3 06	B	19 41	VIR	28
325	21	Tu.	6 42	D	4 18	A	9 36	30	9½	10	5 17	E	3 49	B	19 54	LIB	29
326	22	W.	6 43	D	4 17	A	9 34	30	10¼	10¾	6 28	E	4 38	B	20 08	LIB	0
327	23	Th.	6 44	D	4 16	A	9 32	29	11	11¾	7 37	E	5 35	B	20 20	OPH	1
328	24	Fr.	6 45	D	4 16	A	9 31	29	—	12	8 40	E	6 39	B	20 32	SAG	2
329	25	Sa.	6 47	D	4 15	A	9 28	29	12½	12¾	9 36	E	7 47	B	20 44	SAG	3
330	26	A	6 48	D	4 15	A	9 27	29	1½	1¾	10 24	E	8 57	C	20 56	SAG	4
331	27	M.	6 49	E	4 14	A	9 25	28	2½	2¾	11 06	D	10 06	C	21 07	CAP	5
332	28	Tu.	6 50	E	4 14	A	9 24	28	3¼	3¾	11ᴹ43	D	11ᴹ14	C	21 18	CAP	6
333	29	W.	6 51	E	4 13	A	9 22	28	4½	4¾	12ᴹ16	D	— —		21 28	AQU	7
334	30	Th.	6 52	E	4 13	A	9 21	27	5½	5¾	12ᴹ47	C	12ᴹ20	D	21s.38	PSC	8

NOVEMBER hath 30 days. 1995

The geese honked overhead
I ran to catch the skein
To watch them as they fled
In a long wavering line.
– *May Sarton*

D. M.	D. W.	Dates, Feasts, Fasts, Aspects, Tide Heights	*Weather* ↓
1	W.	**All Saints** • Post Office introduced money orders, 1864 • Tides {9.8 10.1	*Now*
2	Th.	**All Souls** • ☌♄☾ • Daniel Boone born, 1734 • Tides {10.0 10.0	*the*
3	Fr.	U.S. Embassy in Teheran, Iran, seized, 52 Americans held hostage, 1979 • {10.3 10.0 •	*tattered*
4	Sa.	Will Rogers born, 1879 • Walter Cronkite born, 1916 • Tides {10.5 10.0 •	*flags*
5	**A**	**22nd S. af. P.** • ☾ at ☋ • "Fawkes plot" never forgot. •	*of*
6	M.	*Beware of a door that has too many keys.* • Adolphe Sax born, 1814 • {10.8 9.9 •	*fall*
7	Tu.	**Full Beaver** ○ • Lewis and Clark first sighted the Pacific Ocean, 1805 • {10.8 9.8 •	*are*
8	W.	The Louvre Museum opened to public in Paris, 1793 • Tides {10.7 — •	*torn by*
9	Th.	Citizens danced in celebration as Berlin Wall opened, 1989 • Carl Sagan born, 1934 •	*blasts*
10	Fr.	**St. Leo the Great** • ☾ rides high • Martin Luther born, 1483 • {9.4 10.3	*from*
11	Sa.	**St. Martin** • **Veterans Day** • Sadie Hawkins Day • ☾ at apo. •	
12	**A**	**23rd S. af. P.** • Indian Summer • {9.0 9.7 •	*Montreal.*
13	M.	Vietnam Veterans Memorial dedicated in Washington, D.C., 1982 • Tides {8.8 9.4	*Snow*
14	Tu.	Claude Monet born, 1840 • Yale Univ. announced plans to admit women, 1968 •	*and*
15	W.	*None so surely pays his debt As wet to cold and cold to wet.* • Tides {8.7 9.0 •	*sleet*
16	Th.	☌♂♃ • Historic weather: –53° F, Lincoln, Mont., 21.5" snow, Helena, Mont., 1959	• *and*
17	Fr.	**St. Hugh of Lincoln** • ☾ on Eq. • Tides {9.2 9.1 •	*freezing*
18	Sa.	**St. Hilda** • Margaret Atwood born, 1939 • Tides {9.6 9.3 •	*rain*
19	**A**	**24th S. af. P.** • ☌♀♃ • Tides {10.2 9.7 •	*glaze*
20	M.	☾ at ☊ • President Lincoln delivered Gettysburg Address, 1863 • {10.8 10.1 •	*the*
21	Tu.	*Only the mediocre are always at their best.* • Tides {11.4 10.4 •	*glowing*
22	W.	♄ stat. • **New** ● • ☌♀♂ • {11.9 10.6	*windowpane.*
23	Th.	**Thanksgiving Day** • ☿ in sup. ☌ • ☾ at perig. • ☌♃☾ •	
24	Fr.	☾ runs low • ☌♂☾ • ☌♀☾ • Tides {— 12.3 •	*Let's*
25	Sa.	Dinner for two at Delmonico's, New York, cost 25¢, 1834 • Tides {10.7 12.1 •	*say*
26	**A**	**25th S. af P.** • ☌♆☾ • ☌♅☾ • {10.6 11.7 •	*a*
27	M.	Curtis P. Brady received first permit to drive a car through Central Park, N.Y., 1889 •	*blessing,*
28	Tu.	Friedrich Engels born, 1820 • Coffee rationing began, 1942 • {10.2 10.7 •	*and*
29	W.	Lord Carnarvon and Howard Carter discovered tomb of King Tutankhamen, 1922 •	*pass the*
30	Th.	**St. Andrew** • ☾ on Eq. • ☌♄☾ • {10.0 9.7 •	*dressing!*

And now you're married, you must be good
And keep your wife in kindling wood. – *Hearth and Home*, 1875

Farmer's Calendar

The job of setting things about the place to rights for winter holds a telescope up to the spring and summer just past, a telescope that you look through at the wrong end. Events, individuals, mishaps, ideas, plans of May through September appear as if at a great distance through the lens of late-autumn chores. It's an effect that stands the Theory of Relativity on its head: Time speeds up, rushes more quickly into the past for the observer who is busy around his home in the fall.

The windowpane that I dislodged in swatting a fly in June, as I fix it in place now, seems to have been knocked loose years ago. When I tear out the frost-killed marigolds, a dank, tough tangle the height of my knee, I remember in spring planting their seeds like tiny porcupine quills; it feels as though that happened in another life. I promised I'd mend that fence. Today the project is as remote as the quest for the Northwest Passage. The lawn chairs must be lugged down to the cellar. The company who sat on them in the August heat have returned to distant cities. Now the air feels not far off snow. That visit might have happened to somebody else, in a former age.

Why should this be? In the spring when you're planting, setting out, opening up, you don't see a sharp image of the winter before receding into the past. You're looking forward then, I guess, letting your life expand. In the fall, however, you're moving inward, seeking warmth and light rather than joy. There's a certain pleasure in doing so, a certain security — but there's also a certain regret. Hence, perhaps, the feeling of remoteness of the life just past that comes in preparing your place for winter.

1995   DECEMBER, THE TWELFTH MONTH

Jupiter and Mars get lost in the Sun's glare, but Venus appears higher in the southwest. By midevening, the Northern Cross pattern of Cygnus the Swan is standing upright on the northwest horizon. Overhead is the constellation Perseus and the Pleiades cluster. High in the southeast, the arrowhead of the Hyades star cluster and orange Aldebaran outline taurus the Bull's face, while following Orion the Hunter up the southeast sky are Procyon and the brightest star of all: Sirius. High in the east, yellow Capella flickers in Auriga; Gemini (the Twins) is low in the east. Look for Geminid meteors after midnight on the 12th and 13th, despite the glare from a gibbous Moon.

O Full Moon	6th day	20th hour	28th min.
☾ Last Quarter	15th day	0 hour	33rd min.
● New Moon	21st day	21st hour	24th min.
☽ First Quarter	28th day	14th hour	7th min.

For an explanation of this page, see "How to Use This Almanac," page 30; for values of Key Letters, see Time Correction Tables, page 186.

Day of Year	Day of Month	Day of Week	☉ Rises h. m.	Key	☉ Sets h. m.	Key	Length of Days h. m.	Sun Fast m.	Full Sea Boston A.M.	Full Sea Boston P.M.	☽ Rises h. m.	Key	☽ Sets h. m.	Key	Declination of Sun °	Place	☽ Age
335	1	Fr.	6 53	E	4 13	A	9 20	27	6½	7	1ᴹ18	C	1ᴹ24	D	21 s.48	PSC	9
336	2	Sa.	6 54	E	4 12	A	9 18	27	7½	8	1 49	C	2 26	E	21 57	PSC	10
337	3	A	6 55	E	4 12	A	9 17	26	8¼	8¾	2 22	B	3 27	E	22 05	PSC	11
338	4	M.	6 56	E	4 12	A	9 16	26	9	9½	2 57	B	4 27	E	22 13	ARI	12
339	5	Tu.	6 57	E	4 12	A	9 15	25	9¾	10¼	3 36	B	5 24	E	22 21	TAU	13
340	6	W.	6 58	E	4 12	A	9 14	25	10½	11	4 18	B	6 19	E	22 28	TAU	14
341	7	Th.	6 59	E	4 12	A	9 13	25	11	11¾	5 05	B	7 10	E	22 35	TAU	15
342	8	Fr.	7 00	E	4 11	A	9 11	24	11¾	—	5 55	B	7 57	E	22 42	ORI	16
343	9	Sa.	7 01	E	4 11	A	9 10	24	12¼	12½	6 47	B	8 40	E	22 49	GEM	17
344	10	A	7 02	E	4 12	A	9 10	23	1	1	7 43	B	9 18	E	22 54	GEM	18
345	11	M.	7 03	E	4 12	A	9 09	23	1¾	1¾	8 39	C	9 53	E	22 59	CAN	19
346	12	Tu.	7 04	E	4 12	A	9 08	22	2½	2½	9 37	C	10 25	D	23 04	CAN	20
347	13	W.	7 05	E	4 12	A	9 07	22	3	3¼	10 36	D	10 55	D	23 08	LEO	21
348	14	Th.	7 05	E	4 12	A	9 07	21	4	4	11ᴹ37	D	11 25	D	23 12	SEX	22
349	15	Fr.	7 06	E	4 12	A	9 06	21	4¾	5	— —	–	11ᴹ54	D	23 16	LEO	23
350	16	Sa.	7 07	E	4 13	A	9 06	20	5½	6	12ᴹ39	D	12ᴹ26	C	23 19	VIR	24
351	17	A	7 08	E	4 13	A	9 05	20	6¼	6¾	1 44	E	12 59	C	23 21	VIR	25
352	18	M.	7 08	E	4 13	A	9 05	19	7¼	7¾	2 52	E	1 38	B	23 23	VIR	26
353	19	Tu.	7 09	E	4 14	A	9 05	19	8	8¾	4 01	E	2 23	B	23 24	LIB	27
354	20	W.	7 09	E	4 14	A	9 05	18	9	9½	5 11	E	3 15	B	23 25	LIB	28
355	21	Th.	7 10	E	4 14	A	9 04	18	9¾	10½	6 18	E	4 16	B	23 25	OPH	0
356	22	Fr.	7 11	E	4 15	A	9 04	17	10¾	11½	7 20	E	5 23	B	23 25	SAG	1
357	23	Sa.	7 11	E	4 15	A	9 04	17	11½	—	8 14	E	6 35	B	23 25	SAG	2
358	24	A	7 11	E	4 16	A	9 05	16	12¼	12½	9 01	E	7 48	C	23 25	CAP	3
359	25	M.	7 12	E	4 17	A	9 05	16	1¼	1½	9 41	D	8 59	D	23 23	AQU	4
360	26	Tu.	7 12	E	4 17	A	9 05	15	2	2¼	10 17	D	10 08	D	23 21	AQU	5
361	27	W.	7 12	E	4 18	A	9 06	15	3	3¼	10 50	D	11ᴹ14	D	23 19	PSC	6
362	28	Th.	7 13	E	4 19	A	9 06	14	4	4¼	11 22	C	— —		23 16	PSC	7
363	29	Fr.	7 13	E	4 19	A	9 06	14	5	5½	11ᴹ53	C	12ᴹ18	E	23 13	PSC	8
364	30	Sa.	7 13	E	4 20	A	9 07	13	6	6½	12ᴹ25	B	1 20	E	23 09	PSC	9
365	31	A	7 13	E	4 21	A	9 08	13	7	7½	12ᴹ59	B	2ᴹ20	E	23 s.05	ARI	10

DECEMBER hath 31 days. 1995

Christmas is coming, the geese are getting fat,
Please to put a penny in the old man's hat;
If you haven't got a penny, a ha'penny will do,
If you haven't got a ha'penny, God bless you!
– *Beggar's Rhyme*

D. M.	D. W.	Dates, Feasts, Fasts, Aspects, Tide Heights	*Weather* ↓
1	Fr.	Rosa Parks arrested for refusing to give up her bus seat to a white man, 1955 • {10.1 / 9.5 •	*Shop*
2	Sa.	☾ at ☋ • Barney Clark received first artificial heart, 1982 • {10.2 / 9.4 •	*early,*
3	A	**1st S. in Advent** • Tides {10.3 / 9.3 •	*dearie —*
4	M.	*The pure and simple truth is rarely pure and never simple.* • Tides {10.4 / 9.3 •	*soon*
5	Tu.	Prohibition repealed, 1933 • Walt Disney born, 1901 •	*you will*
6	W.	St. Nicholas • Full Cold ○ • Ira Gershwin born, 1896 • Tides {10.5 / 9.3 •	*be*
7	Th.	St. Ambrose • Japanese attacked and devastated Pearl Harbor, Hawaii, 1941	*winter-*
8	Fr.	☾ rides high • U.S. and Britain declared war on Japan, 1941 • {10.4 / — •	*weary.*
9	Sa.	☾ at apo. • Clarence Birdseye born, 1886 • Tides {9.2 / 10.2 •	*For*
10	A	**2nd S. in Advent** • "The Gift of the Magi" published, 1905	*though*
11	M.	Fiorello LaGuardia born, 1882 • Joe DiMaggio retired, 1951 • Tides {9.0 / 9.8 •	*the*
12	Tu.	Beethoven paid 19¢ for his first music lesson from Haydn, 1792 •	*temperature's*
13	W.	St. Lucy • *An American in Paris* opened in New York, 1928 • {8.9 / 9.3 •	*above*
14	Th.	*Better a dry morsel and quietness therewith, than a house full of feasting, with strife.* •	*average,*
15	Fr.	☾ on Eq. • Bill of Rights ratified, 1791 • Canadian flag adopted, 1964 •	*so's the*
16	Sa.	☌♀♆ • Earthquake, New Madrid, Mo., changed course of Mississippi River, 1811	*snow,*
17	A	**3rd S. in Advent** • ☾ at ☊ • Tides {9.9 / 9.1 •	*and*
18	M.	☌♃☉ • Ty Cobb born, 1886 • Betty Grable born, 1913 • {10.4 / 9.4 •	*winds*
19	Tu.	Women awarded Rhodes Scholarships for the first time, 1976 • Tides {10.9 / 9.8	*are*
20	W.	☌♀♅ • Ember Day • Branch Rickey born, 1881 • Tides {11.5 / 10.1	*savage.*
21	Th.	St. Thomas • New ● • Joseph Stalin born, 1879 • {12.0 / 10.5 •	*Pray*
22	Fr.	☾ runs low • ☾ at perig. • Winter Solstice • Ember Day • {12.3 / 10.7 •	*we*
23	Sa.	☌☿☾ • ☌♂☾ • ☌♆☾ • ☌♅☾ • ☌☿♂ • Ember Day	
24	A	**4th S. in Advent** • ☌♀☾ • Halcyon Days {10.9 / 12.2	*now,*
25	M.	**Christmas Day** • *A green Christmas, a white Easter.* •	*both*
26	Tu.	St. Stephen • James H. Nason patented coffee percolator, 1865 • {10.7 / 11.2 •	*dudes*
27	W.	St. John • ☾ on Eq. • ☌♄☾ • ☌☿♆ • {10.5 / 10.6 •	*and*
28	Th.	Holy Innocents • Comet Kohoutek made closest approach to Sun, 1973 •	*hicks,*
29	Fr.	*The future is made of the same stuff as the present.* • Tides {10.1 / 9.3 •	*for a*
30	Sa.	–50° F, Bloomfield, Vermont, 1933 • Bo Diddley born, 1928 • {9.9 / 8.9 •	*peaceful*
31	A	*Begin the new year square with every man.* (Robert B. Thomas) • Tides {9.9 / 8.7 •	*'96.*

Farmer's Calendar

From a safe distance, anything that's possible looks easy. It's the theoretical point of view: If you *can* do a thing, you will. Then experience intervenes, and you learn that the street of reality has high curbs.

Nowhere is the gap between the possible and the practical wider than in the beliefs of those who move to the country from places having more complete amenities. Your house is without a modern stove? No problem: There's a woodburning range with an oven. We'll cook the turkey in that. How hard can it be? Need six cords of wood to heat the house in the winter? No problem: We'll cut it on the weekend; after all, there's trees all around. It'll be fun.

You learn fast. I remember the first time a winter storm knocked out our electricity and left us without running water. I took it well at first because there were a couple of feet of fresh snow on the ground. What is snow, I reflected, but water? We don't really need running water; we'll just melt snow. I wasn't wrong, of course, but reality is in the ratios, and the water-to-snow ratio is not favorable to the comfort I felt in the fact that snow is nothing but water. I found that the five-gallon pot, our largest, which we use for lobsters, yielded about a quart of water when filled with snow and heated. That's good news if all you need is a cup of tea, but it's not much help if you want to bathe, do a wash, clean up the dirty dishes. Yes, you *could* melt, say, 1,000 gallons of snow, but you won't. You'll do what I did: Wait disconsolately for the power to come back on and reflect on the difference between the way you know things to be and the way they are.

Jackie Robinson's athletic skills were surpassed only by his courage and determination to succeed in breaking major-league baseball's color barrier.

Fifty years ago, the president of the Brooklyn Dodgers baseball club, Branch Rickey, announced he had hired a player by the name of Jack Roosevelt Robinson, the grandson of a slave. The following, excerpted from the script of KEN BURNS's nine-part film about baseball (written by Geoffrey C. Ward and Ken Burns and aired on PBS nationwide beginning September 18, 1994), covers some of the behind-the-scenes events that led up to that historic, milestone decision . . .

THE

Revolution That Began on Tuesday, October 23, 1945

THE CAST OF SPEAKERS INCLUDES:

RED BARBER:
Play-by-play radio announcer for the Brooklyn Dodgers.

DAN OKRENT:
With Harris Lewine, editor of The Ultimate Baseball Book *(Houghton Mifflin Co.). Now managing editor of* Life *magazine.*

JOHN JORDAN "BUCK" O'NEILL:
Star player and later manager of the Kansas City Monarchs of the Negro Leagues.

SAMMIE HAYNES:
Another star player in the old Negro Leagues.

RACHEL ROBINSON:
Widow of Jackie Robinson.

CLYDE SUKEFORTH:
Chief scout for the Brooklyn Dodgers during the 1940s.

GERALD EARLY:
History professor at Washington University, St. Louis, Missouri.

81

**Dodgers president
Branch Rickey**

**Baseball Commissioner Judge
Kenesaw Mountain Landis**

"What about the Satchel Paiges of the future? Will they be playing in the big leagues? The question becomes more pressing yearly. It has been tossed into old Judge Landis's lap more than once, and the spectacularly adroit manner in which this articulate apostle of Lincoln tosses it out the window is a source of much marvel."

Joe Williams, New York World-Telegram, *August 25, 1944*

"There is no rule, formal or informal, or any understanding — unwritten, subterranean, or sub-anything — against the hiring of Negro players by the teams of organized ball." *Kenesaw Mountain Landis*
(Commissioner of Baseball from 1920 to 1944)

He had helped restore the game's integrity after the Black Sox scandal of 1919.
He had also done all he could to keep it white.
It was true that there had never been any written law banning African-Americans, but Judge Landis had worked ceaselessly to ensure that the old "gentleman's agreement" against hiring them remained firmly in effect. When the Pittsburgh Pirates sought permission to hire slugger Josh Gibson in 1943, Landis bluntly refused: "The colored ball players have their own league. Let them stay in their own league."
When Bill Veeck Jr. attempted to buy the eighth-place Phillies, then restaff it with stars from the Negro League, Landis made sure the team was sold to someone else.
And when Leo Durocher told a newspaperman that he'd seen plenty of blacks good enough for the big leagues, Landis forced him to claim he had been misquoted.
But the hypocrisy of fighting racism abroad while ignoring it at home grew clearer. Pickets appeared at Yankee Stadium with signs reading, "If we are able to stop bullets, why not balls?"

"I've said everything that's going to be said on that subject. The answer is no." *Kenesaw Mountain Landis*

On July 6, 1944, a month after D-Day, a young army lieutenant named Jack Roosevelt Robinson boarded a military bus near Fort Hood, Texas. The driver ordered him to "get to the back of the bus where the colored people belong."
Robinson refused and was court-martialed.
But the army judges found him fully within his rights and acquitted him. "I had learned," Robinson wrote, "that I was in two wars, one against a foreign enemy, the other against prejudice at home."
A few days after Robinson's trial, Kenesaw Mountain Landis died at the age of 78.

RED BARBER: This I know: In March of 1945, Mr. Rickey told me in confidence what only the board of directors of the ball club knew and only his family knew, and now I was going to know, that he was going to bring a black player to the white Dodgers. And Mr. Rickey said that when he was the baseball coach of Ohio Wesleyan University, he took the team down to play a series at South Bend, Indiana, with Notre Dame. And he said, "My best player was my catcher, and he was black. . . . But," said Mr. Rickey, "when we were registering this squad in the hotel, when the black player stepped up to sign the register, the clerk jerked the register back and said, 'We don't register Negroes in this hotel.'" And Rickey said, "I remonstrated and said, 'This is the baseball team from Ohio Wesleyan. We're the guests of Notre Dame University.' He said, 'I don't care who you are. We don't register Negroes in this hotel.' 'Well,' Mr. Rickey said, 'there are two beds in my room, aren't there?' And he said, 'Yes.' 'Well,' he said, 'can't he use one bed and not register him?'" The clerk grudgingly allowed that to happen, and Mr. Rickey took the key, handed it to the black player, and said, "You go up to the room and wait for me. Soon as I get the rest of the team settled, I'll be up." Mr. Rickey said, "When I opened the door, here's this fine young man sitting on the edge of a chair, and he was crying and he was pulling at his hands, and he said, 'Mr. Rickey, it's my skin. If I could just tear it off, I'd be like everyone else.' And

With Robinson, the Dodgers won six National League pennants and the 1955 World Series.

Mr. Rickey told me this day in March of 1945, he said, "All these years, I've heard that boy crying. And now," he said, "I'm going to do something about it."

"This is a particularly good year to campaign against the evils of bigotry, prejudice, and race hatred because we have witnessed the defeat of enemies who tried to found a mastery of the world upon such cruel and fallacious policy."

The New York Times

Judge Landis's replacement as commissioner was a jovial, gregarious senator from Kentucky, Albert Benjamin "Happy" Chandler, who said he took the job because the $50,000 salary was so much more than the $10,000 he'd been making as a United States Senator.

Few thought he would be an improvement. But in April 1945, two black sportswriters, Wendell Smith and Ric Roberts, who had campaigned tirelessly for integration since before the war, called upon the new commissioner to find out where he stood. "If a black boy can make it on Okinawa and Guadalcanal," Chandler told his visitors, "hell, he can make it in baseball."

Still, a secret vote revealed that 15 out of 16 club owners opposed racial integration.

The lone exception was Branch Rickey, who had left St. Louis in 1942 to become president and general manager for the Brooklyn Dodgers.

DAN OKRENT: It was in a narrow, tight, and unenlightened world . . . it was Branch Rickey who said,

Jack's wife, Rachel Robinson

Radio announcer Red Barber

"I'm going to do this. I'm going to integrate baseball. I'm no longer going to allow a part of the population to be excluded." Now Rickey's detractors say he would do anything to win. And it wasn't because he had such a big heart or that he was such a great believer in Civil Rights. He simply wanted to win. Well, there were a lot of men in baseball who wanted to win, and they wouldn't go this far. . . . This is far?. . . I don't think so at all.

"Branch Rickey is a con man, brilliant, fascinating, erudite — but still a con man. I've been listening to him for 25 years. I've always been impressed, seldom enlightened. The trick of the con man is to weave a spell. In this Branch Rickey stands alone. Not since the days of William Jennings Bryan and Billy Sunday has any man fallen so deeply in love with the melodic quality of his own voice."

Joe Williams, New York World-Telegram

Rickey had already transformed the game once by devising the farm system during his quarter of a century as president of the St. Louis Cardinals. He was already rich and in his sixties.

But he loved the challenge of building a new dynasty and he loved Brooklyn — its fierce local loyalties, its distinctive neighborhoods, and devotion to the Dodgers.

Now he was plotting a second, still more sweeping revolution. Rickey believed with equal fervor in fair play and big profits; he was convinced integration would be good for America, for baseball — and for his balance sheet.

BUCK O'NEILL: Branch Rickey had seen us play before 50,000 people in Comiskey Park. You understand? We had played in Yankee Stadium, you know, with 30, 40 thousand people, and we played the Dodgers, at Ebbets Field. So he knew here's a new source of revenue.

"The greatest untapped reservoir of raw material in the history of the game is the black race!" Rickey confided. "The Negroes will make us winners for years to come."

Meanwhile, Rickey's scouts began to scour the black leagues for a likely player.

SAMMIE HAYNES: A race man is a person who is proud of his race. He wants his race to advance. He wants his race to be recognized. That's the type of guy Jackie was. . . That's his whole thing. Recognition. Treat me as I'm supposed to be treated.

Give our people a fair shot at it. We make it, fine. If we don't make it, that's still fine. But give us an equal chance.

That's what a race man is.

Jack Roosevelt Robinson was born in 1919 in Cairo, Georgia, the grandson of a slave and the fifth child of a sharecropper who soon deserted his family. He was brought up by his mother, a domestic, in a white neighborhood in Pasadena, California, where white children pelted him with rocks — until he and his elder brothers began to pelt them back.

RACHEL ROBINSON: Jack, even in high school, was concerned about what was happening to his race. He had that early on. His mother, Mallie Robinson, was an extraordinary woman. And she came up from Georgia with five children and no prospects and just her determination to make it for her kids, that she set the example and set the pace. She was a real pioneer. And so a part of what she gave him was self-esteem. He wore white shirts to UCLA. He was ebony black and at a time when my generation really was not that proud to be black.

But not Jack. And what attracted me to him when we were at UCLA was he walked straight, he held his head up, and he was proud of not just his color, but his people.

At Pasadena Junior College and UCLA, he excelled at every sport he tried: led his basketball league in scoring two years running, beat his own brother's national record at the broad jump, and was one of the country's best running backs in football.... Baseball was relatively low on his list. But he was good enough at it so that when he left the army in 1944, the Kansas City Monarchs offered him a job as short-stop at $400 a month.

SAMMIE HAYNES: Jackie came to the Kansas City Monarchs in 1945. We spring-trained that year in Houston, Texas, and after spring training we went to New Orleans for an exhibition game there. Well, we had more people than seats in the bus. Jack

said, "Look, I'm a rookie. My seat is in the step of the bus. I'm going to earn mine just like everybody else." That's the type of guy that he was.

He hit .387 his first season, and Wendell Smith, still pressing for integration, arranged a tryout for Robinson and two other young Negro League players with the Boston Red Sox. Although Boston manager Joe Cronin was impressed by Robinson's skills, Boston passed up the opportunity to become the first major-league team to integrate. Instead, it would be the last.

By this time Robinson had caught the attention of Branch Rickey. He sent his chief scout, Clyde Sukeforth, a former catcher, to look Robinson over.

CLYDE SUKEFORTH: Well, he called me, and he said, "I want you to see a game in Chicago, Friday night." He said, "Pay in particular attention to a fella named Robinson. Now," he said, "I want you to identify yourself. Tell him who sent you and what you want to see. His arm ... pay in particular attention to his arm."

Sukeforth was impressed and told Robinson that Branch Rickey would like to see him.

CLYDE SUKEFORTH: He came down, and I talked to him at length. He was pouring the questions to me about "why is Rickey interested in me?" And the more you talked to the guy, the more you were impressed with the guy. The determination was written all over him.

Robinson did not know precisely what Rickey had in mind, but he agreed to accompany Sukeforth back to Brooklyn.

RED BARBER: Mr. Rickey, who had never laid eyes on Robinson, sent for him and had him in his office for three hours. Mr. Rickey was not only very intelligent but also very intelligent vocally. He never used profanity. And his strongest expletive was "Judas Priest." But that morning Mr.

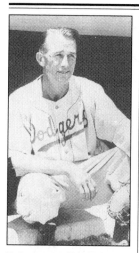

Dodgers scout Clyde Sukeforth

Negro Leagues star "Buck" O'Neill

– photos: National Baseball Library & Archive, Cooperstown, N.Y.

Rickey took Robinson into every possible negative situation he would encounter in all the world of Jim Crowism, et cetera. And he took Robinson into what would happen on the playing field, that he'd be thrown at, at his head, that he would be slid into and spiked, et cetera... he screamed in his face every expletive that Robinson would ever hear. And he said to Robinson. "Do you have the guts not to fight back?" And he said finally, "The only way that you can be the first man to do this, the first black man, is you'll have to promise me that for three years you will not answer back. You cannot win this by a retaliation. You can't echo a curse with a curse, a blow with a blow."

CLYDE SUKEFORTH: So Robinson gave it a little thought before he answered, and that impressed Rickey. If he'd said right off quick, "Oh, I can do that ..." Well, he gave it some thought, and he said, "Mr. Rickey, if you want to take this gamble, I'll promise you there will be no incident." And that was just what Rickey wanted to hear.

RACHEL ROBINSON: He picked Jack because he showed an assertive side of himself, which he would need. He showed the kind of strength to go through things.... He also was a deeply religious man, Mr. Rickey was, and he knew about Jack's religious convictions. So they were kind of alike in that sense. I think he saw the various aspects of the character that attracted him and made him feel that he could come through a scathing experience without being harmed or without giving in, giving up. There was very much of a partnership between them, and they had to agree on these things because they were in it together. Rickey needed Jack as much as Jack needed Rickey. They just had to do it together.

DAN OKRENT: They picked him because of who he was and what he was. Sure, the baseball skill was important, but there were other skilled players — Monte Irvin, who everyone expected to be the first. But Robinson had a determination and an ability to on the one hand turn the other cheek, but on the other hand as he turned the cheek to let his antagonist know that it would come around again.

SAMMIE HAYNES: The one thing that we weren't sure, that Jackie could hold his temper. Jackie had a terrific temper. He knew how to fight and he would fight ... if Jackie can hold down that temper, he can do it. He knew he had the whole black race — so to speak — on his shoulders, so he just said, "I can take it. I can handle it. I will take it for the rest of the country and the guys," and that's why he took all that mess. And it killed him.

On Tuesday, October 23, 1945, Rickey's office made an announcement that it said would affect baseball "from coast to coast."

The Montreal Royals, the Dodgers' top farm club, had hired Jackie Robinson. If he did well for Montreal, he would move up to the Dodgers.

GERALD EARLY: You can almost divide American history in the 20th century: before Robinson and after Robinson. America was defined by baseball. This was our national game. So, the drama of this moment of Robinson coming in is enormous because of the game being tied to the national character, tied to America's sense of its mission and its destiny.

ALMANAC EDITOR'S EPILOGUE:

Jackie Robinson went on to play a full year with the Brooklyn Dodgers' farm club, the Montreal Royals, where he hit .349. Then, in 1947, he joined the Dodgers to become the first black player in the modern-day major leagues. Before he'd even played his first game at Ebbets Field, April 15, 1947, some of his teammates had circulated a petition for signatures saying they'd rather be traded than play with him. During his first season, as well as the several thereafter, he was jeered unmercifully, spiked intentionally, and pitchers threw at his head. He received innumerable death threats (as did his wife), and of course, he was refused at many hotels in which the Dodgers were housed for away games. Throughout his ordeal during those first three years, however, he kept his promise to Branch Rickey not to retaliate. To just take it.

He also played superbly. Over the next ten years, playing mostly at second base, he helped the Dodgers win six National League pennants as well as the 1955

Jackie Robinson made the national pastime a democratic game.

World Series championship. In 1957 he retired from baseball with a lifetime batting average of .311 and in 1962 was elected to the Baseball Hall of Fame in Cooperstown, New York.

Always a civil-rights activist, Robinson after retirement served as chairman of the NAACP Fight for Freedom Fund, was Governor Nelson Rockefeller's special assistant for community affairs, and in 1965 helped found and became chairman of the board of the Freedom National Bank, Harlem's first black chartered and managed commercial bank. He was active in promoting other capital ventures and, on the day diabetes and heart disease ended his life on October 24, 1972, he had planned to participate in a symposium on drug abuse.

Writer George Will, speaking in the Ken Burns film, said, "... all that he did under all that pressure is not just one of the great achievements in the annals of sport but one of the great achievements of the human drama anywhere, anytime." ☐☐

– photo: National Baseball Library & Archive, Cooperstown, N.Y.

Shaker Herb Cabinet

NEW! 🏠

From *The Old Farmer's Almanac*
Farmhouse Collection

A rustic cabinet handcrafted with authentic square nails and etched glass. This sturdy, solid pine cabinet can either be hung from a wall or placed on a counter.

23"wide x 29"high x 9½"deep
#OF94FHC ....only $199

plus $15 shipping and handling

◆ ◆ ◆

ORDER TODAY

CALL TOLL FREE

800-685-3376

S50FSC

or mail order to:

The Old Farmer's Almanac
Farmhouse Collection
P.O. Box 10778
Des Moines, IA 50340-0078

The Only American Fairy

She (occasionally he) is far more American than Santa or the Easter Bunny. And she appears somewhere in this country every single night of the year.

☆ THE BEST WE CAN tell, she was born in America just after the turn of the century. We don't know exactly where. Somewhere a child lost a tooth. And a parent made magic in the night. When the child awoke, a coin lay beneath the pillow, and the tooth was gone. America's only fairy was born. Today, dentistry is the only profession with its own supernatural sprite, and the Tooth Fairy, surely, is one of the only fairies to have its own museum.

In Rosemary Wells's Tooth Fairy Museum in Deerfield, Illinois, more than 500 Tooth Fairy figurines, boxes, banks, pillows, jewelry, T-shirts, and posters are displayed. Paintings of tooth fairies cover the walls. Wells, a former English professor at Northwestern Dental School, has documented 76 books in which the Tooth Fairy figures. Her obsession began when dental-hygiene students wanted to discuss the mythology of dentistry. Her research showed scant studies.

"The Tooth Fairy is more American than Santa Claus and more pervasive than either Santa or the Easter Bunny," Wells says. "Santa Claus and the Easter Bunny appear once a year, tied to a religious belief. The Tooth Fairy appears every night somewhere, tied only to the family traditions." And it's a fairy whose only function is to exchange lost teeth for a gift, usually money. This fairy does only good — no evil spells, no tricks.

Wells has dated the appearance of the American Tooth Fairy back to the early 1900s, although the earliest mention in

Illustration by Molly Peery, age 9

print she's found so far is in a three-act play for children entitled *The Tooth Fairy* from 1927. The most popular image of the Tooth Fairy seems to be of a Tinker Bell-like creature. "There is no one single image," Wells says. "The Tooth Fairy can take on many images, but it's usually like someone the child knows so the child won't by Mel R. Allen

be frightened. In a single-parent family headed by a father, the Tooth Fairy is often a male."

Wells has surveyed more than 2,000 people about their personal Tooth Fairy practices. Some families mark only the loss of the first tooth. Seventy-five percent think of the Tooth Fairy as female. Eighty-five percent put the shed tooth under the pillow. Nearly everyone considers silver coins as especially magical. In 1930, the year Wells was born, the average gift from the Tooth Fairy was a dime. Today, *The Wall Street Journal* reported, 47 percent of respondents to a poll said they give $1 a tooth (which, incidentally, is worth about nine cents compared to its worth in the early 1900s).

The singular Tooth Fairy is firmly established in the United States and has spread to Canada (which has a Tooth Fairy Society), the British Isles, and sections of Spain and North Africa. Australia has the "Fang-Fairy Lady." When *Family Circle* magazine published "Letters to the Tooth Fairy" in 1979, one child wrote, "Dear Tooth Fairy, How long have you been in the tooth fairy business? My mother said they didn't

Illustration by Jacob Jarvela, age 13

have tooth fairies when she was a little girl, and that was a long time ago. . . ."

A Massachusetts boy offered this description: "I think she has a big, huge telescope and a big, huge model of the Earth, and whenever a kid loses a tooth, a light blinks in the house where it's lost. Then she flies down and does her stuff."

A child has 20 deciduous or milk teeth to lose, and doing something special to mark their loss is as old as Egypt. Ancient superstitions and folklore all seem designed to ensure that the old tooth will never again be seen by the child. Different cultures have devised all sorts of ways to accomplish this. The tooth — and especially the first tooth shed — may be thrown up toward the Sun, or into a fire, or sprinkled with salt. In Russia it was put in the mother's apron for safekeeping. In some parts of Mexico, the tooth is hidden in a shoe and is spirited away by a mouse instead of a fairy. Sometimes the tooth is thrown over the roof of the house or is even swallowed by the mother. Some cultures warned of great harm if the tooth remained in sight, as in this old English warning: "If you don't burn the shed tooth, you'll have to search for it in a pail of blood in hell."

Those first teeth are often lost just as the child begins going to school, a double rite of passage. The Tooth Fairy ritual, starting at a time when children still believe in fantasy, gives parents a way of protecting and extending childhood and remembering the child's infancy. The Tooth Fairy, a kindly spirit, helps ease the primitive fear of losing a part of the body. The silver coins represent the act of giving and a touch of magic. As poet John Masefield wrote, "Whoever gives a child a treat, makes joy bells ring in heaven's street."

The Tooth Fairy Museum, 1129 Cherry Street, Deerfield, IL 60015. Open by appointment. Write, or call Dr. Rosemary Wells, 708-945-1129.

For
Good Luck and Good Teeth

☆ Dr. Joseph G. Carter, professor of geology at University of North Carolina in Chapel Hill and a dentist's son, collects dental folklore and customs from around the world. Here are some American folk beliefs about shed baby teeth:

☞ Have your child throw his first lost tooth into the fire while saying: "Fire, fire, give me back a stronger tooth that I may chew a nail." *(Ohio)*

☞ Place your shed tooth under a rock, and you will become a traveler. *(Ohio)*

☞ For good luck and good teeth, throw the shed tooth over a low-hanging roof, and don't look where it lands. *(Ohio)*

☞ Put the tooth in a mouse hole for the mouse to chew it. The child will then have strong, straight teeth like mice. *(Ohio)*

☞ Wrap the tooth in a piece of red flannel and place in the drying oven of the stove. This ensures against catching cold in your jaw. *(Ohio)*

☞ Hide the tooth under a rock so the replacement will be straight and decay free. *(Illinois, Ozarks)*

☞ Place the tooth behind Grandmother's water pitcher so she will be lucky. *(Illinois)*

☞ If you shed your milk teeth before age seven, you will die before age eleven. *(North Carolina)*

☞ Children who drop a shed tooth through a crack in the floor and who keep their tongue out of the socket will some day get a gold tooth. *(North Carolina)*

☞ For good teeth, put the tooth on a piece of charcoal. Throw it over your right shoulder. *(North Carolina)*

☞ Run with a shed tooth around the house, repeating four times, "Beaver, put a new tooth into my jaw." Throw the tooth onto the roof. *(Cherokee Indians)* □□

HANDEDNESS

Leonardo da Vinci and Pablo Picasso were lefties, as were Benjamin Franklin, Albert Einstein, Marilyn Monroe, Queen Victoria, and Joan of Arc.

als tested show a preference for a particular hand, and they are evenly divided between left-handers and right-handers.

Researchers into handedness — or *laterality,* as the medical and scientific communities prefer to describe it — do not yet know why handedness should have evolved among humans in the first place, or even how it is passed along from one generation to the next. Indeed, pairs of identical twins appear to be no more likely to share the same handedness than randomly chosen pairs of unrelated strangers.

But handedness does run in families, in a general way. The newborn child of two right-handed parents, for example, has something like a ten percent chance of turning out left-handed. If Dad is left-handed

– illustrated by Eldon Doty

Pairs of identical twins appear to be no more likely to share the same handedness than random pairs of unrelated strangers.

and Mom is right-handed, the odds of the child being left-handed edge upward by a few percentage points. If Mom is left-handed, however, and Dad is right-handed, the odds rise sharply to 20 percent, or almost double. And if both parents are left-handed, the incidence of left-handedness among the offspring nearly doubles again, to between 35 and 40 percent.

Is handedness somehow preordained, or is it simply learned? Psychologists are now convinced that nature, rather than nurture, is the deciding factor. Until just a few decades ago, however, it was widely believed that left-handedness was simply a bad habit, one that could be rooted out and eradicated if proper "corrective" action was taken early enough. Many adult left-handers retain vivid memories of the forceful, occasionally cruel, and generally fruitless methods used to convert them into right-handers.

The belief that training would carry the day reached its zenith in the turn-of-the-century Ambidextral Culture Society, which energetically promoted training both hands to perform skilled tasks. For a time, it enjoyed a large and influential following, including R. S. S. Baden-Powell, Boer War hero and founder of the Boy Scouts. (Baden-Powell even wrote an introduction to a popular book on ambidextrality, closing with two specimens of his signature, one written with each hand.)

The movement unraveled, however, as it became painfully obvious — as Hemingway's Santiago would later observe — that true ambidextrality is very difficult, if not impossible, for most people to achieve. Still more problematic,

those who did turn the trick were hard pressed to put their ambidextrality to practical use. The movement's most visible legacy seems to be the official Boy Scout handshake — created by Baden-Powell himself — that is still offered and accepted with the left hand.

The ambidextrality fad has run its course, but other half-baked ideas about handedness have appeared to take its place. The most popular notion now making the rounds is that left-handed people are more insightful and creative than right-handers, thanks to a supposed ability to draw directly on the right hemisphere of the brain. Right-handers, by contrast, are seen as the stolid, slavishly rational captives of the left hemisphere.

Unlike most pieces of folklore about handedness, that one at least portrays left-handers in a favorable light. And there is a grain of truth associated with it: The two hemispheres of the brain *do* control motor functions on opposite sides of the body, which is why an injury to the left hemisphere — a stroke, for example — results in paralysis of the right side. But there is no evidence that the distribution of motor functions in the brain has anything to do with handedness or difference in the thought processes.

Still, there probably are some minor differences in the neurological wiring of right- and left-hander brains. One difference shows up in what are sometimes called "veering biases." A right-handed person stirring sugar into a cup of coffee, for example, swirls the spoon in a clockwise direction, while a left-hander stirs counterclockwise. The same pattern carries over into larger-scale movements, as well. Right-handers show a

tendency to bear right upon entering a room, while left-handers typically bear left. The myth of left-handed awkwardness probably has less to do with a lack of grace on the part of left-handers themselves than to the right-handed majority's lack of practice in anticipating their movements.

In some cases, though, that can work to the southpaw's advantage. In sports such as boxing, fencing, and tennis, a left-handed competitor often finds it easier to keep a right-handed opponent off-balance. (However, when two lefties compete against one another, both are at an equal disadvantage.)

But neurological differences are only part of the story. Several studies show left-handers to be disproportionately numerous in architecture, the arts, and among the ranks of chess champions. They also tend to do better than right-handers on tests that measure ability to visualize and manipulate three-dimensional images.

Do these findings mean that left-handers really *are* inherently more creative than right-handers? Probably not. It's more likely that left-handers —

who, from childhood, must learn to adapt to right-handed scissors, ice-cream scoops, writing desks, and other items — simply have more practice solving visual problems, and gravitate naturally to activities where such skills are valued. The frustration lefties experience in using improperly designed tools and machines may also explain why left-handers tend to be both more cautious and more anxious than their right-handed counterparts.

Right-handed scissors and ice-cream scoops can be annoying, but a southpaw who must struggle with a right-handed power saw or rotary meat slicer risks losing more than his or her composure. Not surprisingly, some studies suggest that left-handers suffer more accidental injuries than right-handers, although that has not been conclusively proven.

Lefties can, of course, take some solace from the everyday items that actually favor them. Hand-cranked pencil sharpeners, for example, are cranked with the right hand, enabling a left-handed user to insert a pencil without first shifting it from the preferred writing hand, as a right-hander must. Most

The movement's most visible legacy seems to be the official Boy Scout handshake that is still offered and accepted with the left hand.

Kill Foot Pain Dead!

Total Relief Guaranteed– Risk-Free.

Don't blame foot pain on your shoes! Most foot pain comes from mis-alignment of the bones in your feet.

Foot pain begins when your foot's balance and natural elasticity is gone. Corns, calluses, bunions, even hammertoes can develop, as well as toe cramps, fallen arches, burning skin, tender blisters, flaking and chafing. Ankle, leg, knee, hip - even lower back pain, can result from improper foot alignment. And when your feet hurt, you hurt all over.

Now! No More Foot Pain. Guaranteed!

Featherspring® Foot Supports, a remarkable discovery from Europe are unlike anything you have ever tried. First, they are *custom-formed* for your feet and your feet only! Secondly, they help restore and maintain the elastic support you had when you were younger. They actually help realign your feet, while absorbing shock and relieving pain.

For over 40 years, Feathersprings have brought blessed relief to more than 3,000,000 foot pain sufferers world wide. No other foot support has ever given so much relief to so many people.

It doesn't matter whether you are a woman or man, whether your feet are size 4 or 14, what width your foot is, how low or high your arches are, how old you are or how long you've had foot pain...we know Feathersprings will work for you.

Guaranteed To Kill Your Foot Pain Dead! We'll Prove It To You Risk Free!

If you are bothered by aches and pains of the feet, legs, or lower back, we state without reservation that Feathersprings will bring you relief or *you risk nothing.*

Send today for FREE Fact Kit.

Cut out and mail in the coupon below TODAY for FREE information, including details of our risk-free money back guarantee.

Custom—Formed Feathersprings end foot pain... once and for all!

© Featherspring
712 N. 34th Street,
Seattle, WA 98103-8881

AMAZE YOUR FRIENDS *with* THESE FACTS:

☞ Composer Frederic Chopin and author Samuel Johnson believed it is bad luck to enter a house on the left foot.

☞ Famous lefties include Ben Franklin, Marilyn Monroe, Jack the Ripper, Queen Victoria, Paul McCartney, and Billy the Kid. And don't forget southpaws Lefty Gomez and Lefty Grove.

☞ In any culture, approximately one person in seven is left-handed.

☞ The Boy Scout handshake is done with the left hand because founder Robert Baden-Powell believed in ambidextrality.

☞ A right-handed person stirs sugar into coffee with a clockwise motion.

☞ A left-handed person stirs sugar into coffee with a counterclockwise motion.

☞ Upon entering a room, left-handers typically bear to the left; right-handers bear right.

☞ Women's clothing, with buttons on the left, is most efficiently buttoned by a left-handed wearer or by a right-handed lady's maid (the origin of the convention).

☞ Left-handers are disproportionately represented in architecture, the arts, and among chess champions.

☞ On a typewriter or computer keyboard, the left hand does nearly three-quarters of the work.

☞ Design bias in power tools, automobiles, and other potentially dangerous products may result in more accidents among left-handers.

☞ Studies have shown that people have a difficult time judging whether friends and family members are right- or left-handed. One study found that seven percent of participants could not correctly identify their own handedness.

☞ Safety experts agree that left-handers should be extremely careful when operating power tools, machinery, and cars. (So, they say, should right-handers.)

women's clothing is designed with the buttons on the left, so that it is most efficiently buttoned by a left-handed wearer (or a right-handed lady's maid facing her, which is how the convention got started). And the keyboards on most typewriters and computers are laid out in such a way that the operator's left hand is responsible for nearly three-quarters of the work.

But in the end, examples like those simply underscore the fact that we live in an overwhelmingly right-handed world. Under the circumstances, the left-handed minority's refusal to knuckle under and *be* overwhelmed — despite centuries of distrust, scorn, and ridicule — has to be seen as inspiring.

And even though the righties have the upper hand at the moment, it's possible that the shoe may someday be on the other foot. Some researchers speculate that the small but consistent pool of left-handers in the population may represent a sort of evolutionary ace in the hole — a hedge against the possibility that an unforeseeable turn of events may someday work against the survival of the right-handed variety of *Homo sapiens*.

That may sound unlikely, and it probably is. But maybe, just maybe, the southpaws will one day inherit the Earth. They certainly will have earned it.

□□

Cowboys Sang to the Cows

The old-time tunes of the West, with a
simple rhythm to match a horse's gait,
have given way to the big western swing
bands with their fancy chord progressions,
guitar runs, and drum riffs. But there are
those who still remember . . .

BY CHRISTINE SCHULTZ

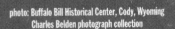

All day they've pushed 200 cattle toward greener pastures in Hamilton Dome, Wyoming, and now the animals won't quiet in the corral at Cottonwood Creek. The fire cracks, the fiddle jumps, the cattle just keep lowing. It's time, Skip Gorman decides, to sing a lullaby. He chooses one from the turn of the century. The old cowboy songs are what he and his partner, Ron Kane, know best and what they've been hired by the High Island Ranch to play for the two dozen guests who have paid to help drive cattle 35 miles to the summer grazing land. With a nod to Ron, Skip Gorman begins to sing "The Night-Herding Song."

> *Oh, say, little dogies, when are you goin' to lay down*
> *And quit this forever siftin' around?*
> *My limbs are weary, my seat is sore;*
> *Oh, lay down, dogies, like you've laid before,*
> *Lay down, little dogies, lay down.*

The men sing it slowly, with feeling, two voices rising from the wide open plain. When they've finished, the cows have settled. For a time, the night is as still as the stars.

On a night much like this one in March of 1889, a young cowboy named Nathan Howard "Jack" Thorp crossed the Pecos River in search of stray horses. He rode into camp to the sound of a cowboy singing "Dodgin' Joe," a song about the fastest cutting horse in Texas. Jack, who played a little music himself, wanted to learn more. The cowboys sang what they could remember — a handful of stand-bys that everyone knew and a few stray verses of others. Jack wrote them all down. They sat singing at the fire till the tunes clung to Jack like the smell of wood smoke to his clothes. By morning he'd decided to give up hunting horses and round up harmonies instead. His decision would make him the first man to systematically set down in writing what had been an oral tradition.

During the next year, with a man-dolin-banjo and notepad tucked in his bedroll, Jack rode 1,500 miles through the Southwest. He gathered a verse here, another there, piecing together a puzzle of the West. Every county had its own songs, and every cowboy had his own verse. What the singers couldn't remember, they made up. They shaped poetry during horseback days and bunkhouse nights. They rhymed tales of wild pranks and lost partners and fit the words to popular tunes they'd learned as boys. Jack collected lyrics wherever he found them: "The Prospector" scratched on an old ranch-house door; "A Man Named Hods" from a cowpuncher on the Rio Grande; "Old-Time Cowboy" from an old-timer who claimed someone's calf got caught up in his rope as he dragged it along.

The songs ran from English ballads to Negro spirituals, German lieder to Irish reels. There were some with enough spirit to rouse a slow dogie and others with enough rhythm to match a horse's gait. And though most cowboys couldn't carry a tune, no one seemed to mind. They sang to pass the time, to calm a skittish mount, or ease a weary soul. "I never did hear a cowboy with a real good voice," Jack Thorp once wrote. "If he had one to start with, he always lost it bawling at cattle, or sleeping out in the open, or tellin' the judge he didn't steal that horse."

On an 1898 drive from Chimney

Jack Thorp wasn't the first to sing the cowboy songs, but he was the first to write them down. His collection was published in 1908.

A song like "The Old Chisholm Trail" was seldom the same song twice — the more whiskey, the more verses, the more variety.

Lake, New Mexico, to Higgins, Texas, Jack scratched the story of "Little Joe the Wrangler" on a paper bag, set the words to "The Little Old Log Cabin in the Lane," and sang it to the men. He performed it later at Uncle Johnny Root's saloon in Weed, New Mexico, and the song caught on like a prairie fire. Men who heard about the boy who died in a stampede swore they knew Little Joe. The tune would become one of the oral tradition's most popular pieces.

In 1908 Jack printed "Little Joe," together with other songs, in a slim volume titled *Songs of the Cowboys.* Though the collection lacked melody lines, it nonetheless was the first of its kind. Jack sold all the copies he could of the 2,000 he'd had printed, charging 50¢ apiece. What he couldn't sell, he gave away, not knowing that at the century's end they'd sell for thousands of dollars each.

A lot of the songs from that volume were picked up two years later by folklorist John Lomax, who had better luck at distributing his own collection, called *Cowboy Songs and Other Frontier Ballads.* Though Jack had laid the groundwork, it was Lomax's songbook that became the cowboy singers' bible and standardized the tunes.

Folklorists look at such moments and worry that they change history forever, that they stop the natural evolution of the "folk process." But in this case, they needn't have been concerned. The songs refused to be roped in by print. Where there was a singing cowboy, there was always a new twist. A song like "The Old Chisholm Trail," sung from the border of Mexico to the Canadian line, was seldom the same song twice — the more whiskey, the more verses, the more variety. And certainly there was always spice; cowboys liked their songs with a kick. As Jack Thorp said, the lyrics weren't always "parlor talk."

Obscenities would remain a part of the tradition, but in other ways western music was about to take a turn. In 1925 Carl T. Sprague carried the cowboy flavor to New Jersey to cut a single with RCA Victor. He sang of a cowboy who hoped to get back to see his mother when the ranch work was all done in the fall. But, as the song goes, a stampede let loose and the cowboy's saddle horse "did stumble and upon him did fall, and he'll not see his mother when the work's all done this fall." The tragedy struck a popular chord in America that year, and people purchased close to a million copies of "When the Work's All Done This Fall." "That recording marked the beginning of the cowboy music industry," says Skip Gorman. "It's probably why they wear cowboy hats in Nashville today."

A few years later the yodeling brakeman, Jimmy Rogers, moved to Texas and fancied himself a real Texas cowboy; he was the first to make a million dollars in country music. Victor signed more cowboy artists, including Jules Verne Allen, who'd ridden in Wild West shows and rodeos and who billed himself as "The Original Singing Cowboy." Hollywood followed with the first singing cowboy of the silver screen, the rodeo rider Ken Maynard, who starred in *The Wagon Master.* Before long America was taken with sweet-voiced singers like

Gene Autry and Roy Rogers. By the 1930s, the happy-go-lucky image portrayed by Hollywood had migrated far from its origins in the 1870s cattle drives.

Other influences were soon at work. In the following decades "cowboy" musicians took their cues from Hollywood and Nashville and Broadway. Cowboy music became "Western" music, then "Western swing," and listeners started hearing horns schooled in the jazz tradition. Even when bands used the old lyrics, they incorporated modern technique — fancy chord progressions, electric guitar runs, drum riffs — until some popular groups had little more in common with old-time cowboys than their hats. These days, when bands gather in

The lyrics weren't always "parlor talk."

Nevada for the annual Western Folklife Center's cowboy music gathering, it's the big western swing bands and country-western groups that draw the crowds. Only a few traditionalists have stayed true to the old cowboy style.

Just as barbed-wire fences reconfigured the open plains, modern influences have changed the songs of the cattle-drive generation. But, in fact, the West has always been reimagined and romanticized as far back as Buffalo Bill's Wild West Show in 1883. And all along, cowboys have been lamenting the change — often through songs like "The Last Longhorn."

The cowboys and the longhorns
Who pardnered in eighty-four
Have gone to their last round-up
Over on the other shore.
They answered well their purpose,
But their glory must fade and go,
Because men say there's better things
In the modern cattle show.

On a Wyoming summer night at 3,000 feet, Skip Gorman and Ron Kane re-create the old flavor — with a twang in the voice, tinny mandolin, and a low-droning fiddle. The moan of cows and the snap of the fire add to the mood, and it's hard to know what century it is. Just outside the rim of fire, his face hidden in the shadow of his hat, sits Nate Brown. He's cowboyed for more than seven decades on the next ranch over — a place he likes to call "Belly Acres." He's a link to the old ways, helping less experienced dudes learn the ropes. When he's riding in the saddle, Nate still sings to himself the songs he learned as a boy from his cousins and neighboring cowboys. He looks at the two musicians and gives them a grin. "That's just how my grand-daddy played it."

At high noon the next day Ron Kane is tucked in among a patch of cottonwoods with the fiddle tucked under his chin. He plays a tune in the key of G called "Jenny and the Cotton Patch." Having herded cattle all morning, many dudes are sacked out in the sun, hats tipped over their faces. They seem oblivious to the cattle mooing like the horns in a Dallas traffic jam. "Some of the old recordings sound just like this," Ron says, "with the cows mooing in back. There weren't any buttons to push, so the songs sound pretty rough." Still, it's what he loves. "Some people collect stamps," he says, "some people collect salt shakers. I collect old tunes."

His tunes may sound raw to people accustomed to modern music, but they come from a tradition where many learned to play by ear on the trail without formal training. They found it easier to tune a violin to an open chord, down lower so it whined, and to use three or four basic chords. Out of that

Jules Verne Allen, who'd ridden in Wild West shows, recorded for RCA Victor as "The Original Singing Cowboy."

custom grew a sound as fresh as the smell of sage and sweet clover, a sound that evoked the wide-open feel of light chasing shadow across a valley. A musician could grow old trying to capture that wildness, while in the process his heart grew young.

The author especially thanks High Island Ranch. For more information on their cattle drives: P.O. Box 7A, Hamilton Dome, WY 82427; 307-867-2374.

THAT Old-Time Cowboy Sound

Recordings

☞ *Powder River.* Skip Gorman and Ron Kane. Folk Legacy, Sharon, Connecticut.

☞ *Trail to Mexico.* Skip Gorman. Folk Legacy, Sharon, Connecticut.

☞ *Rolling Up Hill from Texas.* Buck Ramsey. Fiel Publications, Lubbock, Texas.

☞ *My Home Was in Texas.* Buck Ramsey. Fiel Publications, Lubbock, Texas.

☞ *Cowboy Songs.* Bunkhouse Orchestra (Deseret String Band). Gibbs-Smith, Salt Lake City, Utah.

☞ *Red Steer.* Deseret String Band. Okehdokee Recordings, Salt Lake City, Utah.

☞ *A Greener Prairie.* Skip Gorman. The Rounder Records Group, Cambridge, Massachusetts.

Books

☞ Cannon, Hal, ed. *Cowboy Poetry: A Gathering.* Salt Lake City: Peregrine Smith Books, 1985.

☞ Logsdon, Guy. *The Whorehouse Bells Were Ringing.* Urbana: University of Illinois Press, 1989.

☞ Lomax, John and Allan. *Cowboy Songs and Other Frontier Ballads.* New York: Macmillan Company, 1986. (Reprint of 1910 collection)

☞ Ohrlin, Glenn. *The Hell-Bound Train: A Cowboy Songbook.* Urbana: University of Illinois Press, 1973.

☞ Thorp, N. Howard. *Songs of the Cowboys.* Lincoln: University of Nebraska Press, 1984. (Reprint of 1908 collection)

☞ Tinsley, Jim Bob. *He Was Singin' This Song.* Orlando: University of Florida, 1981.

☞ White, John I. *Git Along Little Dogies.* Urbana: University of Illinois Press, 1975. □□

E=mc²

SO WHAT?

T he problem with the theory of relativity is not so much that it is difficult to understand, but that it is almost impossible to believe. What it says about reality so contradicts common sense and everyday experience that it seems absurd.

Most normal people (i.e., people who aren't physicists) live in a Newtonian universe, whether they call it that or not. In the 17th century, Isaac Newton, using the calculus he invented for the purpose, was able to describe how the physical universe works through the force of gravitation. His mathematical laws explained everything from the fall of an apple to the elliptical orbits of the planets around the Sun. His system was so complete and satisfying that it came as a revelation to people of his time. It seemed that there was little left to discover. Alexander Pope wrote:

Nature and Nature's laws lay hid in night:
God said, Let Newton be! *and all was light.*

Fundamental to the Newtonian world view is that space and time are absolutes. They are the unchanging stage on which all the events of the universe are acted out.

But Newton was wrong. On the human scale, even on the scale of the solar system, Newton's laws work almost perfectly. *Almost* perfectly. With extremely sophisticated instruments, scientists can now detect slight discrepancies here. But on the scale of massive stars and galaxies and clusters of galaxies, the discrepancies are enormous.

Scientists of Newton's time, of course, didn't have these instruments, and they didn't know of the existence of galaxies, let alone clusters of galaxies. Even so, a clue

Ever wondered what Einstein's 90-year-old "theory of relativity" really means to you and me? Like, is it even possible for us to understand? Well, here's a pretty good attempt at a simple explanation . . .

by Michael McNierney

to the fact that not all was right with the Newtonian system was present for those who could see. And Newton himself was the one to see it. The haunting question he could not answer was: How do light and gravitational force travel through the emptiness of space?

The attempt to answer this question led to the theory of relativity.

Light moves so fast that for centuries attempts to measure its speed seemed to indicate that it propagated instantaneously. Across a park, you see a batter hit a ball. A moment later, you hear the crack of the bat. Sound obviously has a speed, but light seems instantaneous. For a long time, technology was simply too crude to measure light's speed, which was finally determined to move at about 186,272 miles per second. (Sound moves at about 12.5 miles per second.)

Light behaves like a wave. (It also behaves like particles, but that story would get us into quantum physics.) Scientists reasoned that sound waves are carried in the air. Water waves are carried in water. Therefore, although space is empty, light waves must be carried in something. This conclusion led to the theory of the luminiferous ether — a light-carrying "substance" in space.

Determining if your boat is moving through the water is easy: You can look for the bow wave or put your hand in the water and feel motion. On this analogy, 19th-century scientists tried to detect an ether wind or drift as the Earth moved through space. Many attempts were made, and finally, in July 1887, the definitive experiment was performed by Albert Michelson and Edward Morley. The results shocked the scientific world. They could find no ether wind.

Scientists scrambled to find an explanation for the failure of the experiment. Almost no one wanted to consider the most obvious explanation: There is no ether.

Physics had reached a frustrating dilemma. If the ether existed, then why couldn't it be detected experimentally? If it didn't exist, then *why* didn't it exist? In 1905 the answer was provided by a theory that not only solved the problem of the ether, but also made far-ranging predictions in other areas.

The theory belonged to an obscure man of 26 working as a "technical expert third class" in the Swiss patent office in Bern.

Albert Einstein had been a dreamy child, not even speaking until he was three years old. He failed his first college entrance exam, but finally graduated in 1900 with mediocre grades (he preferred playing the violin and hanging out in cafés to studying). He ended up working in the patent office after trying, and failing, to get a job as a scientist or high school teacher.

Einstein had been fascinated with physics since he was a child and never stopped thinking about the subject. He applied himself to the problem of light and the ether wind and wrote a short paper on it entitled "On the Electrodynamics of Moving Bodies." After Max Planck, a renowned physicist and editor of a German journal of physics, read the paper submitted by this unknown young man, he knew immediately that the standard view of the world had changed forever. Einstein's paper set forth what would later be known as the special theory of relativity.

In his paper, Einstein offered and proved two postulates:

1. The ether, if it exists, cannot be detected;

Einstein failed his first college entrance exam, but finally graduated in 1900 with mediocre grades (he preferred playing the violin and hanging out in cafés).

2. The speed of light is always constant relative to an observer.

Neither of these will seem all that dramatic to a nonphysicist, but the deductions and conclusions that follow from them are earthshaking. Relativity can't be completely explained or comprehended without mathematics, but we can at least sketch out an idea of what the Einsteinian, relativistic universe is like. Incidentally, don't be misled by the word "theory." Relativity was only a theory when Einstein published it, but it is a fact now. Its truth has been repeatedly verified by experiment.

Einstein discovered two extraordinary facts about light (and about all other electromagnetic radiation). The first is that its speed never changes, even if an observer is moving directly toward the light source or directly away from it. This means that the light leaving a star travels at 186,272 miles per second relative to you even if you are approaching or separating from the star at a speed of 186,271 miles per second!

This kind of behavior is not true of anything else, including other types of waves. If two cars approach each other head on, each traveling at 60 miles per hour, the speed of the other car relative to each observer is 120 miles per hour. Or if they are traveling parallel to each other, the relative speed of each is 0 miles per hour. This principle also applies to sound waves. Yet with light, the relative speed remains constant.

The second fact that Einstein discovered about light is that the speed of light — 186,272 miles per second — is the speed limit of the universe. Nothing can travel faster than that.

This brings us to the heart of the special theory of relativity and the most famous formula in the history of science: $E=mc^2$. In simple terms, what this equation says is that energy and mass are equivalent; they are the same thing in different forms. Mass is frozen energy. $E=mc^2$ means that equivalent energy (E) is equal to mass (m) times the speed of light (c) squared.

You are familiar with the implications of this equation, even if you don't realize it. If you will recall a little of your high school algebra, you can figure it out for yourself. You know that the speed of light is a very large number. Multiply it by itself and you get an astronomically large number. If you substitute even a small number for the mass in the equation, just a few pounds, say, and multiply it by the squared speed of light, the result is another enormous number. And this is E, the pure energy that is equivalent to those few ounces of mass.

Take 110 pounds of uranium. If you drop it on a house, it will crash through the roof, but that's about all the damage it will do. Put it into a special device (military-speak for "bomb") that converts it to pure energy, however, and you level the city of Hiroshima. All forms of nuclear power are implied in that simple equation.

The reason nothing can exceed the speed of light is that the faster an object goes, the more its mass increases. As it approaches light speed, its mass approaches the infinite, and since energy is required to move a mass, the energy needed also approaches the infinite. It would take an infinite amount of energy to move something, anything, faster than light, and that is of course more energy than is available in the entire universe. Faster-than-light travel is therefore impossible.

In 1916, 11 years after Einstein published his special theory, he introduced the general theory of relativity to the scientific world. Building on his earlier work, he now finished off the Newtonian world view for good.

The implications of general relativity are still being worked out in the realm of quasars, pulsars, and black holes. But what the combined general and special theories say is that on the largest scale of the universe there is no such thing as gravitation or independent, absolute space or time. Everything exists in space-time, which is the three dimensions of space plus the fourth dimension of time. Space-time is curved in the vicinity of mass — the greater the mass, the greater the curve. What Newton thought of as the mysterious force of gravitation is not a force at all. It is the sliding and falling of a body along the curves made by a more massive body in space-time.

The Earth, for example, is sliding along the walls of space-time curved around the mass of the Sun. Great mass can even bend light. Black holes, formed in the collapse of huge stars, contain the mass of their parent stars in incredibly dense spheres of matter only a few miles in diameter. Space-time is so curved in their vicinity that not even light can escape; it is curved back on itself.

If your mind is beginning to feel a little scrambled, don't worry. General relativity is not comprehensible without the mathematics. It's a little like trying to hear music from a verbal description. We just have to trust the physicists when they say it is true.

Some people have rejected the whole idea of relativity because they think that it makes *everything* relative, even values, or even that God does not exist because there is no such thing as good and evil. This is an unfortunate misunderstanding. The theory of relativity has nothing whatsoever to say about spiritual values; it describes only the physical universe.

But what a universe! It's a place of infinite mystery and awe. Albert Einstein, himself a deeply religious man, drew unlimited inspiration from the universe he had discovered. "I want to know," he said, "how God created this world. I am not interested in this or that phenomenon. . . . I want to know His thoughts, the rest are details." □□

While the Bass Get SMARTER and We All Get DUMBER

In the meantime, here's the problem: Dumb fish are easier to catch so they're being all caught up. Those remaining are the smart fish that are hard to catch. Solution: breed more really dumb fish. It's actually happening in Texas.

by Al Levine

– illustrated by Jan North / represented by Creative Freelancers

Until recently the ability to catch fish was considered a birthright of human beings. And why not? If you go merely by the size of the brain, fishermen ought to be considered a tad more intelligent than a fish. We've got a three-pound brain; theirs is just a few ounces. And ours is so much more developed.

In recent years, however, fish appear to be turning the tide. Fishing no longer is the simple exercise that Grandpa used to enjoy. It has become so difficult to catch anything that some large, usually productive lakes are referred to locally as the Dead Sea.

The situation in Texas, where bass are the number-one sport fish, became so frustrating about five years ago that Dr. Gary Garrett, a research biologist, initiated a project at the state fish hatchery in response to complaints that certain reservoirs were becoming more difficult to fish.

Through two generations of breeding, he determined that there definitely was something genetically different between a group of fish that was easy to catch and a group that was difficult. "The dumb bass is not really that — it's a matter of an aggressive fish versus a wary fish," he said.

"What was happening was that the aggressive fish, the fish easiest to catch — what people considered the dumb ones — were being taken out of the breeding cycle, leaving only the wary, smart ones that weren't being caught," said Garrett.

"As far as dumb and smart goes, it may be that the fish easiest to catch are actually the ones you want to leave as breeding stock.

These fish, the supposedly dumb ones, are the most aggressive, the best fed, the fastest, and the healthiest. The supposedly smart ones are scared of their shadow and don't grow as large as the others. Why this is we don't know. You know research: You answer one question and you raise ten more."

Garrett, who has become known as the man breeding a dumber bass, uncovered these facts: Before the selective breeding process, eight percent of the allegedly dumber bass went after a baited hook in a 40-hour fishing period. After selective breeding, that number jumped to 11 percent.

In the same period of fishing research, before selective breeding, 22 percent of the supposedly smarter bass refused to take a line at all; after selective breeding, an amazing 48 percent of the smarter bass would never take a lure.

Conclusion: Through two generations of selective breeding, the dumb bass got dumber and the smart bass got a lot more nervous. "I'm sure you might find the same results with trout or walleye," Garrett said.

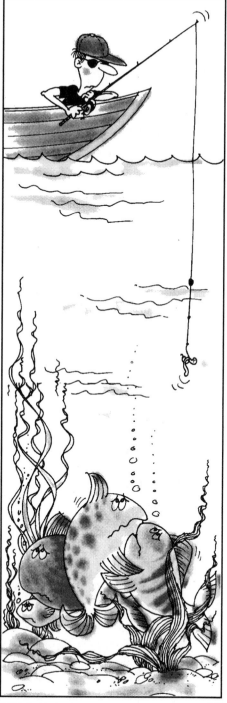

Until Garrett's efforts to breed more easy-to-catch (i.e., dumb) fish take hold, some new gadgets may finally have fish mesmerized into being caught. Fishermen are trying to compensate for smart fish by going high-tech. There are plastic baits that rattle and hum, release air bubbles to simulate a live worm, and come in exotic colors and flavors ("P enzyme-enriched, with the new super finesse twitch," reads one package).

One lure guarantees you'll catch five times more fish or you can get your $3.79 back. The latest rage is the Flying Lure, a box of colored plastic things that swim to the fish instead of away. Its "forward swimming motion is the result of its precisely balanced hydrodynamic design," says a line in the 36-page manual that tells you how to use the lure. If you don't understand the manual, send in the coupon for a free one-hour video lesson. (This isn't rocket science, you see. It's more serious.)

Recently a fisherman claimed that he played country music on his boat to attract crappies. "They like Travis Tritt," he said.

Some lures are so grotesque that you have to wonder about the keen eyesight fish are supposed to possess. And the way they are marketed raises the question: Are fish looking for dinner or a date? The headline above a photo of a lure in a current magazine reads, "What pure, unadulterated sex looks like to a walleye." The copy about Phred's Shadeaux goes on, "Wanna see a walleye pant? Then fish the most alluring shad bait yet hatched.... With its gleaming, sexy exterior. And its unique come-hither wiggle."

They've even taken the guesswork out of selecting the right color worm. "You can use the color chart," said Junior Collis, who runs his own fishing service at Lake Sinclair, Georgia. "You put this probe thing in the water, and it'll tell you what color worm to use according to the depth of the water. It's 60 percent right."

Certainly the idiosyncrasies of fishermen are based on respect for fish brains. "There was this couple that I used to guide," said Jack Wingate, who's operated a fish camp in south Georgia for 35 years. "The lady would set a pan of water with a bar of Ivory soap in it down between her feet, and she'd wash her plastic worm after every other cast. Then she'd wash her hands. And she'd catch 75 percent of the fish.

"I've seen fishermen get gas on their hands, then pour the lemon and ice tea out of their Thermos bottle, get the lemon, and scrub their hands and rub the worms and lures with it, trying to remove the gas and human scent."

Recently a fisherman claimed he played country music on his boat to attract crappies. "They like Travis Tritt," Melvin P. Merritt maintains.

According to Dr. Bob Reinert, fisheries professor at the University of Georgia, "The difference between an expert fisherman and one who isn't is this: When the nonexpert gets skunked, he says, 'I just didn't catch anything today.' The expert has all the excuses." But a dumb fish that gets away may be inexcusable. "We like to say," Dr. Reinert said, "fish are not as smart as we think they are, but neither are we."

Fish, which for so long suffered from poor self-esteem as just a bunch of bottom-dwellers, now get a lot of respect for being smart. But in the eternal battle of wits between man and fish, there is optimism that man may be narrowing the gap. □□

Best Fishing Days, 1995
(and other fishing lore from the files of
The Old Farmer's Almanac*)*

Probably the best fishing time is when the ocean tides are restless before their turn and in the first hour of ebbing. All fish in all waters — salt or fresh — feed most heavily at that time.

Best temperatures for fish species vary widely, of course, and are chiefly important if you are going to have your own fish pond. Best temperatures for brook trout are 45° to 65° F. Brown trout and rainbows are more tolerant of higher temperatures. Smallmouth black bass do best in cool water. Horned pout take what they find.

Most of us go fishing when we can get off, not because it is the best time. But there are best times:

☞ One hour before and one hour after high tide, and one hour before and one hour after low tide. (The times of high tides are given on pages 52-78 and corrected for your locality on pages 194-195. Inland, the times for high tides would correspond with the times the Moon is due south. Low tides are halfway between high tides.)

☞ "The morning rise" — after sunup for a spell — and "the evening rise" — just before sundown and the hour or so after.

☞ Still water or a ripple is better than a wind at both times.

☞ When there is a hatch of flies — caddis or mayflies, commonly. (The fisherman will have to match the hatching flies with *his* fly — or go fishless.)

☞ When the breeze is from a westerly quarter rather than north or east.

☞ When the barometer is steady or on the rise. (But, of course, even in a three-day driving northeaster the fish isn't going to give up feeding. His hunger clock keeps right on working, and the smart fisherman will find something he wants.)

☞ When the Moon is between new and full.

MOON BETWEEN NEW & FULL, 1995

Jan. 1 - 16	June 27 - July 12
Jan. 30 - Feb. 15	July 27 - Aug. 10
March 1 - 16	Aug. 25 - Sept. 8
March 30 - April 15	Sept. 24 - Oct. 8
April 29 - May 14	Oct. 23 - Nov. 7
May 29 - June 12	Nov. 22 - Dec. 6
Dec. 21-Jan. 5, 1996	

GENERAL WEATHER FORECAST
1994-1995

(For details see regional forecasts beginning on page 120.)

November through March is expected to be extremely variable, with dramatic monthly swings in temperature and precipitation in many areas. Much of the eastern two-thirds of the country will experience a cold and wet November, warmer than normal weather in December and January, and cold and blustery weather returning later in February and continuing through March. Despite this variability, five-month averages will be just above normal in New England, the eastern Great Lakes, the Atlantic seaboard, the Ohio and lower Mississippi River valleys, the southern Great Plains, and the southern states. The western Great Lakes, central Great Plains, and central California should be close to normal or slightly below for the season. The Rocky Mountains, Pacific Northwest, and upper Great Plains will be consistently colder than normal, with above-normal snowfall.

Near record amounts of snow are anticipated for the upper Great Plains, Great Lakes, New York, New England, and much of the Appalachians, as well as the higher elevations of the western part of the country, including southern California.

Precipitation totals for the winter will be well above normal for much of the country, but well below normal from the central Great Plains to the Gulf of Mexico, in portions of Florida, and in the extreme Northwest.

April through October: Spring will be generally cooler than normal over the whole country; the few exceptions to this are portions of the south Atlantic seaboard, the upper Ohio River valley, central Great Lakes, and a few parts of the central Great Plains. Most of the country may be drier than normal, particularly so over much of the central United States and southern Florida. Only the Northeast and Southwest, as well as a few isolated areas, will have above-normal rainfall for the season.

Summer is expected to be warmer than normal over the eastern two-thirds of the country, near normal in the West, and cool along the California coast. Most of the country will also be drier than normal, particularly through the central third from the upper Great Plains to the Gulf, with possible drought over sections of Texas, the lower Great Plains, and the lower Mississippi River valley. The central Atlantic seaboard may expect above-normal rainfall.

Early fall will be quite variable but average out colder and drier than normal over the eastern two-thirds of the country except for rains in Florida, while the western third should be warmer and drier than normal.

– Beth Krommes

U.S. WEATHER REGIONS

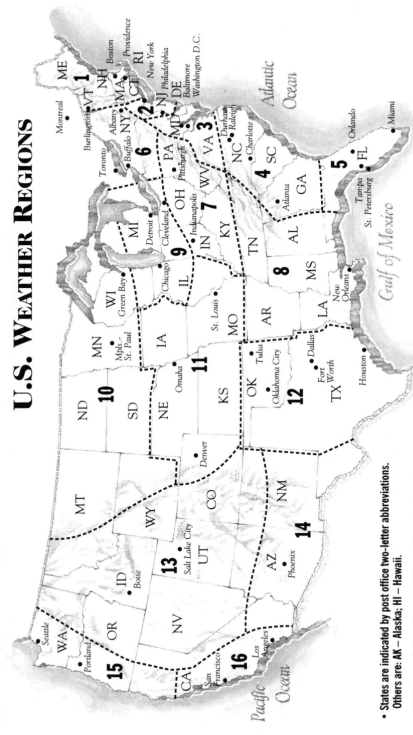

- States are indicated by post office two-letter abbreviations. Others are: AK – Alaska; HI – Hawaii.

- Weather predictions for each of the numbered regions shown begin on page 120.

1 NEW ENGLAND

For regional boundaries, see map page 119.

SUMMARY: *The period from November through March will see great variability in temperature with above-normal snowfall. November will be cold and snowy. December will continue to see frequent outbreaks of Canadian cold and heavy snows. Although the period from December through mid-February will see spells of unusually mild weather, watch for severe cold waves from mid-December through early January and at the beginning of February. Mid-February through March is expected to be cold and snowy.*

Spring will vary within the region. Southern New England will enjoy warm April weather, especially during the second half of the month, while northern New England will remain cool. May will be cool and wet throughout the region. June will be warmer than normal south and east but cool north with frequent light precipitation.

July through September will be warmer than normal with frequent heat waves. Despite a dry July, rainfall will be close to normal east and south. Watch for heavy thundershowers during August and a possible offshore tropical storm in early September. The northwest may be dry. October will be sunny and dry.

NOV. 1994: Temp. 45° (0.5° below avg.; 2° below inland); Precip. 7" (2.5" above avg.). 1-3 Cold, rain, snow inland. 4-5 Milder, sprinkles. 6-8 Heavy rain, snow. 9-11 Cold. 12-14 Rain, seasonable. 15-17 Sunny, seasonable. 18-20 Mild, rain. 21-23 Cold, snow. 24-26 Clear, cold. 27-28 Showers, mild. 29-30 Cold, snow.

DEC. 1994: Temp. 35° (1° above avg.); Precip. 4" (Avg.; 0.5" above north). 1-2 Snowstorm. 3-4 Clear, cold. 5-9 Sunny, mild. 10-13 Rain, then clear; mild. 14-17 Light snow. 18-19 Snowstorm, cold. 20-22 Severe cold. 23-26 Snow, cold. 27-28 Sunny and mild. 29-31 Light snow, seasonable.

JAN. 1995: Temp. 31° (3° above avg.); Precip. 4" (0.5" above avg.; 2" above north). 1-2 Clear, severe cold. 3-5 Snow, rain south; milder. 6-7 Cold, flurries. 8-11 Heavy snow, rain southeast. 12-14 Clear, cold. 15-18 Flurries, mild. 19-25 Rain, snow north; mild. 26-27 Cold. 28-31 Rain; snow inland.

FEB. 1995: Temp. 31° (0.5° above avg.; 3° above inland); Precip. 4.5" (1" above avg.). 1-3 Rain turning to snow. 4-5 Severe cold. 6-8 Sunny, mild. 9-10 Freezing rain, snow mountains. 11-15 Light snow, mild. 16-17 Coastal storm, heavy snow north. 18-20 Clear, cold. 21-23 Northeaster, heavy snow. 24-25 Seasonable. 26-28 Snow, cold.

MAR. 1995: Temp. 35.5° (3° below avg.); Precip. 5" (1" above avg.; 0.5" below inland). 1-3 Seasonable. 4-8 Flurries, cold nights. 9-12 Snowstorm, seasonable. 13-15 Flurries. 16-17 Freezing rain, heavy snow north. 18-21 Cold wave, flurries. 22-23 Clearing, seasonable. 24-29 Periods of freezing rain and snow. 30-31 Sunny, springlike.

APR. 1995: Temp. 49° (1° above avg.; 2° below west); Precip. 2.5" (1" below avg.). 1-5 Sunny, seasonable. 6-8 Rain, snow mountains; seasonable. 9-11 Sunny, mild, then rain. 12-17 Sunny, warming; few sprinkles. 18-20 Cold wave, rain. 21-27 Clear, warm. 28-30 Sprinkles, cool.

MAY 1995: Temp. 55° (3° below avg.); Precip. 5" (2" above avg.; 0.5" above inland). 1-4 Heavy rain, light north; cool. 5-9 Clear, seasonable. 10-12 Sprinkles, cool. 13-15 Sunny and warm. 16-17 Heavy rain, cool. 18-21 Intermittent light rain, cool. 22-25 Sunny, seasonable. 26-27 Rain, cold. 28-29 Clear, warm. 30-31 Rain, cool.

JUNE 1995: Temp. 69° (1.5° above avg.; 1° below north); Precip. 2.5" (0.5" below avg.; 0.5" above inland). 1-2 Sunny, warm. 3-7 Rain, turning heavy; cool. 8-13 Clear, warm, then showers. 14-17 Rain, cool. 18-21 Clear, warm. 22-23 Thunderstorms. 24-26 Light showers, cool. 27-29 Clear, warm; rain south. 30 Rain.

JULY 1995: Temp. 76.5° (3° above avg.); Precip. 1.5" (1.5" below avg.). 1-2 Rain ending, warm. 3-5 Cool. 6-7 Rain, warmer. 8-14 Sunny, hot; few sprinkles. 15-16 Heavy rain, cool. 17-23 Sunny, hot. 24-25 Rain, cool, then sunny and hot. 26-27 Showers, cool. 28-29 Clear, hot. 30-31 Seasonable, sunny.

AUG. 1995: Temp. 73° (1° above avg.); Precip. 6.5" (3" above avg.; 1" below west). 1-3 Thundershowers, warm. 4-5 Cool. 6-9 Clear and warm, showers south. 10-12 Heavy rain, cool. 13-14 Cool, sprinkles. 15-18 Rain, heavy south; seasonable. 19-20 Sunny, warm. 21-22 Rain. 23-26 Clear, pleasant. 27-28 Showers, cool. 29-31 Clear, hot.

SEPT. 1995: Temp. 69° (4° above avg.); Precip. 1.5" (1.5" below avg.; avg. central). 1-3 Clear and hot. 4-5 Showers, cool. 6-8 Offshore hurricane. 9-11 Sunny, warm. 12-14 Cold, light rain. 15-18 Clear, warm. 19-21 Cold, rain. 22-25 Sunny and pleasant, then thundershowers. 26-28 Cold, showers. 29-30 Clear, seasonable.

OCT. 1995: Temp. 55° (Avg.); Precip. 1.5" (1.5" below avg.). 1-2 Showers, seasonable. 3-5 Clear, warm. 6-9 Cooler; then rain. 10-11 Sunny, warm. 12-15 Cool; showers inland. 16-19 Clear, sprinkles west and north. 20-23 Sunny, seasonable. 24-26 Cold, rain; snow north. 27-29 Sunny, warm. 30-31 Cold, snow north.

GREATER NEW YORK–NEW JERSEY

For regional boundaries, see map page 119.

SUMMARY: *The period from November through March will begin with a cold and snowy November and early December. December will then turn mild, but watch for a heavy snowstorm just after midmonth, followed by a severe cold wave shortly before Christmas. Frequent mild spells will then dominate through January and the first half of February, with above-normal precipitation but below-normal snowfall during this time. More seasonable temperatures the latter half of February will be followed by a cold and snowy March. Total snowfall for the winter will be above average in the north and west.*

April through June will be wet with frequent thundershowers, as well as a possible Northeaster up the eastern seaboard at the end of April. Temperatures will fluctuate considerably from the mean, but will average close to normal in the north, below normal south.

July through September will be warm and wet with frequent thunderstorms in July and August, particularly in the north and west, and a possible tropical hurricane off the coast in early September. July will be hot in the north.

October will be cooler and drier than normal, particularly in the south, with cold spells more than balancing the warm periods in the first and third weeks.

NOV. 1994: Temp. 46° (1° below avg.; 2° below south); Precip. 7" (3" above avg.; 2" above south). 1-2 Rain, cool. 3-5 Few showers, milder. 6-8 Rain, cold. 9-11 Clear, warm; frost nights. 12-13 Rain, cool. 14-17 Sunny, seasonable. 18-21 Warm, showers. 22-25 Rain then snow. 26-28 Sunny, mild. 29-30 Rain, snow west; cold.

DEC. 1994: Temp. 38° (1° above avg.); Precip. 4.5" (1" above avg.). 1-2 Snowstorm. 3-6 Mild days, cold nights. 7-8 Mild. 9-11 Rain, warm. 12-14 Rain, cold. 15-18 Cold, frost. 19-20 Heavy snow, cold. 21-23 Partial clearing, mild then seasonable. 24-26 Heavy rain, mild then seasonable. 27-29 Cloudy. 30-31 Cold, light snow.

JAN. 1995: Temp. 34° (3° above avg.); Precip. 4" (1" above avg.). 1-3 Clearing, milder. 4-6 Light rain. 7-11 Freezing rain, then snow. 12-13 Sunny, seasonable. 14-16 Freezing rain, snow west. 17-19 Mild and sunny. 20-24 Showers, mild. 25-26 Sunny, warm. 27-29 Heavy rain, snow inland. 30-31 Clear, warm.

FEB. 1995: Temp. 34.5° (1.5° above avg.); Precip. 3" (0.5" above avg.; avg. south). 1-3 Snowstorm, cold. 4-6 Clearing, mild. 7-11 Heavy rain, cool. 12-15 Sunny, mild. 16-17 Freezing rain, snow inland; cold. 18-20 Clear, cold nights. 21-23 Rain, snow inland. 24-28 Seasonable.

MAR. 1995: Temp. 39.5° (2° below avg.; 3° below south); Precip. 4.5" (1" above avg.; avg. south). 1-5 Sunny, few sprinkles. 6-7 Snowstorm, cold. 8-12 Cold, then snow, heavy north. 13-15 Sunny, warming. 16-17 Rain, warm south cooling. 18-20 Cold, snow north. 21-23 Seasonable. 24-25 Rain, warm south. 26-29 Cold; rain, snow north. 30-31 Sunny, mild.

APR. 1995: Temp. 52.5° (1° above avg.; 1° below south); Precip. 3.5" (Avg.; 1" above south). 1-3 Seasonable; showers, cool south. 4-6 Sunny, warm. 7-9 Rain, then sunny and mild. 10-12 Rain, cold. 13-15 Sunny, cool; few showers. 16-17 Cold. 18-20 Heavy rain, then cool. 21-28 Sunny, warm. 29-30 Northeaster, rain; cold.

MAY 1995: Temp. 60° (2° below avg.; 3° below south); Precip. 6" (2" above avg.). 1-3 Northeaster, cold. 4-9 Seasonable; few showers. 10-14 Cool, then warming, showers. 15-17 Cold, heavy rain. 18-20 Sunny, warm; few sprinkles. 21-22 Clear, cooling. 23-25 Rain, cool. 26-28 Sunny, warm. 29-31 Rain; cool north.

JUNE 1995: Temp. 71.5° (0.5° above avg.; 0.5° below south); Precip. 4" (0.5° above avg.; 1" below south). 1-3 Sunny, warm. 4-6 Cold, heavy rain. 7-8 Clear, warm. 9-10 Showers. 11-13 Clear, warm. 14-16 Rain, cool. 17-18 Warm days, cool nights. 19-23 Sunny, hot. 24-27 Cold, heavy rain. 28-30 Clear, hot.

JULY 1995: Temp. 79° (3° above avg.; 0.5° above south); Precip. 4" (Avg.; 1" above south). 1-3 Clear, seasonable. 4-5 Cold; rain south. 6-12 Sunny, hot; showers. 13-15 Thundershowers, mild. 16-18 Hot and humid. 19-21 Hot. 22-25 Showers. 26-27 Thundershowers, hot. 28-31 Clear, seasonable.

AUG. 1995: Temp. 76° (0.5° above avg.; 1° below south); Precip. 5" (1.5" above avg.; 0.5" above south). 1-3 Showers, hot. 4-6 Milder. 7-10 Showers, then clearing. 11-15 Showers, mild. 16-20 Rain, then clearing. 21-22 Thundershowers. 23-25 Sunny, warm. 26-28 Rain, cool. 29-31 Clear, warm.

SEPT. 1995: Temp. 70° (2° above avg.; avg. south); Precip. 3" (0.5° below avg.; 1" above south). 1-5 Rain; hot then mild. 6-8 Decaying tropical storm. 9-10 Sunny, seasonable. 11-13 Cool, showers. 14-18 Clear, hot. 19-22 Rain then clearing. 23-24 Rain, cooling. 25-27 Clear, cool. 28-30 Rain, seasonable.

OCT. 1995: Temp. 58° (1° above avg.; 2° below south); Precip. 1" (2" below avg.). 1-2 Clear, seasonable. 3-6 Sunny, warm. 7-8 Rain, cool. 9-10 Clear, warm. 11-14 Cool. 15-16 Showers. 17-20 Clear, warm. 21-23 Sunny, mild. 24-26 Cold; rain, snow west. 27-31 Sunny and warm.

MIDDLE ATLANTIC COAST

For regional boundaries, see map page 119.

SUMMARY: *The period from November through March will see considerable variability in temperature from month to month. Precipitation will be average or above normal in every month, with above-normal winter snowfall, especially in the west and north. November will be cold with about twice the normal snowfall, despite brief mild periods. December will be mostly warm and wet, but cold and snowy from midmonth to near Christmas. Mild spells in January will relieve cold periods in between, with above-normal precipitation but below-normal snowfall. February will begin with a severe cold wave, then return to milder temperatures. March will be mostly cold and wet, with some flooding in the southeast.*

April through June should be colder than normal, with above-normal rainfall in the north but slightly below south. Throughout the period temperatures will be quite variable. Frequent cold and wet spells will dominate in April despite a week of warm weather toward the end of the month. May will also be relatively chilly and wet. June will see more extended sunny and warm periods.

July through September will be wetter than normal, with below-normal temperatures in the west, but above east. Thunderstorms will be common during hot spells in July and August. Watch for a possible cold wave from the Prairies at the end of August and for heavy rainfall from a possible decaying hurricane in the Carolinas in early September. October will be fairly dry and cool.

NOV. 1994: Temp. 47° (3° below avg.); Precip. 4.5" (1.5" above avg.). 1-2 Rain, seasonable. 3-5 Warm then showers. 6-8 Rain changing to snow and freezing rain. 9-10 Sunny, seasonable. 11-12 Heavy rain, cold. 13-15 Clear, mild. 16-18 Sunny, warm. 19-21 Rain, cold. 22-24 Cold, frost. 25-27 Clear, mild. 28-30 Freezing rain, snow west.

DEC. 1994: Temp. 40.5° (1° above avg.); Precip. 4" (1" above avg.). 1-2 Rain ending, cold. 3-7 Clear; cold nights. 8-11 Rain, warm. 12-15 Showers, cool. 16-18 Light snow, cold. 19-20 Snowstorm, cold. 21-23 Clearing then snowstorm. 24-26 Freezing rain, snow north. 27-29 Sunny, seasonable. 30-31 Cold, snow.

JAN. 1995: Temp. 38° (3° above avg.); Precip. 3.5" (1" above avg.; 0.5" above south). 1-4 Mild, light rain. 5-7 Seasonable. 8-10 Freezing rain, snow inland. 11-14 Seasonable; showers south. 15-16 Heavy rain, snow inland. 17-20 Clear, warm. 21-25 Rain, snow north, mild. 26-28 Cold, snow. 29-30 Clear, warm. 31 Snowstorm.

FEB. 1995: Temp. 39.5° (2° above avg.); Precip. 3" (Avg.; 1" above south). 1-3 Snow, cold. 4-7 Sunny, mild. 8-10 Rain, seasonable. 11-15 Clear, mild; cold nights. 16-18 Cold, freezing rain. 19-20 Seasonable; rain south. 21-22 Freezing rain, snow inland. 23-25 Clear, seasonable. 26-28 Freezing rain and snow.

MAR. 1995: Temp. 44° (3° below avg.); Precip. 3.5" (Avg.; 1" above south). 1-3 Cold then seasonable. 4-6 Freezing rain, snow. 7-9 Snow then rain, cold. 10-14 Sunny, cold. 15-16 Rain, mild. 17-20 Cold, flurries. 21-23 Clear, milder. 24-26 Rain, warm. 27-29 Cold, rain and snow. 30-31 Clearing, mild.

APR. 1995: Temp. 55.5° (1° below avg.); Precip. 3.5" (1" above avg.; avg. south). 1-3 Cold, light rain. 4-5 Clear, warm. 6-7 Thundershowers. 8-9 Sunny, warm. 10-12 Rain, cold. 13-15 Clearing, seasonable. 16-17 Cold. 18-20 Rain, then cold. 21-24 Clear, warming. 25-27

Sunny, warm. 28-30 Cold, heavy rain.

MAY 1995: Temp. 64° (2° below avg.); Precip. 5.5" (2" above avg.). 1-3 Rain, cold. 4-6 Clear, warm. 7-9 Sunny, seasonable. 10-11 Light rain. 12-14 Clear, warm. 15-17 Cold, rain. 18-20 Showers, seasonable. 21-23 Cold. 24-26 Rain, heavy north; mild. 27-28 Sunny, seasonable. 29-31 Heavy rain.

JUNE 1995: Temp. 75.5° (Avg.; 1° above south); Precip. 2.5" (1" below avg.). 1-2 Clear, warm. 3-6 Cold; rain, heavy north. 7-9 Showers, warming. 10-13 Clear, hot. 14-16 Cool, sprinkles. 17-19 Sunny, hot. 20-23 Clear, hot. 24-25 Cold. 26-28 Rain, cold. 29-30 Clear, hot.

JULY 1995: Temp. 80.5° (0.5° above avg.; 1° above south); Precip. 5" (1" above avg.; avg. south). 1-3 Clear, hot. 4-6 Rain, cool. 7-10 Seasonable, then sprinkles. 11-12 Mild. 13-15 Rain. 16-19 Sunny, hot. 20-23 Few showers, hot. 24-27 Clear, hot, thundershowers north. 28-31 Showers, hot.

AUG. 1995: Temp. 77.5° (1° below avg.; avg. south); Precip. 4.5" (0.5" above avg.; 1.5" above south). 1-3 Sunny, hot; rain north. 4-7 Cool, rain south. 8-9 Clear, seasonable. 10-15 Rain, mild. 16-17 Clear, seasonable. 18-22 Rain, locally heavy; mild. 23-26 Seasonable; showers south. 27-29 Cold. 30-31 Sunny, mild.

SEPT. 1995: Temp. 71° (0.5° below avg.; 1° above south); Precip. 4.5" (1" above avg.). 1-4 Sunny, warm, showers. 5-7 Rain from decaying hurricane; cooling. 8-10 Sunny, warm. 11-13 Cool. 14-17 Clear, hot. 18-19 Cooling. 20-22 Showers, then sunny, warm. 23-25 Rain, seasonable. 26-28 Cool, showers. 29-30 Clear.

OCT. 1995: Temp. 57.5° (2° below avg.; 1° below south); Precip. 1" (2" below avg.). 1-3 Sunny. 4-6 Clear, warm. 7-8 Cold, thundershowers. 9-11 Clear, warm. 12-15 Cold, then rain. 16-19 Clear. 20-21 Sunny, seasonable. 22-25 Cold, snow flurries. 26-28 Clear, warm. 29-31 Sunny, seasonable.

PIEDMONT & SOUTHEAST COAST

For regional boundaries, see map page 119.

SUMMARY: *The period from November through March will get off to a cold start with periods of freezing rain and snow in the mountains in November and December. Warm periods may dominate January and much of February despite several cold and wet spells. Precipitation will vary somewhat within the region, with the south being generally wetter than the north. March will be mostly chilly and quite wet, coming in like a lion and going out like a lamb.*

April through June will be variable: cool in April, warmer in May and June. Cold and wet spells in April and early May will offset the sunny and warm periods at midmonth and over the final week of April. In May it will be cool and wet in the north but warmer and drier central and south. June will be cool and dry in the north, warmer central, and warm and wet south.

July through September will be wet central and north, but drier south. It will be cool inland, warmer east and south. Hot spells are anticipated in late July and early August. Offshore tropical storms may bring heavy rains during the first half of August and the latter half of September. Watch for a hurricane in the Carolinas the first week of September.

October will be cold, with little rainfall after midmonth.

NOV. 1994: Temp. 49° (3° below avg.; 1° below south); Precip. 3.5" (0.5" above avg.). 1-2 Sunny, mild. 3-5 Rain, warm. 6-8 Cold, rain north. 9-11 Cold, rain. 12-14 Clear, warming; frost nights. 15-18 Warm, rain. 19-21 Cold, rain. 22-24 Clear, cold; heavy frost. 25-27 Sunny, mild. 28-30 Cold, rain.

DEC. 1994: Temp. 44° (1° above avg.; 2° above south); Precip. 4.5" (1" above avg.; 0.5" above south). 1-5 Clearing, warm; frost nights. 6-8 Rain, warm. 9-11 Rain, warm. 12-15 Clear, cool. 16-18 Light rain, cool. 19-21 Cold, snow. 22-24 Snowstorm. 25-27 Sunny, seasonable. 28-29 Showers. 30-31 Cold, flurries.

JAN. 1995: Temp. 43° (4° above avg.); Precip. 3" (0.5" below avg.; 2" below south). 1-2 Flurries. 3-6 Warm; sprinkles. 7-9 Rain, seasonable. 10-14 Snow, then rain, warming. 15-16 Seasonable. 17-20 Sunny, warm. 21-23 Cool. 24-27 Cold, rain south. 28-31 Heavy rain, warm.

FEB. 1995: Temp. 44° (1.5° above avg.); Precip. 3" (0.5" below avg.; 1" above south). 1-3 Cold wave, hard frost. 4-7 Warming, rain. 8-11 Sunny, seasonable. 12-15 Sunny, warm. 16-20 Rain, snow north; cold. 21-23 Clear, cold nights. 24-26 Few showers; seasonable. 27-28 Cold, snow north.

MAR. 1995: Temp. 50° (1° below avg.); Precip. 7" (3" above avg.). 1-3 Cold; rain, snow inland. 4-5 Sunny, mild. 6-8 Thunderstorms, cool. 9-13 Sunny, mild. 14-16 Heavy rain. 17-18 Sunny, warm. 19-21 Cold. 22-26 Warmer, few showers. 27-29 Cold, rain. 30-31 Sunny, seasonable.

APR. 1995: Temp. 59° (0.5° below avg.; 1.5° below south); Precip. 2.5" (Avg.; 1" below south). 1-3 Sunny, pleasant. 4-6 Rain, seasonable. 7-8 Clear, warm. 9-11 Cold. 12-16 Sunny, warm. 17-18 Rain, cold. 19-21 Clear, cold. 22-27 Sunny, warm. 28-30 Rain, heavy east; cold.

MAY 1995: Temp. 69° (1.5° above avg.); Precip. 3" (1" below avg.; 0.5" above south). 1-3 Rain, warm. 4-8 Sunny, warm. 9-14 Warm, thundershowers south. 15-17 Cold, rain. 18-21 Clearing, warm. 22-25 Light rain, seasonable. 26-28 Clear, warm. 29-31 Rain, heavy north; warm.

JUNE 1995: Temp. 78° (2° above avg.); Precip. 2.5" (1" below avg.; 1" above south). 1-2 Sunny, seasonable. 3-5 Cold, rain. 6-9 Clear, seasonable. 10-15 Sunny, warm; showers. 16-18 Clear, cool; warm south. 19-21 Few showers; warm. 22-24 Hot, thundershowers. 25-27 Sunny, cool. 28-30 Clear, hot.

JULY 1995: Temp. 80° (1° above avg.; 2° above south); Precip. 3.5" (0.5" below avg.; 2" below south). 1-3 Hot then seasonable, showers. 4-6 Showers, mild. 7-10 Sunny, seasonable; showers south. 11-14 Mild, showers north. 15-22 Sunny, hot; showers north. 23-27 Hot; rain then clearing south, sprinkles north. 28-30 Showers, seasonable. 31 Sunny, warm.

AUG. 1995: Temp. 78° (Avg.; 1° above south); Precip. 5" (1.5" above avg.; avg. south). 1-2 Clear, hot. 3-6 Rain, mild. 7-9 Sunny, seasonable. 10-14 Rain, mild. 15-18 Sunny, showers south; hot. 19-22 Showers then clearing, hot. 23-26 Clear, warm. 27-29 Light rain, cooler. 30-31 Clear, pleasant.

SEPT. 1995: Temp. 71.5° (1° below avg.; avg. south); Precip. 5.5" (2" above avg.; 0.5" above south). 1-4 Showers, mild. 5-6 Possible hurricane, seasonable. 7-10 Clear, pleasant. 11-14 Sunny, mild. 15-17 Rain, seasonable. 18-21 Clear, warm. 22-26 Rain, cool. 27-28 Rain, offshore tropical storm. 29-30 Clear, mild.

OCT. 1995: Temp. 61° (1° below avg.; avg. south); Precip. 2" (1.5" below avg.). 1-3 Clear and pleasant. 4-6 Sunny, quite hot. 7-9 Scattered light showers, cold wave. 10-11 Clear, warm. 12-15 Offshore tropical storm, cold. 16-18 Sunny. 19-22 Warm. 23-26 Cold, frost north. 27-29 Clear, warm. 30-31 Clear.

5 FLORIDA

For regional boundaries, see map page 119.

SUMMARY: *The period from November through March will start out cool, turn warm and relatively dry during December and January, and then moderate to near-normal temperatures in February and March. November will be colder than normal, with frost in the north just before midmonth. December through January will be variable with the sunny and warm periods outshining the cold and rainy ones. Following a cold and rainy beginning in February, with a hard frost in the north, sunny and warm spells will alternate frequently with cold and rainy ones on through March. Rain will be heavy in central and northern sections.*

April through June will start out with somewhat cool temperatures and relatively dry conditions in central and southern sections, warmer and wetter in the north. April will be milder than normal, while May will be closer to normal in temperature. June will be hot. Watch for heavy thundershowers in the north during late May and early June.

July through September will be warm across the region; central and southern sections will be dry while the north will have near-normal precipitation. Heavy thunderstorms are anticipated in the south in early July and over the region in August, with possible heavy rain in early September in the northeast due to an offshore hurricane.

October will be mild and wet, with heavy rain in the south and cool temperatures in the north.

NOV. 1994: Temp. 66° (2° below avg.); Precip. 4" (2" above avg.; avg. north; 1" below south). 1-5 Sunny, warm; showers. 6-8 Cold. 9-10 Seasonable, rain north. 11-13 Cold, frost north. 14-18 Sunny, warm. 19-21 Rain, heavy central and north, cold. 22-24 Clear, cold, frost north. 25-27 Seasonable, showers south. 28-30 Sunny, warm.

DEC. 1994: Temp. 65° (2.5° above avg.); Precip. 2" (Avg.; 0.5" below south). 1-3 Cool, light rain. 4-5 Sunny, warm. 6-8 Rain central and north, warm. 9-12 Sunny, warm, few showers. 13-15 Cold, rain north. 16-18 Sunny, warm. 19-21 Cold; rain, heavy north. 22-24 Warming. 25-27 Rain, cool. 28-29 Sunny, warm. 30-31 Cold, rain.

JAN. 1995: Temp. 63° (3° above avg.); Precip. 0.5" (2" below avg.). 1-8 Clearing, warm. 9-11 Cold, sprinkles. 12-13 Sunny, seasonable. 14-16 Cold, rain north. 17-20 Clearing, warm. 21-25 Sunny, pleasant. 26-28 Seasonable; rain north. 29-31 Warm; rain.

FEB. 1995: Temp. 60° (1° below avg.; 1° above north); Precip. 4" (1" above avg.; 0.5" below south). 1-3 Cold, rain; frost north. 4-5 Sunny, warming. 6-8 Heavy rain, warm. 9-12 Clear, cool; showers north. 13-19 Sunny, warm. 20-22 Heavy rain north and central, cool. 23-25 Sunny, pleasant. 26-28 Showers, cool.

MAR. 1995: Temp. 66° (0.5° below avg.; 1° above south); Precip. 6" (3" above avg.; 0.5" below south). 1-4 Heavy rain, cold. 5-8 Sunny, warm, few showers. 9-13 Cool. 14-18 Seasonable, few showers. 19-21 Heavy rain, cold. 22-25 Sunny, warm, few sprinkles. 26-28 Clear, warm. 29-31 Rain, cold.

APR. 1995: Temp. 69° (2° below avg.); Precip. 1.5" (1" above avg.). 1-2 Rain ending, seasonable. 3-8 Sunny, warm, showers north. 9-11 Cold, few showers. 12-14 Clear, cold nights. 15-17 Sunny, warm. 18-19 Showers, heavy north. 20-22 Clear, cold. 23-27 Sunny. 28-30 Rain, locally heavy; seasonable.

MAY 1995: Temp. 76° (1° below avg.; 1° above north); Precip. 3" (0.5" below avg.; 2" above north). 1-2 Rain, cool. 3-6 Clearing, seasonable. 7-15 Sunny, warm. 16-18 Rain, cool. 19-20 Clearing, warm. 21-26 Rain south, thunderstorms north; warm. 27-29 Showers, heavy north. 30-31 Cool, showers.

JUNE 1995: Temp. 82° (1° above avg.); Precip. 3" (4" below avg.; 1" above north). 1-4 Showers, heavy north; seasonable. 5-10 Sunny, few showers; warm. 11-17 Sunny, hot; showers. 18-21 Showers, hot. 22-26 Showers, heavier north, warm. 27-30 Sunny, hot, few showers.

JULY 1995: Temp. 83° (1° above avg.; 2° above south); Precip. 5" (2" below avg.; 1" above south). 1-5 Sunny, hot, local showers. 6-9 Showers, heavy south; seasonable. 10-13 Sunny, few showers. 14-19 Showers central and south; cool. 20-22 Showers south, dry north; seasonable. 23-31 Sunny, warm; showers north.

AUG. 1995: Temp. 82.5° (Avg.; 1° above north); Precip. 6" (1" below avg.; 2" below south). 1-4 Showers; hot north. 5-7 Showers, seasonable. 8-11 Thunderstorms; warm. 12-16 Hot south; showers north. 17-20 Few showers; warm. 21-26 Few showers; seasonable. 27-31 Heavy showers, mild.

SEPT. 1995: Temp. 81° (Avg.; 1° above south); Precip. 5" (1" below avg.; 1" above north). 1-4 Showers, sunny south; cool north. 5-7 Possible offshore hurricane, hot. 8-15 Showers, seasonable. 16-21 Sunny, warm; rain south. 22-26 Heavy showers; warm. 27-30 Showers north, cooler; sunny, warm south.

OCT. 1995: Temp. 75° (Avg.; 2° below south); Precip. 4.5" (2" above avg.; 5" above south; avg. north). 1-3 Rain south, sprinkles north. 4-5 Clear, warm. 6-10 Rain south, light north. 11-14 Rain, cool. 15-17 Clear, cool north, mild south. 18-21 Rain, warm. 22-26 Rain, cool north. 27-31 Sunny, warm north, rain south.

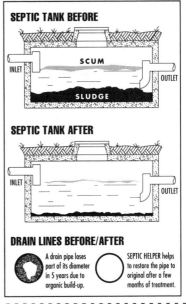

UPSTATE NEW YORK

For regional boundaries, see map page 119.

SUMMARY: *The period from November through March will see wide swings in temperature, with above-normal snowfall for the season as a whole. November and the beginning of December may see frequent Canadian outbreaks with heavy snows, interspersed with brief but more seasonable spells during the first and last weeks of November and an even milder one near mid-month. Mid-December will enjoy another mild spell, but watch for severe winter weather with heavy snows the week before Christmas and at year's end. The latter half of January and early February will see frequent mild spells. However, cold and snowy spells after mid-February and before and after mid-March will prolong the winter.*

April will start out cold and damp but moderate as the month goes on. May is expected to be cool with ample rainfall. June will fluctuate above and below normal, with frequent rains from coastal sections in the east, but quite dry west.

July through September should be warmer than normal, particularly in July. Drought conditions may develop in the west. August temperatures will remain near normal and the month will be comparatively dry. Heat waves will bring September temperatures to above normal; eastern sections will get heavy rain the first week due to a decaying hurricane.

October may be cooler than normal, with cold rain before midmonth and light snow after.

NOV. 1994: Temp. 37° (3° below avg.); Precip. 4" (1" above avg.). 1-3 Sprinkles then clear, warm. 4-5 Cold. 6-8 Snowstorm. 9-11 Sunny, cold. 12-13 Freezing rain, snow mountains. 14-18 Clearing, mild. 19-22 Rain then snow, cold. 23-25 Light snow, cold nights. 26-27 Sunny, seasonable. 28-30 Snow, cold.

DEC. 1994: Temp. 27° (0.5° above avg.); Precip. 3" (Avg.). 1-2 Snow, cold. 3-5 Clear, seasonable. 6-9 Sunny, mild. 10-11 Rain, cool. 12-15 Freezing rain, snow; seasonable. 16-19 Cold, light snow. 20 Snowstorm, cold. 21-22 Clear, severe cold. 23-26 Snow, seasonable. 27-29 Clearing. 30-31 Snow, cold.

JAN. 1995: Temp. 24° (3° above avg.); Precip. 3" (0.5° above avg.; 1" above south). 1-5 Freezing rain and snow north, mild south. 6-9 Flurries, seasonable. 10-13 Clear, cold. 14-16 Snow, seasonable. 17-20 Mild, freezing rain. 21-24 Intermittent freezing rain and snow. 25-28 Snow, cold. 29-31 Mild; rain, snow.

FEB. 1995: Temp. 25.5° (2° above avg.); Precip. 2.5" (Avg.). 1-3 Cold wave, flurries. 4-8 Sunny, mild; sprinkles. 9-12 Snow, cold. 13-15 Mild, sunny; sprinkles. 16-19 Severe cold, flurries. 20-21 Seasonable. 22-23 Snowstorm. 24-25 Clearing, seasonable. 26-28 Light snow.

MAR. 1995: Temp. 31° (3° below avg.; 1° below west); Precip. 2.5" (0.5" below avg.). 1-2 Clear, cold nights. 3-5 Seasonable, light snow. 6-8 Cold. 9-11 Snowstorm. 12-15 Clearing, mild. 16-17 Heavy rain, snow mountains; cold. 18-20 Light snow, cold. 21-23 Drizzle, flurries. 24-26 Mild south, snow north. 27-29 Freezing rain. 30-31 Mild, showers.

APR. 1995: Temp. 47° (1° above avg.; avg. south); Precip. 3.5" (0.5" above avg.; avg. south). 1-3 Freezing rain, snow. 4-6 Mild, sprinkles. 7-9 Rain, snow mountains.; seasonable. 10-12 Freezing rain, snow north. 13-15 Mild, sprinkles. 16-20 Cold; rain. 21-27

Clearing, warm. 28-30 Cool, light rain.

MAY 1995: Temp. 55° (2.5° below avg.); Precip. 4" (0.5" above avg.). 1-4 Clear, pleasant. 5-8 Cool, cold nights. 9-11 Clear, warm. 12-13 Showers, cool. 14-15 Sunny, warm. 16-21 Rain, cool. 22-24 Sunny, seasonable. 25-27 Cold, rain. 28-29 Clear, warm. 30-31 Cool, rain.

JUNE 1995: Temp. 67° (Avg.); Precip. 4.5" (1" above avg.; 1" below west). 1-2 Clear, warm. 3-5 Cold, rain. 6-7 Coastal storm; dry west. 8-13 Showers, warm. 14-16 Cold, rain. 17-21 Sunny, warm showers east. 22-25 Cool, rain east. 26-28 Showers, warming. 29-30 Hot, showers.

JULY 1995: Temp. 74° (2° above avg.); Precip. 2.5" (0.5" below avg.). 1-3 Showers, cool. 4-5 Rain east, sunny west; seasonable. 6-8 Clear, hot. 9-10 Rain, seasonable. 11-12 Sunny, hot. 13-15 Cold; rain east. 16-20 Clear, hot. 21-25 Sunny, warm; showers east. 26-27 Showers, warm. 28-31 Sunny, mild.

AUG. 1995: Temp. 70° (Avg.); Precip. 3.5" (1" below avg.). 1-3 Rain, cool. 4-6 Clear; cold nights. 7-9 Warm, showers east. 10-11 Cool, local showers. 12-14 Sunny, warm. 15-18 Mild, showers. 19-20 Clear, warm. 21-22 Rain, seasonable. 23-25 Clear; cool nights. 26-27 Rain, cool. 28-31 Sunny, hot.

SEPT. 1995: Temp. 64° (2.5° above avg.); Precip. 3.5" (0.5" above avg.; 0.5" below south). 1-2 Clear, hot. 3-5 Cool; sprinkles. 6-8 Heavy rain. 9-10 Sunny, warm. 11-13 Cold. 14-18 Clear, hot. 19-21 Thunderstorms, cool. 22-25 Showers, cool. 26-28 Cold, showers. 29-30 Few sprinkles; seasonable.

OCT. 1995: Temp. 49° (1° below avg.); Precip. 1" (1.5" below avg.). 1-2 Cool, showers. 3-6 Sunny, warm. 7-8 Rain, cold. 9-10 Showers, seasonable. 11-12 Rain, snow mountains. 13-15 Cold. 16-19 Clear, seasonable. 20-23 Rain, cool. 24-25 Snow, cold. 26-28 Sunny, mild. 29-31 Cold, then warming.

Sand, cat-hairs, dust and dust-mites...
Nothing gets by the
8-lb. ORECK XL!

The favorite vacuum of over 50,000 hotels and more than 1 million professional and private users. Now you can use this powerful vac to clean your home better than ever before.

Exclusive 5-Way Filtering System assures hypo-allergenic cleaning. Ideal for those who suffer from dust-related or allergic discomforts. There's virtually no after dust. Its unique top-fill action carries the litter up through the handle and deposits it on the inside top of the bag. Yesterday's dirt can't seep out. And the steel-tube top-fill performance works without hoses to crack, leak or break... ever.

The ORECK seems to float across your floors. The easy-glide feature propels the vac forward. Cuts cleaning time in half.

The lightest full-size vac available. It weighs just 8 pounds. So stairs are a snap. It's super-powerful, with twice the cleaning power: the fast, double helical brushes revolve at 6,500 times a minute – much faster than other commercial models.

ORECK's Helping Hand® handle orthopedically designed on the principles of ergonomics. To put it simply: no need to squeeze your hand or bend the wrist. A godsend for arthritics.

Exclusive New Microsweep® gets bare floors super clean, without any hoses, attachments or adjustments.

A full 10-year Guarantee against breakage or burnout of the housing PLUS a full 3-year Warranty on the extended life motor.

What more could you ask? How about complete information FREE without cost or obligation... and a chance to use ORECK's finance plan with no interest and no finance charge. Better yet, we'll let you try the ORECK XL in your home for 15 days. If you don't love it, you don't keep it.

Made in USA.

FREE with purchase

Super Compact Canister Vac
The 4-lb. dynamo you've seen on TV. The motor's so powerful it lifts a 16-lb. bowling ball! Hand-holdable and comfortable. Cleans under refrigerators... car seats... books... ceilings... even typewriter, computer and piano keys. With 8 accessories. Yours FREE when you purchase an ORECK XL upright. Offer limited, so act now.

A

Call toll-free 1-800-989-4200 Ext. 66076
Or mail coupon today. No salesperson will visit.

GREATER OHIO VALLEY

For regional boundaries, see map page 119.

SUMMARY: *The period from November through March will be variable, with cold and snowy weather in November, December, and March bracketing the relatively mild months of January and February. Eastern sections can expect well above normal snowfall for the winter, while western areas will be drier than normal. November will provide a vigorous start to winter with several cold waves and heavy snows punctuating mild and wet spells. December will begin wet and mild, then turn cold and stormy. Mild spells will dominate much of January and the first half of February. Frequent cold and snowy periods are then expected to prevail on through March.*

April through June will also be variable, particularly April and May. Cold waves with rain and snow will overshadow sunny and warm spells in April. May will begin sunny and warm, then turn cold and wet. June will be warm with frequent showers in northern and eastern sections but drier conditions elsewhere.

July through September will be warmer and drier than normal, with drought conditions in some southern sections. July will be warm and dry except for thundershower activity through the month. August will see close to normal temperatures, with the main shower activity in the second and third weeks. September will have several sunny, warm periods. October will be dry and mostly cool.

NOV. 1994: Temp. 39° (4° below avg.); Precip. 4.5" (1" above avg.). 1-3 Sunny, seasonable; showers west. 4-7 Cold, snow. 8-10 Snowstorm, cold. 11-12 Clear, cold. 13-15 Sunny, seasonable. 16-18 Heavy rain, warm. 19-21 Rain turning to snow, cold. 22-24 Clear, cold. 25-27 Rain, warm. 28-30 Cold, freezing rain.

DEC. 1994: Temp. 34° (Avg.; 1° above east); Precip. 4.5" (1.5" above avg.). 1-2 Cold, snow. 3-6 Sunny, warm. 7-9 Mild; rain, heavy west. 10-12 Warm, rain. 13-15 Cold, rain. 16-18 Snow, cold. 19-20 Clear, cold. 21-23 Snowstorm. 24-25 Clear, cold. 26-29 Rain, snow north. 30-31 Clear, cold.

JAN. 1995: Temp. 45° (4.5° above avg.); Precip. 3.5" (1" above avg.). 1-4 Warm, rain, heavy west. 5-7 Cold, snow. 8-10 Clear, cold; flurries. 11-12 Sunny, mild. 13-15 Seasonable. 16-20 Sunny; warm, rain east. 21-24 Mild, showers. 25-28 Cold, snow. 29-31 Heavy rain, warm.

FEB. 1995: Temp. 35° (2° above avg.); Precip. 3" (0.5" above avg.). 1-3 Cold, light snow. 4-8 Rain, snow north; mild. 9-11 Cold, snow north. 12-15 Sunny, mild, snow east. 16-20 Cold; freezing rain, snow north. 21-23 Mild, rain. 24-26 Cold, light snow north. 27-28 Clear, cold.

MAR. 1995: Temp. 41° (3° below avg.); Precip. 4.5" (0.5" above avg.). 1-4 Sunny, mild. 5-7 Cold, freezing rain, snow north. 8-9 Sunny, seasonable. 10-12 Cold, snow east. 13-17 Mild, rain. 18-21 Cold, light snow. 22-24 Rain, milder. 25-27 Heavy rain, warm. 28-29 Cold. 30-31 Sunny, seasonable.

APR. 1995: Temp. 53° (1° below avg.); Precip. 4" (Avg.; 0.5" above east). 1-2 Cold, sprinkles. 3-6 Warm, rain. 7-9 Heavy rain, cold. 10-11 Clearing, cold. 12-14 Sunny, warm. 15-18 Rain, cold then seasonable. 19-20 Cold. 21-25

Sunny, warm. 26-28 Rain, mild. 29-30 Cold.

MAY 1995: Temp. 63° (1° below avg.); Precip. 4" (0.5" below avg.; 1" above east). 1-3 Clearing, warm. 4-10 Sunny, warm; showers east. 11-13 Showers, mild. 14-17 Cold, heavy rain. 18-20 Warm, sunny. 21-25 Cool; rain, heavy east. 26-27 Sunny, warm. 28-31 Rain, locally heavy; mild.

JUNE 1995: Temp. 74° (2° above avg.); Precip. 3.5" (Avg.). 1-3 Sunny, cool, rain north and east. 4-7 Seasonable; rain north. 8-12 Clear, hot; sprinkles north. 13-16 Rain, cool; hot and dry south. 17-22 Clear, hot, showers north. 23-26 Rain, mild north and east; dry south. 27-30 Clear, hot.

JULY 1995: Temp. 79° (3° above avg.); Precip. 4" (Avg.; 1" below east). 1-3 Clear, hot. 4-7 Rain west; hot. 8-11 Sunny, hot. 12-15 Showers, then clearing and mild. 16-18 Clear, hot. 19-22 Showers, seasonable. 23-26 Clear, hot. 27-29 Sunny. 30-31 Sunny, hot.

AUG. 1995: Temp. 75° (0.5° above avg.); Precip. 3" (0.5" below avg.; 1" above east). 1-2 Clear, hot; rain east. 3-5 Showers, seasonable. 6-10 Hot, then milder; few sprinkles. 11-14 Clear, seasonable; rain east. 15-20 Rain, then warming. 21-25 Warm, rain east. 26-28 Clear, cool. 29-31 Sunny, warm.

SEPT. 1995: Temp. 69° (1° above avg.); Precip. 2.5" (0.5" below avg.; 1" below east). 1-5 Sunny, warm, sprinkles. 6-8 Rain, mild. 9-10 Clear, warm. 11-12 Mild. 13-17 Clear, hot. 18-20 Rain, heavy west; seasonable. 21-25 Showers, cool. 26-28 Clear, cool. 29-30 Sunny, cool.

OCT. 1995: Temp. 55.5° (1° below avg.); Precip. 2" (1" below avg.). 1-6 Clear, warm. 7-9 Showers, cool. 10-12 Rain, cold. 13-15 Cold. 16-18 Sunny, warm. 19-21 Cool, rain north. 22-24 Cold, hard frost north. 25-31 Sunny, warm.

DEEP SOUTH

For regional boundaries, see map page 119.

SUMMARY: *The period from November through March will see great variability in temperature and precipitation from month to month as well as within the region. Cold waves will dominate warm spells in November, particularly in the north. Precipitation in November will be below average. The first half of December will be mostly mild, but then the weather will turn cold and blustery for the rest of the month, with above-average precipitation. January will be mostly mild, with little severe cold. Precipitation will be below average in southern sections. Relatively cold weather will return in February and especially in March. Precipitation will be below normal except for northern regions in February.*

Spring will start with a cold April, with significant rain in the second half of the month. May will be unseasonably warm during the first half, then dominated by cold spells and rain in the latter half. After the first few days, June should be mostly sunny and warm.

The summer will seem warmer than normal weather in July and August and moderate temperatures in September. Much of the region except the east may experience drought conditions through June and July; the dryness will continue in southern sections during August and September. Watch for an offshore tropical storm bringing rain to eastern sections in early September.

Early fall will be cool and dry with many sunny days.

NOV. 1994: Temp. 55° (1° below avg.; 4° below north); Precip. 3" (2" below avg.; 1" below north). 1-3 Rain, then sunny, warm. 4-6 Cold, snowstorm. 7-9 Clearing, mild. 10-11 Cold, snow. 12-15 Warm days, cold nights. 16-18 Rain, warm. 19-21 Cold; freezing rain, snow north. 22-27 Warming, cold nights. 28-30 Rain north, showers south; cold.

DEC. 1994: Temp. 50° (2° above avg.; avg. north); Precip. 6.5" (0.5" above avg.). 1-2 Cold, rain. 3-6 Sunny, warm. 7-9 Rain, warm. 10-11 Warm, sunny. 12-14 Cold, freezing rain. 15-17 Seasonable, sunny. 18-20 Cold, snowstorm. 21-22 Sunny, cold. 23-25 Cold, freezing rain, heavy south. 26-28 Sunny, warm. 29-31 Freezing rain, cold.

JAN. 1995: Temp. 50° (5° above avg.); Precip. 3" (2" below avg.; 0.5" above north). 1-6 Sunny, warm. 7-9 Cold; freezing rain. 10-13 Clearing, mild. 14-15 Cold, rain, sleet. 16-19 Sunny, warm. 20-24 Showers, warm. 25-27 Rain, seasonable. 28-30 Clear, warm. 31 Rain.

FEB. 1995: Temp. 52° (4° above avg.; 1° above north); Precip. 3" (1.5" below avg.; 1" above north). 1-2 Cold; rain, snow north. 3-5 Clearing, warm. 6-10 Rain, cool. 11-15 Sunny, warm. 16-18 Rain, cool. 19-22 Cold, rain, then clearing. 23-24 Clear, warm. 25-28 Cold, few showers.

MAR. 1995: Temp. 55° (1.5° below avg.; 3° below north); Precip. 4" (1.5" below avg.; 0.5" below north). 1-2 Showers, cool. 3-5 Clear, warm. 6-8 Cold wave, heavy rain. 9-13 Sunny; warming, cold nights. 14-15 Heavy rain, cooler. 16-18 Sunny, mild. 19-21 Cold wave, sprinkles. 22-23 Rain, seasonable. 24-26 Clear, very warm. 27-28 Cold and rainy. 29-31 Clear, seasonable.

APR. 1995: Temp. 61.5° (3° below avg.; 4° below north); Precip. 3.5" (2" below avg.). 1-2 Sunny and mild. 3-5 Rain, seasonable. 6-7 Clear. 8-10 Cold, rain. 11-13 Sunny, warm. 14-18 Cold, heavy rain. 19-22 Clear, warming; cold nights. 23-25 Sunny, warm. 26-30 Cold;

rain, then clearing north.

MAY 1995: Temp. 72° (Avg.); Precip. 4" (1" below avg.). 1-3 Sunny, warm; showers south. 4-13 Clear, hot. 14-16 Cold; rain, heavy north. 17-21 Clearing, warm. 22-24 Thundershowers, cooler. 25-27 Sunny, warm. 28-30 Thundershowers, seasonable. 31 Showers.

JUNE 1995: Temp. 81° (2° above avg.); Precip. 3.5" (0.5" above avg.; 1" below north). 1-3 Cold; rain, heavy south. 4-8 Sunny, hot. 9-11 Showers, hot. 12-14 Clear, hot, showers south. 15-23 Clear, drought possible central and west. 24-26 Showers south and east. 27-30 Clear, hot.

JULY 1995: Temp. 81.5° (2° above avg.; 1° above north). 2.5" (2" below avg.). 1-5 Clear, hot; few showers. 6-8 Cooler, showers. 9-11 Clear, hot. 12-14 Showers south and east; seasonable. 15-19 Sunny, hot. 20-22 Thundershowers, seasonable. 23-28 Sunny, very hot. 29-31 Hot, few showers.

AUG. 1995: Temp. 84° (3° above avg.; 2° above north); Precip. 3" (1" below avg.; 0.5" above north). 1-2 Near record heat. 3-5 Showers, hot. 6-9 Clear, hot. 10-15 Showers, seasonable. 16-21 Sunny, hot; then showers. 22-24 Showers, heavy south. 25-28 Sprinkles, seasonable. 29-31 Sunny, hot.

SEPT. 1995: Temp. 76° (Avg.; 0.5° below north); Precip. 2.5" (1" below avg.). 1-2 Clear, hot. 3-5 Sunny, very hot; possible rain east from tropical storm. 6-8 Cold, rain. 9-16 Clear, hot north. 17-19 Rain, seasonable. 20-21 Sunny, warm. 22-24 Rain, seasonable. 25-27 Partly cloudy, warm. 28-30 Clear, pleasant.

OCT. 1995: Temp. 62.5° (2° below avg.; 3° below north); Precip. 1" (2" below avg.). 1-5 Clear, warm. 6-9 Sunny, seasonable. 10-14 Cold; rain, heavy east. 15-18 Clear, warm. 19-20 Cold north. 21-23 Warm days, cold nights. 24-26 Cold. 27-31 Clear, warm.

JESUS, THE WORLD'S SAVIOR

"NEVER BEFORE in human experience has there been such a dire need for a competent ruler. We need one who would be able to lead the hate-infected nations of earth out of the cross-currents of selfishness and despair, into the wholesome atmosphere of trust and goodwill. Without this there can be no lasting peace on earth, and no security—either for individuals or for nations."

This quotation was taken from a booklet entitled, *"JESUS, THE WORLD'S SAVIOR."*

HOW will this leadership be found?

WILL it be through a democratic process?

HOW will the desperate need for security, peace, health, and happiness be satisfied?

You are invited to send for your *FREE COPY* of this booklet. Write for it today. There is no obligation. Use the convenient coupon supplied:

THE BIBLE ANSWERS, DEPT. F
BOX 60, GENERAL POST OFFICE
NEW YORK, NY 10116

☐ Please send me a *FREE COPY* of *"Jesus, the World's Savior."*

NAME...

ADRESS..

CITY/STATE/ZIP.............................

....

WATER WELL DRILL KIT

Thousands of happy gardeners and homeowners have discovered the Hydra-Drill secret. They drilled their own wells and their gardens prove it! You can, too. Call or write us today and we'll send you a big, free package of information about drilling your own well with the Hydra-Drill.

Call Toll Free
1-800-333-7762
(Ask for Operator 7615)

Also, ask about our "How To..." videotape!
Or Clip Coupon and Mail Today!

DeepRock 7615 Anderson Road
Opelika, AL 36802

☐ **YES!** Send the FREE INFORMATION PACKAGE. and the illustrated guide *HOW TO DRILL YOUR OWN WATER WELL.*

Print Name

Address

City/State/Zip

Phone (must have)   © 1995 DeepRock

CHICAGO & SOUTHERN GREAT LAKES

For regional boundaries, see map page 119.

SUMMARY: *The period from November through March will see great variability in temperature, with November and March considerably colder than normal, although the seasonal average will be close to normal. Precipitation and snowfall totals will be well above normal in the east but near normal west. November will have well below normal temperatures and excess precipitation, with cold waves and heavy snows. The latter half of December will also be cold and snowy following a mild first half. January through mid-February will be dominated by several mild spells despite cold snaps at the end of January and in early February. Cold and snowy periods will then prevail on through March.*

April through June should be close to normal in temperature, with below-normal precipitation in the north but well above in the south. April's temperatures will vary between long cold spells and brief mild ones; precipitation will be above normal except in the northwest. May will be mild and dry during the first part, followed by cool and wet spells the second and third weeks. Thereafter, frequent warm and dry periods are expected in the east, warm and wet in the west.

July through September will be drier than normal, particularly in the east, with well above normal temperatures during July and September. July will see frequent hot spells interspersed with showers, particularly in the west, while August will have near-normal temperatures in the east but below west. September will be warm and dry, with heat waves at the beginning and middle of the month. October will be mostly chilly and dry.

NOV. 1994: Temp. 36.5° (5° below avg.; 3° below east); Precip. 3.5" (0.5" above avg.). 1-3 Rain, seasonable. 4-9 Snow, cold. 10-12 Snowstorm, cold. 13-15 Sunny, seasonable. 16-18 Rain, mild. 19-22 Heavy snow, cold. 23-26 Snow, cold, then seasonable. 27-30 Cold, snow.

DEC. 1994: Temp. 27.5° (0.5° below avg.; avg. east); Precip. 2.8" (Avg.). 1-6 Sunny, mild. 7-9 Snow, rain south; cold. 10-11 Sprinkles, mild. 12-15 Cold, light snow. 16-18 Cold wave, snow. 19-21 Severe cold, snow. 22-26 Seasonable, then heavy snow. 27-31 Snow.

JAN. 1995: Temp. 26° (4° above avg.); Precip. 2" (0.5" above avg.). 1-5 Turning mild, light freezing rain. 6-9 Seasonable, snow. 10-15 Seasonable then snow. 16-18 Sunny, mild. 19-21 Mild, rain. 22-25 Cold, snow. 26-28 Cold, flurries. 29-31 Seasonable, snow east.

FEB. 1995: Temp. 29° (2° above avg.); Precip. 1" (0.5" below avg.). 1-3 Very cold, light snow. 4-5 Sunny, mild. 6-9 Cold; snow. 10-12 Sunny, mild; light snow east. 13-16 Clear, mild. 17-23 Seasonable, cold east. 24-26 Snow, colder. 27-28 Clearing, mild.

MAR. 1995: Temp. 35° (3° below avg.); Precip. 3.5" (0.5" above avg.). 1-3 Clear; seasonable, warm south. 4-7 Cold, light snow. 8-12 Cold, clearing; snow east. 13-16 Mild; snow south. 17-20 Cold, flurrries. 21-25 Seasonable; rain, snow north. 26-28 Heavy snow, cold. 29-31 Clearing; then cold, flurries.

APR. 1995: Temp. 48.5° (1° below avg.); Precip. 3.5" (0.5" below avg.; 0.5" above east). 1-2 Snow east; seasonable. 3-6 Rain, mild. 7-10 Cold; snow north, rain south. 11-13 Clearing, warm. 14-19 Cold; snow, rain south. 20-26 Sunny, warm. 27-30 Cold, rain.

MAY 1995: Temp. 59.5° (1° below avg.); Precip. 3" (0.5" below avg.). 1-5 Sunny, warm. 6-7 Seasonable. 8-10 Clear, very warm. 11-16 Cold, rainy. 17-19 Intermittent rain. 20-24 Cool; showers west, sunny east. 25-29 Rain, seasonably warm. 30-31 Few showers.

JUNE 1995: Temp. 71.5° (1° above avg.; 2° above east); Precip. 4" (Avg.; 1" below east). 1-3 Clear, cool, showers south. 4-8 Seasonable, few showers. 9-12 Sunny, hot. 13-16 Thunderstorms, milder. 17-23 Warm; showers west, sunny east. 24-26 Rain, cool. 27-30 Clear, hot.

JULY 1995: Temp. 78° (3° above avg.); Precip. 3" (1" below avg.; avg. east). 1-3 Clear, hot. 4-6 Showers, seasonable. 7-10 Clear, hot. 11-13 Showers, mild. 14-17 Sunny, hot. 18-20 Seasonable, showers west. 21-26 Showers, heavy east, hot. 27-29 Sunny, seasonable. 30-31 Clear, hot.

AUG. 1995: Temp. 72.5° (1° below avg.); Precip. 4" (Avg.; 1" below east). 1-3 Showers, mild. 4-7 Sunny, warm. 8-10 Showers, cool. 11-13 Sunny, seasonable. 14-16 Heavy thundershowers. 17-19 Sunny, mild. 20-21 Showers, warm. 22-24 Clear, hot. 25-27 Cool, heavy showers. 28-31 Clear, hot.

SEPT. 1995: Temp. 67.5° (1.5° above avg.); Precip. 2" (1.5" below avg.; 0.5" below east). 1-3 Sunny, hot. 4-7 Heavy rain, cool. 8-9 Sunny, seasonable. 10-11 Cool. 12-17 Clear, hot. 18-20 Rain, cooling. 21-24 Heavy rain, cooler. 25-27 Clear, cool, few showers. 28-30 Sunny.

OCT. 1995: Temp. 52.5° (1.5° below avg.; 0.5° below east); Precip. 1.5" (1" below avg.). 1-5 Sunny, warm. 6-8 Cool, rain north. 9-11 Clear, cold; frost. 12-14 Warming, few showers. 15-17 Clear, warm. 18-21 Freezing rain, cold. 22-23 Clear, cold. 24-25 Snowstorm north, hard frost. 26-31 Clear, warm.

NORTHERN GREAT PLAINS-GREAT LAKES

For regional boundaries, see map page 119.

SUMMARY: *The period from November through March will see great variability in temperature from month to month, with especially cold weather early and late in the season and colder than normal temperatures overall. Precipitation and snowfall will be above normal, particularly in southern and eastern sections. Despite mild spells at mid-November, at Thanksgiving, and for the first third of December, the two months will be characterized by cold periods with heavy snows. January will average warmer than normal in the east and below normal west, with above-normal snowfall. A cold wave will end January and begin February. Milder weather will then prevail until the third week in February, when generally cold and snowy conditions will take over through March.*

April and May, and June in the west, are expected to be fairly dry. Temperatures will be cool in April and June and warm in May, although each month will see considerable variability. In April, expect sunny and warm spells before and after midmonth and cold periods otherwise. The first third of May will be sunny and warm. June will have cool and wet periods at the beginning, middle, and end, with warm spells in between.

July and August temperatures will fluctuate but will be close to normal on average, and it will be drier than normal in the two months in the west, near normal in the east. September will be relatively hot and dry, especially in the west. October will see alternating mild and cold spells, including cold waves with snow before and after midmonth.

NOV. 1994: Temp. 30° (3° below avg.); Precip. 2" (0.5" above avg.; 0.5" below west). Cold, snow. 5-9 Severe cold; snow, flurries west. 10-16 Sunny, mild. 17-21 Cold, snow. 22-24 Mild; flurries east. 25-27 Severe cold, flurries west. 28-30 Milder, snow east.

DEC. 1994: Temp. 18° (Avg.; 3° below west); Precip. 1" (Avg.; 1" above west). 1-6 Sunny, mild. 7-9 Seasonable, snow. 10-12 Snowstorm, cold. 13-14 Clearing, seasonable. 15-17 Cold, snow. 18-21 Severe cold, snow west. 22-26 Snow, heavy east; cold. 27-28 Milder, flurries. 29-31 Very cold, light snow.

JAN. 1995: Temp. 14° (2° above avg.; 2° below west); Precip. 1.5" (0.5" above avg.). 1-3 Mild, light snow. 4-6 Cold; flurries, snow west. 7-12 Seasonable, flurries east. 13-18 Mild; snow, then clearing. 19-22 Seasonable, snow, heavy west. 23-31 Seasonable then cold; snow, blizzard west.

FEB. 1995: Temp. 20° (2° above avg.; avg. southwest); Precip. 1" (Avg.; 1" above southwest). 1-2 Severe cold, flurries. 3-7 Sunny, warm. 8-11 Seasonable, flurries. 12-14 Mild, light snow. 15-17 Sunny, warmer. 18-21 Seasonable; snow west. 22-24 Blizzard; cold. 25-28 Flurries, clearing; cold.

MAR. 1995: Temp. 27° (4° below avg.; 7° below west); Precip. 2.5" (0.5" above avg.; avg. west). 1-2 Sunny, seasonable. 3-5 Cold, flurries. 6-8 Cold, snow. 9-11 Clearing, seasonable. 12-14 Cold, snow east. 15-17 Snow, heavy west; cold. 18-22 Clear, cold. 23-25 Light snow. 26-28 Cold; snow, heavy east. 29-31 Clearing, cold.

APR. 1995: Temp. 44.5° (2° below avg.); Precip. 1.5" (1" below avg.). 1-3 Sunny, seasonable. 4-8 Snow, cold. 9-11 Sunny, mild. 12-14 Cold, snow. 15-18 Clearing, mild; showers east. 19-24 Sunny, warm. 25-27 Light rain, mild. 28-30 Clear, warm.

MAY 1995: Temp. 60.5° (2° above avg.); Precip. 2" (1.5" below avg.). 1-8 Sunny; hot; few showers west. 9-11 Seasonable, rain west. 12-16 Cold; rain, snow west. 17-18 Sunny, warm. 19-23 Cool; few showers. 24-27 Light rain, then cool. 28-31 Rain, cool.

JUNE 1995: Temp. 67° (1° below avg.; avg. west); Precip. 4.5" (0.5" above avg.; 0.5" below west). 1-4 Cold, rain. 5-8 Warm; then showers, cool. 9-11 Clear, hot. 12-14 Rain, seasonable. 15-17 Showers, hot west. 18-21 Rain, mild west. 22-24 Clear, warm. 25-27 Rain, cool, then warming. 28-30 Rain, cool.

JULY 1995: Temp. 73.5° (Avg.); Precip. 4" (0.5" above avg.; 0.5" below west). 1-3 Showers, warming. 4-7 Sunny, warm; showers. 8-10 Clear, hot. 11-13 Rain, mild. 14-16 Showers, warm. 17-19 Rain, cool. 20-22 Sunny, hot. 23-25 Heavy showers, hot. 26-28 Showers, milder. 29-31 Sunny, hot, few showers.

AUG. 1995: Temp. 69.5° (1° below avg.; avg. west); Precip. 3" (0.5" below avg.). 1-3 Warm, showers. 4-6 Clear, hot. 7-9 Rain, cool. 10-12 Showers, mild. 13-15 Heavy showers. 16-18 Sunny, hot. 19-21 Warm; showers west. 22-24 Seasonable, few showers. 25-26 Sunny west, showers east. 27-31 Clearing, hot.

SEPT. 1995: Temp. 63° (2.5° above avg.); Precip. 1.5" (1" below avg.). 1-3 Seasonable, rain. 4-6 Cold, rain. 7-9 Clear, hot. 10-12 Seasonable, showers west. 13-17 Clear, hot; showers west. 18-22 Warm, few showers. 23-27 Cool, few showers. 28-30 Clear, hot.

OCT. 1995: Temp. 48.5° (0.5° below avg.; 1° above west); Precip. 1" (1" below avg.). 1-4 Sunny, warm. 5-7 Cold nights; showers east. 8-11 Cold, light snow. 12-16 Sunny, warm. 17-21 Cold, snow. 22-23 Clear, mild. 24-26 Cold. 27-30 Clear, warm. 31 Cold.

CENTRAL GREAT PLAINS

For regional boundaries, see map page 119.

SUMMARY: *The period from November through March is expected to start out cold, moderate dramatically during January and February, and then return to cold and stormy weather in March. The north will be colder than the south; precipitation will be below normal west and south, but above northeast. November will be unusually cold due to severe cold snaps. Continued departures from normal are expected in December, which will be warmer in the first half and cold in the latter half, with snow. Warm spells in January and February will counter a few brief cold snaps. March will bring cold and wet weather with above-normal snowfall in the north and a blizzard near the end of the month.*

April and May will be cooler than normal. June will be consistently warm. It will be drier than normal over much of the region during this period except for far eastern sections. Expect large temperature variations during April and May before the warm weather of June arrives. A warm spell at the beginning of April may result in flooding in the north from the March snows. May will also begin with a warm spell.

July and September will be warmer than normal except in the northeast due primarily to frequent hot spells in both months, particularly in central and western sections in September. August will be closer to normal in temperature. It will get progressively drier throughout this period except for a wet August in some central sections.

Early fall may be warm west and cool east and drier than normal overall.

NOV. 1994: Temp. 34° (5° below avg.; 2° below west); Precip. 2" (Avg.; 0.5" below west). 1-2 Rain. 3-8 Cold, flurries. 9-11 Clearing north, snowstorm south. 12-15 Sunny, warm. 16-18 Rain changing to snow. 19-21 Severe cold, flurries. 22-25 Clear, mild. 26-28 Cold; freezing rain, snow. 29-30 Mild, rain, snow.

DEC. 1994: Temp. 22.5° (2° below avg.; avg. south); Precip. 1" (0.5" below avg.; 1" below south). 1-6 Clear, warm. 7-9 Cool, sprinkles, then warm. 10-15 Cold, freezing rain and snow. 16-18 Snowstorm, cold. 19-23 Flurries, cold. 24-26 Snow, cold. 27-29 Flurries, cold. 30-31 Seasonable, snow east.

JAN. 1995: Temp. 21° (2° above avg.; 5° above south); Precip. 1" (Avg.; 0.5" below south). 1-4 Sunny, mild. 5-7 Clear, cold. 8-10 Snowstorm. 11-15 Seasonable; flurries north. 16-19 Sunny, warm; freezing rain north. 20-22 Clear, mild; sprinkles southeast. 23-25 Snow, seasonable. 26-28 Cold, snow. 29-31 Sunny, mild.

FEB. 1995: Temp. 29° (4° above avg.); Precip. 1" (0.5" below avg.). 1-3 Cold, flurries. 4-6 Sunny, mild. 7-9 Snow north, rain south. 10-16 Clear, warm. 17-19 Snowstorm, freezing rain south. 20-22 Seasonable; sunny, mild south. 23-28 Snow, rain south; cold.

MAR. 1995: Temp. 32° (5° below avg.); Precip. 3" (1" above avg.; avg. south). 1-3 Sunny, mild. 4-6 Light snow, rain. 7-9 Cold; snowstorm. 10-12 Clear, seasonable. 13-15 Snow, rain south. 16-18 Cold, snow. 19-21 Sunny, mild. 22-24 Showers, seasonable. 25-28 Cold, blizzard. 29-31 Cold.

APR. 1995: Temp. 48° (3° below avg.); Precip. 3" (0.5" below avg.; 0.5" above south). 1-3 Clear, warm. 4-6 Cool, showers. 7-9 Cold; snow north, freezing rain south. 10-12 Clear, warm. 13-18 Cold, freezing rain and snow. 19-21

Clear, warm. 22-25 Showers, warm. 26-28 Cold; rain, flooding. 29-30 Seasonable.

MAY 1995: Temp. 62° (0.5° below avg.); Precip. 4" (0.5" above avg.; 1" below south). 1-4 Clear, warm. 5-8 Rain, hot. 9-11 Seasonable. 12-14 Cold, rain. 15-19 Clear, warm; rain north. 20-22 Cold; rain. 23-25 Seasonable. 26-28 Rain, heavy north. 29-31 Sunny, warm.

JUNE 1995: Temp. 74° (2° above avg.); Precip. 4" (0.5" below avg.; 2" below west). 1-2 Cold, rain. 3-6 Seasonable; showers south. 7-9 Warm, showers. 10-14 Warm; showers east. 15-22 Sunny, hot, showers north. 23-26 Mild, showers east. 27-30 Hot, few showers.

JULY 1995: Temp. 76.5° (Avg.; 2° above southeast); Precip. 4.5" (0.5" above avg.; 1" above west). 1-2 Hot, showers north. 3-5 Sunny, hot. 6-8 Rain, seasonable. 9-10 Clear, hot. 11-13 Cool, rain. 14-16 Sunny, hot. 17-19 Mild, rainy. 20-22 Showers, heavy east; seasonable. 23-26 Clear, hot. 27-28 Showers west. 29-31 Clear, hot.

AUG. 1995: Temp. 73° (1° below avg.; 1° above west); Precip. 4.5" (Avg.; 1" below south). 1-3 Mild, showers. 4-8 Seasonable; showers. 9-16 Showers, mild. 17-19 Sunny. 20-24 Clear north, showers south; warm. 25-27 Clear, warm; showers central. 28-31 Sunny, hot.

SEPT. 1995: Temp. 67° (2° above avg.); Precip. 2.5" (1" below avg.; 2" below south). 1-4 Rain north, sunny east; hot. 5-7 Cool, rain east. 8-11 Clear, hot, then seasonable. 12-17 Clear, hot. 18-19 Showers, cool. 20-21 Clear, hot. 22-27 Sprinkles, cool. 28-30 Clear.

OCT. 1995: Temp. 52.5° (1° below avg.; 1° above west); Precip. 0.5" (2" below avg.). 1-5 Clear, hot. 6-8 Cool. 9-11 Cold, frost north. 12-16 Sunny, pleasant. 17-19 Cool, sprinkles. 20-23 Clear, cold nights. 24-26 Frost. 27-31 Clear, warm.

THE OLD FARMER'S ALMANAC

**Always useful. Always familiar.
And always fun!**

*Enjoy our famous weather
forecasts, planting guides,
how-to tips and techniques,
and fascinating feature stories!*

Here's just a sample of a what we plan to share with you next year . . .

1995 Old Farmer's Almanac
Available September 13, 1994

All-new facts, forecasts, and features for 1995, including *The Most Prayed-For Man in World War II. Prizewinning Recipes from Food Festivals. The Healthiest Vegetable of All.* How to grow it and how to cook it. *The Revolution That Began on Tuesday, October 23, 1945*... plus lots more.

1995 Gardener's Companion
Available January 17, 1995

A Roundup on Roses, growing hints, location advice, and where to get hardy antique roses. *Heirloom Onions*: where to get them, and why they're good to grow. *How to Grow a Living Hedge*. *Backyard Cash Crops*: growing flowers and pumpkins for profits. *Eat Your Greens. An Herb Sampler*: practical uses, lore, and superstitions about herbs.

1995 HomeOwner's Companion
Available March 7, 1995

NEW! A comprehensive companion about practical house matters, questions, problems, and expenses. Features include: *Six Great Myths of Home Repair: What You Shouldn't Try to Fix and Why, How to Talk to Your Fuse Box, Mistakes to Avoid in Getting Your House Ready to Sell*, plus tips, quizzes, contests, and lots more!

1996 Hearth & Home Companion
Available July 18, 1995

The Most Incredible Recipe for Sticky Buns. Making Money from Your Kitchen. An expert chef lists common cooking advice that's actually "nonsense"! *How to Eat Embarrassing Foods.* Plus favorite recipes, reader tips for saving money, useful charts, and other information of special interest in the heart of the house, the kitchen.

✔ **YES! I WANT TO RESERVE THE PUBLICATIONS INDICATED BELOW.**

Quantity	Description	Price	Total
	1995 OLD FARMER'S ALMANAC (#0F95B0F available 9/13/94)	$3.95 each	
	1995 GARDENER'S COMPANION (#0F95BGC available 1/17/95)	$2.99 each	
	1995 HOMEOWNER'S COMPANION (#0F95BH0 available 3/7/95)	$2.99 each	
	1996 HEARTH & HOME COMPANION (#0F95BHH available 7/18/95)	$2.99 each	
	Total Books Ordered	SUBTOTAL	$

SEND NO MONEY NOW! We will gladly bill you later when we ship your book(s).

Please charge my credit card: ⬤ ☐ MC ▭ ☐ Visa

Card # _____

Signature _____

AMOUNT DUE	$
Add $1.95 postage & handling per delivery date	$
TOTAL AMOUNT DUE	$

Mail to: **The Old Farmer's Almanac**

P.O. Box 10778 • Des Moines, IA 50340-0778   Or call toll-free: **800-685-3376** S5OFPUB

TEXAS-OKLAHOMA

For regional boundaries, see map page 119.

SUMMARY: *The period from November through March is expected to be extremely variable, starting colder than normal, moderating during the middle months, and then returning to cold conditions. The warm months will bring seasonal averages to above normal except for northern and western sections, which may be close to normal. Precipitation will be well below normal except in the far west and in the southeast during February. November will be cold and snowy central and north and close to normal in temperature in the south, but dry. A warm beginning in December will be followed by cold spells, with below-normal precipitation. Much of January and the first half of February will be warm and dry, causing some drought conditions. Cold waves should dominate the latter half of February and all of March, but with little precipitation except in the far north and eastern sections.*

April through June will be colder and drier than normal with a possible continuing drought in central and western sections. Considerable variation in temperatures will continue on through mid-June, when warm weather will begin to dominate.

Starting in July, the weather will become progressively warmer and drier, with most of the shower activity occurring in early and mid-July and early August. September will see a few cool spells and an intense cold front at the end of the month.

October will turn cold, and dry conditions will continue. Drought may still be severe.

NOV. 1994: Temp. 53° (3° below avg.; avg. south); Precip. 2" (Avg.; 1" below south). 1-3 Showers, warm. 4-6 Cold; rain, snow north. 7-8 Seasonable. 9-11 Cold; rain, snow north. 12-15 Clear, warm. 16-18 Sunny; showers north. 19-21 Hard frost, snow north. 22-26 Warm, sunny. 27-30 Cold; rain south, snow north.

DEC. 1994: Temp. 47° (Avg.; 2° above south); Precip. 1" (1" below avg.). 1-2 Clear, warm; rain east. 3-9 Clear, mild. 10-13 Cold; rain, snow north. 14-15 Cold nights, frost. 16-19 Warm then hard frost; showers. 20-22 Sunny, warm. 23-25 Hard frost, flurries. 26-29 Sunny, mild. 30-31 Cold, flurries.

JAN. 1995: Temp. 48° (5° above avg.); Precip. 1.3" (0.5" below avg.; 1.5" below south). 1-5 Sunny, warm. 6-8 Cold, rain and snow north. 9-11 Clear, warm. 12-14 Seasonable. 15-24 Warm; sprinkles north. 25-26 Cold; snow north, rain east. 27-31 Clear, warm.

FEB. 1995: Temp. 53° (4° above avg.); Precip. 1" (1" below avg.; 2" above southeast). 1-2 Cold, showers east. 3-5 Clear, warm. 6-8 Rain north and east. 9-14 Clear, warm. 15-17 Hot, showers north. 18-20 Cold; rain east, snow north. 21-23 Clear, warm. 24-26 Showers, seasonable. 27-28 Cold; rain, snow north.

MAR. 1995: Temp. 53.5° (3° below avg.; 1° below south); Precip. 2" (1" below avg.). 1-2 Storm ending. 3-5 Clear, warm. 6-8 Cold, rain east, snow north. 9-13 Seasonable. 14-16 Rain; dry central. 17-20 Sunny, cool. 21-23 Rain, warm. 24-26 Cold. 27-29 Sunny, seasonable. 30-31 Showers, cool.

APR. 1995: Temp. 61.5° (4° below avg.); Precip. 4.5" (1" above avg.; 3" above southeast). 1-3 Showers east, warm. 4-6 Rain east and northwest, seasonable. 7-8 Cold, rain north. 9-12 Sunny, warm. 13-17 Cold, rain east. 18-22 Clear, mild. 23-27 Rain east, showers west.

28-30 Sunny; cool nights.

MAY 1995: Temp. 72° (2° below avg.); Precip. 4.5" (0.5" below avg.; 2" below east and south). 1-2 Clear, warm. 3-6 Showers central, warm. 7-13 Clear, hot. 14-16 Cold, showers. 17-20 Sunny, warm. 21-24 Cold, rain central. 25-26 Clear, seasonable. 27-29 Rain north and coast, mild. 30-31 Showers, seasonable.

JUNE 1995: Temp. 82° (0.5° above avg.; 1° below south); Precip. 2" (1" below avg.). 1-3 Cold; rain, heavy Gulf. 4-8 Warm, showers. 9-11 Seasonable, rain Gulf and north. 12-15 Sunny, hot; showers coast. 16-19 Clear, hot. 20-23 Hot, showers north. 24-28 Clear, hot, showers west and east. 29-30 Sunny, hot.

JULY 1995: Temp. 84.5° (1° below avg.; avg. south); Precip. 1.5" (1" below avg.; 1" above southeast). 1-5 Seasonable; few showers. 6-10 Sunny, hot. 11-13 Mild, showers west. 14-17 Clear, seasonable. 18-22 Mild, showers. 23-26 Sunny, seasonable. 27-31 Clear, hot.

AUG. 1995: Temp. 87° (2° above avg.); Precip. 1" (1.5" below avg.). 1-5 Hot north, showers west. 6-8 Warm, dry. 9-12 Hot central; few showers. 13-15 Clear, hot. 16-18 Sunny, hot; showers north. 19-22 Hot, dry. 23-25 Seasonable. 26-28 Showers. 29-31 Clear, hot.

SEPT. 1995: Temp. 79.5° (2° above avg.; avg. west); Precip. 1.4" (2" below avg.; 0.5" below southwest). 1-6 Clear, hot; showers north. 7-10 Sunny; cool nights. 11-17 Warm; rain south. 18-20 Sunny, hot. 21-24 Clear, hot, showers east. 25-27 Cold, rain. 28-30 Seasonable.

OCT. 1995: Temp. 65° (2° below avg.; avg. northeast); Precip. 1" (2.5" below avg.; 1" below west). 1-8 Clear, hot. 9-11 Cold; thundershowers south. 12-14 Seasonable; cold nights. 15-18 Clear, warm. 19-21 Cold, rain north. 22-25 Sunny, dry. 26-28 Cold. 29-31 Clear.

GET IN ON THE PROFITS OF SMALL ENGINE SERVICE AND REPAIR

START YOUR OWN MONEY MAKING BUSINESS & BEAT INFLATION!

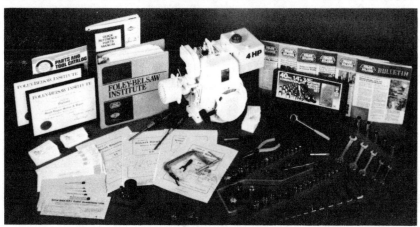

You get all this Professional equipment with your course,
PLUS 4 H.P. Engine... ALL YOURS TO KEEP... All at NO EXTRA COST.

Work part time, full time right at home. In just a short time, you can be ready to join one of the fastest growing industries in America... an industry where qualified men are making from **$25.00 to $30.00 per hour.** Because the small engine industry has grown so quickly, an acute shortage of qualified Small Engine Professionals exists throughout the country. When you see how many small engines are in use today, it's easy to understand why qualified men command such high prices — as much as $49.95 for a simple tune-up that takes less than an hour.

65-million small engines are in service today!

That's right — there are over sixty-five million 2-cycle and 4-cycle small engines in service across the U.S.A.! With fully accredited and approved Foley-Belsaw training, you can soon have the skill and knowledge to make top money servicing these engines. Homeowners and businessmen will seek you out and pay you well to service and repair their lawn mowers, tillers, edgers, power rakes, garden tractors, chain saws, mini-bikes, go-carts, snowmobiles... the list is almost endless.

No experience necessary.

We guide you every step of the way, including tested and proven instructions on how to get business, what to charge, how to get free advertising, where to get supplies wholesale... all the 'tricks of the trade'... all the inside facts you need to assure success right from the start.

Send today for FREE facts!

You risk nothing by accepting this offer to find out how Foley-Belsaw training can give you the skills you need to increase your income in a high-profit, recession-proof business of your own.
Just fill in and mail coupon below (or send postcard) to receive full information and details by return mail. DO IT TODAY!

FOLEY-BELSAW INSTITUTE
6301 Equitable Rd., Dept. 52402
Kansas City, Mo. 64120

NO OBLIGATION... NO SALESMAN WILL CALL

RUSH COUPON TODAY FOR THIS FACT-FILLED FREE BOOKLET!

Tells how you quickly train to be your own boss in a profitable Spare time or Full time business of your own PLUS complete details on our 30 DAY NO RISK Trial Offer!

YOUR OPPORTUNITIES IN SMALL ENGINE REPAIR

FOLEY-BELSAW INSTITUTE
6301 EQUITABLE RD., DEPT. 52402
KANSAS CITY, MO. 64120

☐ YES, please send me the FREE booklet that gives full details about starting my own business in Small Engine Repair. I understand there is no obligation and that no salesman will call.

NAME _____

ADDRESS _____

CITY _____

STATE _____ ZIP _____

ROCKY MOUNTAINS

For regional boundaries, see map page 119.

SUMMARY: *The period from November through March will be much colder than normal in every month, with well above normal precipitation and near-record amounts of snowfall except in the far north. November through mid-December will see frequent cold fronts bringing ample precipitation, primarily as snow, alternating with brief sunny and mild spells. Following a cold period the second week of December, temperatures should be closer to normal until a cold spell arrives during early January, bringing double the normal snowfall. The first half of February may be relatively mild and dry before cold and storms set in through March.*

April through June temperatures will be quite variable, but will average on the cool side except in the north in April and in central sections in May. Precipitation will be below normal except for northern sections, where showers will be frequent in May and June.

July will be a relatively cool month, August and September will be warmer than usual. Precipitation, primarily from thundershowers, will be generally below normal except during July in northern and western sections.

Early fall will be warm and dry.

NOV. 1994: Temp. 39° (2° below avg.; 1° below west); Precip. 1.5" (Avg.). 1-2 Sunny, seasonable. 3-5 Cold, rain south. 6-10 Seasonable; warm west. 11-14 Clear, warm. 15-19 Cold, rain; heavy snow mountains. 20-23 Clear, warm. 24-26 Cold; snow. 27-29 Very cold; snow. 30 Clearing.

DEC. 1994: Temp. 27° (3° below avg.); Precip. 2" (0.5" above avg.; 0.5" below south and west). 1-5 Warm; rain, snow north. 6-8 Rain, snow higher elevations. 9-10 Snow. 11-13 Clear, cold. 14-16 Sunny, cold. 17-21 Light snow, then clearing. 22-24 Cold; snow central and south. 25-26 Sunny, mild. 27-29 Cold, snow. 30-31 Milder.

JAN. 1995: Temp. 27° (1° below avg.; 4° below north and west); Precip. 3" (2" above avg.; 4" above south; avg. north). 1-5 Snow, cold. 6-10 Clear, cold. 11-13 Snow. 14-19 Snow, heavy west and mountains. 20-23 Cold; snow, heavy south. 24-28 Milder, snow. 29-31 Freezing rain, snow mountains.

FEB. 1995: Temp. 31° (3° below avg.); Precip. 1.5" (0.5" above avg.; 0.5" below south and west). 1-3 Seasonable, mild south. 4-7 Rain, snow mountains; mild. 8-15 Sunny then snow south. 16-18 Cold; snow. 19-20 Clear, seasonable. 21-23 Cold, snow. 24-28 Cold, snow.

MAR. 1995: Temp. 35° (7° below avg.); Precip. 3" (1" above avg.). 1-3 Seasonable; snow north. 4-7 Cold; snow. 8-9 Clear, cold. 10-13 Cold, flurries. 14-16 Cold wave, snowstorm. 17-21 Milder, cold nights; snow. 22-25 Snow, light north; cold. 26-27 Clear, very cold. 28-31 Mild; rain, snow mountains.

APR. 1995: Temp. 49° (0.5° below avg.); Precip. 2" (Avg.; 0.5" above west). 1-5 Rain, snow mountains. 6-11 Sunny, warm. 12-16 Cold; rain, snow mountains, then seasonable. 17-19 Cold; rain. 20-22 Clear, warm. 23-25 Cold, rain. 26-30 Sunny, warm.

MAY 1995: Temp. 59° (Avg.; 1° below west); Precip. 1.3" (0.5" below avg.; 0.5" above north). 1-4 Cold, rain. 5-10 Warm; rain, cold north. 11-14 Cool, showers. 15-18 Sunny, warm. 19-21 Cool, rain. 22-24 Warm, sunny. 25-27 Cold, rain. 28-31 Warm, then rain south.

JUNE 1995: Temp. 68° (1° below avg.; 2° below north and west); Precip. 1" (Avg.; 0.5" below west). 1-5 Seasonable, sprinkles north. 6-8 Warm north; cool, rain south. 9-14 Warm; showers north. 15-19 Sunny; rain, cool north. 20-23 Clear, hot. 24-27 Cool, rain north. 28-30 Very cool, rain north.

JULY 1995: Temp. 75° (3° below avg.); Precip. 0.5" (0.5" below avg.; 0.5" above west and north). 1-2 Cool, rain. 3-5 Warm south; cool, rain north. 6-8 Clear, warm. 9-11 Cool, showers. 12-14 Sunny, warm. 15-19 Showers, cool. 20-22 Sunny, warm. 23-26 Cool, showers north; clear, warm south. 27-31 Few showers.

AUG. 1995: Temp. 77° (1° above avg.); Precip. 1" (Avg.; 0.5" below north and west). 1-5 Thunderstorms, mild. 6-9 Sunny, hot; few showers. 10-13 Showers, seasonable. 14-15 Sunny south, rain north. 16-22 Warm north, thundershowers south. 23-28 Hot, showers. 29-31 Thundershowers, cool.

SEPT. 1995: Temp. 67° (2° above avg.); Precip. 0.2" (1" below avg.; 0.5" above south and west). 1-3 Clear north, showers south; seasonable. 4-7 Clear, warm. 8-11 Sunny, warm; showers north. 12-14 Rain, warm. 15-18 Frost, snow east. 19-23 Clear, warm. 24-26 Cold, rain south; warm north. 27-30 Sunny, warm.

OCT. 1995: Temp. 57° (4° above avg.); Precip. 0" (1.5" below avg.). 1-3 Mild, sprinkles. 4-8 Sunny, warm. 9-11 Sunny, cooling. 12-16 Clear, warm. 17-19 Cooling, showers north. 20-23 Clear, warm. 24-25 Sprinkles, seasonable. 26-31 Clear, warm.

SOUTHWEST DESERT

For regional boundaries, see map page 119.

SUMMARY: *The period from November through March will have great variability, but overall will be colder than normal in the west but warmer in the east with above-normal precipitation throughout. November will see cold fronts early and late in the month; it will be colder and wetter than normal in the west. Variable weather will characterize December with warm periods at the beginning and end and cold spells in between. Following a cold beginning, January through mid-February will be warmer than normal before cold and wet sets in to last through March.*

April through June will be cooler than normal, particularly in northern sections, with above-normal precipitation over the region. A warm first half of April will be followed by cold fronts and rain through early May. Unseasonably hot weather lasting past midmonth will precede a brief cold wave. June will see few significant departures from normal.

July and August will be warmer than normal across the south, but below normal north, with below-normal precipitation over the region. Expect cool shower activity in the east in mid-July and especially cool nighttime temperatures in early and mid-July in northern sections. The first half of September will be warm and dry before a cold front moves in.

Early fall will be mostly sunny, warm, and dry.

NOV. 1994: Temp. 61° (1° below avg.; 0.5° above east); Precip. 1" (0.5" above avg.; 2" above south). 1-4 Cool; rain south. 5-10 Sunny, warm; frost east. 11-13 Clear, seasonable. 14-16 Cool, rain. 17-19 Sunny, mild. 20-22 Cold, frost east. 23-25 Mild. 26-28 Cold, rain central. 29-30 Clear, cold nights.

DEC. 1994: Temp. 52° (2° below avg.; 1° above east); Precip. 0.5" (0.5" below avg.). 1-5 Clear, warm. 6-8 Sunny, seasonable. 9-12 Cold; rain, snow mountains. 13-15 Clearing, warming. 16-18 Rain, cool. 19-21 Clear; cold nights, frost. 22-23 Rain, cold. 24-26 Clear, hard frost. 27-30 Clear, warm. 31 Sprinkles, mild.

JAN. 1995: Temp. 52° (1.5° below avg.; 3° above east); Precip. 1" (0.3" above avg.; 0.5" below south and east). 1-4 Cool, rain. 5-9 Hard frost. 10-11 Sprinkles, cool. 12-15 Sunny, warm. 16-17 Rain; cool. 18-20 Clearing, seasonable. 21-24 Rain, snow mountains. 25-29 Clear, warm. 30-31 Sprinkles, seasonable.

FEB. 1995: Temp. 55° (3° below avg.; 0.5° below east); Precip. 0.4" (0.3" below avg.; 0.5" above east). 1-5 Sunny, warm. 6-9 Clear, cold nights; frost. 10-12 Warm. 13-15 Showers, cool. 16-19 Hard frost; rain east. 20-21 Sunny, seasonable. 22-24 Frost. 25-28 Cold nights.

MAR. 1995: Temp. 58° (4° below avg.); Precip. 2" (1" above avg.). 1-4 Sunny, warm. 5-6 Rain, cold. 7-9 Clear, cold nights. 10-12 Clear, warm. 13-18 Cold; rain. 19-20 Sunny, warm. 21-24 Cold, rain; then mild. 25-27 Cold, frost. 28-31 Clear, turning warm.

APR. 1995: Temp. 69° (1° below avg.); Precip. 1.2" (1" above avg.). 1-5 Sunny, warm. 6-11 Clear, hot. 12-14 Scattered showers, seasonable. 15-16 Cold, rain. 17-20 Sunny. 21-23 Clear, very warm. 24-26 Cold; rain. 27-30 Sunny, warm, then showers.

MAY 1995: Temp. 77° (2° below avg.; 1° below east); Precip. 0.5" (0.5" above avg.; avg. east). 1-4 Cold, rain. 5-10 Clear, hot. 11-13 Sunny, warm. 14-18 Clear, hot. 19-22 Cold, few sprinkles. 23-25 Clearing, warm. 26-29 Seasonable. 30-31 Hot, showers; cool, rain east.

JUNE 1995: Temp. 85° (3° below avg.; 1° above east); Precip. 0" (Avg.). 1-4 Hot, few showers; warm east. 5-7 Thundershowers, cool. 8-10 Sunny, hot. 11-13 Clear, hot. 14-17 Thundershowers, sprinkles east. 18-20 Clear, hot. 21-24 Clear, hot. 25-27 Sunny, seasonable. 28-30 Mild, rain east.

JULY 1995: Temp. 90° (3.5° below avg.; 1° below east); Precip. 0.5" (0.5" below avg.; 0.5" above east). 1-2 Warm; rain east. 3-6 Clear, seasonable. 7-9 Thundershowers, milder. 10-12 Showers, locally heavy; cool east. 13-18 Clear, hot; showers east. 19-23 Sunny, hot. 24-26 Clear, seasonable. 27-31 Few showers, milder.

AUG. 1995: Temp. 91° (0.5° below avg.; 2° above east); Precip. 1.3" (0.3" above avg.; 0.5" below east). 1-3 Showers, mild. 4-7 Clear, hot. 8-10 Showers, seasonable. 11-15 Sunny, hot, then showers. 16-20 Showers, heavy south and east; mild. 21-24 Few showers, seasonable. 25-27 Sunny, hot. 28-31 Showers, seasonable.

SEPT. 1995: Temp. 86.5° (1° above avg.; 3° above east); Precip. 0.5" (0.5" below avg.; 1" below east). 1-3 Showers, hot. 4-13 Clear, heat wave; few sprinkles. 14-17 Cold; sunny, cool. 18-23 Sunny, hot, sprinkles. 24-27 Rain, sprinkles east; seasonable. 28-30 Clear, hot.

OCT. 1995: Temp. 77.5° (3° above avg.); Precip. 0" (0.5" below avg.). 1-3 Showers, seasonable. 4-7 Sunny, warming. 8-10 Clear, hot. 11-13 Mild, cool east. 14-18 Sunny, warm. 19-27 Clear, warm; cool east. 28-31 Clear, warm.

PACIFIC NORTHWEST

For regional boundaries, see map page 119.

SUMMARY: *The period from November through March will see below-normal temperature averages in every month. It will be drier than normal in the north, but wetter south, while snowfall will be well above normal over the region. Following a mild and dry start, November will turn wintry; this weather will prevail with increasing vigor through December and January with well above normal snowfall even at the lower elevations due to increasingly cold temperatures. Despite the snow, precipitation will generally be below normal except for southern sections. Following a milder first half of February, colder than normal periods will return through March.*

April through June will be variable. April will be mostly sunny and warm following a cool and wet beginning. May will be cool and wet the first half with sunny and warm spells the latter half. June will see periods of clear, warm weather alternating with cool and dry spells.

July will have variable temperatures that will average just below normal. August should be fairly dry and warm during the first half, cool later in the month. September is anticipated to be drier than normal, particularly in central and northern sections, with variable temperatures.

October should be warm and dry with drought developing in southern sections.

NOV. 1994: Temp. 45° (1° below avg.); Precip. 4" (1" below avg.; avg. southeast). 1-5 Cool, showers. 6-8 Rain, mild. 9-12 Showers; mild. 13-16 Rain, snow mountains. 17-19 Cold, snow mountains. 20-22 Warm north, seasonable south. 23-25 Cold rain, snow higher elevations. 26-28 Clearing, cold. 29-30 Sunny, warm.

DEC. 1994: Temp. 39° (1° below avg.; avg. south); Precip. 6" (Avg.; 2" above south). 1-6 Rain, snow mountains. 7-10 Cold; freezing rain, heavy snow. 11-13 Clear, cold. 14-15 Showers, seasonable. 16-18 Clear, cold nights. 19-23 Freezing rain turning to snow, heavy mountains. 24-26 Rain, seasonable. 27-29 Clear, cold. 30-31 Snow, heavy south.

JAN. 1995: Temp. 35.5° (4° below avg.); Precip. 4.5" (1" below avg.; 2" above south). 1-2 Freezing rain, seasonable. 3-9 Cold; snow. 10-12 Seasonable, freezing drizzle. 13-15 Cold; snow, heavy mountains. 16-19 Seasonable, freezing rain. 20-23 Showers. 24-29 Cold; snow. 30-31 Warm, sprinkles.

FEB. 1995: Temp. 42.5° (1° below avg.); Precip. 4.5" (0.5" above avg.; avg. north). 1-5 Mild; rain, snow mountains. 6-9 Cold; freezing rain, snow. 10-14 Warm days, cold nights. 15-18 Cold; snow. 19-25 Cold, freezing rain, snow. 26-28 Seasonable; snow mountains.

MAR. 1995: Temp. 45° (2° below avg.); Precip. 4" (0.5" above avg.; 1" below southwest). 1-5 Rain and snow, cool. 6-9 Rain, snow higher elevations; cool. 10-12 Sunny, mild. 13-17 Heavy rain, snow mountains; cool. 18-20 Sunny, mild. 21-24 Freezing rain, heavy snow; cold. 25-27 Sunny, cold nights. 28-31 Rain, snow mountains; seasonable.

APR. 1995: Temp. 51.5° (0.5° above avg.; 1° below north and south); Precip. 1.5" (1" below avg.). 1-6 Cold; rain, snow mountains. 7-10 Clear, warm. 11-13 Cold, clear. 14-16 Sunny, warm. 17-19 Rain, cool. 20-22 Clear, warm. 23-24 Rain, cool. 25-29 Mild. 30 Cooling, showers.

MAY 1995: Temp. 56° (1° below avg.); Precip. 2" (Avg.; 0.5" above north). 1-4 Cold; rain, snow higher elevations. 5-7 Rain, heavy north; mild. 8-10 Sunny, seasonable. 11-13 Rain, heavy south, snow mountains. 14-17 Warm, showers. 18-19 Cool, rain. 20-22 Clear, very warm. 23-25 Rain, locally heavy; cool. 26-29 Sunny, pleasant. 30-31 Clear, warm.

JUNE 1995: Temp. 61° (2.5° below avg.); Precip. 1.5" (Avg.; 0.5" below north). 1-5 Cool, sprinkles. 6-8 Sunny, warm. 9-11 Showers, seasonable. 12-14 Clear, warm. 15-18 Cold, rain, then clearing, milder. 19-20 Cold, rain. 21-23 Sunny, warm. 24-26 Rain, cool. 27-30 Scattered showers, seasonable.

JULY 1995: Temp. 67° (1° below avg.); Precip. 0.5" (Avg.; 0.5" above south). 1-5 Heavy rain, cool. 6-8 Clear, warm. 9-10 Cool, scattered showers. 11-14 Clear, hot. 15-17 Sunny, warm. 18-20 Clear, warm. 21-23 Sunny, pleasant. 24-26 Cool, sprinkles. 27-29 Warm, rain north. 30-31 Clear, warm.

AUG. 1995: Temp. 68.5° (Avg.; 1° below north and south); Precip. 0.5" (0.5" below avg.). 1-5 Clear, warm. 6-8 Clear, hot. 9-11 Cool, few showers. 12-17 Sunny, warm. 18-20 Showers, cool. 21-24 Clearing, warm. 25-27 Sunny, warm. 28-31 Cooling, rain.

SEPT. 1995: Temp. 64° (1° above avg.; 1° below north and south); Precip. 0.5" (1" below avg.; avg. south). 1-4 Clear, seasonable. 5-8 Sunny, warm; hot south. 9-11 Cool, showers. 12-14 Rain, cold. 15-17 Clearing; mild, cold nights. 18-21 Clear, warm. 22-27 Sunny, warm; hot south. 28-30 Mild.

OCT. 1995: Temp. 56.5° (2° above avg.; avg. southwest); Precip. 0.5" (2" below avg.). 1-4 Sunny, few showers north. 5-10 Clear, warm. 11-13 Seasonable, sprinkles. 14-17 Sunny. 18-21 Clear, cool nights. 22-28 Showers, then rain; mild. 29-31 Clear, turning cold.

CALIFORNIA

For regional boundaries, see map page 119.

SUMMARY: *The period from November through March will be variable. The season will start warm and end up cooler than normal; precipitation will be substantial during November, December, and January before drier conditions set in. Snowfall in both the Sierra Nevada and San Gabriel Mountains will be above normal for the season. Following a sunny and warm first half of November, frequent cold waves and abundant moisture will prevail, particularly before and after mid-December and over most of January, with heavy snow in the higher elevations. February will be mild the first half, dry and cold the second half. March may begin and end warm and sunny, but cold and rainy weather will dominate, with heavy snows in the mountains.*

April and May will be slightly cooler than normal with close to average precipitation except for the north coast, which will get less rain than usual. June will be dominated by cool spells, with rainfall mostly in the north.

July through September will be cooler than normal along the coast, but slightly above normal inland and with below-normal rainfall. Other than a cool spell at the beginning of July and another in mid-September, temperatures will be close to the mean.

October will be warm inland, cool along the coast, and relatively dry.

NOV. 1994: Temp. 56° (1° above avg.; 2° above inland); Precip. 3" (Avg.; 0.5" below inland). 1-4 Showers, mild. 5-10 Clear, warm. 11-13 Cooling. 14-16 Rain north, heavy snow mountains; sunny south. 17-21 Warm days, cold nights. 22-24 Rain, snow mountains, cold. 25-28 Clear, cold; showers north. 29-30 Rain; sunny south.

DEC. 1994: Temp. 51° (1.5° above avg.; 1° below south); Precip. 5" (2" above avg.; 1" above inland; 0.5" below south). 1-3 Sunny, warm. 4-9 Rain, cold. 10-14 Sunny; cold nights, frost inland. 15-17 Showers, seasonable. 18-20 Cool inland. 21-23 Rain. 24-26 Warm, cold nights; frost inland. 27-31 Showers, cool.

JAN. 1995: Temp. 47.5° (1° below avg.; avg. inland); Precip. 8" (4" above avg.; 2" above inland). 1-3 Heavy rain, heavy snow mountains; cold. 4-9 Clear, cold; hard frost inland. 10-13 Rain, cold; heavy snow mountains. 14-21 Rain, heavy snow higher elevations. 22-24 Rain, seasonable. 25-27 Seasonable. 28-30 Rain, heavy snow mountains. 31 Clear, mild.

FEB. 1995: Temp. 51.5° (0.5° below avg.; 1° below inland); Precip. 2.5" (0.5" below avg.; 2" below south). 1-3 Cold; clear, warm south. 4-6 Rain; sunny south; seasonable. 7-10 Sunny, warm south; cool inland. 11-14 Sunny, mild; showers south. 15-16 Rain, snow mountains; cool. 17-20 Sunny, seasonable. 21-26 Cold; rain, snow mountains. 27-28 Clear, seasonable.

MAR. 1995: Temp. 52° (1.5° below avg.; 3° below inland); Precip. 4" (1" above avg.; 2" above south). 1-4 Sunny, warm. 5-9 Rain, cold; snow mountains. 10-12 Rain, snow mountains. 13-18 Clearing, then cold, rain. 19-21 Rain, snow mountains; cold. 22-24 Rain, warming. 25-28 Clear, warm, cold nights. 29-31 Clear, warm.

APR. 1995: Temp. 55.5° (Avg.; 1° below south); Precip. 1.5" (Avg.; 0.5" above inland and south). 1-2 Clear, warm. 3-6 Cool. 7-10 Clear, warm. 11-17 Cool; showers, snow mountains. 18-20 Sunny, warm. 21-23 Clear, warm. 24-25 Seasonable, showers south. 26-28 Sunny, pleasant. 29-30 Showers, cool.

MAY 1995: Temp. 57.5° (0.5° below avg.); Precip. 0.2" (Avg.). 1-4 Cold, sprinkles. 5-10 Seasonable, warm south. 11-13 Cool; light rain north. 14-19 Clear, seasonable; warm south. 20-23 Clear, warm. 24-25 Sunny, mild. 26-31 Clear; hot interior.

JUNE 1995: Temp. 58.5° (3° below avg.; 5° below inland); Precip. 0.1" (Avg.). 1-4 Seasonable; drizzle south. 5-9 Clear, warm. 10-15 Cold, sprinkles north. 16-18 Sunny, cool. 19-21 Clear, hot inland. 22-25 Sunny, seasonable. 26-28 Cool, sprinkles. 29-30 Clear, mild.

JULY 1995: Temp. 59.5° (3° below avg.); Precip. 0" (Avg.). 1-3 Cool, rain. 4-6 Clear, warm. 7-11 Sunny; hot inland. 12-17 Sunny; mild inland, warm south. 18-21 Hot inland, warm coast; sprinkles. 22-27 Clear; hot. 28-31 Seasonable, hot south.

AUG. 1995: Temp. 60.5° (3° below avg.; avg. inland); Precip. 0" (Avg.). 1-2 Clear, hot. 3-5 Cooler, sprinkles. 6-9 Hot, then seasonable. 10-12 Clear, warm. 13-17 Cool. 18-20 Clearing, hot. 21-27 Sunny, hot. 28-31 Sunny; hot south.

SEPT. 1995: Temp. 63.5° (1° below avg.; 1° above inland); Precip. 0" (Avg.). 1-2 Clear; hot south. 3-6 Clear, hot. 7-9 Seasonable, hot south. 10-12 Sprinkles; hot south. 13-15 Cold, sprinkles. 16-18 Clearing, hot. 19-24 Clear, warm, then sprinkles. 25-30 Clear, hot, milder south.

OCT. 1995: Temp. 59° (2° below avg.; 3° above inland); Precip. 0" (1" above avg.). 1-3 Clear, hot; light rain south. 4-6 Hot inland, sprinkles north coast. 7-12 Hot inland, warm south coast. 13-15 Cool, rain. 16-19 Warm inland, sprinkles coast. 20-25 Light rain. 26-28 Sprinkles, cool. 29-31 Clear, warm.

He was with our troops in North Africa, Sicily, Italy, and on the beaches of Normandy. Finally, before he landed with the Marines on Okinawa 50 years ago this coming April, he wrote, "I feel that I've used up my chances."

The Most
PRAYED-FOR MAN
IN WORLD WAR II

His feelings had always reflected stark reality . . .

T hey weren't heroic figures as they moved forward one at a time, a few seconds apart. You think of attackers as being savage and bold. These men were hesitant and cautious. They were really the hunters, but they looked like the hunted. There was a confused excitement and a grim anxiety in their faces. They seemed terribly pathetic to me. They weren't warriors. They were American boys who by mere chance of fate had wound up with guns in their hands, sneaking up a death-laden street in a strange and shattered city in a faraway country in a driving rain."
                                        – Ernie Pyle column published July 13, 1944

☐ IF YOU STAND OUTSIDE THE TWO-STORY, WHITE FRAME HOUSE on Main Street in the small town of Dana, Indiana, you can see the men walking slowly toward the front door. They are in their seventies now. Some are older. They have turned off U.S. Highway 36, the Ernie Pyle Memorial Highway, searching Dana's Main Street for the house where, in 1900, Ernie Pyle was born.

There's a good chance that if you're under 40, you have only the vaguest idea who Ernie Pyle was. His war was a long time ago. He never fired a shot during World War II, yet generals said he helped win the war. General Omar Bradley said his men fought longer and braver when they knew Ernie Pyle was nearby. The *Saturday Evening Post* called him "the most prayed-for man with the armed forces." And when a Japanese machine gun killed him on April 18, 1945, never before or since has the country so mourned a writer.

He was a shy man who on his best day weighed 110 pounds.

Surrounded by soldiers, Ernie Pyle listened to news on a Navy transport two days before the invasion of Okinawa — his last assignment.

✦ ✦ ✦

BY MEL R. ALLEN

– photo, opposite page: official U.S. Navy photograph. All photos courtesy Ernie Pyle State Historic Site

"Dead men had been coming down the mountain all evening, lashed onto the backs of mules. They came lying belly down across the wooden pack saddle ..."

He hated to be cold and dirty, yet lived by choice in cold and dirty foxholes because that is where the soldiers lived. He loved the foot soldiers. One soldier who landed with Pyle in Normandy wrote his mother: "It was not that his column told us things we did not know or feel, but the fact that we knew you folks at home could read it and get to know and understand."

The house in Dana is now the Ernie Pyle State Historic Site, and the old soldiers have not forgotten what he meant to them. "Ernie was their spokesman," said Evelyn Hobson, curator of the museum since 1978. "He wrote about the soldier boy, not strategy, not about generals. A lot of these men couldn't talk about the war for years. Now they bring their children and their grandchildren. Now they will talk about the war. And they want to see Ernie again."

Inside they find the clothes he wore during his last days and the duffel bag with "Ernie Pyle, war correspondent" stenciled on the side. Here is the coat with ripped-out elbows he once wore to a tea with First Lady Eleanor Roosevelt. Here is the old Underwood portable he used during

Pyle writing his column in Normandy during an air assault after D-Day, 1944.

his roving reporter days before the war.

In one room a mannequin looking eerily like the thin, gray-haired, sad-faced reporter reads Pyle's most famous war dispatch, about the death of the beloved Captain Henry Waskow from Belton, Texas:

"I was at the foot of the mule trail the night they brought Capt. Waskow down. The moon was nearly full, and you could see far up the trail, and even partway across the valley. Soldiers made shadows as they walked.

"Dead men had been coming down the mountain all evening, lashed onto the backs of mules. They came lying belly down across the wooden pack saddle, their heads hanging down on the left side of the mule, their stiffened legs sticking awkwardly from the other side, bobbing up and down as the mule walked ..."

Many leave the house in tears. A few years ago Leonard Bessman came from Madison, Wisconsin. "I just wanted to be where Ernie's things were," Mr. Bessman said. Pyle had written three columns about him: "His bravery was a byword among us long before he was captured ..." After the war Mr. Bessman became a judge in Wisconsin. When he retired, a plaque in his honor was hung in the courthouse. On the plaque were Ernie Pyle's words.

He was the only child of William and Maria Pyle ("the best chicken raiser and cake baker in the neighborhood"), farmers born to the Midwestern soil. In 1909, when he was nine, he started driving a team of horses in the field. As a boy, he felt the long afternoons would never end. He yearned for freedom from the farm, and as soon as he was old enough, he took flight.

He attended the University of Indiana, and because a friend said the easiest courses were in the journalism school, he studied journalism. He left school only a few months shy of graduation to become a cub reporter on a small Indiana paper, which he soon left to join the fledgling Scripps-Howard *Washington Daily News.* He was the best headline writer on the staff, so for five years he worked the desk. But he hungered to report, and in 1928, when aviators still held America enthralled, he assigned himself a column on aviation. He wrote of danger and fear, the grief of widows and colleagues. Amelia Earhart once was asked if she knew Ernie Pyle. "Not to know Ernie Pyle," she said, "is to admit that you yourself are unknown in aviation."

The column ended when he reluctantly became managing editor in 1932. He loathed indoor work, and three years later he convinced his bosses to give him a column unlike any other. He could go anywhere, do anything. Just write 600 words a day, six days a week. He started in August 1935 in Flemington, New Jersey, writing about Bruno Hauptmann and the Lindbergh baby kidnapping. Then he headed for New England and into Canada. Within a year he had driven his Ford roadster through all 48 states.

He had married Geraldine Siebolds, a Minnesota girl, in 1925. He called her "That girl who rides with me" in his column, and together they crossed the continent 20 times. They had no home. Once they tried counting the hotels they had slept in and stopped at 800.

"Our travel is a means of escape. We don't have to stay and face anything out. If we don't like a place, we can move on. ... Stability cloaks you with a thousand little personal responsibilities, and we have been able to flee from them."

He talked to ordinary people about their lives, and they told him their stories. He packed his columns, published under "Hoosier Vagabond," with details of what he saw and heard and smelled and touched and tasted. He observed America

Ernie Pyle (right) with two of his heroes, General Omar Bradley (left) and General Dwight D. Eisenhower.

for everyone. Slowly and surely he was painting a portrait of America, and slowly he was gaining readers. A column that began only in his *Washington Daily News* grew to over 70 newspapers and some three million readers. His prose was as clean and unpretentious as the man. People said it reminded them of personal letters home from a best friend.

"The store clerks in New Orleans, in that last crowded, destroying week before Christmas, are sweeter and kinder than it is possible for human beings to be. ... The prettiest girls are in Salt Lake City. The best-dressed women, outside the coastal cities, are in Memphis. ... The nicest rain is in Seattle. The American town with the most spectacular setting is Ouray, Colorado, completely cupped by terrifically towering mountains. The most beautiful single scene on this continent is Lake Louise, in Canada."

He who had seen so much bloodshed in war stood there holding her as blood soaked both of them, until the doctors could come and save her.

Only rarely in those years did he write of "important" issues, the news on the front pages. He said he didn't care about those things, and once he went five weeks without reading a newspaper. But that changed in November 1940, when he traveled alone to London, then under siege by the German Luftwaffe. He saw London "stabbed with great fires, shaken by explosions, its dark regions along the Thames sparkling with the pinpoints of white-hot bombs, all of it roofed over with a ceiling of pink that held bursting shells, balloons, flares, and the grind of vicious engines. . . . These things all went together to make the most hateful, most beautiful single scene I have ever known."

Ernie and his comrades in the 1st Marine Division after landing on Okinawa, 1945.

His London reporting brought him new and unexpected prominence. What Ernie Pyle achieved in London was what he had tried to do from the start: "making people at home see what I see."

When he returned from England, he tried to roam again through his own land, but now found the stories too tame, lacking in drama and urgency. And unknown to all but a handful of close friends, his personal life was coming apart.

Almost from the beginning of their marriage, his wife had suffered long bouts of depression. She drank. She took pills. She withdrew into despondency. Physical ills plagued her, and a constant life of strange hotels only increased her isolation. Then the dark periods passed, and she resumed her task of buoying Ernie's spirits and keeping his own self-doubts about his talent from sinking too low.

After London, Jerry's mental illness grew graver. Ernie took three months unpaid leave to be with her. They loved the Southwest more than any other region, so they built a small house in Albuquerque. Despite the house, Jerry's grief proved impenetrable, and in desperation they divorced in April 1941. Ernie told friends it was a last-ditch effort to shock his wife into some semblance of normalcy. It was then he left for war, and with his life in turmoil, he would set down words that touched a nation.

Ernie landed in North Africa, and his reporting from that campaign earned him a Pulitzer. He remarried Jerry by proxy in 1943, a friend standing in his stead. "If anything should happen to me before this war is over," he wrote a friend, "I wanted to go out that way — as we were."

Now his column ran in 250 newspapers and was read by 14 million people. He had never needed much money, but after a collection of his war columns, *Here Is Your War,* became a best-seller, he had thousands. A movie company began a film with Burgess Meredith playing Ernie.

By then he had lived and marched with the army through Sicily and Italy, had landed with them on Normandy, and stayed with them as they liberated Paris. From Paris he wrote his readers that he just couldn't see another man die. He had to leave the war. In the summer of 1944 he came back to the States. He was home only a short while when Jerry tried to stab herself to death with scissors. He who had seen so much bloodshed in war stood there holding her as blood soaked both of them, until the doctors could come and save her.

The war in Europe was all but over, but the Pacific called. He dreaded going back, but knew he must. "You begin to feel that you can't go on forever without being hit. I feel that I've used up my chances, and I hate it," he wrote.

The night before he was to land with the Marines on Okinawa another correspondent, Lisle Shoemaker, found him sorting gear into two stacks, one to go back to New Mexico. Shoemaker asked why. "Because I'm going to get killed," Pyle replied. "I'm on another invasion," he wrote Jerry. "I never intended to. But I feel I must cover the Marines, and the only way to do it honestly is to go with them."

After he landed safely on Okinawa, he wrote again: "I will never make another landing." When the Marines invaded the tiny island of IeShima, just west of Okinawa, he waited until the beachhead was secured. He wrote his father he finally believed he might make it home alive.

On the morning of April 18, 1945, he rode in a jeep with Colonel Joseph B. Coolidge along a narrow road. A sniper opened fire with a machine gun. Ernie and Coolidge scampered for safety in a shallow ditch. The sniper did not fire. For ten years Ernie Pyle had been looking around and asking questions. He raised his head, just above the rim of the ditch and called out across the road to see if the other soldiers he had been riding with were OK.

The sniper fired again.

Nellie Hendrix had grown up next door to Ernie. She came from a family of eight

The house where Ernie Pyle was born, now a State Historic Site in Dana, Indiana.

children, and Ernie had been an only child, so he loved going to her house to play. The radio told her Ernie had been killed. She walked across the field to be with his dad and aunt. When she arrived, she realized they knew nothing. Mr. Pyle was sitting in his black rocking chair. Nellie leaned over and said quietly, "Let's turn on the radio."

President Harry Truman insisted on telling America himself that Ernie had been killed. A soldier built him a crude wood coffin, and he was buried along with 200 others in a shallow grave. Later his body was reburied in National Memorial Cemetery of the Pacific in Punchbowl Crater, Hawaii. Jerry never recovered and a few months later died from pneumonia. Among her personal effects was a telegram signed simply, "A soldier's wife." "I knew him not," she wrote, "but I loved him." □□

On April 18, 1995, the Ernie Pyle State Historic Site will dedicate a new museum housed in a World War II Quonset hut. Write P.O. Box 338, Dana, Indiana 47847; 317-665-3633.

For further reading, all four of Ernie Pyle's war collections can be found at most libraries. Lee G. Miller's The Story of Ernie Pyle *is long out of print, but can also be found at many libraries. More recent collections are* Ernie's War, the Best of Ernie Pyle's World War II Dispatches, *and* Ernie's America, the Best of Ernie Pyle's 1930s Travel Dispatches. *Both books are edited with biographical essays by David Nichols and published by Random House.*

Sweet potatoes have amazing virtues that not everyone knows about. So perhaps this is the year to learn how best to grow them and how best to cook them . . .

by Georgia Orcutt

The Healthiest Vegetable of All

S weet potatoes are many things to many people. One woman we know used its fiery orange flesh as a color swatch for her kitchen wall. While making supper one night, she cut into a baked sweet potato and saw at last the color she'd been searching for. She popped a slice into a plastic container and headed for the paint store. "The man mixing the paint looked at me strangely," she reported, "but I got the accent color I wanted for one wall."

SWEET POTATO

To nutritionists, sweet potatoes are food for thought. By some measures they rank as the healthiest vegetable we can eat. An excellent source of vitamin A and a good source of vitamin C, high in iron and dietary fiber, sweet potatoes also provide their eaters with potassium and vitamin B_6. Of special note is their high percentage of beta-carotene — four times the recommended daily allowance per cup. (Beta-carotene, which the body converts to vitamin A, is especially valued for its ability to reduce the risk of certain cancers.)

To George Washington Carver, the

 sweet potato was the key to unending possibilities. Before World War I, he urged rural southern farmers to think beyond cotton and grow this easy, cheaply raised crop with its high nutritional rewards. To cut back on the use of precious wartime wheat, Carver recommended using two cups of cooked, mashed sweet potato for every six cups of flour in preparing bread. And he went to Washington in 1918 to extol the virtues of sweet potato flour, but the end of the war curtailed the commercial application of his ideas.

To gardeners, especially those in the South, sweet potatoes have earned their place as an easy, economical, and tasty crop. Most at home in USDA Zones 8, 9, and 10, sweet potatoes prefer rather poor, dry, sandy soil and need it to be nice and loose, so they have room to develop. They like moisture, but don't enjoy being constantly wet. In fact, they like resisting drought. When planted in rich, acid soils, they tend to make all leaves and very poor fruit.

Sweet potatoes are planted from slips or sprouts, which you can buy from mail order seed and plant purveyors or start yourself: A month before warm weather (60° F nights) sets in, suspend a sweet potato on toothpicks in a glass with its lower half in water. As shoots develop, cut them off, root them in water, and plant them. (A sweet potato suspended in water also makes a remarkable houseplant, sending out rampant vines and delighting kids of all ages.)

Depending on the variety, sweet potatoes need 120 to 150 frost-free growing days. Some gardeners prefer planting them in mounds about 16 inches apart, leaving room for their trailing vines. Keep at least two leaves from each slip above ground and water them well after planting. When the plant tops turn black after the first frost, they are ready to harvest. (In areas where there is no frost, they are ready for harvest four months after planting.) Dig them carefully and handle them as you would eggs. Their tender skins bruise easily.

For northern gardeners, sweet potatoes offer a true challenge that has been successfully met as far north as Canada. One gardener in the Yukon plants sweet potatoes in a lean-to cold frame against his house and reaps a small but rewarding yield. Another Canadian grower reports harvesting one sweet potato that weighed ten pounds.

Ken Allan of the Garden Research Exchange in Kingston, Ontario, advocates growing sweet potatoes in USDA Zones 6b, 5a, and 5b under clear plastic mulch, which warms the soil and retains heat. "Make a slit to plant them, and use sand or sawdust to keep the plastic close to the ground around the slit," he advises. "You don't want to have a flap for the air to come in and out. That's just like leaving a door open in your garden." If May brings some warm days, Allan recommends planting sweet potatoes by the 15th. As to variety, he's sold on Georgia Jets.

Proper curing enhances sweet potato flavor by converting starch to sugar and hardening their skins for storage.

The late James Crockett advocated planting sweet potatoes in bushel baskets, one slip per basket. He noted that sweet potatoes grown in such confinement often outproduced those allowed to roam in garden soil. And if early frost threatens, you can simply move the baskets to a warmer spot.

Although it may be tricky to grow sweet potatoes in the North, they are, ironically, well suited to storage in colder climates. "The sweet potato is an ideal root crop for those northern gardeners with central heating in their homes," says Allan. "Temperatures of 55° to 60° F are ideal for long keeping. If you see a sweet potato with sunken circular spots, that's a sign that it has been stored at too cold a temperature. Below 50° F they suffer chilling injury and develop a hard core and spotting."

Proper curing enhances sweet potato flavor by converting starch to sugar and hardening their skins for storage. Unlike new potatoes, which are a delicacy, newly harvested sweet potatoes are watery and bland. To cure home-grown sweet potatoes, keep them at 90° F for five to ten days at high humidity. Some people use heaters in closets; others get good results from an incubator or a carefully monitored light bulb in a box. Allan puts his crop in brown paper bags, folds over the tops, and puts them in his back bedroom with a 1,500-watt heater. "I suppose a sauna would work well, too," he said.

To the cook, sweet potatoes are easier than pie. They can simply be scrubbed, poked with a fork in a few places, and baked at 400° F for 35 minutes to one hour, until they give a bit when you squeeze them. In the microwave a whole sweet potato baked on high will be ready in four to six minutes. (Let it stand five minutes to soften.)

Sweet Potato Facts

☞ Never put sweet potatoes in your refrigerator unless they have first been cooked. They will develop a hard core and sunken spots and will spoil much faster than if you keep them at room temperature.

☞ Leading varieties are Beauregard, Jewel, Centennial, Georgia Red, Nugget, and New Jersey Orange.

☞ One cup of cooked sweet potato provides 30 milligrams (50,000 IU) of beta-carotene. (It would take 23 cups of broccoli to provide the same amount.)

☞ One medium sweet potato contains 135 to 155 calories.

☞ The ranking states for production of sweet potatoes for 1992 were California, North Carolina, Louisiana, Texas, Alabama, Georgia, Mississippi, New Jersey, South Carolina, and Virginia, according to the USDA.

☞ The per capita consumption of sweet potatoes is approximately six pounds.

☞ The National Cancer Society cites sweet potatoes as an excellent food to aid in the prevention of several common types of cancer.

Sweet potatoes can also be steamed or boiled whole and unpeeled for about 40 minutes or until tender, but they are tastier baked.

Immerse cut raw sweet potatoes in water until you're ready to cook them; they will darken otherwise. As a general rule, don't substitute sweet potatoes for regular potatoes in recipes (the two aren't related). Sweet potatoes don't hold together the way potatoes do, and their strong flavor can overwhelm a dish meant for a milder potato taste. But they make a fine substitute for pumpkin, especially in desserts.

There is one thing a sweet potato is not. And that is a potato. Unrelated to its white namesake, the sweet potato is a member of the morning-glory family (*Convolvulaceae*), genus *Ipomoea batatus*. It also is not a tuber, but a fleshy root originating in South and Central America. Many varieties were being grown by the time Columbus came to America in 1492. Ships' logs from the early 16th century note sweet potatoes traveling from Honduras to Spain, where their popularity grew to Europe and beyond.

The Great Yam Scam

☞ Are sweet potatoes the same as yams? No . . . and yes. Literally and botanically speaking, the two are not related. Yams are large, starchy, edible tuberous roots that belong to the genus <u>Dioscorea</u>. They grow in tropical and subtropical countries and require eight to ten months of warm weather to mature. Yams can grow two to three feet long and some can weigh as much as 80 pounds. According to horticulturist U. P. Hedrick, the word <u>yam</u> means "to eat" in the dialect of Guinea. In the United States today it is possible to find true yams in some urban Hispanic markets.

Both the yam and the sweet potato grow underground and have yellowish-orange flesh, but there the similarity ends. Yet the two became entwined in this country by household vernacular in part through the work of a publicity campaign. Earlier this century, sweet potato promoters attached the word <u>yam</u> to the deep orange, moist-fleshed varieties of sweet potatoes and left the words <u>sweet potato</u> to the smaller, yellowish, and drier-fleshed varieties. The two types of sweet potato are interchangeable in cooking, but bring different tastes, textures, and colors to your plate. Centennial and Puerto Rico are two popular moist-fleshed (formerly called yam) varieties; Nemagold, New Jersey Orange, and Nugget have the lighter and drier (sweet potato) flesh.

Today it is common to find either or both words used in supermarkets, although sweet potato promoters wish we would all stop saying yam. The North Carolina SweetPotato Commission currently urges the world to spell "sweetpotato" as one word. But it's an uphill battle. If your Mama called them yams, for certain you will, too.

Y A M

Recipes

Pork and Sweet Potato Stir-Fry

- 1 pork tenderloin (about 12 ounces)
- 2 tablespoons oil
- 2 medium sweet potatoes, finely diced or julienned
- 1 medium yellow pepper, chopped
- 1 medium sweet red pepper, chopped
- 8 ounces fresh or frozen snow peas
- 2 cloves garlic, minced
- 1 tablespoon grated fresh gingerroot
- 2 tablespoons soy sauce
- 3 tablespoons water
- 1 tablespoon cornstarch
- 2 tablespoons hoisin sauce (available in Oriental section of supermarket)

Cut pork diagonally into ¼-inch slices. Have remaining ingredients ready. Stir-fry pork in hot oil over high heat until no longer pink. Add sweet potatoes and toss until they begin to soften. Add peppers, snow peas, garlic, and gingerroot and continue stir-frying until peppers are crisp-tender. Combine soy sauce, water, and cornstarch in a small jar, shake well, and add to pan, stirring well. Cover pan, lower heat, and cook briefly, then uncover and stir in hoisin sauce. Serve with rice or noodles. **Makes 6 servings.**

Sweet Potato-Chocolate Nut Cake

The colors and flavor of this moist cake are a knockout. The recipe is adapted from The Victory Garden Cookbook *by Marian Morash (Knopf, New York, 1982).*

- 4 ounces semisweet chocolate
- 1 teaspoon vanilla extract
- 3 cups flour
- 1½ cups sugar
- 2 teaspoons baking powder
- 2 teaspoons baking soda
- 1½ teaspoons cinnamon
- ¾ teaspoon ground ginger
- ¼ teaspoon ground cloves
- ¼ teaspoon freshly grated nutmeg
- ½ teaspoon salt
- 2 cups mashed cooked sweet potatoes
- 1½ cups vegetable oil
- 4 eggs
- 1 cup chopped nuts

Butter and lightly flour a 10-inch tube pan. Place chocolate and vanilla in a small saucepan and set, covered, in a larger pan that you've just filled with boiling water.

Sift together all dry ingredients and set aside. In a large bowl beat the sweet potatoes and oil together, then beat in the eggs one by one until well blended. Slowly add dry ingredients and mix well; stir in nuts. Put one-third of the mixture in another bowl and stir in the chocolate, which should be melted smooth by now. Alternate the batters in the tube pan, as you would for a marble cake. With a knife, cut through the two batters to swirl together slightly. Bake in a preheated 350° F oven for 1 to 1¼ hours, or until the sides have shrunk away from the pan, the top is springy, and tester comes out dry. Let cool 10 minutes and then remove from the pan and cool on a rack. If desired, drizzle with a thin confectioners' sugar glaze (beat 2 to 3 tablespoons boiling water into 1½ cups confectioners' sugar). □□

Sources

Fred's Plant Farm, P.O. Box 707, Dresden, TN 38225. Sells 14 varieties of sweet potato plants, minimum order 50 plants (get together with your neighbors). Write for a price list. 800-243-9377.

The following mail order nurseries offer at least four varieties of sweet potatoes, minimum order 12 plants; all sell special collections that allow you to buy three or four plants of different varieties in that dozen:

☞ Henry Field's Seed & Nursery Co., 415 North Burnett, Shenandoah, IA 51602.

☞ Gurney's Seed & Nursery Co., 110 Capital St., Yankton, SD 57079.

☞ J.W. Jung Seed Co., 335 S. High St., Randolph, WI 53957.

☞ Park Seed Co., Cokesbury Rd., Greenwood, SC 29647.

☞ R.H. Shumway's, P.O. Box 1, Graniteville, SC 29829.

Cooking with Sweet Potatoes. This handy booklet includes 57 different ways to prepare sweet potatoes. Send a self-addressed, stamped No. 10 business-size envelope plus 50¢ for handling to: Harold H. Hoecker, Executive Secretary, Sweet Potato Council of the U.S., Inc., P.O. Box 14, McHenry, MD 21541.

Discover The World of Herbs For A Healthier Tomorrow!

SEND FOR YOUR FREE
1995 HERBALIST CATALOG!

Featuring Over 500 *Natural* Home Remedies!

Herbs! The 1995 Herbalist Catalog features over 500 different herbs for helping you lead a healthier, more active life! These ancient healers have been used by mankind for over 4000 years to soothe pain, increase energy look & feel your very best. Herbs work safely & gently so they do not have dangerous side-effects on your body as many synthetic chemicals do.

Join the millions of people who have discovered the health benefits of natural and delicious herb teas...without the side-effects and costly doctor bills! Choose from over 500 different herb remedies, all backed by The Herbalist's famous guarantee--<u>your money back if you are not completely satisfied.</u>

- America's oldest and largest supplier of herbs and herbal products
- Hundreds of Natural Products, Health Aids, Personal Care Products and Vitamins

Send Today for your FREE Catalog of natural home remedies!

THE HERBALIST CATALOG
"A Family Tradition Since 1910"

☐ **YES! Please Send me my FREE** FC2
copy of the 1995 Herbalist Catalog

HERBALIST, P.O. Box 5 Dept OFAN Hammond, IN 46325

Mr/Mrs/Ms _____

Address _____

City _____

State _____ Zip _____

"Keeping America Healthy Since 1910"

PRIZEWINNING RECIPES ☞ FROM AMERICA'S FOOD FESTIVALS

BY POLLY BANNISTER

– illustrated by Sara Mintz Zwicker

☞ Throughout the year, around the country, thousands of festivals and celebrations honor local harvests and regional cooking. Communities gather together — some for a day, like Idaho Spud Day, others for as long as a month, like the Mushroom Festival in Pennsylvania — to pay tribute to their bounty. Activities include parades, concerts, eating contests, beauty pageants, and in one case, a mashed potato tug-of-war! But the highlight is always the food — available in great supply and freshly prepared with pride and love. Here are a few of the best recipes from those festivals.

STOCKTON ASPARAGUS FESTIVAL

Every year during the last weekend in April, Stockton, California, holds a two-day event honoring this delicate vegetable (a member of the lily family). Stockton, located in the San Joaquin-Sacramento delta region, calls itself the asparagus capital of the world. The region supplies nearly 70 percent of the nation's fresh market asparagus. Cook-off finalist recipes can be found in two cookbooks available from the Stockton Asparagus Festival, 46 West Fremont St., Stockton, California, 95202; 800-350-1987 or 209-943-1987. ASPARAGUS ALL WAYS . . . ALWAYS, $13 plus $2 postage, and COOK-OFF FINALIST RECIPES, $10 plus $2 postage.

Asparagus Lasagna *(Liz Rotert)*

1 to 2 pounds fresh asparagus, cleaned and cut into 1-inch pieces
2 green onions, chopped
4 cups fresh mushrooms, washed and chopped
3 tablespoons butter
¼ cup flour
1 teaspoon salt
¼ teaspoon cayenne pepper
2¼ cups milk
8 ounces lasagna noodles
black pepper
2 cups cottage cheese
8 ounces Monterey Jack cheese, shredded
½ to 1 cup Parmesan cheese, grated

Preheat oven to 325° F. Cook asparagus to crisptender, drain, and let cool. Sauté onions and mushrooms in butter until soft, about 5 minutes. Blend in flour, salt, and cayenne pepper. Gradually stir in milk, and cook sauce until thickened for an additional 5 minutes. Cook lasagna noodles according to package directions. Spread ½ cup mushroom sauce in greased 9x13-inch pan and add a layer of noodles, seasoned with fresh ground black pepper. Add a third of the remaining ingredients (asparagus, cottage cheese, Jack cheese, a third of the remaining mushroom sauce, and Parmesan cheese), then another layer of noodles. Repeat twice. Bake for 45 minutes. Let stand for 20 minutes before cutting. *Serves 8.*

ARIZONA STATE CHAMPIONSHIP CHILI COOK-OFF

Over 150 chili cookers from Arizona, Nevada, and California compete in Bullhead City, Arizona, on the last Saturday in April. Nearly 10,000 fans gather to sample the hot stuff. Each cook must make at least one-half gallon of chili, from which one quart is reserved for judging. The rest of the chili is for festival goers who "buy" a cup and spoon for a dollar's charitable donation.

The cook-off winner, who does not reveal his or her recipe, goes on to the World's Championship Chili Cook-Off, sponsored by the International Chili Society the first weekend in October. Here the winner receives $25,000! Nearly all the contestants prepare "real" chili — a mixture of beef, onions, garlic, chili pepper, and cumin, based on the traditional Texas trail cook's specialty. (Beans were occasionally added to stretch the stew if there were too many cowboys to feed.) For 25 world-

class winning recipes, send a self-addressed envelope, with 58¢ postage, to: International Chili Society, P.O. Box 2966, Newport Beach, CA 92663; 714-631-1780. Here's a favorite:

Ram Tough Chili

(Dusty Hudspeth)

2 pounds beef chuck, coarsely ground
1 tablespoon oil
1 8-ounce can tomato sauce
1 medium onion, finely chopped
1 teaspoon garlic powder, or 5 cloves minced fresh garlic
¼ cup chili powder
1 teaspoon oregano
1½ teaspoons salt
2 teaspoons ground cumin
¼ teaspoon Tabasco sauce
½ teaspoon cayenne pepper

Brown meat in oil in covered 2-quart pan. Add tomato sauce, onion, and garlic powder. Cover and simmer for 30 minutes, stirring occasionally. Add remaining ingredients and simmer for 1 hour, stirring occasionally. Add water if too thick. Serve with side dishes of pinto beans, chopped onions, and grated cheddar cheese. *Serves 6.*

IDAHO SPUD DAY

For 65 years the small town of Shelley has been celebrating Idaho's potato harvest. On the third Saturday in September, 10,000 people gather to eat free baked potatoes, watch potato digging and peeling contests, and enjoy a parade, talent show, and mashed potato tug-of-war. In 1992 a team of five speedy peelers peeled 1,064 pounds, 6 ounces of Idaho russets in 45 minutes. The highlight of the day is the Dutch oven cook-off where six teams of chefs cook over hot coals (charcoal briquettes), using camp ovens (a cast-iron pot, often with swing handle, legs, and a flat, rimmed lid).

These cooks tell us camp-style Dutch oven cooking is easy. The rule of thumb is that each coal or charcoal briquette is worth about 25 degrees of heat. When coals are hot, place specified number of briquettes under the pot and on the lid. To learn more, contact the International Dutch Oven Society, 1104 Thrushwood, Logan, UT 84321; 801-752-2631. DUTCH OVEN COOKBOOK is available from the Society for $8.95 plus $2.50 postage and handling.

For information about Spud Day, contact the Shelley Chamber of Commerce, P.O. Box 301, Shelley, ID 83274; 208-357-7662. CREATIVE POTATO COOKBOOK is available for $4.95, including postage, from Pioneer Publications, P.O. Box P, Shelley, ID 83274.

Dutch Oven Pork Loin and Potatoes

(John R. Darrington)

16-inch Dutch oven with flat lid
4- to 6-pound pork loin roast
salt and pepper
10 pounds Idaho potatoes
4 large onions
1 apple (garnish)
1 sprig parsley (garnish)

Season roast with salt and pepper and place in Dutch oven. Brown over 8 to 10 coals, then cover and place 10 to 12 coals on lid. Cook for 1½ hours. Peel and cut potatoes and onions into large chunks and season with salt and pepper in a mixing bowl. Remove roast from heat, scoop off drippings, and stir into potatoes and onions. Return roast to Dutch oven and pack potato-onion mixture around it. Cook with same number of hot coals as above for 1 to 1½ hours or until done. To avoid hot spots, turn lid and oven a quarter turn every 15 minutes. Garnish with chopped parsley and fresh apple wedges. *Serves 6 to 8.*

SPINACH FESTIVAL

Crystal City, Texas, holds its annual spinach festival on the second weekend in November. During this time, townspeople (many of whom work in the local Del Monte plant processing the leafy green vegetable) build giant spinach salads, wear spinach hats and T-shirts, and sample cook-off dishes prepared by contestants whose ages range from ten to 80. Crystal City, located southwest of San Antonio in a region known as the winter garden of Texas, has a giant statue of Popeye next to the city hall and was officially proclaimed the Spinach Capital of the World in 1937 by Popeye's inventor, E. C. Segar. For information write: Crystal City Festival Association, P.O. Box 100, Crystal City, TX 78839; 210-374-3161.

Crepes Filled with Spinach Vera Cruz
(Dale Barker)

Basic crepes:
1 cup flour
2 eggs
1¾ cups milk
½ teaspoon salt
1 tablespoon butter, melted

Filling:
1 cup cooked fresh spinach, or 1 10-ounce package frozen chopped spinach, cooked
3 strips bacon
½ cup chopped onion
2 medium tomatoes, peeled, seeded, and chopped
1 cup sour cream
1 cup Monterey Jack cheese, grated
dash of Tabasco sauce
salt and pepper

Mix flour, eggs, milk, salt, and butter together in blender or food processor. Brush a 4- to 6-inch skillet (or crepe pan) with butter. Pour in about 1½ tablespoons batter and tilt pan so batter covers bottom. Cook quickly on both sides. Butter pan after each crepe. Set cooked crepes aside.

Preheat oven to 350° F. Cook spinach according to package directions, drain, and squeeze dry. Cook bacon in large, heavy skillet and remove. In about 2 tablespoons of bacon fat, sauté chopped onion, then add spinach, tomatoes, and crumbled bacon. Stir in sour cream and three-quarters of the Jack cheese, Tabasco, dash of salt and pepper, and mix thoroughly. Heat until cheese is melted. Place about 2 tablespoons of spinach filling on each crepe, roll up, and place seam side down in a buttered 9x13-inch baking dish. Put a little additional filling on top and sprinkle with remaining grated Monterey Jack cheese. Heat in oven until bubbly. ***Makes 12 crepes.***

WILD RICE FESTIVAL

The Minnesota towns of Kelliher and Waskish produce over three million pounds of wild rice annually. Locals leave their paddies the second weekend of every July to celebrate the "caviar of grains."

(Wild rice is the only cereal grain native to North America.) Festival highlights include a wild-rice pancake breakfast, food show and recipe contest, a trike race, a parade, wild-rice supper, and the Minnesota State Wild Rice

Queen pageant and sunset dance. For information, contact the Kelliher-Waskish Wild Rice Festival, Box 2, Kelliher, MN 56650; 218-647-8649. WILD RICE COLLECTIONS cookbook available from above address for $5.50 plus $1 shipping.

Wild Rice and Carrot Muffins
(Marje Barnard)

¾ cup white flour
¾ cup whole wheat flour
2 teaspoons baking powder
½ teaspoon salt
1 teaspoon cinnamon
½ teaspoon nutmeg
½ cup brown sugar
1 cup cooked wild rice
1 egg, lightly beaten
¾ cup milk
⅓ cup vegetable oil
1 cup carrots, grated

Topping:

1 tablespoon sugar mixed
    with ¼ teaspoon
    cinnamon

Preheat oven to 400° F. Combine flours, baking powder, salt, cinnamon, nutmeg, and brown sugar in a mixing bowl. Add cooked wild rice to dry ingredients and toss to coat rice. In another bowl mix the egg with milk and oil, add the grated carrots. Stir wet ingredients into the dry ingredients, mixing just enough to blend well. Divide batter into greased muffin tins. Sprinkle cinnamon-sugar topping over muffin batter. Bake for 20 to 25 minutes. Cool on wire rack. *Makes 12 muffins.*

NATIONAL CHERRY FESTIVAL

Traverse City, Michigan, has been home to this cherry festival for nearly 70 years. The state produces 70 percent of the world's cherries. For a week in early July, just-picked sweet cherries are everywhere in the Grand Traverse Bay area. Pie-eating contests for children and adults are held every day. And if you're not too full, there is a Taste of Cherries cook-off, a Very Cherry luncheon, and orchard tours where you can eat all you pick. Cool Whip, Sara Lee, and Minute Maid sponsor big parades and exhibits, while bands from all over the Midwest entertain and compete. Information: National Cherry Festival, P.O. Box 141, 108 W. Grandview Parkway, Traverse City, MI 49684; 616-947-4230. They offer a little cherry cookbook, TASTE OF CHERRIES, for $2 (shipping included), and good sources for cherry products of all kinds.

Endive Salad with Cherries, Roquefort, and Walnuts *(Joy Cassens)*

½ cup walnuts
1 small head endive, rinsed
    and drained
1 small butterhead lettuce,
    rinsed and drained
¾ cup walnut oil
3 tablespoons sherry or
    red wine vinegar
1 tablespoon lemon juice
salt and pepper
½ cup fresh sweet cherries,
    rinsed and pitted
4 ounces Roquefort cheese,
    crumbled
2 tablespoons minced
    chives

Toast whole walnuts in oven or toaster oven at 350° F for 15 minutes; chop. Tear endive and lettuce into bite-sized pieces and place in large salad bowl. In a small container mix walnut oil, vinegar, and lemon juice; beat with wire whisk until well blended. Season with salt and freshly ground black pepper. Drizzle dressing over salad and toss until lettuce is well coated. Arrange lettuce and endive on salad plates. Top each serving with a portion of cherries, walnuts, Roquefort cheese, and chives. (This salad tastes best when dressing is well chilled before tossing.) *Serves 4 to 6.*

☐☐

Amazing VITASEX ® Formula for MEN & WOMEN

GUARANTEED TO
RENEW VIGOR

REVIVE "YOUR" LOVE LIFE

This amazing formula renews your vigor and may be the fastest, safest, and surest vitamin, mineral tonic and stimulant formula ever released by medical science. Yes, many men and women who have taken these miracle tablets after a tiring working day have found new strength and potency to the point it has made the relationship come alive again. These potent VitaSex tablets are the reason many couples are enjoying a happier home life after years of dragging through each day.

REVITALIZE ENERGY, POTENCY, AND VIGOR

Start today to renew your strength, potency and vigor with the first tablets you take. You don't have to wait days to get results. You get almost immediate new surges of energy because this revolutionary new product is designed to start working instantly. And you won't experience hypertension and jittery energy that accompanies other drugs that you see advertised in certain magazines and newspapers.

AMAZING RESULTS

VITASEX® is a **scientifically formulated** tonic and stimulant that gives you the EXTRA measure of nutrients and stimulant that you may need to revitalize vigor, energy and stamina. Therefore, you'll also experience the exhilarating, rewarding lift of HEALTHY BODY FUNCTION.

Yes, now instead of being left out of the "good times" you can:

• **Restore healthy body function . . .**
• **Improve your desire and performance . . .**
• **Renew your strength, potency and vigor . . .**
• **And win the desire of your mate regardless of age, or age differences.**

Results with VITASEX have **proven** that it gets guaranteed results! Anyone in good health can renew their strength, stamina and vigor with VITASEX®. **Yes, success in every case.**

VITASEX® — A Personal Relations™ Health Product sold in durg stores. Ask your Pharmacist or order direct. Druggist inquiries appreciated.

RENEW VIGOR WITH THE FASTEST, SUREST, AND SAFEST TONIC AND STIMULANT FORMULA OUR MEDICAL SCIENTISTS HAVE EVER DEVELOPED — ABSOLUTELY GUARANTEED!

In fact, the only way VitaSex® won't work for you is by not using them! It's guaranteed to work for you, even if you've had a problem for years. Even if other formulas have failed you. Even if nothing you've tried in the past had any lasting effect!

That's why we can make this 100% no-risk guarantee. This potent formula must work for you or your money will be refunded (less postage of course), and you can keep the first bottle free. ACT NOW!

For Our Fastest Service
Call 919-554-4014

Quality • Research • Integrity • Since 1888

Tummy hurt? Gutwort. Toothache? Toothwort, tied around your neck. Madness looming? Madwort. Baby coming soon? Milkwort. Hernia? Rupturewort, good also for worms. Spider bite? The hairy-stemmed spiderwort. Warts? Well, wartwort, of course!

You get the idea. Despite the warning of Jean Baptiste Molière (1622-1673) that "Nearly all men die of their remedies and not of their illnesses," some of these ancient herbal cures continue to enjoy medical repute. Plants with the suffix "wort" seem particularly useful. (Properly pronounced "wurt," although it's commonly rhymed with "court," wort is from the Old English *wyrt* meaning simply root, herb, or plant.) And most are either native to or naturalized in North America, where they now grace roadsides and formal herb gardens alike.

MUGWORT *(Artemisia)* is named for Artemis, Greek goddess of the Moon, the chase, and chastity, and was once the main ingredient in absinthe. Called the eldest of worts, mugwort grows wild from Nova Scotia to Michigan. True to Artemis, who loved the chase, mugwort was thought to protect travelers from fatigue, lightning, sunstroke, the Evil Eye, plague, wild beasts, and even carbuncles. Placed under a horse's saddle, it refreshed the steed. Walkers stuffed it in their shoes. The Druids of Devon and Cornwall used it to lure the Sun's warmth back to Earth. American Indians put a leaf in one nostril to cure headaches. Nicholas Culpeper, in his *Complete Herbal* of 1653, advised mugwort "for a good time" or the smoke of it under a child's bed "to make him merry." Also known as wormwood, it's an aromatic moth repellent.

Gardeners like the perennial mugwort or wormwood for its fragrance and silvery foliage. Useful as an edging plant, it tolerates dry or poor soils and partial shade. The white mugwort *(Artemisia lactiflora)* has creamy-white flowers and green foliage.

SNEEZEWORT *(Achillea ptarmica)*, used as snuff, or woundwort *(Achillea millefolium)*, both better known as yarrow, are probably the most commonly recognized of the worts. Named for Achilles, who was taught its healing powers by the centaur, woundwort was used to staunch the flow of blood during the

IF IT'S A "WORT," IT MUST BE USEFUL

And the most useful "wort" plants are those whose old-time names describe what they were specifically grown for back in the old days. Here are a dozen examples . . .

by Martha White

Battle of Troy as well as in the American Civil War. Folklore values it for self-esteem, heartache, love charms, to conjure the Devil, and against insomnia. American Indians use it to postpone baldness, the Chinese throw the fortune-telling I Ching with its stems, and in India it's a fever remedy. Brought to weddings, it's supposed to ensure seven years of love, but any woman caught gathering it may be labeled a witch.

In your garden, woundwort is the more common of the yarrows, a rapidly spreading white to red flower that blooms midsummer to early fall. Sneezewort has white, ball-shaped flowers in early summer, and both types are good for cutting and drying and excellent as border plants.

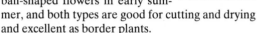

SAINT-JOHN'S-WORT *(Hypericum)* is a yellow-flowered herb named for St. John the Baptist, who celebrates his feast day June 24, when the plant is in bloom. The Greek *hyper,* above, and *eikon,* picture, refer to the custom of hanging the herb over images to ward off evil. It also decorated cottage windows and doorways as a lightning protection, to cure bedwetting, and to promote healthy crops. Like woundwort, Saint-John's-wort was utilized on battlefields for over 2,000 years and was used extensively during the American Civil War.

Today, Saint-John's-wort goes into Hypericin, an experimental AIDS drug being researched in the United States, Germany, and the Soviet Union. An ointment of the herb is prescribed for skin complaints and burns.

A spreading, woody perennial, Saint-John's-wort is often seen in well-drained rock gardens, banks, and edgings. Some claim it will turn on you if it's cut after sunset, however, and a fairy horse (see Ragwort) will carry you off until daybreak.

LUNGWORT is known variously as *Pulmonaria* (Latin for lung), *Verbascum,* and *Mertensia.* It comes from the family *Scrophulariaceae,* from *scrofula,* an old term for swollen glands, later recognized as tuberculosis. By the old Doctrine of Signatures — which decreed that each plant displays an external sign indicating what it is effective for — lungwort was

thought to cure lung ailments because its spotted leaves resembled diseased lungs. Ulysses carried it against the wiles of Circe, and Quaker girls rubbed it against their cheeks to simulate rouge. In India it was used against coughs, and in many countries against TB. Also called the tinder plant, hag's taper, or witch's candle, it was recommended for use both by and against witches.

Originally an Old World plant, it now grows wild from Canada to Florida and west of the Rockies. The garden variety *(Pulmonaria)* is a low, spreading perennial with speckled leaves, pink buds, and blue flowers that open in the spring. *Mertensia,* also called Virginia bluebells or cowslip, is valued for its ability to bloom in dense shade and may be planted among ferns as a ground cover.

BARRENWORT *(Epimedium)* was prescribed primarily for men, especially in China, where it was considered an aphrodisiac to increase sperm production and restore vigor. In gardens, it's generally used as a shade-tolerant ground cover to prevent soil erosion. The foliage goes from pink or reddish to autumn yellow, red, and bronze.

BIRTHWORT takes its Greek name *Aristolochia* from the words meaning "best for childbirth." Some assign it to the Doctrine of Signatures, saying the curved flower and base resemble a human fetus in the right position for birth. Greeks, Romans, Arabs, Hindus, and American Indians used birthwort to aid parturition. North American varieties are found in the warmer regions only and include the Virginia snakeroot (good for snakebite, some say) and the pelican flower.

MOTHERWORT, or *Leonurus* for lion's tail, came originally from Siberia but has naturalized to most of the United States and grows in wastelands as a coarse perennial weed up to five feet tall. Culpeper said motherwort, governed by Venus, would make "women joyful mothers of children" and settle their wombs. Modern research suggests it's more apt to prevent motherhood than promote it: It's a uterine stimulant

. . . folklore claims it as the steed of fairies and witches. In Ireland, leprechauns were thought to bury their treasure beneath

RAGWORT.

and trigger to the menses, but it might aid in expelling the afterbirth. Greeks and Romans used it for heart palpitations, and in Japan it's thought to promote longevity.

MOONWORT,

also supposed to regulate a woman's menses and stay bleeding or vomiting, is an early spring herb that withers in hot weather. It's otherwise known as grape fern (*Botrychium*), referring to the bunched, grapelike appearance of the spore-bearing organs. Folklore suggests it could open locks and unshoe horses. Culpeper related a story of the herb he called "Unshoe the Horse" wherein "were found thirty horse shoes, pulled off from the feet of the Earl of Essex's horses, being there drawn up in a body, and no reason known, which caused much admiration, and the herb described usually grows upon heaths."

RAGWORT *(Senecio)*, known also as

Saint-James's-wort, staggerwort, or stammerwort, flowers in pastures in June and July, but is rarely cultivated. Culpeper recommended it to heal "old and filthy ulcers of the privities" and folklore claims it as the steed of fairies and witches. In Ireland, leprechauns were thought to bury their treasure beneath ragwort.

SOAPWORT *(Saponaria)* was grown

in Colonial American gardens and its lathering sap used for shampoo. Indians found that bits of the plant, thrown into small pools, would stupefy fish. Herbal gardeners use the perennial for a trailing ground cover in dry, stony areas. Its bright pink flowers bloom in showy summer clusters.

BACKWORT or BRUISEWORT

(Symphytum) was another colonial transplant to Salem and the Boston Common, known commonly now as comfrey and seen in informal borders. Poultices of the mucilaginous root were used for healing bruises and were thought to help set broken bones. Some know it as boneset or knitback. A vigorous, clump-forming perennial, it thrives in moist soils and shows loose, branching, purplish flowers.

COUGHWORT, better known as

coltsfoot (*Tussilago,* for cough dispeller), is the wort that came to symbolize all herbal medicine. Images of it were hung on the doors of French apothecaries to advertise their trade. Similar to its kin the dandelion, and rivaling it in early spring appearance, coughwort is still used in cough-drop formulas and as a main ingredient of a British herb tobacco.

Finally, lest you sneeze at these few herbs and weeds, keep in mind that they are a bare sampling of the many wonderful worts. Look for the insectivorous bladderwort, feverwort (being researched as an anticancer agent), lousewort (wood betony; worn about the neck, it wards off catastrophe), liverwort, masterwort, and moneywort. There's nailwort, pilewort, stitchwort (don't pick it; it's the rightful property of the pixies), and swallowwort, each with a story of its own, and that still doesn't name them all. While others grow white gardens, be the first to sport a wort garden. □□

COMPLETE HOME CIDER PRESS and fruit grinder, 3 models to choose from, completely assembled or in kit form. The secret is the cast iron "APPLE EATER" grinder which reduces the fruit to a fine pulp and will grind a bushel of whole apples in 5 minutes. Tub holds full bushel of pulped fruit. Heavy 1½" acme screw and cast iron crossbeam. Hardwood construction. Call or send $1.00 for catalog.

HAPPY VALLEY RANCH (913)849-3103
16577 W.327 DEPT 17 • PAOLA, KS 66071

RAINY DAY AMUSEMENTS

Answers on page 174.

The winner of the 1994 Old and New Mathematical Puzzles was Robert L. Henderson of Belleville, Michigan, with 98 points. Runner-up was Kenneth Harbison from Rochester, New York. Congratulations to both! For explanations and Prize-Set answers, send $1 and a self-addressed, stamped envelope to "Puzzle Answers," *The Old Farmers Almanac,* P.O. Box 520, Dublin, NH 03444.

For 1995 we embark on a new puzzle department, offering a blend of our old Rainy Day Amusements and Mathematical Puzzles sections to bring you a variety of popular brainteasers. Young and old alike will find something here to while away a rainy day. Have fun!

1. Fractured Franklin

The Right-Hand Calendar Pages of *The Old Farmer's Almanac* contain proverbs and maxims scattered throughout the year. Some of our favorites include those attributed to Benjamin Franklin, one of our country's early almanac makers. Here are 20 of Franklin's pithy sayings, but with a twist — we've split each adage and mixed them up. The object is to match the beginning of one saying with its correct ending. For example, "Fish and visitors stink after three days." The first half of Number 1 matches the second half of Number 13, as indicated by the number written in the first blank. So here it is — your chance to match wits with Ben Franklin! — *Teresa M. Hackett*

1. ___13___ **Fish and visitors** shall rise up with fleas.

2. _____ **If your head is wax,** the doctor takes the fee.

3. _____ **Many foxes grow grey, but** are dead.

4. _____ **Half wits talk much, but** wise men eat them.

5. _____ **An empty bag** don't wait for Time.

6. _____ **There are lazy minds** without pains.

7. _____ **If you have time** the bee has a sting.

8. _____ **Hunger is** the best possession.

9. _____ **No gains** as well as lazy bodies.

10. _____ **Fools make feasts and** we know the worth of water.

11. _____ **All blood is** the best pickle.

12. _____ **A true friend is** alike ancient.

13. _____ **Great spenders** stink after three days.

14. _____ **He that lieth down with dogs** takes care.

15. _____ **He that takes a wife** say little.

16. _____ **The discontented man** cannot stand upright.

17. _____ **God heals and** finds no easy chair.

18. _____ **When the well's dry** few grow good.

19. _____ **Three may keep a secret if two of them** are bad lenders.

20. _____ **Honey is sweet, but** don't walk in the Sun.

2. Thirty-Four in a Four-by-Four

Arrange the numbers 1 through 16, inclusive, in a 4x4-block square so as to add up to 34 in every direction (including diagonally).

3. The Four-Part 45

The number 45 has some curious properties. Among others, it may be divided into four parts in such manner that if you add two to the first, subtract two from the second, multiply the third by two, and divide the fourth by two, all the results will be equal. What are the four parts?

Word Charades

Word charades are just like the party game, except that the clues are given in riddling verse, or prose, rather than acted out. When the verse mentions "my first, second, or third," it refers to the separate parts or syllables of the word to be guessed. "My whole," of course, refers to the word as a whole.

4. My first asserts your power to do,
My second that you've done it.
Pray be my whole and tell us now
All that you know about it.

5. My first is counted by people, but not every day.
My second's in fool, but never in flay.
My last is avoidance of something or someone,
While my whole is corruption that comes by the ton.

6. I am found in a jail; I belong to a fire;
And am seen in a gutter abounding in mire;
Put my last letter third, and then 'twill be found;
I belong to a king, without changing my sound.

7. My first is all-embracing, right and left and front and back,

And my second may be many or a unit, but alack!
My first and third without my second moan and sigh; but once it's there,
My whole incites to mirth, to wit, to banishment of care;
A constant guide, a cheerful friend throughout the changing year;
Seed-time and harvest shall not fail with this companion dear!

8. Medical Melodies

We were having a lovely time recently at a doctors' convention until we tried to play a song on the jukebox. Much to our befuddlement — and the medicos' amusement — all of the song titles had been "translated" into medical terminology. For example, the song "Heart Attack" appeared on the listing as "Cardiac Arrest." The titles of 20 popular songs appear below. How many of them can you match with their medical equivalents in the list on the next page?

– Teresa M. Hackett

____ **1.** I've Got You Under My Skin
____ **2.** Smooth Operator
____ **3.** Silver Threads and Golden Needles
____ **4.** At This Moment
____ **5.** The Beat Goes On
____ **6.** Greensleeves
____ **7.** Put Your Head on My Shoulder
____ **8.** Take Good Care of My Baby
____ **9.** Spinout
____ **10.** Dizzy
____ **11.** You Talk Too Much
____ **12.** Steam Heat
____ **13.** Two Faces Have I
____ **14.** Another Sleepless Night
____ **15.** Doctor's Orders
____ **16.** Crying
____ **17.** Change of Heart
____ **18.** Mr. Sandman
____ **19.** Talk to the Animals
____ **20.** Try to Remember

(continued on next page)

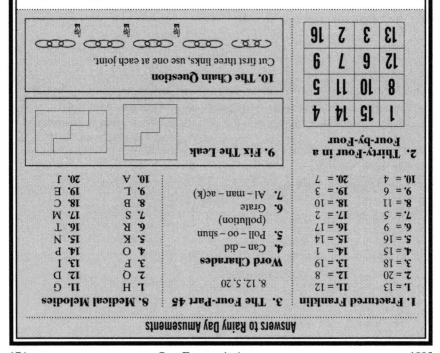

WINNING RECIPES
in the 1994 RECIPE CONTEST

The Best Original Main-Dish Recipes Featuring Eggs

FIRST PRIZE
Cheesy-Chive Eggs

1 tablespoon melted butter
4 ounces cream cheese, softened and cut
   into 4 pieces
4 teaspoons chopped fresh chives
4 large eggs
½ teaspoon salt
½ teaspoon white pepper
4 tablespoons half-and-half
6 tablespoons grated sharp cheddar cheese

Garnish:
2 tablespoons chopped fresh parsley
1 large tomato, seeded and chopped
1 medium avocado, chopped and
   combined with 1 tablespoon lemon juice

Preheat oven to 350° F. Brush four ramekins or custard cups with melted butter. Place 1 portion of cream cheese in each cup, and sprinkle 1 teaspoon chives over each. Add 1 slightly beaten egg to each cup. Sprinkle each egg with ⅛ teaspoon salt and ⅛ teaspoon white pepper. Gently add 1 tablespoon of half-and-half to each cup. Sprinkle 1½ tablespoons cheese over each cup.

Fill a 9x11-inch baking pan with 1 inch of hot water. Set cups in pan. Bake 20 minutes until eggs are set. Remove egg cups from water and garnish tops with parsley, tomato, and avocado. Serve with warm croissants and fresh fruit.

Serves 4.
– Nikki Peden,
Winter Park,
Florida

SECOND PRIZE
Creamy Smoked Salmon Tart

5 frozen phyllo pastry sheets, thawed
3 tablespoons unsalted butter, melted
4 large egg yolks
1 heaping tablespoon Dijon mustard
3 large eggs
1 cup half-and-half
1 cup whipping cream
6 ounces smoked salmon (lox), diced
4 scallions, chopped
1 to 2 tablespoons chopped fresh dill or
   1 teaspoon dried
dill or parsley sprigs for garnish, or use thin
   lime or lemon slices

Generously butter a deep 9½-inch pie plate. Place 1 phyllo sheet on your work surface (cover remaining pieces with damp towel or plastic wrap). Brush the sheet lightly with butter and fold in half lengthwise. Brush folded surface with butter. Cut in half crosswise. Place 1 phyllo rectangle buttered side down in pie plate, covering bottom and letting it overhang the edge by ½ inch. Brush top of phyllo dough in pie plate with butter. Place second phyllo rectangle crosswise in pie plate, covering bottom and letting it overhang the remainder of the pie plate by ½ inch; brush with butter. Repeat process with remaining 4 phyllo sheets. Fold overhanging pastry under to form crust edge flush with edge of pie plate. Brush with butter. (Can be prepared a day ahead, if covered and refrigerated.)

Preheat oven to 350° F. Whisk egg yolks and mustard in medium bowl to blend; beat in eggs, half-and-half, cream, salmon, scallions, and dill. Salt and pepper to taste (remember that the salmon is quite salty). Pour mixture into prepared crust and bake until center is set, about 50 minutes. Transfer to rack and cool. Garnish and serve at room temperature or slightly warm. **Serves 6 to 8.**

– Diane Halferty, Seattle, Washington

THIRD PRIZE

East Texas-Pennsylvania Ranch Eggs

Molé Sauce:
1 small onion, chopped
1 small red pepper, chopped
1 tablespoon cooking oil
2 cups chopped fresh or canned tomatoes
1 tablespoon chopped fresh parsley
2 tablespoons chopped cilantro
½ teaspoon cinnamon
½ teaspoon cumin
½ teaspoon oregano
1 ounce semisweet chocolate
chili pepper (to taste)

6 small flour tortillas
2 cups Molé Sauce (see above)
6 eggs
8 ounces shredded cheese (Monterey Jack, Colby, cheddar)

Make sauce: Sauté chopped onion and red pepper in 1 tablespoon oil; add tomatoes and all remaining sauce ingredients. Cook 15 minutes over low heat.

Preheat oven to 350° F. Place tortillas on the bottom of a large oiled casserole dish (try not to overlap). Cover each tortilla with Molé sauce. Crack and put one egg on top of each sauce-covered tortilla. Cover with shredded cheese and bake for 30 minutes. **Serves 6.**

– David Rheinauer, Macungie, Pennsylvania

HONORABLE MENTION

French Toast Strata

2 tablespoons butter or margarine
1 large cooking apple, peeled and coarsely chopped
½ cup seedless raisins
½ cup coarsely chopped walnuts
¼ cup granulated sugar
½ teaspoon ground cinnamon
¼ teaspoon ground nutmeg
1 cup sour cream, divided
6 eggs
1½ cups milk
¼ cup maple syrup
half of a 1-pound loaf of French or Italian bread, cut into ½-inch-thick slices, slices halved

Melt the butter or margarine in a medium nonstick skillet over medium-high heat. Sauté the apple until just softened, about 3 minutes, and remove from heat. Stir in the raisins, walnuts, sugar, cinnamon, nutmeg, and ½ cup sour cream.

In a medium bowl beat the eggs, milk, maple syrup, and remaining ½ cup sour cream. In a buttered 10-inch pie plate or 9-inch square baking dish, layer half the bread; spread apple-sour cream mixture over the bread and then layer with remaining bread. Pour egg-milk mixture over. Cover and chill in refrigerator for 2 to 24 hours.

Preheat oven to 325° F. Bake strata in preheated oven 50 to 60 minutes, or until set and lightly browned. Let stand 10 minutes before cutting. **Serves 6 to 8.**

– Julie DeMatteo, Clementon, New Jersey

ANNOUNCING

The **1995 RECIPE CONTEST**

Family-Tradition Ethnic Desserts

For 1995, cash prizes (first prize, $50; second prize, $25; third prize, $15) plus baskets of *Old Farmer's Almanac* brand-name foods will be awarded for the best original recipes for ethnic desserts that have been part of your family's traditions. Please include a sentence or two describing the history of each recipe. All entries become the property of Yankee Publishing Incorporated, which reserves all rights to the materials submitted. Winners will be announced in the 1996 edition of *The Old Farmer's Almanac.* Deadline is February 1, 1995. Address: Recipe Contest, *The Old Farmer's Almanac,* P.O. Box 520, Dublin, NH 03444.

WINNING ESSAYS

in the 1994 ESSAY CONTEST

One Thing I Wish I Had Never Done

FIRST PRIZE

As a young lad growing up in the corn country of rural Indiana, I ordered an item once from an ad in a comic book. It was sneezing powder, and all it took was a dare from an uncle of mine to get me to place a generous pinch into my grandfather's handkerchief.

Grandpa hadn't needed his hanky until right about lunchtime, and as we saw him reaching for the tattered old piece of blue-and-white cloth, we could barely hold a straight face. The instant he pressed it to his nose, he broke into a sneezing frenzy the likes of which I have never seen before or since. About the third or fourth sneeze his upper plate flew out of his mouth like a shot, and across the dining table it slid — right between the chicken legs and the roastin' ears and onto the hardwood kitchen floor with a resounding crack. I reluctantly peeked under the table to see two pieces where there should have been one, the break running straight as an arrow between the two front teeth. Grandpa was a loving and patient man, and thanks to his sense of humor we (my uncle and I) were able to forgo a trip to the woodshed. Gramps had really been looking forward to those roastin' ears.

– Scott Magill, Chapmansboro, Tennessee

SECOND PRIZE

There's no way to improve on the old home remedy for skunk odors. Tomato juice works best, no ifs, ands, or buts about it. The first time my dog came in reeking of skunk, I foolishly discarded the tried-and-true method and attempted to come up with a more modern, scientific approach. I wish I never had.

Since baking soda is effective for removing refrigerator odors, I made a paste of baking soda and liberally applied it to the dog. She still smelled.

Since vinegar successfully attacks sink smells, I poured a gallon of it over the pasty mutt. Too late I remembered those science experiments we did in grade school. I had created a chemical reaction.

The dog had a few reactions, too. Her skin began to bubble and foam. She turned into a giant fizzy. Her nostrils flared, her jowls quivered. She whined in confusion, broke off the chain, ran three laps around the house, and hid under the car.

After coaxing her out to rinse off the foaming mess, she still smelled like a skunk — but more like a pickled skunk!

– Debbie Bixby, Riddle, Oregon

THIRD PRIZE

When I was growing up, there was a hard-and-fast rule in our family: You had to eat what was on your plate before you could be excused. On rare occasions, Mom served green peas — a nightmare for a child who grew up raising rabbits that were fed alfalfa pellets. The thought of . . . how could anyone?

I had been sitting at the table, moving peas from one side of my plate to the other, trying to convince my parents I had eaten some. They weren't convinced. So, after the rest of the family had finished, I found myself sitting alone and staring at the peas, now coated with a white film.

My mind became filled with how to dispose of them without actually swallowing them. My shorts didn't have pockets, and I was desperate for a solution.

I turned in my chair and there it was: an electrical outlet. I picked up a pea, held it next to the outlet, and with a butter knife I pushed it in. Not a smart thing to do. I started shaking, the lights went out, and smoke went up the wall. Dad ran into the kitchen, picked up a broom, and knocked me across the room. The melted remains of the butter knife fell to the floor.

From that day forward I never had to eat green peas. And I had a whole new outlook on life, a view from the other side of the table.

– Cindy Hayes, Edmond, Oklahoma

HONORABLE MENTION

I was making a surprise birthday dinner for my husband and was busy baking a chocolate cake with chocolate frosting, my husband's favorite. Where could I hide this beautiful cake, complete with candles?

I looked around the kitchen and spied the dryer. The perfect place to hide a cake! Into the dryer went my surprise. Then, for some unknown reason, call it habit, call it stupidity, I pushed the dryer knob. The dryer flipped on and off. The cake flipped, and I flipped, really losing my cool.

By pure luck the plate wasn't broken, and half the cake didn't look too bad. Tearfully I put the cake back together. We did eat it. In retrospect, I wouldn't expect anyone to eat "dryer cake" again. But then, I don't plan to make another one.

– Ruth Bixby, Cuba, New York

ANNOUNCING
The 1995 ESSAY CONTEST

The Best Tried-and-True Way to Cure a Headache

For 1995, cash prizes (first prize, $50; second prize, $25; third prize, $15) will be awarded for the best 200-word essays on this topic: "The Best Tried-and-True Way to Cure a Headache." All entries become the property of Yankee Publishing Incorporated, which reserves all rights to the materials submitted. Winners will be announced in the 1996 edition of *The Old Farmer's Almanac.* Deadline is February 1, 1995. Address: Essay Contest, *The Old Farmer's Almanac,* P.O. Box 520, Dublin, NH 03444.

Secrets of the Zodiac

Famous Debowelled Man of the Signs

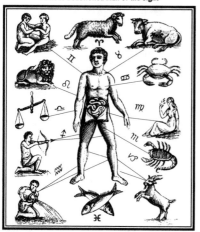

Ancient astrologers associated each of the signs with a part of the body over which they felt the sign held some influence. The first sign of the zodiac — Aries — was attributed to the head, with the rest of the signs moving down the body, ending with Pisces at the feet.

♈	Aries, head.	ARI Mar. 21-Apr. 20
♉	Taurus, neck.	TAU Apr. 21-May 20
♊	Gemini, arms.	GEM May 21-June 20
♋	Cancer, breast.	CAN June 21-July 22
♌	Leo, heart.	LEO July 23-Aug. 22
♍	Virgo, belly.	VIR Aug. 23-Sept. 22
♎	Libra, reins.	LIB Sept. 23-Oct. 22
♏	Scorpio, secrets.	SCO Oct. 23-Nov. 22
♐	Sagittarius, thighs.	SAG Nov. 23-Dec. 21
♑	Capricorn, knees.	CAP Dec. 22-Jan. 19
♒	Aquarius, legs.	AQU Jan. 20-Feb. 19
♓	Pisces, feet.	PSC Feb. 20-Mar. 20

Astrology and Astronomy

In ancient times, astrology and astronomy were the same science. "Wise men" looked into the heavens, noted the passage of planets through the vault of the sky, and summarily attached meaning to these events; their counsel was sought by kings.

During the Middle Ages and beyond, the separation of church and state and the rise of science had a negative effect on astrology. Matters of the spirit were given over to religious institutions, and the business of everyday living was subjected to the scientific model. Astronomy became solely the study of the physical properties of the universe.

Yet astrology persists. This ancient art attempts to explain human behavior and even predict the future according to the astrological placement of the two luminaries (the Sun and the Moon) and the eight known planets (Mercury, Venus, Mars, Jupiter, Saturn, Uranus, Neptune, and Pluto) in the 12 signs of the zodiac. It is important to note that *the planetary placements through the signs of the zodiac are not the same astrologically as they are astronomically.* This is because astrologers figure according to a 26,000-year cycle they have identified as the Great Ages; astronomy takes into account precession of the equinoxes and the actual placement of the planets and constellations in the heavens.

Astrologers believe we have spent the past 2,000 years in the Age of Pisces, exploring the realm of compassion and religion. We are now poised on the brink of the Age of Aquarius. Astrologers believe this age will be one of intuition and self-knowledge. As Aquarius is concerned with all of humanity, global awareness and male-female equality will increase.

Astrology as a Tool

Astrology is the study of cycles. Just as the Moon waxes and wanes, everything in life is in a state of flux. An astrologer can provide an individual birth chart to describe a person's initial orientation in time and space. An individual's Sun sign (the astrological sign in which the Sun was located at birth) will describe the active, conscious personality; one's work should be compatible with the qualities of this sign. The Moon, on the other hand, shows the passive personality as well as the habits. One's emotional well-being is nourished by the qualities of the sign the Moon occupied at birth.

Many readers have asked us which signs are best suited for various activities. Astrologers use Moon signs for this determination; a month-by-month chart showing appropriate times for certain activities is provided on page 182. (To find the astrological place of the Moon in the zodiac, as well as detailed gardening information, see page 183. *Do not confuse this with the astronomical position of the Moon, as listed on the Left-Hand Calendar Pages [52-78]; because of precession and other factors the astrological and astronomical zodiacs do not agree.*)

A MONTH-BY-MONTH ASTROLOGICAL TIMETABLE FOR 1995

Herewith we provide the following yearlong chart, based on the Moon signs, showing the appropriate times each month for certain activities. **BY CELESTE LONGACRE**

	JAN.	FEB.	MAR.	APR.	MAY	JUNE	JULY	AUG.	SEPT.	OCT.	NOV.	DEC.
Give up smoking	17, 22	18, 27	26, 30	22, 26	19, 24	15, 19	17, 26	13, 23	10, 20	17, 21	13, 18	11, 16
Begin diet to lose weight	17, 22	18, 27	26, 30	22, 26	19, 24	15, 19	17, 26	13, 23	10, 20	17, 21	13, 18	11, 16
Begin diet to gain weight	2, 7	3, 13	2, 7, 12	6, 13	6, 11	2, 7, 11, 30	4, 9	1, 9, 28	1, 5	3, 7, 30	3, 26, 30	24, 28
Buy clothes	17, 18, 22, 23	14, 15, 18, 19	13, 14, 17, 18	9, 10, 14, 15	7, 8, 11, 12	3, 4, 8, 9	1, 5, 6, 28, 29	1, 2, 24, 25, 26	20, 21, 25, 26	18, 19, 22, 23	14, 15, 19, 20	11, 12, 16, 17
Seek favors	3, 4, 31	27, 28	26, 27	22, 23	19, 20	16, 17	13, 14	10, 11	6, 7	3, 4, 31	1, 27, 28	24, 25
Dental care	20, 21	16, 17	8, 9	12, 13	9, 10	5, 6	3, 4	26, 27	27, 28	20, 21	16, 17	14, 15
End old projects	1, 30	27, 28	29, 30	28, 29	27, 28	26, 27	25, 26	24, 25	22, 23	22, 23	21, 22	20, 21
Hair care	22, 23	18, 19	17, 18	14, 15	11, 12	8, 9	5, 6	1, 2, 29	25, 26	22, 23	19, 20	16, 17
Seek pleasures	24, 25	20, 21	19, 20	16, 17	13, 14	10, 11	7, 8	3, 4	1, 27, 28	25, 26	21, 22	18, 19
Start a new project	2, 3	1, 2	2, 3	1, 30	1, 2	29, 30	29, 30	27, 28	25, 26	26, 27	23, 24	23, 24
Fishing	26, 27	22, 23	22, 23	18, 19	15, 16	12, 13	9, 10	6, 7	2, 3, 29, 30	26, 27	23, 24	20, 21
Breed	24, 25	20, 21	19, 20	16, 17	13, 14	10, 11	7, 8	3, 4	1, 27, 28	25, 26	21, 22	18, 19
Destroy pests/weeds	7, 8, 9	4, 5	3, 4, 31	1, 27, 28	24, 25	20, 21	17, 18, 19	14, 15	10, 11	8, 9	4, 5	1, 2, 29, 30
Graft or pollinate	6, 15, 16	2, 3, 11, 12	1, 2, 11, 12	7, 8, 25, 26	4, 5, 22, 23	1, 2, 18, 19	15, 16, 25, 26	12, 13, 22, 23	8, 9, 18, 19	5, 6, 15, 16	2, 3, 11, 30	9, 10, 26, 27
Harvest above-ground crops	10, 11	7, 8	6, 7	2, 3	9, 10	6, 7	3, 4	3, 4	27, 28	25, 26	2, 3	4, 5
Harvest root crops	20, 21	16, 17	20, 21	16, 17	27, 28	23, 24	20, 21	16, 17	13, 14	10, 11, 12	8, 17, 18	13, 14, 15
Begin logging	1, 2, 29, 30	25, 26	24, 25	20, 21, 22	18, 19	14, 15	12, 13	8, 9	4, 5	2, 3, 30	25, 26	23, 24
Prune or cut hay	8, 9	4, 5	3, 4, 5	1, 27, 28	25, 26, 27	21, 22	17, 18, 19	14, 15, 16	11, 12	8, 9	4, 5	1, 2, 29
Seed grain	5, 6, 7	2, 3	2, 11, 12	7, 8	4, 5, 6	1, 2, 29	8, 9	3, 4, 31	8, 27, 28	5, 6, 7, 26	2, 3, 30	27, 28
Set posts or pour concrete	1, 2, 29, 30	25, 26	24, 25	20, 21, 22	18, 19	14, 15	12, 13	8, 9	4, 5	2, 3, 30	25, 26	23, 24
Slaughter	24, 25	21, 22	20, 21	16, 17	13, 14	10, 11	7, 8	3, 4, 31	27, 28	24, 25	21, 22	18, 19
Wean	26, 27	22, 23	22, 23	18, 19	15, 16	12, 13	9, 10	5, 6, 7	2, 3	26, 27	23, 24	20, 21
Castrate animals	3, 4	27, 28	26, 27	22, 23	19, 20	16, 17	13, 14	10, 11	6, 7	3, 4	27, 28	24, 25

GARDENING BY THE MOON'S SIGN

Astrology is not the same science as astronomy. The actual sign placements of planets differ drastically between these two bodies of knowledge. For a fuller explanation see "Secrets of the Zodiac," page 180. The *astrological* placement of the Moon, by sign, is given in the chart below. For planting, the most fertile signs are the three water signs: Cancer, Scorpio, and Pisces. Taurus, Virgo, and Capricorn would be good second choices for sowing. Above-ground crops like to be planted between the new Moon and full Moon (waxing), whereas the root and below-ground crops prefer to be sown after the full Moon and before the new Moon (waning). The dates for the Moon's phases can be found on pages 52-78.

Weeding and plowing are best done when the Moon occupies the signs of Aries, Gemini, Leo, Sagittarius, or Aquarius. Insect pests can also be handled at those times. Transplanting and grafting are best done under a Cancer, Scorpio, or Pisces Moon. Pruning is best done under an Aries, Leo, or Sagittarius Moon, with growth encouraged during the waxing stage and discouraged during waning. Clean out the garden shed when the Moon occupies Virgo so the work will flow smoothly. Fences or permanent beds can be built or mended when Capricorn predominates. Avoid indecision when under the Libra Moon.

MOON'S PLACE IN THE ASTROLOGICAL ZODIAC

	NOV. 94	DEC. 94	JAN. 95	FEB. 95	MAR. 95	APR. 95	MAY 95	JUNE 95	JULY 95	AUG. 95	SEPT. 95	OCT. 95	NOV. 95	DEC. 95
1	LIB	SCO	CAP	PSC	PSC	ARI	GEM	CAN	LEO	LIB	SCO	CAP	PSC	ARI
2	LIB	SAG	CAP	PSC	PSC	TAU	GEM	CAN	VIR	LIB	SAG	CAP	PSC	ARI
3	SCO	SAG	AQU	PSC	ARI	TAU	GEM	LEO	VIR	SCO	SAG	AQU	PSC	TAU
4	SCO	CAP	AQU	ARI	ARI	GEM	CAN	LEO	VIR	SCO	CAP	AQU	ARI	TAU
5	SAG	CAP	PSC	ARI	TAU	GEM	CAN	VIR	LIB	SAG	CAP	PSC	ARI	TAU
6	SAG	AQU	PSC	TAU	TAU	GEM	LEO	VIR	LIB	SAG	AQU	PSC	TAU	GEM
7	CAP	AQU	ARI	TAU	TAU	CAN	LEO	LIB	SCO	CAP	AQU	ARI	TAU	GEM
8	CAP	PSC	ARI	TAU	GEM	CAN	LEO	LIB	SCO	CAP	PSC	ARI	GEM	CAN
9	AQU	PSC	ARI	GEM	GEM	LEO	VIR	LIB	SAG	AQU	PSC	ARI	GEM	CAN
10	AQU	PSC	TAU	GEM	CAN	LEO	VIR	SCO	SAG	AQU	AQU	ARI	TAU	GEM	CAN
11	PSC	ARI	TAU	CAN	CAN	VIR	LIB	SCO	CAP	AQU	ARI	TAU	CAN	LEO
12	PSC	ARI	GEM	CAN	CAN	VIR	LIB	SAG	CAP	PSC	TAU	CAN	LEO
13	PSC	TAU	GEM	LEO	LEO	VIR	SCO	SAG	AQU	PSC	TAU	GEM	CAN	VIR
14	ARI	TAU	GEM	LEO	LEO	LIB	SCO	CAP	AQU	ARI	TAU	GEM	LEO	VIR
15	ARI	TAU	CAN	LEO	VIR	LIB	SAG	CAP	PSC	ARI	GEM	CAN	LEO	VIR
16	TAU	GEM	CAN	VIR	VIR	SCO	SAG	AQU	PSC	TAU	GEM	CAN	VIR	LIB
17	TAU	GEM	LEO	VIR	LIB	SCO	CAP	AQU	ARI	TAU	CAN	LEO	VIR	LIB
18	TAU	CAN	LEO	LIB	LIB	SAG	CAP	PSC	ARI	GEM	CAN	LEO	LIB	SCO
19	GEM	CAN	VIR	LIB	SCO	SAG	AQU	PSC	ARI	GEM	CAN	LEO	LIB	SCO
20	GEM	CAN	VIR	SCO	SCO	CAP	AQU	ARI	TAU	GEM	LEO	VIR	LIB	SAG
21	CAN	LEO	VIR	SCO	SAG	CAP	PSC	ARI	TAU	CAN	LEO	VIR	SCO	SAG
22	CAN	LEO	LIB	SAG	SAG	AQU	PSC	TAU	GEM	CAN	VIR	LIB	SCO	CAP
23	CAN	VIR	LIB	SAG	SAG	AQU	PSC	TAU	GEM	CAN	VIR	LIB	SAG	CAP
24	LEO	VIR	SCO	CAP	CAP	PSC	ARI	TAU	GEM	LEO	VIR	SCO	SAG	AQU
25	LEO	LIB	SCO	CAP	CAP	PSC	ARI	GEM	CAN	LEO	LIB	SCO	CAP	AQU
26	VIR	LIB	SAG	CAP	AQU	ARI	TAU	GEM	CAN	VIR	LIB	SAG	CAP	PSC
27	VIR	LIB	SAG	AQU	AQU	ARI	TAU	CAN	LEO	VIR	SCO	SAG	AQU	PSC
28	LIB	SCO	CAP	AQU	PSC	ARI	TAU	CAN	LEO	LIB	SCO	CAP	AQU	ARI
29	LIB	SCO	CAP	—	PSC	TAU	GEM	CAN	LEO	LIB	SAG	CAP	PSC	ARI
30	SCO	SAG	AQU	—	ARI	TAU	GEM	LEO	VIR	SCO	SAG	AQU	PSC	ARI
31	—	SAG	AQU	—	ARI	—	CAN	—	VIR	SCO	—	AQU	—	TAU

The ASTROLOGER'S GUIDE TO THE

ARIES
(March 21-April 20)

You love the chase. Quick, alert, and able, you enjoy the challenge of meeting new people and broadening your so- cial base. You are good at beginnings, and commitment comes from you when you feel no threat to your own freedom. You want your relationships to remain interesting. **Best matches:** Leo, Sagittarius, Aries, Gemini, or Aquarius. Libra can balance you, while Scorpio and Capricorn intrigue you.

TAURUS
(April 21-May 20)

You seek monogamy. Loyal, steadfast, and trustworthy, you enjoy the special security that comes with a reliable relationship. You love to snuggle in your nest and will spend countless hours (and dollars) making it exceedingly comfortable. You also possess an excellent sense of taste and often provide your mate with the most delectable entrées. **Best matches:** Capricorn, Virgo, Taurus, Cancer, or Pisces. Scorpio can balance you; you like Leo's style and Libra's grace.

by Celeste Longacre

GEMINI
(May 21-June 20)

You want diversity. Witty, spontaneous, and entertaining, you (like your element, the air) want to dance, dazzle, and leave a wake. You thrive on movement and change. Ideas are very important to you and you desire a partner who will stimulate and challenge your mind. You will stay only with a person who allows you to maintain your freedom. **Best matches:** Aquarius, Libra, Aries, Leo, or Gemini. Sagittarius can balance you, and Virgo shares your love for words.

CANCER
(June 21-July 22)

You desire a home and family. Sympathetic, kind, and loyal, you see your loved ones as the clan that makes life worth living. You honor traditions and cling to mementos. You are a good catch, as you will place your partner's needs above all others. You want a mate who shares your wish for a dynasty and who will return your steadfast devotion. **Best matches:** Scorpio, Pisces, Cancer, Taurus, or Virgo. Capricorn can balance you, and Leo is more similar to you than you might suspect.

LEO
(July 23-August 22)

You seek somebody special. Dashing, vibrant, and full of personality, you have the ability to dazzle and charm. Often found in the center of your own group of admirers, your stories are legendary and adventurous. You want an admiring partner who will appreciate your humor and generosity. **Best matches:** Aries, Sagittarius, Libra, Gemini, or Leo. Aquarius can balance you, while Pisces and Cancer bring out your protective nature (Capricorn and Scorpio also fascinate you).

VIRGO
(August 23-September 22)

You prefer reliability. Organized, efficient, and capable, you can be counted on to remember the details and do the job right. Never sloppy or unkempt with externals, you want a partner who will respect your boundaries, participate in the upkeep of the residence, and squeeze the toothpaste from the bottom. You yourself always strive for perfection. Your hope is that your mate does, too. **Best matches:** Virgo, Taurus, Capricorn, or Cancer. Pisces can balance you, while Gemini shares your love of words, and Libra is more similar than you might suspect.

PERFECT MATE (How to Find One or Be One)

LIBRA
(September 23-October 22)

You want a true partnership. Graceful, social, and polite, you are always concerned with your impact upon others. More than any other sign, you have a constant need to be relating outward and will interact with your environment when other humans are not present. You therefore seek a mate to keep you company at home as well as out and about. **Best matches:** Libra, Gemini, Aquarius, Pisces, or Leo. Aries can balance you, while Taurus intrigues you, and Virgo is quite similar.

SCORPIO
(October 23-November 22)

You desire depth. Mysterious, magnetic, and powerful, you seek an emotional bond as well as a

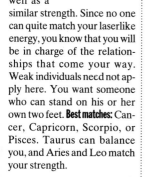

similar strength. Since no one can quite match your laserlike energy, you know that you will be in charge of the relationships that come your way. Weak individuals need not apply here. You want someone who can stand on his or her own two feet. **Best matches:** Cancer, Capricorn, Scorpio, or Pisces. Taurus can balance you, and Aries and Leo match your strength.

SAGITTARIUS
(November 23-December 21)

You seek a companion. Philosophical, energetic, and adventuresome, you treat life as a big game. Setting goals, meeting them, and setting new goals keep you going. You love the outdoors, the country, and the city and are often quite athletic. You want a partner who can keep up with your travels

but not one who will inhibit you. Freedom is very important to you. **Best matches:** Sagittarius, Aries, Leo, or Aquarius. Gemini can balance you, and Virgo appreciates your honesty.

CAPRICORN
(December 22-January 19)

You desire stability. Diligent, capable, and organized, you want life to fit into a structured pattern. You are well aware that society has many levels and you are not interested in landing on the bottom. Seeking a partner who shares this intention, you need to know what you can expect. Security is important. **Best matches:** Taurus, Virgo, Pisces, Scorpio, and Capricorn. Cancer can balance you and Aries' spontaneity attracts you.

AQUARIUS
(January 20-February 19)

You want excitement. Flamboyant, independent, and eccentric, you have a strong

need to be different from everybody else. Able to visualize the future and act accordingly, you are not particularly interested in the mundane or tradition. (Please note: You rare conservative types should go back and read Capricorn.) Freedom is important to you, and you won't stay with a mate who tries to tie you down. **Best matches:** Sagittarius, Gemini, Aries, or Aquarius. Leo can balance you, and Libra charms you.

PISCES
(February 20-March 20)

You seek acceptance. Gentle, considerate, and kind, your sensitive nature is unusually open to outside influences. You need a partner who will take the time to inquire about your day and understands

your periodic retreats into solitude. A bit of a tether can provide a grounded outlet for your creative energies. Warmth and a soft touch fill out the bill nicely. **Best matches:** Taurus, Cancer, Scorpio, Pisces, and Capricorn. Virgo can balance you, while you enjoy Leo's protectiveness and Libra's tactfulness. □□

Times, Tides, Frosts, and When to Plant

TIME CORRECTION TABLES

The times of sunrise/sunset, moonrise/moonset, and the rising and setting times of the planets and bright stars, are given for **Boston only** on pages 52-78, 40, and 44. Use the **Key Letter** shown to the right of each time on those pages with these tables to find the number of minutes that should be added to or subtracted from Boston time to give the correct time for your city. (Because of the complexities of calculation for different locations, times may not be precise to the minute.) If your city is not listed, find the city closest to you in both latitude and longitude and use those figures. **Boston's latitude is 42° 22' and longitude is 71° 03'.** Canadian cities appear at the end of the list. For a more complete explanation of the usage of Key Letters and these tables, see "How to Use This Almanac," page 30.

Time Zone Code: Atlantic Std. is -1; Eastern Std. is 0; Central Std. is 1; Mountain Std. is 2; Pacific Std. is 3; Alaska Std. is 4; Hawaii-Aleutian Std. is 5.

City	North Latitude ° '	West Longitude ° '	Time Zone Code	A min.	B min.	C min.	D min.	E min.
Aberdeen, SD	45 28	98 29	1	+37	+44	+49	+54	+59
Akron, OH	41 5	81 31	0	+46	+43	+41	+39	+37
Albany, NY	42 39	73 45	0	+ 9	+10	+10	+11	+11
Albert Lea, MN	43 39	93 22	1	+24	+26	+28	+31	+33
Albuquerque, NM	35 5	106 39	2	+45	+32	+22	+11	+ 2
Alexandria, LA	31 18	92 27	1	+58	+40	+26	+ 9	− 3
Allentown-Bethlehem, PA	40 36	75 28	0	+23	+20	+17	+14	+12
Amarillo, TX	35 12	101 50	1	+85	+73	+63	+52	+43
Anchorage, AK	61 10	149 59	4	−46	+27	+71	+122	+171
Asheville, NC	35 36	82 33	0	+67	+55	+46	+35	+27
Atlanta, GA	33 45	84 24	0	+79	+65	+53	+40	+30
Atlantic City, NJ	39 22	74 26	0	+23	+17	+13	+ 8	+ 4
Augusta, GA	33 28	81 58	0	+70	+55	+44	+30	+19
Augusta, ME	44 19	69 46	0	−12	− 8	− 5	− 1	0
Austin, TX	30 16	97 45	1	+82	+62	+47	+29	+15
Bakersfield, CA	35 23	119 1	3	+33	+21	+12	+ 1	− 7
Baltimore, MD	39 17	76 37	0	+32	+26	+22	+17	+13
Bangor, ME	44 48	68 46	0	−18	−13	− 9	− 5	− 1
Barstow, CA	34 54	117 1	3	+27	+14	+ 4	− 7	−16
Baton Rouge, LA	30 27	91 11	1	+55	+36	+21	+ 3	−10
Beaumont, TX	30 5	94 6	1	+67	+48	+32	+14	0
Bellingham, WA	48 45	122 29	3	0	+13	+24	+37	+47
Bemidji, MN	47 28	94 53	1	+14	+26	+34	+44	+52
Berlin, NH	44 28	71 11	0	− 7	− 3	0	+ 3	+ 7
Billings, MT	45 47	108 30	2	+16	+23	+29	+35	+40
Biloxi, MS	30 24	88 53	1	+46	+27	+11	− 5	−19
Binghamton, NY	42 6	75 55	0	+20	+19	+19	+18	+18
Birmingham, AL	33 31	86 49	1	+30	+15	+ 3	−10	−20
Bismarck, ND	46 48	100 47	1	+41	+50	+58	+66	+73
Boise, ID	43 37	116 12	2	+55	+58	+60	+62	+64
Brattleboro, VT	42 51	72 34	0	+ 4	+ 5	+ 5	+ 6	+ 7
Bridgeport, CT	41 11	73 11	0	+12	+10	+ 8	+ 6	+ 4
Brockton, MA	42 5	71 1	0	0	0	0	0	− 1
Brownsville, TX	25 54	97 30	1	+91	+66	+46	+23	+ 5
Buffalo, NY	42 53	78 52	0	+29	+30	+30	+31	+32
Burlington, VT	44 29	73 13	0	0	+ 4	+ 8	+12	+15
Butte, MT	46 1	112 32	2	+31	+39	+45	+52	+57
Cairo, IL	37 0	89 11	1	+29	+20	+12	+ 4	− 2
Camden, NJ	39 57	75 7	0	+24	+19	+16	+12	+ 9
Canton, OH	40 48	81 23	0	+46	+43	+41	+38	+36
Cape May, NJ	38 56	74 56	0	+26	+20	+15	+ 9	+ 5
Carson City–Reno, NV	39 10	119 46	3	+25	+19	+14	+ 9	+ 5

City	North Latitude ° '		West Longitude ° '		Time Zone Code	Key Letters				
						A min.	B min.	C min.	D min.	E min.
Casper, WY	42	51	106	19	2	+19	+19	+20	+21	+22
Chadron, NE	42	50	103	0	2	+ 5	+ 6	+ 7	+ 8	+ 9
Charleston, SC	32	47	79	56	0	+64	+48	+36	+21	+10
Charleston, WV	38	21	81	38	0	+55	+48	+42	+35	+30
Charlotte, NC	35	14	80	51	0	+61	+49	+39	+28	+19
Charlottesville, VA	38	2	78	30	0	+43	+35	+29	+22	+17
Chattanooga, TN	35	3	85	19	0	+79	+67	+57	+45	+36
Cheboygan, MI	45	39	84	29	0	+40	+47	+53	+59	+64
Cheyenne, WY	41	8	104	49	2	+19	+16	+14	+12	+11
Chicago-Oak Park, IL	41	52	87	38	1	+ 7	+ 6	+ 6	+ 5	+ 4
Cincinnati-Hamilton, OH	39	6	84	31	0	+64	+58	+53	+48	+44
Cleveland-Lakewood, OH	41	30	81	42	0	+45	+43	+42	+40	+39
Columbia, SC	34	0	81	2	0	+65	+51	+40	+27	+17
Columbus, OH	39	57	83	1	0	+55	+51	+47	+43	+40
Cordova, AK	60	33	145	45	4	−55	+13	+55	+103	+149
Corpus Christi, TX	27	48	97	24	1	+86	+64	+46	+25	+ 9
Craig, CO	40	31	107	33	2	+32	+28	+25	+22	+20
Dallas-Fort Worth, TX	32	47	96	48	1	+71	+55	+43	+28	+17
Danville, IL	40	8	87	37	1	+13	+ 9	+ 6	+ 2	0
Danville, VA	36	36	79	23	0	+51	+41	+33	+24	+17
Davenport, IA	41	32	90	35	1	+20	+19	+17	+16	+15
Dayton, OH	39	45	84	10	0	+61	+56	+52	+48	+44
Decatur, AL	34	36	86	59	1	+27	+14	+ 4	− 7	−17
Decatur, IL	39	51	88	57	1	+19	+15	+11	+ 7	+ 4
Denver-Boulder, CO	39	44	104	59	2	+24	+19	+15	+11	+ 7
Des Moines, IA	41	35	93	37	1	+32	+31	+30	+28	+27
Detroit-Dearborn, MI	42	20	83	3	0	+47	+47	+47	+47	+47
Dubuque, IA	42	30	90	41	1	+17	+18	+18	+18	+18
Duluth, MN	46	47	92	6	1	+ 6	+16	+23	+31	+38
Durham, NC	36	0	78	55	0	+51	+40	+31	+21	+13
Eastport, ME	44	54	67	0	0	−26	−20	−16	−11	− 8
Eau Claire, WI	44	49	91	30	1	+12	+17	+21	+25	+29
El Paso, TX	31	45	106	29	2	+53	+35	+22	+ 6	− 6
Elko, NV	40	50	115	46	3	+ 3	0	− 1	− 3	− 5
Ellsworth, ME	44	33	68	25	0	−18	−14	−10	− 6	− 3
Erie, PA	42	7	80	5	0	+36	+36	+35	+35	+35
Eugene, OR	44	3	123	6	3	+21	+24	+27	+30	+33
Fairbanks, AK	64	48	147	51	4	−127	+ 2	+61	+131	+205
Fall River– New Bedford, MA	41	42	71	9	0	+ 2	+ 1	0	0	− 1
Fargo, ND	46	53	96	47	1	+24	+34	+42	+50	+57
Flagstaff, AZ	35	12	111	39	2	+64	+52	+42	+31	+22
Flint, MI	43	1	83	41	0	+47	+49	+50	+51	+52
Fort Randall, AK	55	10	162	47	4	+62	+99	+124	+153	+179
Fort Scott, KS	37	50	94	42	1	+49	+41	+34	+27	+21
Fort Smith, AR	35	23	94	25	1	+55	+43	+33	+22	+14
Fort Wayne, IN	41	4	85	9	0	+60	+58	+56	+54	+52
Fort Yukon, AK	66	34	145	16	4	+30	−18	+50	+131	+227
Fresno, CA	36	44	119	47	3	+32	+22	+15	+ 6	0
Gallup, NM	35	32	108	45	2	+52	+40	+31	+20	+11
Galveston, TX	29	18	94	48	1	+72	+52	+35	+16	+ 1
Gary, IN	41	36	87	20	1	+ 7	+ 6	+ 4	+ 3	+ 2
Glasgow, MT	48	12	106	38	2	− 1	+11	+21	+32	+42
Grand Forks, ND	47	55	97	3	1	+21	+33	+43	+53	+62
Grand Island, NE	40	55	98	21	1	+53	+51	+49	+46	+44
Grand Junction, CO	39	4	108	33	2	+40	+34	+29	+24	+20
Great Falls, MT	47	30	111	17	2	+20	+31	+39	+49	+58

City	North Latitude ° '		West Longitude ° '		Time Zone Code	Key Letters A min.	B min.	C min.	D min.	E min.
Green Bay, WI	44	31	88	0	1	0	+ 3	+ 7	+11	+14
Greensboro, NC	36	4	79	47	0	+54	+43	+35	+25	+17
Hagerstown, MD	39	39	77	43	0	+35	+30	+26	+22	+18
Harrisburg, PA	40	16	76	53	0	+30	+26	+23	+19	+16
Hartford-New Britain, CT..	41	46	72	41	0	+ 8	+ 7	+ 6	+ 5	+ 4
Helena, MT	46	36	112	2	2	+27	+36	+43	+51	+57
Hilo, HI	19	44	155	5	5	+94	+62	+37	+ 7	−15
Honolulu, HI	21	18	157	52	5	+102	+72	+48	+19	− 1
Houston, TX	29	45	95	22	1	+73	+53	+37	+19	+ 5
Indianapolis, IN	39	46	86	10	0	+69	+64	+60	+56	+52
Ironwood, MI	46	27	90	9	1	0	+ 9	+15	+23	+29
Jackson, MI	42	15	84	24	0	+53	+53	+53	+52	+52
Jackson, MS	32	18	90	11	1	+46	+30	+17	+ 1	−10
Jacksonville, FL	30	20	81	40	0	+77	+58	+43	+25	+11
Jefferson City, MO	38	34	92	10	1	+36	+29	+24	+18	+13
Joplin, MO	37	6	94	30	1	+50	+41	+33	+25	+18
Juneau, AK	58	18	134	25	4	−76	−23	+10	+49	+86
Kalamazoo, MI	42	17	85	35	0	+58	+57	+57	+57	+57
Kanab, UT	37	3	112	32	2	+62	+53	+46	+37	+30
Kansas City, MO	39	1	94	20	1	+44	+37	+33	+27	+23
Keene, NH	42	56	72	17	0	+ 2	+ 3	+ 4	+ 5	+ 6
Ketchikan, AK	55	21	131	39	4	−62	−25	0	+29	+56
Knoxville, TN	35	58	83	55	0	+71	+60	+51	+41	+33
Kodiak, AK	57	47	152	24	4	0	+49	+82	+120	+154
LaCrosse, WI	43	48	91	15	1	+15	+18	+20	+22	+25
Lake Charles, LA	30	14	93	13	1	+64	+44	+29	+11	− 2
Lanai City, HI	20	50	156	55	5	+99	+69	+44	+15	− 6
Lancaster, PA	40	2	76	18	0	+28	+24	+20	+17	+13
Lansing, MI	42	44	84	33	0	+52	+53	+53	+54	+54
Las Cruces, NM	32	19	106	47	2	+53	+36	+23	+ 8	− 3
Las Vegas, NV	36	10	115	9	3	+16	+ 4	− 3	−13	−20
Lawrence-Lowell, MA	42	42	71	10	0	0	0	0	0	+ 1
Lewiston, ID	46	25	117	1	3	−12	− 3	+ 2	+10	+17
Lexington-Frankfort, KY.	38	3	84	30	0	+67	+59	+53	+46	+41
Liberal, KS	37	3	100	55	1	+76	+66	+59	+51	+44
Lihue, HI	21	59	159	23	5	+107	+77	+54	+26	+ 5
Lincoln, NE	40	49	96	41	1	+47	+44	+42	+39	+37
Little Rock, AR	34	45	92	17	1	+48	+35	+25	+13	+ 4
Los Angeles incl. Pasadena and Santa Monica, CA...	34	3	118	14	3	+34	+20	+ 9	− 3	−13
Louisville, KY	38	15	85	46	0	+72	+64	+58	+52	+46
Macon, GA	32	50	83	38	0	+79	+63	+50	+36	+24
Madison, WI	43	4	89	23	1	+10	+11	+12	+14	+15
Manchester-Concord, NH..	42	59	71	28	0	0	0	+ 1	+ 2	+ 3
McAllen, TX	26	12	98	14	1	+93	+69	+49	+26	+9
McGrath, AK	62	58	155	36	4	−52	+42	+93	+152	+213
Memphis, TN	35	9	90	3	1	+38	+26	+16	+ 5	− 3
Meridian, MS	32	22	88	42	1	+40	+24	+11	− 4	−15
Miami, FL	25	47	80	12	0	+88	+57	+37	+14	− 3
Miles City, MT	46	25	105	51	2	+ 3	+11	+18	+26	+32
Milwaukee, WI	43	2	87	54	1	+ 4	+ 6	+ 7	+ 8	+ 9
Minneapolis-St. Paul, MN	44	59	93	16	1	+18	+24	+28	+33	+37
Minot, ND	48	14	101	18	1	+36	+50	+59	+71	+81
Moab, UT	38	35	109	33	2	+46	+39	+33	+27	+22
Mobile, AL	30	42	88	3	1	+42	+23	+ 8	− 8	−22
Monroe, LA	32	30	92	7	1	+53	+37	+24	+ 9	− 1
Montgomery, AL	32	23	86	19	1	+31	+14	+ 1	−13	−25

City	North Latitude ° '		West Longitude ° '		Time Zone Code	Key Letters				
						A min.	B min.	C min.	D min.	E min.
Muncie, IN	40	12	85	23	0	+64	+60	+57	+53	+50
Nashville, TN	36	10	86	47	1	+22	+11	+ 3	− 6	−14
New Haven, CT	41	18	72	56	0	+11	+ 8	+ 7	+ 5	+ 4
New London, CT	41	22	72	6	0	+ 7	+ 5	+ 4	+ 2	+ 1
New Orleans, LA	29	57	90	4	1	+52	+32	+16	− 1	−15
New York, NY	40	45	74	0	0	+17	+14	+11	+ 9	+ 6
Newark–Irvington– East Orange, NJ	40	44	74	10	0	+17	+14	+12	+ 9	+ 7
Nome, AK	64	30	165	25	4	−48	+74	+132	+199	+271
Norfolk, VA	36	51	76	17	0	+38	+28	+21	+12	+ 5
North Platte, NE	41	8	100	46	1	+62	+60	+58	+56	+54
Norwalk-Stamford, CT	41	7	73	22	0	+13	+10	+ 9	+ 7	+ 5
Oakley, KS	39	8	100	51	1	+69	+63	+59	+53	+49
Ogden, UT	41	13	111	58	2	+47	+45	+43	+41	+40
Ogdensburg, NY	44	42	75	30	0	+ 8	+13	+17	+21	+25
Oklahoma City, OK	35	28	97	31	1	+67	+55	+46	+35	+26
Omaha, NE	41	16	95	56	1	+43	+40	+39	+37	+36
Orlando, FL	28	32	81	22	0	+80	+59	+42	+22	+ 6
Ortonville, MN	45	19	96	27	1	+30	+36	+40	+46	+51
Oshkosh, WI	44	1	88	33	1	+ 3	+ 6	+ 9	+12	+15
Parkersburg, WV	39	16	81	34	0	+52	+46	+42	+36	+32
Paterson, NJ	40	55	74	10	0	+17	+14	+12	+ 9	+ 7
Pendleton, OR	45	40	118	47	3	− 1	+ 4	+10	+16	+21
Pensacola, FL	30	25	87	13	1	+39	+20	+ 5	−12	−26
Peoria, IL	40	42	89	36	1	+19	+16	+14	+11	+ 9
Philadelphia-Chester, PA	39	57	75	9	0	+24	+19	+16	+12	+ 9
Phoenix, AZ	33	27	112	4	2	+71	+56	+44	+30	+20
Pierre, SD	44	22	100	21	1	+49	+53	+56	+60	+63
Pittsburgh-McKeesport, PA.	40	26	80	0	0	+42	+38	+35	+32	+29
Pittsfield, MA	42	27	73	15	0	+ 8	+ 8	+ 8	+ 8	+ 8
Pocatello, ID	42	52	112	27	2	+43	+44	+45	+46	+46
Poplar Bluff, MO	36	46	90	24	1	+35	+25	+17	+ 8	+ 1
Portland, ME	43	40	70	15	0	− 8	− 5	− 3	− 1	0
Portland, OR	45	31	122	41	3	+14 .	+20	+25	+31	+36
Portsmouth, NH	43	5	70	45	0	− 4	− 2	− 1	0	0
Presque Isle, ME	46	41	68	1	0	−29	−19	−12	− 4	+ 2
Providence, RI	41	50	71	25	0	+ 3	+ 2	+ 1	0	0
Pueblo, CO	38	16	104	37	2	+27	+20	+14	+ 7	+ 2
Raleigh, NC	35	47	78	38	0	+51	+39	+30	+20	+12
Rapid City, SD	44	5	103	14	2	+ 2	+ 5	+ 8	+11	+13
Reading, PA	40	20	75	56	0	+26	+22	+19	+16	+13
Redding, CA	40	35	122	24	3	+31	+27	+25	+22	+19
Richmond, VA	37	32	77	26	0	+41	+32	+25	+17	+11
Roanoke, VA	37	16	79	57	0	+51	+42	+35	+27	+21
Roswell, NM	33	24	104	32	2	+41	+26	+14	0	−10
Rutland, VT	43	37	72	58	0	+ 2	+ 5	+ 7	+ 9	+11
Sacramento, CA	38	35	121	30	3	+34	+27	+21	+15	+10
Salem, OR	44	57	123	1	3	+17	+23	+27	+31	+35
Salina, KS	38	50	97	37	1	+57	+51	+46	+40	+35
Salisbury, MD	38	22	75	36	0	+31	+23	+18	+11	+ 6
Salt Lake City, UT	40	45	111	53	2	+48	+45	+43	+40	+38
San Antonio, TX	29	25	98	30	1	+87	+66	+50	+31	+16
San Diego, CA	32	43	117	9	3	+33	+17	+ 4	− 9	−21
San Francisco incl. Oak- land and San Jose, CA	37	47	122	25	3	+40	+31	+25	+18	+12
Santa Fe, NM	35	41	105	56	2	+40	+28	+19	+ 9	0
Savannah, GA	32	5	81	6	0	+70	+54	+40	+25	+13

City	North Latitude ° '		West Longitude ° '		Time Zone Code	Key Letters				
						A min.	B min.	C min.	D min.	E min.
Scranton–Wilkes Barre, PA.	41	25	75	40	0	+21	+19	+18	+16	+15
Seattle-Tacoma-Olympia, WA..................	47	37	122	20	3	+ 3	+15	+24	+34	+42
Sheridan, WY	44	48	106	58	2	+14	+19	+23	+27	+31
Shreveport, LA................	32	31	93	45	1	+60	+44	+31	+16	+ 4
Sioux Falls, SD	43	33	96	44	1	+38	+40	+42	+44	+46
South Bend, IN.................	41	41	86	15	0	+62	+61	+60	+59	+58
Spartanburg, SC	34	56	81	57	0	+66	+53	+43	+32	+23
Spokane, WA	47	40	117	24	3	−16	− 4	+ 4	+14	+23
Springfield, IL..................	39	48	89	39	1	+22	+18	+14	+10	+ 6
Springfield-Holyoke, MA	42	6	72	36	0	+ 6	+ 6	+ 6	+ 5	+ 5
Springfield, MO...............	37	13	93	18	1	+45	+36	+29	+20	+14
St. Johnsbury, VT...........	44	25	72	1	0	− 4	0	+ 3	+ 7	+10
St. Joseph, MO	39	46	94	50	1	+43	+38	+35	+30	+27
St. Louis, MO...................	38	37	90	12	1	+28	+21	+16	+10	+ 5
St. Petersburg, FL	27	46	82	39	0	+87	+65	+47	+26	+10
Syracuse, NY	43	3	76	9	0	+17	+19	+20	+21	+22
Tallahassee, FL.................	30	27	84	17	0	+87	+68	+53	+35	+22
Tampa, FL.......................	27	57	82	27	0	+86	+64	+46	+25	+ 9
Terre Haute, IN................	39	28	87	24	0	+74	+69	+65	+60	+56
Texarkana, AR.................	33	26	94	3	1	+59	+44	+32	+18	+ 8
Toledo, OH	41	39	83	33	0	+52	+50	+49	+48	+47
Topeka, KS	39	3	95	40	1	+49	+43	+38	+32	+28
Traverse City, MI.............	44	46	85	38	0	+49	+54	+57	+62	+65
Trenton, NJ......................	40	13	74	46	0	+21	+17	+14	+11	+ 8
Trinidad, CO....................	37	10	104	31	2	+30	+21	+13	+ 5	0
Tucson, AZ	32	13	110	58	2	+70	+53	+40	+24	+12
Tulsa, OK	36	9	95	60	1	+59	+48	+40	+30	+22
Tupelo, MS......................	34	16	88	34	1	+35	+21	+10	− 2	−11
Vernal, UT.......................	40	27	109	32	2	+40	+36	+33	+30	+28
Walla Walla, WA	46	4	118	20	3	− 5	+ 2	+ 8	+15	+21
Washington, DC...............	38	54	77	1	0	+35	+28	+23	+18	+13
Waterbury-Meriden, CT..	41	33	73	3	0	+10	+ 9	+ 7	+ 6	+ 5
Waterloo, IA....................	42	30	92	20	1	+24	+24	+24	+25	+25
Wausau, WI	44	58	89	38	1	+ 4	+ 9	+13	+18	+22
West Palm Beach, FL	26	43	80	3	0	+79	+55	+36	+14	− 2
Wichita, KS	37	42	97	20	1	+60	+51	+45	+37	+31
Williston, ND...................	48	9	103	37	1	+46	+59	+69	+80	+90
Wilmington, DE	39	45	75	33	0	+26	+21	+18	+13	+10
Wilmington, NC	34	14	77	55	0	+52	+38	+27	+15	+ 5
Winchester, VA................	39	11	78	10	0	+38	+33	+28	+23	+19
Worcester, MA.................	42	16	71	48	0	+ 3	+ 2	+ 2	+ 2	+ 2
York, PA	39	58	76	43	0	+30	+26	+22	+18	+15
Youngstown, OH	41	6	80	39	0	+42	40	+38	+36	+34
Yuma, AZ.........................	32	43	114	37	2	+83	+67	+54	+40	+28
CANADA										
Calgary, AB	51	5	114	5	2	+13	+35	+50	+68	+84
Edmonton, AB	53	34	113	25	2	− 3	+26	+47	+72	+93
Halifax, NS.......................	44	38	63	35	−1	+21	+26	+29	+33	+37
Montreal, PQ	45	28	73	39	0	− 1	+ 4	+ 9	+15	+20
Ottawa, ON......................	45	25	75	43	0	+ 6	+13	+18	+23	+28
Saint John, NB.................	45	16	66	3	−1	+28	+34	+39	+44	+49
Saskatoon, SK..................	52	10	106	40	1	+37	+63	+80	+101	+119
Sydney, NS	46	10	60	10	−1	+ 1	+ 9	+15	+23	+28
Thunder Bay, ON	48	27	89	12	0	+47	+61	+71	+83	+93
Toronto, ON.....................	43	39	79	23	0	+28	+30	+32	+35	+37
Vancouver, BC.................	49	13	123	6	3	0	+15	+26	+40	+52
Winnipeg, MB	49	53	97	10	1	+12	+30	+43	+58	+71

THE TWILIGHT ZONE

How to Determine the Length of Twilight and the Times of Dawn and Dark

Twilight begins (or ends) when the Sun is about 18 degrees below the horizon, and the latitude of a place, together with the time of year, determines the length of twilight. To find the latitude of your city, or the city nearest you, consult the **Time Correction Tables,** page 186. Check the figures against the chart at right for the appropriate date, and you will have the length of twilight in your area.

It is also possible to determine the times dawn will break and darkness descend by applying the length of twilight taken from the chart at right, to the times of sunrise and sunset at any specific place. (Follow the instructions given in "How to Use This Almanac," page 30, to determine sunrise/sunset times for a given locality.) **Subtract** the length of twilight from the time of sunrise for dawn. **Add** the length of twilight to the time of sunset for dark.

Latitude	25° N to 30° N	31° N to 36° N	37° N to 42° N	43° N to 47° N	48° N to 49° N
	H M	H M	H M	H M	H M
Jan. 1 to Apr. 10	1 20	1 26	1 33	1 42	1 50
Apr. 11 to May 2	1 23	1 28	1 39	1 51	2 04
May 3 to May 14	1 26	1 34	1 47	2 02	2 22
May 15 to May 25	1 29	1 38	1 52	2 13	2 42
May 26 to July 22	1 32	1 43	1 59	2 27	—
July 23 to Aug. 3	1 29	1 38	1 52	2 13	2 42
Aug. 4 to Aug. 14	1 26	1 34	1 47	2 02	2 22
Aug. 15 to Sept. 5	1 23	1 28	1 39	1 51	2 04
Sept. 6 to Dec. 31	1 20	1 26	1 33	1 42	1 50

	Boston, MA (latitude 42° 22')	San Diego, CA (latitude 32° 43')
Sunrise, August 1	4:36 A.M.	5:09 A.M.
Length of twilight	−1:52	−1:38
Dawn breaks	2:44 A.M., EST	3:31 A.M., PST
Sunset, August 1	7:04 P.M.	6:55 P.M.
Length of twilight	+1:52	+1:38
Dark descends	8:56 P.M., EST	8:33 P.M., PST

TIDAL GLOSSARY

Apogean Tide: A monthly tide of decreased range that occurs when the Moon is farthest from the Earth (at apogee).

Diurnal: Applies to a location that normally experiences one high water and one low water during a tidal day of approximately 24 hours.

Mean Lower Low Water: The arithmetic mean of the lesser of a daily pair of low waters, observed over a specific 19-year cycle called the National Tidal Datum Epoch.

Neap Tide: A tide of decreased range occurring twice a month when the Moon is in quadrature (during the first and last quarter Moons, when the Sun and Moon are at right angles to each other relative to the Earth).

Perigean Tide: A monthly tide of increased range that occurs when the Moon is closest to the Earth (at perigee).

Semidiurnal: Having a period of half a tidal day. East Coast tides, for example, are semidiurnal, with two highs and two lows in approximately 24 hours.

Spring Tide: Named not for the season of spring, but from the German *springen* (to leap up). This tide of increased range occurs at times of syzygy (q.v.) each month. A spring tide also brings a lower low water.

Syzygy: Occurs twice a month when the Sun and Moon are in conjunction (lined up on the same side of the Earth at the new Moon) and when they are in opposition (on opposite sides of the Earth at the full Moon, though usually not so directly in line as to produce an eclipse). In either case, the gravitational effects of the Sun and Moon reinforce each other and tidal range is increased.

Vanishing Tide: A mixed tide of considerable inequality in the two highs or two lows, so that the "high low" may become indistinguishable from the "low high" or vice versa. The result is a vanishing tide, where no significant difference is apparent.

TIDE CORRECTIONS

Many factors affect the time and height of the tides: the coastal configuration, the time of the Moon's southing (crossing the meridian) at the place, and the phase of the Moon. This table of tidal corrections is a sufficiently accurate guide to the times and heights of the high water at the places shown. (Low tides occur approximately 6.25 hours before and after high tides.) No figures are shown for the West Coast or the Gulf of Mexico, since the method used in compiling this table does not apply there. For such places and elsewhere where precise accuracy is required, consult the Tide Tables published annually by the National Ocean Service, 1305 E. West Highway, Silver Spring, MD 20910; telephone 301-713-2815.

The figures for Full Sea on the Left-Hand Calendar Pages 52-78 are the times of high tide at Commonwealth Pier in Boston Harbor. (Where a dash is shown under Full Sea, it indicates that time of high water has occurred after midnight and so is recorded on the next date.) The heights of these tides are given on the Right-Hand Calendar Pages 53-79. The heights are reckoned from Mean Lower Low Water, and each day listed has a set of figures—upper for the morning, lower for the evening. To obtain the time and height of high water at any of the following places, apply the time difference to the daily times of high water at Boston (pages 52-78) and the height difference to the heights at Boston (pages 53-79).

	Time Difference: Hr. Min.	Height Feet
MAINE		
Bar Harbor	−0 34	+0.9
Belfast	−0 20	+0.4
Boothbay Harbor	−0 18	−0.8
Chebeague Island	−0 16	−0.6
Eastport	−0 28	+8.4
Kennebunkport	+0 04	−1.0
Machias	−0 28	+2.8
Monhegan Island	−0 25	−0.8
Old Orchard	0 00	−0.8
Portland	−0 12	−0.6
Rockland	−0 28	+0.1
Stonington	−0 30	+0.1
York	−0 09	−1.0
NEW HAMPSHIRE		
Hampton	+0 02	−1.3
Portsmouth	+0 11	−1.5
Rye Beach	−0 09	−0.9

	Time Difference: Hr. Min.	Height Feet
MASSACHUSETTS		
Annisquam	−0 02	−1.1
Beverly Farms	0 00	−0.5
Boston	0 00	0.0
Cape Cod Canal:		
East Entrance	−0 01	−0.8
West Entrance	−2 16	−5.9
Chatham Outer Coast	+0 30	−2.8
Inside	+1 54	*0.4
Cohasset	+0 02	−0.07
Cotuit Highlands	+1 15	*0.3
Dennis Port	+1 01	*0.4
Duxbury (Gurnet Pt.)	+0 02	−0.3
Fall River	−3 03	−5.0
Gloucester	−0 03	−0.8
Hingham	+0 07	0.0
Hull	+0 03	−0.2
Hyannis Port	+1 01	*0.3
Magnolia (Manchester)	−0 02	−0.7
Marblehead	−0 02	−0.4
Marion	−3 22	−5.4
Monument Beach	−3 08	−5.4
Nahant	−0 01	−0.5
Nantasket	+0 04	−0.1
Nantucket	−0 56	*0.3
Nauset Beach	+0 30	*0.6
New Bedford	−3 24	−5.7
Newburyport	+0 19	−1.8
Oak Bluffs	+0 30	*0.2
Onset (R.R. Bridge)	−2 16	−5.9
Plymouth	+0 05	0.0
Provincetown	+0 14	−0.4
Revere Beach	−0 01	−0.3
Rockport	−0 08	−1.0
Salem	0 00	−0.5
Scituate	−0 05	−0.7
Wareham	−3 09	−5.3
Wellfleet	+0 12	+0.5
West Falmouth	−3 10	−5.4
Westport Harbor	−3 22	−6.4
Woods Hole Little		
Harbor	−2 50	*0.2
Oceanographic Institute	−3 07	*0.2
RHODE ISLAND		
Bristol	−3 24	−5.3
Sakonnet	−3 44	−5.6
Narragansett Pier	−3 42	−6.2
Newport	−3 34	−5.9
Pt. Judith	−3 41	−6.3
Providence	−3 20	−4.8
Watch Hill	−2 50	−6.8
CONNECTICUT		
Bridgeport	+0 01	−2.6

Difference: Hr. Min.	Time	Height Feet		Difference: Hr. Min.	Time	Height Feet
Madison	–0 22	–2.3	Hatteras:			
New Haven	–0 11	–3.2	Ocean	–4 26	–6.0
New London	–1 54	–6.7	Inlet	–4 03	–7.4
Norwalk	+0 01	–2.2	Kitty Hawk	–4 14	–6.2
Old Lyme			**SOUTH CAROLINA**			
(Highway Bridge)	–0 30	–6.2	Charleston	–3 22	–4.3
Stamford	+0 01	–2.2	Georgetown	–1 48	*0.36
Stonington	–2 27	–6.6	Hilton Head	–3 22	–2.9
NEW YORK			Myrtle Beach	–3 49	–4.4
Coney Island	–3 33	–4.9	St. Helena			
Fire Island Lt.	–2 43	*0.1	Harbor Entrance	–3 15	–3.4
Long Beach	–3 11	–5.7	**GEORGIA**			
Montauk Harbor	–2 19	–7.4	Jekyll Island	–3 46	–2.9
New York City (Battery)	–2 43	–5.0	Saint Simon's Island	–2 50	–2.9
Oyster Bay	+0 04	–1.8	Savannah Beach:			
Port Chester	–0 09	–2.2	River Entrance	–3 14	–5.5
Port Washington	–0 01	–2.1	Tybee Light	–3 22	–2.7
Sag Harbor	–0 55	–6.8	**FLORIDA**			
Southampton	–4 20	*0.2	Cape Canaveral	–3 59	–6.0
(Shinnecock Inlet)			Daytona Beach	–3 28	–5.3
Willets Point	0 00	–2.3	Fort Lauderdale	–2 50	–7.2
NEW JERSEY			Fort Pierce Inlet	–3 32	–6.9
Asbury Park	–4 04	–5.3	Jacksonville			
Atlantic City	–3 56	–5.5	Railroad Bridge	–6 55	*0.10
Bay Head (Sea Girt)	–4 04	–5.3	Miami Harbor Entrance	–3 18	–7.0
Beach Haven	–1 43	*0.24	St. Augustine	–2 55	–4.9
Cape May	–3 28	–5.3	**CANADA**			
Ocean City	–3 06	–5.9	Alberton, P.E.I.	–5 45**	–7.5
Sandy Hook	–3 30	–5.0	Charlottetown, P.E.I.	–0 45**	–3.5
Seaside Park	–4 03	–5.4	Halifax, N.S.	–3 23	–4.5
PENNSYLVANIA			North Sydney, N.S.	–3 15	–6.5
Philadelphia	+2 40	–3.5	Saint John, N.B.	+0 30	–8.0
DELAWARE			St. John's, Nfld.	–4 00	–6.5
Cape Henlopen	–2 48	–5.3	Yarmouth, N.S.	–0 40	+3.0
Rehoboth Beach	–3 37	–5.7				
Wilmington	+1 56	–3.8				

* Where the difference in the "Height/Feet" column is so marked, height at Boston should be multiplied by this ratio.

** Varies widely; accurate only within 1½ hours. Consult local tide tables for precise times and heights.

Example: The conversion of the times and heights of the tides at Boston to those of Cape May, New Jersey, is given below:

Sample tide calculation July 10, 1995:

High tide Boston (p. 68)	8:45 A.M., EST
Correction for Cape May	–3:28 hrs.
High tide Cape May	5:17 A.M., EST
Tide height Boston (p. 69)	9.9 ft.
Correction for Cape May	–5.3 ft.
Tide height Cape May	4.6 ft.

MARYLAND

Annapolis	+6 23	–8.5
Baltimore	+7 59	–8.3
Cambridge	+5 05	–7.8
Havre de Grace	+11 21	–7.7
Point No Point	+2 28	–8.1
Prince Frederick		
(Plum Point)	+4 25	–8.5

VIRGINIA

Cape Charles	–2 20	–7.0
Hampton Roads	–2 02	–6.9
Norfolk	–2 06	–6.6
Virginia Beach	–4 00	–6.0
Yorktown	–2 13	–7.0

NORTH CAROLINA

Cape Fear	–3 55	–5.0
Cape Lookout	–4 28	–5.7
Currituck	–4 10	–5.8

OUTDOOR PLANTING TABLE

1 9 9 5

The best time to plant flowers and vegetables that bear crops above the ground is during the *light* of the Moon; that is, between the day the Moon is new to the day it is full. Flowering bulbs and vegetables that bear crops below ground should be planted during the *dark* of the Moon; that is, from the day

after it is full to the day before it is new again. The dates given here are based on the safe periods for planting in areas that receive frost, and the Moon's phases for 1995. Consult page 198 for dates of frosts and length of growing season. See calendar pages 52-78 for the exact days of the new and full Moons.

– Beth Krommes

☞ Above-Ground Crops Marked (*)   ☞ E means Early   ☞ L means Late

	Planting Dates	Moon Favorable	Planting Dates	Moon Favorable	Planting Dates	Moon Favorable
*Barley	5/15-6/21	5/29-6/12	3/15-4/7	3/15-16, 3/30-4/7	2/15-3/7	2/15, 3/1-7
*Beans (E)	5/7-6/21	5/7-14, 5/29-6/12	4/15-30	4/15, 4/29-30	3/15-4/7	3/15-16, 3/30-4/7
(L)	6/15-7/15	6/27-7/12	7/1-21	7/1-12	8/7-31	8/7-10, 8/25-31
Beets (E)	5/1-15	5/15	3/15-4/3	3/17-29	2/7-28	2/16-28
(L)	7/15-8/15	7/15-26, 8/11-15	8/15-31	8/15-24	9/1-30	9/9-23
*Broccoli (E)	5/15-31	5/29-31	3/7-31	3/7-16, 3/30-31	2/15-3/15	2/15, 3/1-15
Plants (L)	6/15-7/7	6/27-7/7	8/1-20	8/1-10	9/7-30	9/7-8, 9/24-30
*Brussels Sprouts	5/15-31	5/29-31	3/7-4/15	3/7-16, 3/30-4/15	2/11-3/20	2/11-15, 3/1-16
*Cabbage Plants	5/15-31	5/29-31	3/7-4/15	3/7-16, 3/30-4/15	2/11-3/20	2/11-15, 3/1-16
Carrots (E)	5/15-31	5/15-28	3/7-31	3/17-29	2/15-3/7	2/16-28
(L)	6/15-7/21	6/15-26, 7/13-21	7/7-31	7/13-26	8/1-9/7	8/11-24
*Cauliflower (E)	5/15-31	5/29-31	3/15-4/7	3/15-16, 3/30-4/7	2/15-3/7	2/15, 3/1-7
Plants (L)	6/15-7/21	6/27-7/12	7/1-8/7	7/1-12, 7/27-8/7	8/7-31	8/7-10, 8/25-31
*Celery Plants (E)	5/15-6/30	5/29-6/12, 6/27-30	3/7-31	3/7-16, 3/30-31	2/15-28	2/15
(L)	7/15-8/15	7/27-8/10	8/15-9/7	8/25-9/7	9/15-30	9/24-30
*Collards (E)	5/15-31	5/29-31	3/7-4/7	3/7-16, 3/30-4/7	2/11-3/20	2/11-15, 3/1-16
(L)	7/1-8/7	7/1-12, 7/27-8/7	8/15-31	8/25-31	9/7-30	9/7-8, 9/24-30
*Corn, Sweet (E)	5/10-6/15	5/10-14, 5/29-6/12	4/1-15	4/1-15	3/15-31	3/15-16, 3/30-31
(L)	6/15-30	6/27-30	7/7-21	7/7-12	8/7-31	8/7-10, 8/25-31
*Cucumber	5/7-6/20	5/7-14, 5/29-6/12	4/7-5/15	4/7-15, 4/29-5/14	3/7-4/15	3/7-16, 3/30-4/15
*Eggplant Plants	6/1-30	6/1-12, 6/27-30	4/7-5/15	4/7-15, 4/29-5/14	3/7-4/15	3/7-16, 3/30-4/15
*Endive (E)	5/15-31	5/29-31	4/7-5/15	4/7-15, 4/29-5/14	2/15-3/20	2/15, 3/1-16
(L)	6/7-30	6/7-12, 6/27-30	7/15-8/15	7/27-8/10	8/15-9/7	8/25-9/7
*Flowers (All)	5/7-6/21	5/7-14, 5/29-6/12	4/15-30	4/15, 4/29-30	3/15-4/7	3/15-16, 3/30-4/7
*Kale (E)	5/15-31	5/29-31	3/7-4/7	3/7-16, 3/30-4/7	2/11-3/20	2/11-15, 3/1-16

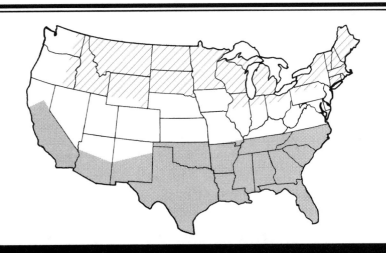

	Planting Dates	Moon Favorable	Planting Dates	Moon Favorable	Planting Dates	Moon Favorable
*Kale (L)	7/1-8/7	7/1-12, 7/27-8/7	8/15-31	8/25-31	9/7-30	9/7-8, 9/24-30
Leek Plants	5/15-31	5/15-28	3/7-4/7	3/17-29	2/15-4/15	2/16-28, 3/17-29
*Lettuce	5/15-6/30	5/29-6/12, 6/27-30	3/1-31	3/1-16, 3/30-31	2/15-3/7	2/15, 3/1-7
*Muskmelon	5/15-6/30	5/29-6/12, 6/27-30	4/15-5/7	4/15, 4/29-5/7	3/15-4/7	3/15-16, 3/30-4/7
Onion Sets	5/15-6/7	5/15-28	3/1-31	3/17-29	2/1-28	2/16-28
*Parsley	5/15-31	5/29-31	3/1-31	3/1-16, 3/30-31	2/20-3/15	3/1-15
Parsnips	4/1-30	4/16-28	3/7-31	3/17-29	1/15-2/4	1/17-29
*Peas (E)	4/15-5/7	4/15, 4/29-5/7	3/7-31	3/7-16, 3/30-31	1/15-2/7	1/15-16, 1/30-2/7
(L)	7/15-31	7/27-31	8/7-31	8/7-10, 8/25-31	9/15-30	9/24-30
*Pepper Plants	5/15-6/30	5/29-6/12, 6/27-30	4/1-30	4/1-15, 4/29-30	3/1-20	3/1-16
Potato	5/1-31	5/15-28	4/1-30	4/16-28	2/10-28	2/16-28
*Pumpkin	5/15-31	5/29-31	4/23-5/15	4/29-5/14	3/7-20	3/7-16
Radish (E)	4/15-30	4/16-28	3/7-31	3/17-29	1/21-3/1	1/21-29, 2/16-28
(L)	8/15-31	8/15-24	9/7-30	9/9-23	10/1-21	10/9-21
*Spinach (E)	5/15-31	5/29-31	3/15-4/20	3/15-16, 3/30-4/15	2/7-3/15	2/7-15, 3/1-15
(L)	7/15-9/7	7/27-8/10, 8/25-9/7	8/1-9/15	8/1-10, 8/25-9/8	10/1-21	10/1-8
*Squash	5/15-6/15	5/29-6/12	4/15-30	4/15, 4/29-30	3/15-4/15	3/15-16, 3/30-4/15
Sweet Potatoes	5/15-6/15	5/15-28, 6/13-15	4/21-30	4/21-28	3/23-4/6	3/23-29
*Swiss Chard	5/1-31	5/1-14, 5/29-31	3/15-4/15	3/15-16, 3/30-4/15	2/7-3/15	2/7-15, 3/1-15
*Tomato Plants	5/15-31	5/29-31	4/7-30	4/7-15, 4/29-30	3/7-20	3/7-16
Turnips (E)	4/7-30	4/16-28	3/15-31	3/17-29	1/20-2/15	1/20-29
(L)	7/1-8/15	7/13-26, 8/11-15	8/1-20	8/11-20	9/1-10/15	9/9-23, 10/9-15
*Watermelon	5/15-6/30	5/29-6/12, 6/27-30	4/15-5/7	4/15, 4/29-5/7	3/15-4/7	3/15-16, 3/30-4/7
*Wheat, Winter	8/11-9/15	8/25-9/8	9/15-10/20	9/24-10/8	10/15-12/7	10/23-11/7, 11/22-12/6
Spring	4/7-30	4/7-15, 4/29-30	3/1-20	3/1-16	2/15-28	2/15

FROSTS AND GROWING SEASONS

Courtesy of National Climatic Center

Dates given are normal averages for a light freeze (32° F); local weather and topography may cause considerable variations. The possibility of frost occurring after the spring dates and before the fall dates is 50 percent. The classification of freeze temperatures is usually based on their effect on plants, with the following commonly accepted categories: **Light freeze:** 29° F to 32° F — tender plants killed, with little destructive effect on other vegetation. **Moderate freeze:** 25° F to 28° F — widely destructive effect on most vegetation, with heavy damage to fruit blossoms, tender, and semihardy plants. **Severe freeze:** 24° F and colder — heavy damage to most plants.

CITY	Growing Season (Days)	Last Frost Spring	First Frost Fall	CITY	Growing Season (Days)	Last Frost Spring	First Frost Fall
Mobile, AL	272	Feb. 27	Nov. 26	North Platte, NE	136	May 11	Sept. 24
Juneau, AK	133	May 16	Sept. 26	Las Vegas, NV	259	Mar. 7	Nov. 21
Phoenix, AZ	308	Feb. 5	Dec. 15	Concord, NH	121	May 23	Sept. 22
Tucson, AZ	273	Feb. 28	Nov. 29	Newark, NJ	219	Apr. 4	Nov. 10
Pine Bluff, AR	234	Mar. 19	Nov. 8	Carlsbad, NM	223	Mar. 29	Nov. 7
Eureka, CA	324	Jan. 30	Dec. 15	Los Alamos, NM	157	May 8	Oct. 13
Sacramento, CA	289	Feb. 14	Dec. 1	Albany, NY	144	May 7	Sept. 29
San Francisco, CA	*	*	*	Syracuse, NY	170	Apr. 28	Oct. 16
Denver, CO	157	May 3	Oct. 8	Fayetteville, NC	212	Apr. 2	Oct. 31
Hartford, CT	167	Apr. 25	Oct. 10	Bismarck, ND	129	May 14	Sept. 20
Wilmington, DE	198	Apr. 13	Oct. 29	Akron, OH	168	May 3	Oct. 18
Miami, FL	*	*	*	Cincinnati, OH	195	Apr. 14	Oct. 27
Tampa, FL	338	Jan. 28	Jan. 3	Lawton, OK	217	Apr. 1	Nov. 5
Athens, GA	224	Mar. 28	Nov. 8	Tulsa, OK	218	Mar. 30	Nov. 4
Savannah, GA	250	Mar. 10	Nov. 15	Pendleton, OR	188	Apr. 15	Oct. 21
Boise, ID	153	May 8	Oct. 9	Portland, OR	217	Apr. 3	Nov. 7
Chicago, IL	187	Apr. 22	Oct. 26	Carlisle, PA	182	Apr. 20	Oct. 20
Springfield, IL	185	Apr. 17	Oct. 19	Williamsport, PA	168	Apr. 29	Oct. 15
Indianapolis, IN	180	Apr. 22	Oct. 20	Kingston, RI	144	May 8	Sept. 30
South Bend, IN	169	May 1	Oct. 18	Charleston, SC	253	Mar. 11	Nov. 20
Atlantic, IA	141	May 9	Sept. 28	Columbia, SC	211	Apr. 4	Nov. 2
Cedar Rapids, IA	161	Apr. 29	Oct. 7	Rapid City, SD	145	May 7	Sept. 29
Topeka, KS	175	Apr. 21	Oct. 14	Memphis, TN	228	Mar. 23	Nov. 7
Lexington, KY	190	Apr. 17	Oct. 25	Nashville, TN	207	Apr. 5	Oct. 29
Monroe, LA	242	Mar. 9	Nov. 7	Amarillo, TX	197	Apr. 14	Oct. 29
New Orleans, LA	288	Feb. 20	Dec. 5	Denton, TX	231	Mar. 25	Nov. 12
Portland, ME	143	May 10	Sept. 30	San Antonio, TX	265	Mar. 3	Nov. 24
Baltimore, MD	231	Mar. 26	Nov. 13	Cedar City, UT	134	May 20	Oct. 2
Worcester, MA	172	Apr. 27	Oct. 17	Spanish Fork, UT	156	May 8	Oct. 12
Lansing, MI	140	May 13	Sept. 30	Burlington, VT	142	May 11	Oct. 1
Marquette, MI	159	May 12	Oct. 19	Norfolk, VA	239	Mar. 23	Nov. 17
Duluth, MN	122	May 21	Sept. 21	Richmond, VA	198	Apr. 10	Oct. 26
Willmar, MN	152	May 4	Oct. 4	Seattle, WA	232	Mar. 24	Nov. 11
Columbus, MS	215	Mar. 27	Oct. 29	Spokane, WA	153	May 4	Oct. 5
Vicksburg, MS	250	Mar. 13	Nov. 18	Parkersburg, WV	175	Apr. 25	Oct. 18
Jefferson City, MO	173	Apr. 26	Oct. 16	Green Bay, WI	143	May 12	Oct. 2
Fort Peck, MT	146	May 5	Sept. 28	Janesville, WI	164	Apr. 28	Oct. 10
Helena, MT	122	May 18	Sept. 18	Casper, WY	123	May 22	Sept. 22
Blair, NE	165	Apr. 27	Oct. 10	*Frosts do not occur every year			

IRRITABLE BOWEL?

(Special) If you suffer bowel problems such as constipation, bloating, diarrhea, gas, stomach cramps, heartburn, pain and discomfort associated with foods, you should know about a new book, *Gastro-Intestinal Health.*

The book contains the latest up-to-date information on the bowel—how it functions, what can go wrong, how it can best be treated, and how to protect yourself from irritable bowel problems. The book gives you specific facts on the latest natural and alternative remedies that can bring prompt and lasting relief without the use of dangerous drugs. You'll learn all about these new remedies and find out how and why they work. You'll discover what you can do to avoid irritable bowel and stomach problems, what foods actually promote healing of an irritable bowel, and what to avoid at all costs. The book even explains a simple technique that has helped thousands rid themselves of irritable bowel problems, yet is little-known to most people—even doctors.

The book also explains how the bowel works, how food is digested, how specific foods affect the bowel, why certain foods and activities cause problems, and why over 20 million people suffer irritable bowel problems.

Written by a medical doctor, the book covers actual case histories of people who suffered irritable bowel problems and how they were able to overcome their problems.

Many Americans are putting up with troublesome irritable bowel and stomach problems because they are unaware of new natural treatments and the welcome relief that is now available.

Get all the facts. Order this book today. The book is being made available for only $12.95 *(plus $3 postage and handling)*. To order, send your name and address with payment to: United Research Publishers, 103 North Highway 101, Dept. FAA-2, Encinitas, CA 92024. You may return the book within 30 days for a refund if not satisfied.

The OLD FARMER'S GENERAL STORE

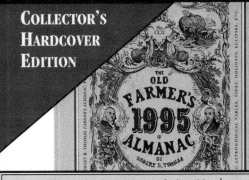

THE LAST WORD ON TOMATOES

FOR 1995

Here's the scoop on all the latest tomato research projects, covering the waterfront on taste, shape, size, color, genetic engineering, heirloom varieties, mulching, and even outer-space tomatoes.

BY MARTIN P. WATERMAN

BEATING YOUR NEIGHBORS TO THE BITE

Enjoying a friendly rivalry over that first ripe tomato? Try growing Sub Arctic Maxi, which can offer up a ripe tomato in as little as 48 days after transplanting. Although this variety was created especially for northern gardeners, it can also be used in warmer climes. Not surprisingly, some of the genetic material used in breeding hardier, earlier tomatoes is coming from the former Soviet Union. Every year we seem to gain a few days over the year before. Per-

SIMPLIFY: JUST USE CONTAINERS

Tomato breeders are developing varieties that will thrive in a pot on the patio or balcony. The cherry tomato Sweet 100, known for its sweetness, will produce as many as 300 tomatoes per plant. Husky Gold is a dwarf, ideal for container planting because of its compactness, and a heavy producer of tasty fruit that averages about eight ounces apiece.

One key to container planting is liberal use of mulch to conserve moisture and keep the soil cool. White containers are best for warm climates; dark, for cool. Container gardening allows people with handicaps or even just creaky joints to enjoy the pleasures of gardening without strenuous physical activity. If frost threatens, the plants can be brought indoors or simply covered with large plastic bags. And weeding is a breeze.

New Kinds on the Block

You might try Yellow Stuffer, shaped like a square bell pepper and amenable to a savory stuffing (perhaps rice, feta cheese, and basil?). Another novelty is Jersey Giant, a long, tapering tomato that can grow as large as 12 ounces. At the other extreme is Red Currant, a tomato plant with tiny, pea-sized fruit that can be eaten by the handful like berries.

Angora is a conversation starter: The plants (which do bear tasty fruit) have grayish-white fuzz all over the stems and leaves. If you like the look, use them as edible ornamentals in the flower garden. (No, you cannot make angora sweaters from the fuzz.)

Pink, orange, and striped tomatoes are turning up in seed catalogs. One favorite is Lemon Boy, with its mild, sweet flavor and unusual color. Also worth a try for a new look in salads is Snowball, a white tomato.

haps someday the tomatoes will be ready with the lettuce for those early salad days of summer. (Dream on . . .)

Giants from the Earth

When the big beefsteaks are not big enough, try one of the giants like Magnum, a product of test seed developed by large-vegetable specialist Bernard Lavery, who grew a five-pound Magnum from the seed. Then there are the tall tomato plants such as Trip-L-Crop, one of the most vigorous and productive tomatoes you can grow. It is not unusual for this indeterminate plant to grow more than 12 feet (some have reached 24), so either gather up some tall stakes and a ladder or grow the tomato against a house or wall. The red fruit weigh up to a pound apiece.

Breeding for Taste

Many research projects focus on issues most important to commercial growers, such as uniformity and spoilage, but the USDA South Atlantic Citrus and Subtropical Products Laboratory in Winter Haven, Florida, is looking at the all-important quality of taste. Little is known about the 400 or so compounds called flavor volatiles that have been identified in the tomato and how they are affected by culture and breeding in creating flavor. One of the basic studies has been simply to identify which tomatoes have the best flavors by analyzing sugar and acid content and by using ordinary folks as panelists. Once a better chemical definition of tomato flavor and aroma is found, tomato breeders may be able to select cultivars for their taste as well as other desirable characteristics.

RETURN OF THE NATIVES

Although many heirloom varieties are not cosmetically perfect, they make up for it in superior flavor, keeping qualities, and disease resistance. Astute gardeners have never stopped growing them. One favorite, always a big hit at the county fair, is Watermelon Beefsteak, a mid-season tomato with large, pink, oblong fruit. The variety has been around for more than 100 years.

Purple Calabash, which some historians have traced back to the 16th century, features rosy-purple fruits that turn bronze or brown when ripe. This old variety is said to be one of the most intensely flavored tomatoes available.

PETUNIAS AND TOMATOES: THE ODD COUPLE

If scientists have their way, tomato plants of the future will contain petunia genes. Petunia foliage is deadly to various insects. Larvae of the tobacco horn worm, for instance, die within four days of eating petunia leaves. Scientists hope to transfer the genes that make petunias toxic into plants of economic significance, particularly the tomato and the potato. (We hope they create an insect-resistant tomato rather than a petunia with funny red fruit.)

MULCH MAGIC

Scientists at the USDA lab in Beltsville, Maryland, got dramatic results when they replaced traditional black polyethylene mulch with hairy vetch. Tomato yield increased by 138 percent! In addition, insect problems were nearly eliminated and less fertilizer and pesticides were needed. Vetch, a nitrogen-fixing legume, also added beneficial organic matter to the soil.

Although black plastic mulch promotes an early crop, the plants mulched with vetch produced tomato plants that were greener (desirable because deeper pigmentation is associated with higher nutrient levels) and larger. The study found that control plots with no mulch averaged 19 tons of tomatoes per acre. Fields with paper and plastic mulch yielded 34 and 35 tons per acre, respectively. Fields with the vetch mulch averaged 45 tons per acre.

You can try this at home. Plant hairy vetch in the fall as a ground cover on prepared beds. In the spring, at planting time, mow the vetch to about an inch and immediately plant the tomato

– Jan North

Taming the Wild Galapagos Tomato

A wild tomato from the Galapagos Islands may revolutionize the future of tomatoes. *Lycopersicon cheesmanii* is a bright orange tomato about the size of a pea. It contains as much as 40 times more vitamin A than commercial tomatoes and nearly 40 times the amount of beta-carotene. Growers crossed this little wild tomato with Flora-Dade, a commercial variety grown for fresh markets, to create a hybrid about an inch in diameter with about 30 milligrams of beta-carotene per gram (the common tomato has 1.5 mg. per gram). It will still take about five more generations until a suitable tomato is ready to present to seed producers. Other orange tomatoes already on the market do not have the high vitamin A content, so growers expect the new tomato to be popular with health-conscious consumers.

– Jan North

seedlings. (Do not till the soil.) The vetch cuttings will dry and create a layer of mulch that will suppress weeds but will let water pass through.

Other researchers involved with mulch at a USDA Soil and Water Conservation Research Center in Florence, South Carolina, have found that the color of plastic mulch can make a difference. Researchers already know that northern gardens benefit from black mulch (to warm the soil) while southern gardeners use white plastic to reflect light and prevent heat build-up. Curious scientists painted the plastic mulch red and found that red mulch caused a 20 percent increase in tomato yield over black (later experiments averaged about 12 percent). Colored mulches are already patented, and it is expected they will be available in the near future to commercial and home growers.

Outer-Space Tomatoes

Scientists are working on a tomato plant and culture suitable for the environment of space. With the promise of long-term space travel (three years to Mars), some method of food production must be designed to feed the travelers, and one of the stars of the research has been the tomato. Much of the experimentation is taking place at the Climate Stress Laboratory in Beltsville, Maryland, where botanists are

trying to encourage tomato plants to use more of their resources for creating shoots than roots. The problem is that root-bound plants often limit their own top growth. Scientists hope to use growth hormones to create plants that will not need large root masses in order to produce lots of fruit. □□

Classified Advertising

AGENTS WANTED

WATKINS PRODUCTS has steady & sincere ways to earn extra money. Call 800-828-1868

ASTROLOGY/OCCULT

FREE BIRTHCHART! High resolution with Sun, Moon, planets, nodes, houses, and aspects. Complete interpretation guide also included. Receive this special offer with our 1995 catalog of fine astrological charts/reports. Enclose $1 for postage. Send one birthdate, time, place to: Synergy Services, 2011-K Pepperstone, Greensboro NC 27406

LOVE, LUCK, AND MONEY can be yours. Send now for free catalog. Church Goods, Dept. F, 801 W. Jackson, Chicago IL 60607.

THE MOST COMPLETE metaphysical, magical & psychic power development correspondence course ever offered. Ancient secrets finally revealed by 5,000-year-old magical order. Reasonable rates. Priesthood, 2301 Artesia Blvd. 12-188A, Redondo Beach CA 90278

LEARN WITCHCRAFT for protection, success, and serenity. Gavin and Yvonne Frost, world's foremost witches, now accepting students. Box 1502-0, New Bern NC 28563

BIORHYTHMS — Your physical, emotional, intellectual cycles charted in color. Interpretation guide. Six months ($10). Twelve months ($15). Send name, birthdate. Cycles, Dept. FAB, 2251 Berkely Ave., Schenectady NY 12309

PSYCHIC CAN INFLUENCE others. Removes spells. Restores nature. Brings luck. Rev. Carson Weaver. Telephone: 703-439-8495

AMERICA'S PSYCHIC HOTLINE. Live 1-on-1 with your personal gifted psychic. Fast answers. Average 8 minutes. You'll be delighted and amazed! 1-900-420-2444 ext. 515. $2.98/minute. 18+. Avalon. As seen on TV.

FREE LUCKY NUMBERS. Send birthdate, self-addressed stamped envelope. Mystic, Box 2009-R, Jamestown NC 27282

PROF. NUMEROLOGY Profiles. Ordering/information, SASE. Christine Nichols, 663 So. Bernardo Ave. Suite R, Sunnyvale CA 94087

ZODIACAL LOVE FRAGRANCES. Send birth sign + $15.98 (M.O.) To: Amoré Oils, Box 02-1232, Brooklyn NY 11202

ASTROLOGY — Personalized, comprehensive natal chart $10. Progressed chart for current year $10. Both $15. Send name, birthdate, birth time, birthplace. Cycles, Dept. FAA, 2251 Berkely Ave., Schenectady NY 12309

FREE OCCULT CATALOG. Oils, incense, herbs, books, etc. $2 p/h. Joan Teresa Power Products, Box 442-F, Mars Hill NC 28754

YOUR YEAR according to the cards (common deck). Personal computerized reading using numerology/astrology. Send $22 with name, age, birthdate, and occupation. Influences, Box 2035, Valley Center CA 92082

SPECIALIZED FOR 1995. Read your future. Personalized horoscope $10. Send natal information to: Darla Hlucky, 11710 Blossom, Parma Hts. OH 44130

WORLD'S LARGEST OCCULT, mystic arts, new age, witchcraft, voodoo. Largest supply of good-luck talismans and amulets for every purpose. Thousands of rare, unusual curios and gifts. Set of 3 fascinating 1995 catalogs, $2. By airmail, $3. Worldwide Curio House, Box 17095-A, Minneapolis MN 55417

WITCHCRAFT POWERS can be yours. Let Lady Sabrina help you bring prosperity, love, and happiness to your life. Six home-study courses available. Free information. PO Box 1366, Nashua NH 03061. 603-880-7237

AUTOMOTIVE

ENGINE LIFESAVER. Better compression, gas mileage, performance. Extends engine life. $21.95. Alpha Marketing, Dept. OF, Box 7614, Pine Bluff AR 71611

BEER & WINE MAKING

FREE BEER-MAKING Catalog. Wine too! Middlesex Brewery, 25-13 Old Kings Highway North, Darien CT 06820

LOWEST PRICES Guaranteed. Write for free catalog. Brew City Supplies, PO Box 27729, Milwaukee WI 53227

WINEMAKERS-BEERMAKERS. Free illustrated catalog. Fast service. Large selection. Kraus, Box 7850-YB, Independence MO 64054; 816-254-0242

BOAT KITS & PLANS

BOAT KITS & PLANS. Boatbuilding supplies, 250 designs. Catalog only $3. Clarkcraft, 16-29 Aqualane, Tonawanda NY 14150

BOOKS/MAGAZINES/CATALOGS

FREE COLOR CATALOG, over 260 quality items. Gifts for home, office, weddings, babies, golfers, travelers, etc., many personalized. Lord & Dannbarr, Box 3007-F, Pagosa Springs CO 81147-3007. 303-264-4213

PUBLISH YOUR BOOK! All subjects invited. Attractive books, publicity, advertising, quality service, covering 5 decades of satisfied authors. Send for fact-filled booklet and free manuscript report. Carlton Press, Dept. OA, 11 W. 32nd St., New York NY 10001

BOOKS GALORE! "How-to" books at bargain prices! Catalog $2. K 'n' L Specialties-(FA), PO Box 21804, El Sobrante CA 94826-1804

FREE BOOKLETS: Life, death, soul, resurrection, pollution crisis, hell, Judgment Day, restitution. Bible Standard(OF), PO Box 67, Chester Springs PA 19425-0067

"HOW-TO" books and videos on self-reliance, practical survival, and dozens of other subjects! 64-page catalog describes over 600 titles. Send $2 to: Paladin Press, PO Box 1307-5AZ, Boulder CO 80306

MASTER YOUR MONEY! Compact, categorized, down-to-earth economy guide. Take control with hundreds of proven, powerful "insider" savings techniques. Consumer goods, housing, food, gardening, transportation, utilities, insurance, much more. $9.95. The Frugalist, Box 1759, Evanston IL 60204

SALE. Used books, magazines. List $1. Paying cash for yours. Kelly's, HC86, B-7-OF, Looneyville WV 25259

HOW TO WIN AT BLACKJACK, Roulette, Poker, Lotto, Bingo. Write: Winning, 1302 Cadwell, Bloomington IL 61704

FREE CATALOG. Gifts for all occasions. Beautifully illustrated, 48 pages. Carvers Collectibles, 318 West 100 South FA, Kaysville UT 84037

1,000 NATIVE AMERICAN Catalogs! Complete directory, $8.95. Spotted Horse, PO Box 414, Coosbay OR 97420

FREE! World's most unusual novelty catalog: 2,000 things you never knew existed. Johnson-Smith, F-625, Bradenton FL 34206

FREE CATALOG. Gifts of quality and distinction. Our best to you. The O'Learys, 30 Independence Green, Montpelier VT 05602-3349

BUSINESS OPPORTUNITIES

FREE TAPE AND BOOK on home business with immediate start-up, immediate profits. We drop-ship over 3,500 best-selling products far below wholesale. Great for mail order. SMC, 9401 De Soto Ave., Dept 834-61, Chatsworth CA 91311

RECORD VIDEOTAPES at home. $5,000 monthly possible. No pornography. Free details. Write: CMS Video Company, 210 Lorna Square - #163FA5, Birmingham AL 35216

BUNK BEDS. Clear $300 per day making bunk beds. Start at home in spare time and expand the business at your own pace. Free information. Bunks, PO Box 24705-XE, Edina MN 55424

ADVERTISE to four million people for only $130. Call 1-800-888-4988.

1,000 WEEKLY POSSIBLE: $2 for each envelope you stuff. Rush SASE for free details: Post Scripts, PO Box 39608-FA, Los Angeles CA 90039

MAKE REAL MONEY selling fake tattoos! Free color brochure/sample. Don Ling's Removable Tattoos. 800-247-6817

$32,404 IN BACKYARD Garden! Grow new specialty plants. Free booklet. Growers, Box 1058-FA, Bellingham WA 98227-1058

102 IDEAS for small home-based businesses. Send $1, LSASE to: TBE, 8000 Jemez Trail, Yucca Valley CA 92284

MAIL ORDER MILLIONS. Start your own lucrative mail order business from home. Free information. Call: 609-667-3154

STUFF ENVELOPES for average of $140/100. Send SASE to: Taylors, 22 Waterfront Dr., N. Little Rock AR 72116

U.S. GOVERNMENT GRANTS/ Loans ($5,000-$5,000,000) for your business or education. Free recorded message: 901-759-1720

$80,000 FROM ONE ACRE! Grow ginseng. Sell $60/pound. Free information: Lee's, 5712 Cooper Rd., Indianapolis IN 46208

MAIL ORDER SUCCESS. You cannot fail unless you quit! Money makers. Money savers. Success. Security. Information. Financial independence. Wealth. Satisfaction. Happiness. Knowledge. Achievement. Expect and get the best. Why settle for less? Value offers with substance. Free informative package. Mr. Mailorder, 10 Tinton, Rexdale ONT M9V 2J1

KANGAROO, ALLIGATOR, buffalo, wild boar, venison snack-stick route sales. Free info. Buffalo Bob's, 7800 Computer Ave., Dept XG, Minneapolis MN 55435; 612-831-3936

REVOLUTIONARY Home-Mailing Program that pays two ways. Details! Double-stamped long envelope. WJS, Box 150016-F, Saint Louis MO 63115

WE BUY newspaper clippings. $781.23 weekly. Send stamped envelope. Edwards, Box 467159FA, Atlanta GA 30346

LET THE GOVERNMENT finance your small business. Grants/loans to $500,000. Free recorded message: 707-448-0270 (KE1)

WEALTH IN SILVER/GOLD. Free information. Send name/address. Al Senechal, 35S Bennington Rd., Hancock NH 03449

RUBBER, PLASTIC, molding and casting compounds; techniques, sources. Free information: Castplast, Box 16586, Memphis TN 38186-0586

CARNIVOROUS PLANTS

CARNIVOROUS (INSECT-EATING) plants, seeds, supplies, and books. Peter Paul's Nurseries, Canadaigua NY 14424

COLLECTIBLES/NOSTALGIA

GRACE LIVINGSTON HILL collectors! Write for our free list. Arnold Publication-A, 2440 Bethel Rd., Nicholasville KY 40356. 800-854-8571

OLD-FASHIONED RADIOS, telephones & jukeboxes $49.99 and up. Thomas replica collectibles. Order by phone. Call Music Network Inc., 800-OLD-DAYS, or write: 8024 Claytie Circle, Nashville TN 37221

OLD PICTURE POSTCARDS. Free: How to buy, sell, price, plus directory of 300 postcard dealers. Send SASE bearing three stamps to Postcard Federation, 19 Empire Pl., Greenbelt MD 20770

COMPUTERS/SOFTWARE

FACSIMILE COVER sheets from your PC. Crude, cheap, effective! Information, SASE to: A Scully, 851 Haskell Ave., Rockford IL 61103-6709

CRAFTS

APPAREL FABRICS, Crafting Supplies. Seldom-found Ultrasuede, lace, ribbon, fabric, and remnant packages. Savings to 80%. 55-page catalog $1. Oppenheim's Dept. 598, N. Manchester IN 46962-0052

HANDCRAFTED CLAY jewelry. Color brochure. Send LSASE. DES, #FA95, 112 Randy Rd., Madison TN 37115

INDIAN CRAFTS. Free brochure showing materials used. Recommended to Indian guides, scout troops, etc. Cleveland Leather, 2629 Lorain Ave., Cleveland OH 44113

MOCCASIN MAKING: craft manual, 28 authentic patterns, instructions. Craft Manuals, 173 Blodgett Ln., Arlee MT 59821

BEADS, BEADS, BEADS: gemstone, glass, kits, instructions. Catalog $1. Terre Celeste, Box 4125FA, Kenmore NY 14217

EDUCATION/INSTRUCTION

OLDER PERSON? Need a will? Complete will kit/easy instructions! Only $9.95. Willmaker, 42 Roger Williams Ave., Rumford RI 02916

LEARN SMALL BUSINESS Management. Start your own business or advance in your job. Practical tips from experts. Lifetime Career Schools, Dept. OBO915, 800-326-9221

COLLEGE DEGREE BY MAIL. Save $$$. CBC, Station Sq. Suite 227, Rocky Mount NC 27804. 919-442-1211. Accredited.

UNIVERSITY DEGREES without classes! Accredited Bachelor's, Master's, Doctorates. Free revealing facts! Thorson-FA5, Box 470886, Tulsa OK 74147

HIGH SCHOOL AT HOME. No classes. Low monthly payments. Information free. Our 98th year. Call 800-228-5600 or write American School, Dept #348, 850 E. 58th St., Chicago IL 60637

LEARN FLOWER ARRANGING. Start business or hobby. Free brochure on Home Study Program. Lifetime Career Schools, Dept. OBO294, 101 Harrison St., Archbald PA 18403

FARM AND GARDEN

BREAKTHROUGH! PLANTS also need vitamins for optimal health. Six-month supply $10. Ross Plantioxidants, 8A Western, Ardsley NY 10502

HYDROELECTRIC SYSTEMS since 1973. Free brochure, guide. U.S. $15. WPM, c/o Box 9723, Midland TX; 915-697-6955

STRONG GREENHOUSE plastic. Also tarpaulins, pond liners. Resists hailstones, windstorms. Samples: Bob, Box 42FA, Neche ND 58265. 204-327-5540

FREE GARDENING CATALOG – 4,000 items! Seeds, trees, shrubs, supplies, greenhouses, beneficial insects. Mellinger's, Dept. 720J, Range Rd., North Lima OH 44452-9731

BONSAI PLANTS, pots, tools, books. Send $1 for catalog to: The Bonsai Farm, PO Box 130F, La Vernia TX 78121

LEARN LANDSCAPING at home. Free brochure. Call 800-326-9221 or write Lifetime Career Schools, Dept: OBO115, 101 Harrison St., Archbald PA 18403

SAWMILL $2,995. Saw logs into lumber or beams. Trailers anywhere. Free information. Silvacraft Sawmill, 90 Curtwright, Unit 3, Amherst NY 14221. 800-661-7746 ext. 95

BENEFICIAL INSECTS, organic gardening supplies. Free catalog. The Green Spot, 93 Priest Rd., Barrington NH 03825. 603-942-8925

TROYBILTS. 20% discounts. Stamp for discount parts catalog. Replacement Tines $59. Kelley's, Manilla IN 46150. 317-398-9042

NEW LABOR SAVER! Shovel amplifier gets more done with less back strain. Kit: $7 basic; $9.50 heavy duty; $3 S&H. Plans for $1, $5 total. RH Designs, P.O. Box 804, Leonard TX 75452

FLAGS

FLAGS, FLAGS! American, State, MIA/POW, Confederate, historical, more. Free brochure. Write: Flags & Things, PO Box 356, Dillsburg PA 17019

FOOD AND RECIPES

EUROPEAN-STYLE baked fruit desserts. Five deliciously different recipes. $4 to: Good Taste (22), Box 4, LaGrangeville NY 12540

AMISH CHRISTMAS COOKIES. Authentic Pennsylvania family recipes. Chocolate, molasses, spice. Like no others. SASE, $1. Rheinauer, 2907 Whitemarsh Pl., Macungie PA 18062

LEARN HEALTHY, NUTRITIOUS cooking at home. Selection, preparation, serving of appetizing, nutritious foods. Free brochure. Lifetime Career Schools, Dept. OBO815. 800-326-9221

BUSY DAY recipes (6). Delicious, healthy, fast. Send $2, SASE. Sunderlins, Box 181897, Dallas TX 75218

CHEESE made and aged the old way. Send for brochure. Cheese Haven, PO Box 336, Marblehead OH 43440

CARLA EMERY'S *Old-Fashioned Recipe Book/Encyclopedia of Country Living* back in print. POB 209, Kendrick ID 83537. 800-844-0430

TEX-MEX SALSA! Great for dipping or spicing up your next meal. $2, SASE: Tex-Mex, Rte. 3 Box 104A, Decatur AL 35603

THE BEST OLD Southern forgotten recipes. Cracklin' corn bread, egg pies, others. SASE, $2 M.O. to: A. Smith, PO Box 589, Wilton CA 95693

FOR THE HOME

CUCKOO CLOCKS: Hand-carved German Black Forest. Catalog $1. Terre Celeste Gallery, Box 4125F, Kenmore NY 14217

FLY TRAY. Fits in your windows; 3/16x1/2x16-inch adhesive tray catches flying insects. Also troubleshoot your home for crawling bugs. Send $4.75 per pack of six. PO Box 186, Gridley CA 95948 or call 916-846-3116

TUPPERWARE. Catalog $2. Deducted from first order. Send name & address to: PO Box 176, Brightwaters NY 11718

FLOUR-SACK DISH TOWELS: large, white cotton, washed, hemmed, pressed. 14 for $20, includes shipping, USA. Olson Towels, 10299 Nightingale, Coon Rapids MN 55433

CUSTOM TABLE PADS. All sizes, 80 years experience. Factory prices. Finest quality. Prompt delivery. 800-541-0271 ext. 90

NEW Odor-Z-Way Zeolite Crystal odor remover. Environmentally safe. Various uses: household, carpets, smoke, garbage, animal odors, etc. Especially effective on urine odors. $10.95 for 14 oz., $18 for 2. S&H included. Call Mineral-Right, Inc., Phillipsburg KS 67661. 800-444-6571

GINSENG AND HERBS

SALTLESS SEASONINGS — Spice up your life with herbs! $3.50 ppd., includes 1 packet plus list of blends available. Vail Farm, Vail Rd., Bennington VT 05201

GINSENG 1ST-YEAR ROOTS $18/100, seed $12/oz. VCR about hunting ginseng $24.95. Ginseng OFA, Flagpond TN 37657

FOR INCREASED ENERGY and robust health try all-natural herbs and nutrition supplements. Send $2 for details and catalog. Ridge's Way, 104 South Pine, Seneca SC 29678

GINSENG! GOLDENSEAL! Profitable. Good demand. Quality planting stock. Comfrey. Information $1. William Collins, Viola IA 52350

GOVERNMENT SURPLUS

GOVERNMENT LAND now available for claim. Up to 160 acres/person. Free recorded message: 707-448-1887. (4KE1)

GOVERNMENT-SEIZED vehicles! Buy dirt cheap! Your area! Free details. Surplus, Box 3321, Ft. Smith AR 72913

GOVERNMENT AUCTIONS! Your area. Cars from $100! Seized/surplus trucks, boats, aircraft, more! 800-601-2212 ext. SP590

HEALTH/BEAUTY

FREE CATALOG! National-brand vitamins up to 60% off! Kal, Schiff, Twinlab & more! 800-858-2143

PSORIASIS SUFFERERS. Discouraged? Write for free important information helping thousands. Pixacol, PO Box 347144-OF, Parma OH 44134

GREAT DISCOVERY! Stops cigarette smoking. Guaranteed. Only $5/SASE. Brown's, 3550G Calle Principal, Chico CA 95926

NATURAL MEDICINE for your common ailments with no side effects. Homeopathic medicines are safe for you. Free catalog: Luyties, Box 8080 (Dept. O), St. Louis MO 63156

HERBS for your health. Hundreds from around the world. Free catalog. PO Box 2115, Naples FL 33939

BE SAFE, SECURE! Instantly stop attackers with Defiance Pepper defense spray. $9.95. 800-888-4988. Distributors needed.

DRUGLESS THERAPY Secrets restore body, mind, spirit. Health handbook from America's greatest psychic. Free details. Consultant, PO Box 186, San Clemente CA 92674

POSSIBLE LUPUS RELIEF. Send SASE & $5 M.O. to: A. Smith, PO Box 589, Wilton CA 95693

HELP WANTED

EXCELLENT INCOME! Assemble easy craft products at home. Easy work! Legitimate! Program guaranteed! 800-377-6000 ext. 590

INVENTIONS/PATENTS

INVENTIONS, IDEAS, New Products! Presentation to industry and exhibition at national innovation exposition. Call 800-288-IDEA

PATENT IT ECONOMICALLY! Free details. Licensed since 1958. Ranere Associates, 2008 Fondulac, Richmond VA 23229

MONEY WITH YOUR IDEAS! Learn the secrets about patents! Send for free facts! Invent, 955 Mass. Ave., Box #312, Cambridge MA 02139

INVENTORS. Have an idea? For your free patenting and marketing kit call Freedom Marketing: 800-932-4298.

LOANS BY MAIL/FINANCIAL

FOR MAJOR CREDIT CARD with low interest and liberal approval call today! 800-980-0099 ext. 889

BUSINESS PLANS WRITTEN, financing arranged, venture-capital found. Information $20. DRB Assoc., Box 250 A, Spofford NH 03462

MUSIC/RECORDS/TAPES

ACCORDIONS, CONCERTINAS, button boxes. New, used, buy, sell, trade, repair. Hohners, Martin guitars, lap harps, hammered dulcimers. Catalog $5. Castiglione, Box 40, Warren MI 48090; 313-755-6050

LARGE 7" HARMONICA. Satisfaction guaranteed! Sweet music! Low price! $7.95 plus $3.25 s/h: ECHO, Box 27433FA, Los Angeles CA 90027

MUSICAL STRINGS, Accessories Catalog. Nearly 50% off guitar strings, more! Write for free catalog. Haage Music Co., Dept. B, 7719 Hwy. 76, Kirbyville MO 65679

TRADITIONAL MUSIC, hammered and mountain dulcimer. Celtic, oldtime, and more! Recordings, dulcimer, instruction, accessories. Free catalog. Fishbite Recordings, Box 280632 FA5, San Francisco CA 94128-0632

FIDDLING, FOLK, music instruction, recordings. Free catalog. Captain Fiddle, 4 Elm Court, Newmarket NH 03857. 603-659-2658

PLAY GOSPEL SONGS by ear! Ten lessons $7.98. "Learn Gospel Music!" Chording, runs, fills $8.98. Both $15. Davidsons, 6727FA Metcalf, Shawnee Mission KS 66204

NURSERY STOCK

EVERGREEN TREE SEEDLINGS. Direct from grower. Free catalog. Carino Nurseries, Box 538, Dept. AL, Indiana PA 15701

FRUIT, NUT, ORNAMENTAL trees. Berries, shrubs. Free catalog. Wells Nursery, Box 606, Lindale TX 75771

OF INTEREST TO ALL

BELLS IN YOUR EARS? Amazing natural remedy. 100 capsules $13.95. International Concepts, 60 Martin Creek Ct., Stockbridge GA 30281

COPPER BRACELETS: Solid copper chain link. Beautifully hand polished. Specify 8-, 9-, or 10-inch length. $12.50 each. Touch of Excellence, 75 Forest Ridge Dr., Columbus OH 43235-1410

PERFUME CONCENTRATE 100+, designers included! List + sample. Send $3 cash or M.O. to: Amoré Oils, Box 02-1232, Brooklyn NY 11202

HOME CANNERS. Order everything you need: canners, jars, rubber rings, spices, more. Send $1 for catalog. Home Canning Supply, PO Box 1158-OF, Ramona CA 92065

NEW! FLOWER-of-the-Month Collectibles. Free information. SASE. Welcome Mats, 4 Parkside, Kincheloe MI 49788

ATTENTION, ROSE LOVERS! Gorgeous 5" Porcelain Rose nightlight, exquisitely handcrafted and lit from within by a standard night-light bulb. Specify red or red/white twotone. Send $24.95 plus $3.50 shipping to Dreamboat Annie's, 2220 Bardsdale FA95, Fillmore CA 93015-9710. Money-back satisfaction guarantee!

HEALTH INSURANCE for individuals and the self-employed at affordable group rates. Free information: 800-869-5774

"JUST MARRIED" bumper stickers solve many car-decorating problems. Two/$3, four/$4.95 postpaid. No foreign money! 1776 Enterprises, Box 374FG, Sudbury MA 01776

SUBSCRIBE! Clean humor mininewspaper. Quarterly. Four issues, $4. Chuckle Town USA, Dept A4, Box 47181, Indianapolis IN 46247

SCOTLAND YARD'S Famous Bobby Whistles! Direct from England. Unique, classic, effective! $5.95 + $1.50 hdlg. Gladstone's, OFA, 5 Wylly Ave., Savannah GA 31406

GRANDPA'S PINE TAR, Baking soda, witch hazel, oatmeal, Thylox bar soaps. Timberline, PO Box 57, Walnutport PA 18088

ICE CHOPPER, industrial grade, home or auto. Save time and money. SASE plus $1 for info. Ice Chopper, Box 353, Allston MA 02134-0004

FREE! NEW CATALOG of fine handcrafted items with "Mostly Moose" in mind. Call or write: Mostly Moose, 166 Shephard Rd., Dept. G, Gibsonia PA 15044. 412-444-6674

OLD PHOTOS copied, restored, hand-colored, enlarged. Originals safely returned. Quotes: Photos, OFA95, COY AL 36435

BLUEGRASS, COUNTRY, Gospel videos, recordings, books, and more! Free catalog: NAT-OFA, Box 31557, San Francisco CA 94131

TWELVE-MONTH BIORHYTHM charts. $5. Send birthdate and year. John Morgan, 1208 Harris, Bartlesville OK 74006

OF INTEREST TO WOMEN

144 YARDS BETTER LACE trims $13.50. Twelve delightful patterns. Oppenheim's, Dept. 599, N. Manchester IN 46962-0052

EARN $400 A MONTH at home, spare time, doing only two $10 invisible reweaving, reknitting jobs a day. Good money paid for making cuts, tears disappear from fabrics. Details free. Fabricon, 2051 Montrose, Chicago IL 60618

PERSONALS

RUSSIAN LADIES, truly beautiful, educated, seek relationships. Free color photo brochure. Russia 182, PO Box 888851, Atlanta GA 30356. 404-458-0909

NICE SINGLES with Christian values wish to meet others. Free magazine. Send age, interests. Singles, Box 310-OFA, Allardt TN 38504

JAPANESE, ASIANS, Europeans seek friendship, correspondence! All ages! Free information: Inter-Pacific, Box 304-K, Birmingham MI 48012

NEW AGE contacts, occultists, circles, wicca, companionship, love, etc. America/worldwide. Dollar bill: Dion, Golden Wheel, Liverpool L15 3HT, England

MOTHER DOROTHY, reader and adviser. Advice on all problems — love, marriage, health, business, and nature. Gifted healer, she will remove your sickness, sorrow, pain, bad luck. ESP. Results in 3 days. Write or call about your problems. 404-755-1301. 1214 Gordon St., Atlanta GA 30310

THAI, ASIAN, worldwide ladies desire life mates. Free brochure. TAWL, Box 937(FA), Kailua-Kona HI 96745-0937. Nationwide dateline. 900-726-2038. 18+, $2.49/min.

LATIN AND ORIENTAL LADIES seek friendship, marriage. Free photo brochure. "Latins," Box 1716-FR, Chula Vista CA 91912

GORGEOUS ASIAN WOMEN! Pen pals, romance, marriage! Color photos $1. P.I.C., Box 461873-FA, Los Angeles CA 90046

ASIAN WOMEN desire marriage! Overseas. $2 for details, photos. Sunshine International, Box 5500-YH, Kailua-Kona HI 96745-5500

ATTENTION: SISTER LIGHT, Spartanburg, S.C. One free reading when you call. I will help in all problems. 803-576-9397

ALONE? SINGLE? Farm? Small town background? American traditional values? Looking for that special someone? Contact Stars-N-Stripes Singles, Box 270301, Sappington MO 63126 or 314-742-4320. Confidential. Respectable.

SISTER ADAMS, spiritual healer, will solve problems in love, marriage, business, health, evil influences. If you have talked with others and are disappointed, contact me. 8287 Spanish Fort Blvd., Spanish Fort AL 36527. Immediate results. 205-626-7997

SISTER ANN GIVES ADVICE on all problems. Love, marriage, health, and aura cleansing. Call 205-621-1206. One question answered free.

ASIAN LADIES overseas seek correspondence, romance, marriage. Free photo brochure. PO Box 1245FA, Benicia CA 94510. 707-747-6906

SISTER HOPE SOLVES all problems. Specializing in love affairs. Are you sick? Having bad luck? Bothered by evil spells? Whatever your problem may be, call today. 800-548-0023 or 706-353-9259

NEED HELP DESPERATELY? Mrs. Stevens, Astrologer. Lonely? Unlucky? Unhappy? Helps all. Marriage, love, business, health, stress. I will give you options you never considered, never dreamed of. Immediate results. Call or write now 803-682-9889. Mrs Stevens, PO Box 207, Laurens SC 29360

PEN PAL ADDRESS MAGAZINE! Worldwide! All ages! Fascinating! $3 postpaid. Golden Quill Pen Pal Club, RR 1 Box 55, Blain PA 17006

MOTHER ANDERSON wants to help you with all your problems — large or small. 65 years' experience. 305-380-8353 or 404-382-2143

DO YOU NEED HELP? Call Sister Christian. Where others have failed, call 205-281-1116 now.

FREE BULLETIN! Single men and women! Send two postage stamps to: Cathye, POB 20066, Columbus OH 43220

POULTRY

GOSLINGS, DUCKLINGS, chicks, turkeys, guineas, bantams, pheasants, swans. Books, equipment, medications. Hoffman Hatchery, Gratz PA 17030

PEACOCK CHICKS, swans — everything — you name it. Bantams, pheasants, quail, waterfowl, turkeys, incubators, books: Peacocks $8.95; swans $8.95 plus $3 shipping. Free catalog. Stromberg's Gamebirds Unlimited, Pine River 45 MN 56474.

GOSLINGS, DUCKLINGS, chicks, turkeys, guineas, books. Picture catalog $1, deductible. Pilgrim Goose Hatchery, OF-95, Williamsfield OH 44093

REAL ESTATE

FOR SALE: 5-acre corner building lot in Desert Sky near Douglas Arizona. Price $7,500. Raymond Howard, RFD 9, Bloomfield IA 52537

ARKANSAS — Free Catalog. Natural beauty. Low taxes. The good life for families and retirement. Fitzgerald-Olsen Realtors, PO Box 237-A, Booneville AR 72927. Call toll-free 800-432-4595, ext. 641A

OZARK MOUNTAIN OR LAKE acreages from $30/month. Nothing down, environmental protection codes, huge selection. Free catalog. Woods & Waters, Box 1-FA, Willow Springs MO 65793. 417-469-3187

FORECLOSED HOMES! Your area – ½ price, even less! Move in for nearly nothing! 800-434-5977 ext. GH590

ARKANSAS LAND — Free Lists! Farms, ranches, homes, recreational acreages. Gatlin Farm Agency, Box 790, Waldron AR 72958. 800-562-9078 ext. OFA.

FREE LAND/BUILDINGS legally. All 50 states and D.C. $20 to: R. Romanishin, Rte. 1, Box 57, Greenwood WV 26360

RELIGION

FREE: Two booklets of Bible verses. Vernon-2BF, 11613 N. 31st Dr., Phoenix AZ 85029-3201

FREE ADULT OR CHILDREN'S Bible-study courses. Project Philip, Box 35-A, Muskegon MI 49443

COMFORT AND CONSOLATION. How to cope with tragedy. Free booklet. Clearwater Bible Students, PO Box 8216, Clearwater FL 34618

SEEDS

TOBACCO. Home-growing kit, 50-seed pkg. Instructions included. Smoking, chewing. $11. Homegrown Seeds, PO Box 4205, Pasco WA 99302-4205

FREE LIST. Over 200 varieties pepper seeds — hot, sweet, ornamental. SASE. "Pepper Gal," Box 23006, Ft. Lauderdale FL 33307

RARE HILARIOUS peter, female, and squash pepper seeds. $3 per pkg. Any two $5. All three $7.50 and over 100 other rare seeds. Seeds, Rte. 2 Box 246, Atmore AL 36502

FREE CATALOG. Finest quality vegetable, flower, and herb seed. Burrell, Box 150-FA, Rocky Ford CO 81067

FREE SEED SAMPLES! Exotic plants worldwide. Houseplants, lawn, garden, timber, tobacco, palms, cactus, fruit. Samples, 3421 Bream St., Gautier MS 39553

FREE CATALOG. Unusual seed varieties. Giant Belgium, evergreen, pineapple, tomatoes, and more. We make gardening fun. Glecker Seedman, Metamora OH 43540

COMPLETE LINE of organically grown seeds for sprouting and gardening. Cross Seeds, Bunkerhill KS 67626. 913-483-6163

STATIONERY

STUNNING, UNIQUE, environ-

mentally safe, your message-matching business cards, letterheads, envelopes. 20 pieces $14.95. Information $2. Mr. Graphic, 443 Jefferson St., Waterloo WI 53594

GREETING CARDS REUSED. Assorted sizes of labels/envelopes for reusing 50 plus cards. Recycle kit $11.95 + $3 S&H. Dolphin Greetings, PO Box 3097, Dona Vista FL 32784. 904-357-6855

WANTED

WANTED: AUTOGRAPHS, signed photos, letters, documents of famous people. Gray, Box 5084, Cohituate MA 01778 or 617-426-4912

ANTIQUE PURSES WANTED: Beaded, mesh, needlepoint. Photo or xerox. Bayhouse, Box 40443, Cleveland OH 44140. 216-871-8584

WE BUY ROYALTIES and minerals. Oil, gas, coal, minerals. Please write Marienfeld Royalty Corp., PO Box 25914, Houston TX 77265 or call 800-647-2580

AUTOMOBILE LITERATURE wanted: 1900-1975. I buy automobile sales brochures, manuals, etc. Walter Miller, 6710 Brooklawn, Syracuse NY 13211. 315-432-8282. Fax 315-432-8256

WORK CLOTHES

WORK CLOTHES. Save 80%. Shirts, pants, coveralls. Free folder. Write: Galco, 4004 East 71st St., Dept. OF-1, Cleveland OH 44105

MISCELLANEOUS

CASH FOR OLD RECORDS! Illustrated 72-page catalog, including thousands of specific prices we pay for 78s on common labels (Columbia, Decca, Victor, etc.), information about scarce labels, shipping instructions, etc. Send $2 (refundable). Discollector, Box 691035(FA), San Antonio TX 78269

UPSTATE N.Y. Catskills, Adirondacks vacation land, houses. For list & packet, send $2 + #10 SASE to: G.M.C., Box 585, Pine Hill NY 12465. Buyers's Broker.

SWEET POTATO PLANTS! And free catalog for tobacco products. Fred's Plant Farm, Box 707, Dresden TN 38225

BURIED TREASURE. Sensitive equipment allows locating from distance. Brochure free. Simmons, Box 10057-PA, Wilmington NC 28405

AMERICA'S Highest-quality vitamins at guaranteed wholesale! 48-page catalog. VPI, Box 0818FA, Freeport NY 11520. 800-645-6567

FREE BROCHURES: Herbs, Home Remedies. Send long stamped envelope to: Champion's Pharmacy & Herb Store, 2369 Elvis Presley-FA, Memphis TN 38106

CALENDAR! Until the end of the millennium, 1995 through 2000, at a glance. 2'x3' write-on Mylar surface, includes erasable marker and mounting pins. Send $20 to: MW Enterprises, PO Box 2485, Van Nuys CA 91404

POEMS WANTED for national contest. $15,000 in prizes. Be a published poet. Send one poem, 20 lines or less, any subject, any style, to: Sparrow Grass Poetry Forum, PO Box 193FA, Sisterville WV 26175

BONSAI by Jian Gang Shen. Send inquiries to: Jian Gang Shen, 212 Hillridge, Conroe TX 77385

AMAZING OCCULT DISCOVERIES. Develop supernatural powers, safely, easily. Free experiments. Williamsburg, Box 3483-FAZ, New York, NY 10008

WATKINS Famous vanilla, liniments, health aids, spices. Independent representatives needed, top profits! Free catalog, details. Watkins, Box 440392-F, Kennesaw GA 30144. (494) 974-1097

ANECDOTES
and PLEASANTRIES

A motley collection of useful (and, occasionally, useless) facts, stories, advice, and observations compiled from reader correspondence over the past year.

How Almanac Readers Get Rid of Certain Bugs in the House

(Without Spending Any Money, Of Course)
by Almanac consultant and friend Earl Proulx
of Surry, New Hampshire

Cockroaches, for Instance . . .

☞ Make a trap with a glass jar that's about four inches high. Put some bacon grease and a small chunk of banana in the bottom of the jar. Smear a band of petroleum jelly about ¼-inch wide around the inside of the jar about ½ inch from the top, and stand the jar in the area where the roaches are a problem. The bugs can crawl in, but they can't get out.

☞ Roaches love the area under the refrigerator — especially the drip pan and motor. Vacuum up all dirt and dust from around these areas, and wash out the drip pan often. Any area that is warm and dark or that is the least bit damp will be a home for them.

Or Itsy-Bitsy Spiders . . .

☞ To get rid of spiders, put cedar chips in the toes of old panty hose. Hang the hose from the porch ceiling or other areas where spiders build their webs.

☞ To discourage spiders, spray rubbing alcohol on windowsills or leave perfumed soap chips scattered about.

Maybe You Have Fleas?

☞ This method was mentioned in the Almanac several years ago, but it bears repeating. To catch fleas, place on the floor of the room that is infested a shallow pan filled with water and a little dishwashing liquid. At night, turn on a lamp and focus it right over the pan. Turn off all the other lights in the room. The fleas will jump at the light and fall into the dish. You'll be amazed at the number of fleas you'll catch the first night. Change the solution as needed. Continue the treatment for at least two weeks to get the next generation of fleas after the hatch.

☞ Keep fleas off your dog or cat by sprinkling ½ to 1 teaspoon of brewer's yeast on the animal's food daily or by crushing a tablet of 25 milligrams of vitamin B_1 (thiamin) on the food. Brewer's yeast is available at natural-food stores and pet stores; vitamin B_1 is sold in food stores and drugstores.

☞ To help keep a pet free of fleas and ticks, add 1 teaspoon of vinegar to each quart of the animal's drinking water.

Everyone Has Ants Sometimes . . .

☞ To get rid of ants, mix equal parts borax and confectioners' sugar with enough water to make a syrup. Put this mixture

☞ Should Radios Be Allowed in Automobiles?

As debated 65 years ago, here are the pros and cons.

A grave problem that developed in New Hampshire, spread to Massachusetts, and crept over to Albany, now has all the motor-vehicle commissioners of the eastern states in a wax. It's whether radios should be allowed on cars. Some states don't want to permit them at all — say they distract the driver and disturb the peace. The manufacturers claim that the sound of Rudy Vallee's voice is less disturbing than backseat conversation. Massachusetts leans toward the middle of the road. The Commissioner there thinks the things should be shut off while you are driving, but that you should be allowed to take culture with you into the wilderness. The whole problem is getting very complex, but the upshot is that you'll probably be allowed to take your radio anywhere, with possibly some restriction on the times when you can play it.

written by Nicholas Trott in 1930 (Courtesy of Lawrence Ashmead, New York City)

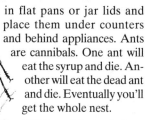

in flat pans or jar lids and place them under counters and behind appliances. Ants are cannibals. One ant will eat the syrup and die. Another will eat the dead ant and die. Eventually you'll get the whole nest.

☞ Wipe cabinets, shelves, countertops, and baseboards with a solution of equal parts white vinegar and water to help keep away ants.

☞ Squirt lemon juice on windowsills and the bottoms of doors to keep ants from coming into the house.

☞ You can discourage those small sugar ants from getting into your kitchen by sprinkling a little red pepper around the baseboards and at the rear of the counters.

Some of the above are taken from Earl Proulx's Yankee Home Hints (Yankee Books, 1993).

In the Event Anyone Would Like Information on the Bathing Habits of Today's College Students . . .

For example, 99.3 percent of college women bathe on Tuesdays between 6:00 and 9:00 P.M.

B ack in the 1980s, while working in an area of energy and water conservation, we conducted a study on the bathing behavior of college students. Approximately 85 percent of the "bathings" were accounted for by three patterns: one shower plus hair wash, one shower only, and two showers plus two hair washes. A mean number of 9.2 gallons of water per

---

shower was used, but when the bathers also washed their hair, this increased to 16.4 gallons. Whether the hair was washed or not, the mean water temperature was 102.4° F and a water temperature of 109° F was found to take care of 90 percent of the showers.

In a survey representing over 2,000 bathing days, we found that 99.3 percent of the men bathed on Saturday night (proof that the Saturday night bath is still in vogue), but to date a "clean" co-ed, a male should do so on Tuesday when 99.3 percent of the women bathed

between 6:00 and 9:00 P.M. The highest of the nonbathing days was Sunday, when eight percent of the men and 7.6 percent of the women shied away from soap and water, casting suspicion on the old adage that cleanliness is next to godliness.

This whole study took on more meaning when, after driving to Moline, Kansas, to deliver an after-dinner address, I checked into a motel only to find a beautiful big tub but no hot water. Complaining of this to the desk, I was informed, "nobody bathes at three o'clock in the afternoon"!

by Frederick H. Rohles, Ph.D., Professor Emeritus at the Institute for Environmental Research, Seaton Hall, Manhattan, Kansas

Let's Hear It for the Royal Canadian Mounted Police!

Happy 75th birthday to you,
Happy birthday to you,
Happy BIRTHDAY, dear Royal Canadian Mounted Police — who always get their man (or woman) and are clean, brave, and now 19,000 members strong — Happy birthday to you.

You can send your birthday cards and/or gifts (the actual birthday is this coming February 1, 1995) to R.C.M.P. Headquarters, 1200 Vanier Parkway, Ottawa, Ont. K1A 0R2.

And speaking of birthdays . . .

Still Another Difference Between Men and Women

In a study published in a recent issue of *Psychosomatic Medicine* (and reported in *The New York Times* by Sandra Blakeslee), it was discovered that elderly women are, statistically speaking, more likely to die from natural causes during the week just after their birthdays. Men, on the other hand, are more likely, statistically speaking, to die of natural

causes during the week just before their birthdays.

Why? Well, according to Dr. David P. Phillips, a sociology professor at the University of California in San Diego who conducted the research, birthdays can be "a deadline or a lifeline." For men, birthdays may be a time of taking stock, assessing one's lifetime achievements and/or failures, and maybe, if near death anyway, they'd just as soon let go before having to think again about things that may not have gone very well. For women, however, birthdays are often a time of increased attention from family and friends. So they may hang on to enjoy one more.

Those are theories. Dr. Phillips said the actual biological causes of prolonging or shortening life around birthdays are not understood. Nonetheless, the statistics, based on 2,745,149 deaths from natural causes, cannot be refuted. Another difference between men and women has been established.

Courtesy of A. G. Frost, Evansville, Indiana

A Scary Happening That Didn't Make the Evening News Last Year

Oh, sure, you may laugh and say this is pretty nutty. But if you'd been there, what would you have done? Would you have been as brave as Officer Oskierko?

As reported in the *Providence Journal Bulletin,* more than 50 workers at the John L. Scott real estate office in Kirkland, Washington, were held hostage one morning last March by a vicious, red-headed, beady-eyed squirrel. They lined one wall holding boxes and coats in front of themselves, and whenever someone attempted to leave the room, the squirrel would charge at them. Finally someone called 911. Officer Steve Oskierko answered the call, but was forced to radio for backup when he split his pants while trying to corner and catch the little beast. Reinforcements arrived with a change of pants for Officer Oskierko, who finally captured the squirrel and turned it over to a local veterinarian who was to test it for rabies. But the squirrel immediately gnawed through its plastic cage, attacked the veterinarian and others in his office, and escaped to the outdoors. As far as anyone knows, it's still on the lam.

Courtesy of A. B. Skinner, Seattle, Washington

It's Nice To Know Someone Got What They Deserved

A true story that'll make you feel good . . .

My aunt, a Manhattanite for many years, recounted to me this true story from her early days in the Big Apple.

When a beloved pet dies in New York City, it must be properly disposed of. No backyard ceremonies permitted. Dumbwaiter or incinerator disposal is also taboo. People are expected to go to the correct facility for the cremation of their pet.

Following the demise of her old dog, my aunt, obeying the rules, carefully packaged the dog's body in a brown box and tied it tightly with string. She walked the three blocks to the subway (thank God the beast was not an Afghan) and waited for the train to the nearest crematorium.

It was rush hour and the subways were jammed to the hilt. The door to the crowded car opened, and she squeezed herself in backward — the box just clearing the door. As the doors began to shut, a man bounded forward and snatched the box from her hands. As the doors slid slowly closed, my aunt, now boxless and dogless, had time only to shout to the thief, "Have a nice day!"

by Micki Warner, Groton, Connecticut

Good News/Bad News About Last Year's California Earthquake

The Good News

Of the million eggs laid on January 17 at the largest egg farm in the United States, located only five miles from the quake's epicenter, only one solitary egg actually broke.

Reported in The Valley Advocate. *Clipping sent by R. C. Benson, Los Angeles, California*

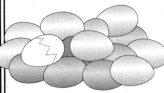

The Bad News

All the personal possessions of the late Charles F. Richter, coinventor of the Richter Scale (which measures the magnitude of earthquakes), were destroyed in the California quake. They included books, papers, and diaries spanning the 1920s to the 1950s, including an account of Richter's meeting with Albert Einstein.

Among the destroyed mementos, too, were home movies that included footage of Mr. Richter and his wife, Lillian, hiking in the nude. "They were nudists," explains Bruce Walport, Richter's nephew and owner of the destroyed Richter house in Granada Hills, "and so they especially liked to walk naked."

Oh.

Courtesy of William Rumford, Chicago, Illinois and The New York Times

Three Rather Astounding Discoveries

They have to do with toilet water, stolen Bibles, and hamsters with a drinking problem . . .

1 Despite the Coriolis force, the inertial force caused by the Earth's rotation that deflects a moving body to the right in the Northern Hemisphere and to the left in the Southern Hemisphere, it turns out that flushed toilet water does NOT spiral down in a different direction in the Southern Hemisphere. North or south, it goes down the same way. Mostly counterclockwise. (Almanac reader J. D. Wallace of Boston, Massachusetts, journeyed to Rio de Janeiro, Brazil, last winter and, after exhaustive testing, concluded the old "clockwise versus counterclockwise" theory was false.)

2 Book retailers report that not only does the Bible continue as the world's best-selling book, with some 2.5 billion copies currently in circulation, but it is also the most commonly shoplifted book in America. (Can anyone explain why?) *Courtesy of Gregory McNamee, Tucson, Arizona*

3 Kudzu, as everyone in the South knows, is a vine that seems to be spreading unchecked almost everywhere south of the Mason-Dixon line. Perhaps fewer people know that for hundreds of years, the Chinese have been using herbal medicine derived from the root of kudzu plants as a way to treat alcohol abuse in humans. Now it seems that Western scientists have extracted two active ingredients from kudzu and have determined they reduce alcohol consumption in Syrian golden hamsters by about 50 percent. This result, we would have to assume, would significantly improve the hamsters' overall health, sense of responsibility, family life, and so on.

Courtesy of William Dicke and The New York Times

Something to Think About While Listening to a Boring Speech

May the following letter, recently received, be your inspiration . . .

Dear *Old Farmer's Almanac,*

If you're trapped in an auditorium with a particularly long-winded politician, time will go by quickly if you try to create the shortest sentence that includes all the letters of the alphabet.

About 15 years ago the *Reader's Digest* printed this sentence, which, the author declared, was the shortest that used words found in the *Oxford English Dic-*

tionary. "Jackdaws love my big sphinx of quartz."

It contains 31 letters and the sentence makes some sense, as, I suppose, an acceptable example should.

Using words found in the *Merriam Webster Dictionary*, one can put together several sentences that are shorter.

A 30-letter one:
Quick frowzy lambs vex the pen judge.

A 29er:
Quick frowzy vamps jinx the big lad.

If common proper names are allowed, the above 29er can be cut to 28:
Quick frowzy vamps jinx glad Beth.

Another 28er,
Vow quick zax dents for jamb glyph!
(a command)

A 29er that reads like a poor headline:
Gulf doves jump by quick-thrown zax.

Haven't found anything better than "quick" and "zax" to use for problem letters. Would love to work in "zephyr-woven flax" someday — but right now I must be off. The mayor has finished his speech.   Sincerely,

Steve Sheffrey

Ann Arbor, Michigan

---

34 Words with Which We'll Say Farewell 'Til Next Year . . .

*Do all the good you can
In all the ways you can
To all the people you can
In every place you can
All the times you can
As long as ever you can.*

Courtesy of David Howe
and Peter Camp

☞If you have something for next year's "Anecdotes and Pleasantries," please send it along to A&P Editor, THE OLD FARMER'S ALMANAC, Dublin, NH 03444. We'll even spring for a little money for anything we actually use. Oh, and if you want it returned, include a self-addressed, stamped envelope. ☐ ☐

Spiders in Motion Indicate Rain

Wife's Confession:
"I had to trick him... and he's happy I did!"

"I had really begun to wonder about him," says Sally S*, 26, who asked that her last name not be published!

"At first I thought it was another woman. Then I wondered if maybe it was something worse."

The problem was her husband, George. "We used to have such good times," Sally recalled fondly of her dating days. "We went dancing and to parties and he could stay up all night."

But, after three years together, the romance began to fade.

George was bringing home a paycheck that should have made them happy, but he was clearly leaving something behind at the job.

"I dreamed of an affair," Sally admits. "But I couldn't picture myself with anyone else."

That's when Sally heard about a pill her best friend's husband was using. "He gets it sent to the office," Laura explained, "so I won't know he buys it. Of course," Laura added with a wicked grin, "if I ever stopped using it, I'd leave him in a minute! That pill has changed my life!"

Pill for men

What was this pill? Amazingly, thousands of men, like Laura's husband, have used it ever since it was first released to men in 1981.

It is called "NSP-270" stories about it have appeared in leading publications. At one time these reports even received an evaluation by the Navy. It was been widely used by both young men and older men — in fact, there are men in their 60's and 70's who count on it.

A happy trick

Laura agreed to "borrow" a few pills for Sally — and find out where her husband was getting them.

At the market, Sally bought a bottle of ordinary vitamins, emptied them out, and put the NSP-270 inside the bottle.

The next morning at breakfast, Sally offered George a "vitamin". He took it and the rest is history.

Later that night when Sally told George what she had done, he offered to buy a six month supply. George now takes his "vitamins" regularly, Sally has her "affair" (with George, of course!), and both Sally and Laura are making extra money selling NSP-270 to their friends!

Men should know!

If a man doesn't yet know about NSP-270, it may be because, like certain personal products, you can't buy it in local stores. But you can order it by mail, if you are over 18.

Write to Frank E. Bush, Inc., Dept. NE-74, Box 5009, Monticello, NY 12701. Be sure to include your name and address. Both checks and money orders are accepted. For orders of $25 or more you may request C.O.D. if your order is to a street address (not a P.O. box).

Send $12.95 for one bottle of NSP-270 (30-day supply), $15.74 for 2 bottles, $21.36 for 3 bottles, $38.85 for 6 bottles or $58.00 for 10 bottles. The company will pay the postage & handling charges on your first order.

If you are ordering 3 bottles or more, they will also send you an interesting book about NSP-270. The product carries a 30-day money back guarantee.

ZOOT SUIT
The

A True Experience

An American alone on a dark night in a remote

town behind the Iron Curtain, gas tank on empty

— and then a sort of miracle. by Nicholas Howe

Not long ago I found a book, a memoir of the mid 1940s in Harlem, when cool first meant hot, when cats were both hep and hip. It was the age of the zoot suit, an outlandish creation: a jacket with immense shoulder pads, shoulder-wide lapels, nipped-in waist, and a flared bottom that reached past the hips. Four pleats and a rib-high waist accentuated the drape of the wide cut and sharply pegged pants. The suit was worn with a flat, broad-brimmed hat, a floppy bow tie, and a gold watch chain looped from vest pocket to shin, and came in pastel colors with black binding at the edges.

The zoot suit was an in-your-face gesture to an America pared to the bone by the wartime economy, the opening statement of a counterculture. Needless to say, a child growing up in rural New England did not see either hep cats or zoot suits.

Forty years after that flowering in Harlem, eastern Europe was tense. On February 11, 1983, I'd filled up the gas tank in Vienna, gotten through the Iron Curtain with great difficulty, and headed diagonally across Czechoslovakia. Evening overtook me, the "Evil Empire" phase of the Cold War was at its most virulent, and I was running out of gas.

The town of Banská Bystrica was my only chance. I was in the middle of a Kafka novel: Only the squares were lit, the streets were empty, the sidewalks were empty, every window was dark. There were no gas stations.

I drove around aimlessly. Finally, in yet another brightly lit and entirely deserted square, I found a taxicab. The driver was asleep, buried in dirty old blankets and a heavy beard. It would probably have been safer to wake up a hibernating bear, but if anyone could find gas late at night, it would be a taxi driver. I knocked on the window.

We had only about eight words in common, but he made me understand that I should follow him. We drove out of the square, me thinking that I had maybe two blocks of travel left in the gas tank — the needle had settled on "Empty" long ago. Many blocks went past in darkness. The houses gave way to an industrial zone. Then we bumped through a railroad yard. I knew my engine could run only for a few more moments.

The rail yard ended, then the paving ended. Soon we were on a sort of cart track through winter fields, and I realized that we were not heading for a gas station. A hillside loomed, and we turned toward a gravel pit. I thought, This is how people disappear in the Eastern Bloc. A dark night, a shot, and a pile of gravel to cover the evidence.

I was as scared as I have ever been in my life. We came to a small house, and my captor stopped. There was no light, but he got out and knocked on the door, then came back and reached for me in my car. After a moment I heard stirrings inside, and words were exchanged that I could not understand. A light went on, there were sounds of something heavy being dragged, a metallic squeak, and small swishing sounds I could not interpret. The door opened and a strong acrid smell overwhelmed me. Mace!

No — *mothballs!* A bandy-legged old man, hardly as high as my elbow and smiling as if his face would break, was standing in the doorway. He was wearing a lavender zoot suit. It was all there: the draped shape, the ruffled shirt, the floppy bow tie, the black trim, even the wide-brimmed flat hat and the gold chain looped to his shin. Hardly able to contain his joy, he pulled me into his tiny house, got out bread and cheese and slivovitz — clear plum brandy so strong it might explode at any moment — and told me his story.

In 1937 things were not good in Banská Bystrica. The Great Depression had fallen on Europe many years earlier; now he decided he'd have a better chance in America and booked passage to New York. A welder by trade, he found work in the Brooklyn Navy Yard, and before long he heard about clubs where Negroes played jazz, people he'd never seen and music he'd never heard. He went up to Harlem one night and decided it was the most amazing thing God ever put on this Earth.

Work at the Navy Yard accelerated under the spur of World War II, he made what seemed to him a considerable fortune, and he went to hear the jazz on Friday nights. The war finally ended, and homesick at last, he came back to Czechoslovakia. But before he left America, he went up to Harlem one more time and bought a lavender zoot suit. It would be, he thought, the only one in Banská Bystrica.

He was right. In fact, he never dared wear it. So he wrapped it up in paper, all of its parts and wonders, and put it away in a trunk. Not many people knew about it, but once he'd shown it to a trusted friend. Years later, that friend was working as a taxi driver and was awakened in the middle of a February night by a person he thought was an American, the only person he'd ever met who might know what a zoot suit was, and he knew where to take him. Just beyond the house of the zoot suit, there was a gas pump. The two old Czech friends wouldn't take a penny for a tankful. □□

– Culver Pictures

1994

JANUARY
S	M	T	W	T	F	S
—	—	—	—	—	—	1
2	3	4	5	6	7	8
9	10	11	12	13	14	15
16	17	18	19	20	21	22
23	24	25	26	27	28	29
30	31	—	—	—	—	—

FEBRUARY
S	M	T	W	T	F	S
—	—	1	2	3	4	5
6	7	8	9	10	11	12
13	14	15	16	17	18	19
20	21	22	23	24	25	26
27	28	—	—	—	—	—

MARCH
S	M	T	W	T	F	S
—	—	1	2	3	4	5
6	7	8	9	10	11	12
13	14	15	16	17	18	19
20	21	22	23	24	25	26
27	28	29	30	31	—	—

APRIL
S	M	T	W	T	F	S
—	—	—	—	—	1	2
3	4	5	6	7	8	9
10	11	12	13	14	15	16
17	18	19	20	21	22	23
24	25	26	27	28	29	30

MAY
S	M	T	W	T	F	S
1	2	3	4	5	6	7
8	9	10	11	12	13	14
15	16	17	18	19	20	21
22	23	24	25	26	27	28
29	30	31	—	—	—	—

JUNE
S	M	T	W	T	F	S
—	—	—	1	2	3	4
5	6	7	8	9	10	11
12	13	14	15	16	17	18
19	20	21	22	23	24	25
26	27	28	29	30	—	—

JULY
S	M	T	W	T	F	S
—	—	—	—	—	1	2
3	4	5	6	7	8	9
10	11	12	13	14	15	16
17	18	19	20	21	22	23
24	25	26	27	28	29	30
31	—	—	—	—	—	—

AUGUST
S	M	T	W	T	F	S
—	1	2	3	4	5	6
7	8	9	10	11	12	13
14	15	16	17	18	19	20
21	22	23	24	25	26	27
28	29	30	31	—	—	—

SEPTEMBER
S	M	T	W	T	F	S
—	—	—	—	1	2	3
4	5	6	7	8	9	10
11	12	13	14	15	16	17
18	19	20	21	22	23	24
25	26	27	28	29	30	—

OCTOBER
S	M	T	W	T	F	S
—	—	—	—	—	—	1
2	3	4	5	6	7	8
9	10	11	12	13	14	15
16	17	18	19	20	21	22
23	24	25	26	27	28	29
30	31	—	—	—	—	—

NOVEMBER
S	M	T	W	T	F	S
—	—	1	2	3	4	5
6	7	8	9	10	11	12
13	14	15	16	17	18	19
20	21	22	23	24	25	26
27	28	29	30	—	—	—

DECEMBER
S	M	T	W	T	F	S
—	—	—	—	1	2	3
4	5	6	7	8	9	10
11	12	13	14	15	16	17
18	19	20	21	22	23	24
25	26	27	28	29	30	31

1995

JANUARY
S	M	T	W	T	F	S
1	2	3	4	5	6	7
8	9	10	11	12	13	14
15	16	17	18	19	20	21
22	23	24	25	26	27	28
29	30	31	—	—	—	—

FEBRUARY
S	M	T	W	T	F	S
—	—	—	1	2	3	4
5	6	7	8	9	10	11
12	13	14	15	16	17	18
19	20	21	22	23	24	25
26	27	28	—	—	—	—

MARCH
S	M	T	W	T	F	S
—	—	—	1	2	3	4
5	6	7	8	9	10	11
12	13	14	15	16	17	18
19	20	21	22	23	24	25
26	27	28	29	30	31	—

APRIL
S	M	T	W	T	F	S
—	—	—	—	—	—	1
2	3	4	5	6	7	8
9	10	11	12	13	14	15
16	17	18	19	20	21	22
23	24	25	26	27	28	29
30	—	—	—	—	—	—

MAY
S	M	T	W	T	F	S
—	1	2	3	4	5	6
7	8	9	10	11	12	13
14	15	16	17	18	19	20
21	22	23	24	25	26	27
28	29	30	31	—	—	—

JUNE
S	M	T	W	T	F	S
—	—	—	—	1	2	3
4	5	6	7	8	9	10
11	12	13	14	15	16	17
18	19	20	21	22	23	24
25	26	27	28	29	30	—

JULY
S	M	T	W	T	F	S
—	—	—	—	—	—	1
2	3	4	5	6	7	8
9	10	11	12	13	14	15
16	17	18	19	20	21	22
23	24	25	26	27	28	29
30	31	—	—	—	—	—

AUGUST
S	M	T	W	T	F	S
—	—	1	2	3	4	5
6	7	8	9	10	11	12
13	14	15	16	17	18	19
20	21	22	23	24	25	26
27	28	29	30	31	—	—

SEPTEMBER
S	M	T	W	T	F	S
—	—	—	—	—	1	2
3	4	5	6	7	8	9
10	11	12	13	14	15	16
17	18	19	20	21	22	23
24	25	26	27	28	29	30

OCTOBER
S	M	T	W	T	F	S
1	2	3	4	5	6	7
8	9	10	11	12	13	14
15	16	17	18	19	20	21
22	23	24	25	26	27	28
29	30	31	—	—	—	—

NOVEMBER
S	M	T	W	T	F	S
—	—	—	1	2	3	4
5	6	7	8	9	10	11
12	13	14	15	16	17	18
19	20	21	22	23	24	25
26	27	28	29	30	—	—

DECEMBER
S	M	T	W	T	F	S
—	—	—	—	—	1	2
3	4	5	6	7	8	9
10	11	12	13	14	15	16
17	18	19	20	21	22	23
24	25	26	27	28	29	30
31	—	—	—	—	—	—

1996

JANUARY
S	M	T	W	T	F	S
—	1	2	3	4	5	6
7	8	9	10	11	12	13
14	15	16	17	18	19	20
21	22	23	24	25	26	27
28	29	30	31	—	—	—

FEBRUARY
S	M	T	W	T	F	S
—	—	—	—	1	2	3
4	5	6	7	8	9	10
11	12	13	14	15	16	17
18	19	20	21	22	23	24
25	26	27	28	29	—	—

MARCH
S	M	T	W	T	F	S
—	—	—	—	—	1	2
3	4	5	6	7	8	9
10	11	12	13	14	15	16
17	18	19	20	21	22	23
24	25	26	27	28	29	30
31	—	—	—	—	—	—

APRIL
S	M	T	W	T	F	S
—	1	2	3	4	5	6
7	8	9	10	11	12	13
14	15	16	17	18	19	20
21	22	23	24	25	26	27
28	29	30	—	—	—	—

MAY
S	M	T	W	T	F	S
—	—	—	1	2	3	4
5	6	7	8	9	10	11
12	13	14	15	16	17	18
19	20	21	22	23	24	25
26	27	28	29	30	31	—

JUNE
S	M	T	W	T	F	S
—	—	—	—	—	—	1
2	3	4	5	6	7	8
9	10	11	12	13	14	15
16	17	18	19	20	21	22
23	24	25	26	27	28	29
30	—	—	—	—	—	—

JULY
S	M	T	W	T	F	S
—	1	2	3	4	5	6
7	8	9	10	11	12	13
14	15	16	17	18	19	20
21	22	23	24	25	26	27
28	29	30	31	—	—	—

AUGUST
S	M	T	W	T	F	S
—	—	—	—	1	2	3
4	5	6	7	8	9	10
11	12	13	14	15	16	17
18	19	20	21	22	23	24
25	26	27	28	29	30	31

SEPTEMBER
S	M	T	W	T	F	S
1	2	3	4	5	6	7
8	9	10	11	12	13	14
15	16	17	18	19	20	21
22	23	24	25	26	27	28
29	30	—	—	—	—	—

OCTOBER
S	M	T	W	T	F	S
—	—	1	2	3	4	5
6	7	8	9	10	11	12
13	14	15	16	17	18	19
20	21	22	23	24	25	26
27	28	29	30	31	—	—

NOVEMBER
S	M	T	W	T	F	S
—	—	—	—	—	1	2
3	4	5	6	7	8	9
10	11	12	13	14	15	16
17	18	19	20	21	22	23
24	25	26	27	28	29	30

DECEMBER
S	M	T	W	T	F	S
1	2	3	4	5	6	7
8	9	10	11	12	13	14
15	16	17	18	19	20	21
22	23	24	25	26	27	28
29	30	31	—	—	—	—

226

I. The Old Farmer's Almanac Great Americans Hall of Fame

Here, for the fourth year in a row, we offer a series of profiles of American men and women chosen for the impact they made on everyday life and for the force of their personalities in pursuing a dream. From Anne Hutchinson, banished by the Puritan fathers for her religious beliefs, to movie mogul Sam Goldwyn, who saw the possibilities in a new entertainment medium, these feisty characters add zest and meaning to our American heritage.

242

II. A Reference Compendium

1995 Great Americans
HALL OF FAME
by Lawrence Doorley

ANNE HUTCHINSON
(1591-1643): Free Thinker

In November of 1637, the General Court of the Massachusetts Bay Colony in Boston brought to trial a 46-year-old wife and mother of 14, Anne Marbury Hutchinson. Mrs. Hutchinson was found guilty of sedition and contempt and banished from the colony; in 1638 she was formally excommunicated from the Boston church.

Who was Anne Hutchinson? And what had she done to deserve such a fate? The woman who was called "the American Jezebel" by Governor John Winthrop was born in 1591 in the small town of Alford in Lincolnshire, England, and lived there for 43 years, the greater part of her life. Anne received an excellent education from her father, Francis Marbury, an Anglican minister; she was a brilliant pupil, schooled in the classics and well versed in the Bible and theology.

When she was 20, her father died, and shortly after, she married William Hutchinson, a prosperous Lincolnshire merchant. Babies arrived every year. Anne became a skilled midwife and herbalist, and one can well imagine the town women relying on her for strength and support.

Early in their married life, the Hutchinsons became followers of a clergyman in the neighboring town of Boston. John Cotton was making a name for himself as a brilliant theologian and eloquent preacher. His fame spread, and crowds flocked to his sermons, but Cotton constantly risked reprisals from the church authorities for his nonconformist views and unorthodox teachings. A constant theme was his belief that adherence to the ordinances of the Bible and a life marked by visible morality together were not enough to become one of "God's elect." It was equally necessary for an individual to be aware of the presence and workings of the Holy Spirit within himself, an acknowledgment Cotton called "the Profession of Grace." Over the years, Anne became one of his most fervent disciples, and she, too, embraced his doctrine — in time carrying it even further.

Dissent was in the air and nowhere more than in Lincolnshire. The county was home to many Puritans, but by 1630 the Crown and church authorities were becoming ever more repressive. That year, John Winthrop and other fellow Puritans set sail for New England, bringing with them their charter as the Massachusetts Bay Company. They were allowed to settle along the coast between the Charles and Merrimack rivers. The next year John Cotton joined them, his fine balancing act with the Anglican church having collapsed. In 1634 the Hutchinsons, 11 children, and other family members also embarked for a new life in Boston.

The Puritan founders of the Massachusetts Bay Colony sought to establish a community bound together in one common faith; to unite themselves into one congregation under Christ; to bind themselves to walk in all ways according to the rule of the Gospel. The ministers preached a personal reformation — a coming closer to God through godly conduct. This was their Covenant of Works. They had no desire to found a haven for dissenters (they were no longer in that category themselves); they desired unity above all. It was later said of them that they walked by the ordinances of God — as interpreted by themselves. But this intertwining of religious and civil life soon caused disaffection, many believing they had exchanged one autocracy for another.

Things went well at first for the Hutchinsons. Quite wealthy, they built a home near that of Governor Winthrop.

Anne, in time, gave birth to her 14th child and revived her practice of midwifery and herbalism.

Soon Anne began gathering the women into her home for the purpose of discussing and debating the Sabbath and lecture-day sermons preached by the town's ministers. Since women could not take part in the discussion groups held by the male members of the church and, in fact, held no offices whatsoever, these gatherings were at first considered rather harmless. But by 1636 Anne was holding forth twice weekly to a group of between 60 and 80 persons, which now included a sizable number of men, many of them prominent citizens, including the governor, Henry Vane. She began proselytizing her belief — the Covenant of Grace. To Anne, conformity with the religious laws and a display of good works did not signify godliness; true sanctifica-

Anne Hutchinson challenged the Puritan authorities over the knotty question of salvation — is it by works or by grace?

— Culver Pictures

tion came from the inner experience of the Holy Spirit. She gathered many converts and her fame spread.

By 1636 the colony was split down the middle. The Hutchinsonians, as they came to be called, scorned those ministers preaching the Covenant of Works, declaring them unfit to preach the Spirit since they lacked it themselves. Only John Cotton and Anne's brother-in-law, John Wheelwright, were deemed worthy since they embraced the Covenant of Grace. John Winthrop later said, "It began to be as common here to distinguish between men by being under the Covenant of Grace or the Covenant of Works, as in other countries between Protestants and Papists."

Both ministers and magistrates were furious at the presumption of this woman. They were also troubled because they perceived that such dismissal of the ordinances of the church to follow a personal quest for grace could render formal religion irrelevant. There was an added fear: Such dissension was a menace to the colony's welfare. England had already threatened to revoke the charter; divisiveness could cost them their independence.

Two events precipitated a showdown: the group's attempt to dismiss a minister of their church and the group's refusal to provide either arms or money for the colony's war against the Pequot Indians. Religious dissent had become civil disobedience. The authorities moved fast, silencing the movement with fines, disenfranchisement, and in some cases, banishment. Anne was brought to trial in November of 1637.

She gave a good account of herself for most of the trial, refuting their charges, matching quotes from the Bible to buttress her arguments. Her mentor, John Cotton, was supportive. But when it seemed she had won, she began to claim revelations from the Almighty: "If you go on in this course . . . you will bring a curse upon you and your posterity." That was enough. Claiming direct revelation was blasphemy; even Cotton sided with the majority. She was remanded to custody, pending banishment.

The next spring she was brought before a church court and, when she refused to confess her sins, was excommunicated. The court commanded her "as a leper to withdraw yourself."

Anne, William, their minor children, and some followers made the hazardous journey to Roger Williams's community in Rhode Island, and there they stayed until William Hutchinson's death in 1642. Then Anne and her children removed themselves to the Dutch settlement on Long Island Sound. In 1643 she and her family were killed in an Indian raid.

Anne Hutchinson occupies a hallowed place in American history. She was the first woman to advocate religious freedom, the first woman preacher. It was her misfortune to be brilliant and progressive in a society that sought conformity.

PETER COOPER
(1791-1883): The Good Rich Man

The 19th century spawned a pack of millionaires, some unprincipled, some unscrupulous, and most ruthless. But there was one shining light among them: Peter Cooper, widely revered as "The Good Rich Man."

Cooper began life in New York City on February 12, 1791, the son of poor parents. When he was still young, his family moved upstate to Peekskill, but Cooper returned at the age of 17 to become apprenticed to a carriage maker. To support his family, young Peter had been obliged to work and had managed only one year of formal education, but he had two untapped assets: a mechanical mind and an unquenchable thirst for education.

– photo courtesy Cooper Union

Peter Cooper's life ran from rags to riches to philanthropy.

gelatin. His wife took over the gelatin operation, mixed fruit with it, and sold it to the better stores in the city.

But Cooper was an anomaly for those days. He adhered to the Golden Rule, paid his employees more than the prevailing wage, treated all his workers with respect, and never went back on his word. He had a horror of debt, regarding bankers as Satan's henchmen. He never borrowed a cent.

Before long his glueworks was netting him the incredible sum of $100,000 a year. He invested in Manhattan real estate, sagely husbanding his resources during booms, waiting until the bottom of the inevitable slump to buy the land. He occasionally fell victim to con men, once paying $150,000 for a large acreage in Baltimore, the lure being that the Baltimore & Ohio Railroad planned to build its shops there. After buying B&O stock, Cooper later learned this was not true, but fate, which often favors the innocent, stepped in. Iron ore was found on the land. Cooper erected a smelter and did a fine business. He attributed his success to luck. "All through my life," he wrote, "good fortune smiled when things seemed darkest."

The B&O was in trouble. It had laid miles of track through rocky hillsides, but had been unable to design a locomotive to negotiate the sharp curves. Cooper went to work and designed the famous "Tom Thumb," the first American locomotive to run on an American railroad. The stock tripled in value. And fate wasn't finished. The smelter land

At night he read every book he could scrounge, in the meantime devising work-saving machines for his employer, who paid him a bonus for his inventions. His apprenticeship completed, he began work for a woolen manufacturer and invented a machine for finishing cloth. His employer gave him a one-third interest in the machine. He produced other work-saving appliances, and by the time he was 30, he had accumulated a nest egg of $3,500.

The panic of 1818-1820 caught many manufacturers overextended. Bankruptcies abounded, and when a bank offered a glueworks to Cooper for $2,000, he bought it. The factory became the foundation of his fortune. A new boom erupted in 1821, and the demand for glue exploded. Cooper, constantly perfecting the operation, soon developed additional products — foot oil, isinglass, and was now valuable real estate, and Cooper sold, taking stock in payment. Eventually he sold the stock for five times its original value. Once more Cooper credited "the purest of good fortune, not my own ability to imagine the future."

As the years passed, money rolled in. Cooper, a shy man, became a celebrity in New York. Always lamenting his lack of formal education, Cooper had resolved that if the Lord favored him with worldly goods, he would help impoverished children. To that end, he became a trustee of the public school system and spent endless hours examining the schools.

But Cooper's most cherished project was the Cooper Union, modeled after a free polytechnical school in Paris. He bought a large parcel of land between Third and Fourth avenues, and in 1859 the first class entered. There was no tuition; the only requirements were poverty and superior intelligence. But Cooper Union was more than a school. There was a spacious public reading room and library and a meeting room for writers, artists, and inventors. And in the Great Hall, New Yorkers heard free lectures from social reformers, scientists, poets, and politicians. "Mathew Brady [the photographer] and Cooper Union helped make me president," said Abraham Lincoln, whose 1860 speech in the Great Hall won him national recognition. U. S. Grant, Grover Cleveland, and Theodore Roosevelt also spoke in the hall, along with Mark Twain, Susan B. Anthony, and Horace Greeley.

At the age of 85, Peter Cooper ran for president as the candidate of the Greenback Party, which not only advocated the issuance of more paper money to benefit working men, but also supported a federal works program to aid the unemployed and strict regulations for railroads, trusts, and stock markets. The Greenbacks lost, but their ideas came to fruition with the election of FDR.

When Peter Cooper died at the age of 92, New York closed down for his funeral, honoring one of the greatest benefactors the city had ever known. Cooper Union is now 135 years old. Tuition is still $0.

HORACE MANN
(1796-1859): Educator and College President

Zealots are not known for their sense of humor. Life — and their cause — is a serious matter. Certainly there were few smiles and little laughter in Horace Mann's early days. Like so many of the poor New England farm boys who rose to prominence in the 19th century, he had a dismal boyhood. He was born on May 4, 1796, on the family farm in Franklin, Massachusetts, and though frail, he was expected to help with farm chores. His formal education was limited to a few weeks per year, for a mere six years, in one-room schools. But luck intervened in the form of an itinerant teacher named Barrett, who appeared at the impoverished farmhouse on a cold January night. He worked cheap — $4 a month, two meals a day, and a cot to sleep on. Horace's widowed mother, yearning to help her son, hired him. In six months this brilliant, eccentric scholar had tutored his pupil so thoroughly that when Horace applied to Brown University in 1816, he was accepted into the sophomore class with a scholarship.

He graduated at the top of his class in 1819 and later entered the Litchfield Law School. Admitted to the bar in 1823, he practiced in Boston and soon became one of the most prosperous lawyers in the city. He married Charlotte Messer, daughter of Brown's president, but his wife died two years later, and devastated, Mann withdrew from all activity.

Finally, friends persuaded him to run for a seat in the state's legislature. He

– photo courtesy Antioch College

Horace Mann's system of universal mandatory public education became the national standard.

It proved a formidable task. He soon realized that the system needed rebuilding from top to bottom. Schools were small, crowded, and shabby, town officials had neither time nor money to improve conditions, and many disillusioned parents tried teaching their children at home. Worst of all were the teachers. Young local females were hired for a pittance, and if they were not available, the town fathers hired the first itinerant to come along. A few, like Barrett, were excellent, but most were surly and ill-educated, hired more for their brute strength than for their academics.

A lesser man might have given up, but Horace Mann was a zealot. He spent the next 12 years visiting schools and gathering data. He visited every hamlet in the state, preaching the value of a good education. He appealed to the New Englander's instinct for turning a dollar. "For the creation of wealth, for the existence of a wealthy nation . . . ," he thundered, "intelligence is the grand condition." In plain words, educate them so they can qualify for the new jobs being generated by the Industrial Revolution.

won easily and spent six years in the House and four in the Senate, the last two as president. In the latter role, he pushed through a landmark education bill, since the dismal state of education in Massachusetts had become his chief cause. The bill established a state board of education and provided for the board to appoint a secretary of education at an annual salary of $1,000 with the secretary making yearly reports to the legislature.

To Mann's surprise, the legislature voted to make him the first secretary. To accept would mean the abandonment of his lucrative law career, but he didn't hesitate. Telling a friend, "Let the next generation be my client," he closed his office and set out to reform the educational system.

Opposition slowly succumbed. Bills were passed, more money was appropriated for education, and teachers' salaries increased. A minimum school year of six months was established; education was made universal and mandatory for all children up to the age of 16 (this latter was bitterly opposed by factory owners dependent on child labor). Mann kept all Massachusetts informed of the changes via his annual reports and Common School Journal. The system eventually became standard for every state.

Meanwhile, in 1843 Mann married Mary Peabody, one of the brilliant daughters of Dr. Nathaniel Peabody of Salem. It proved to be an idyllic May-December union. Mary became his confidante, counselor, and pal. She stood by him when the religious establishment insisted he was advocating a godless system simply because, while he agreed Bible reading should be permissible in public schools, he permitted no discussion of the readings.

The churches lost, and Mann, his mission accomplished, resigned his secretaryship. He was elected to Congress, but quarrelled with Daniel Webster, who later helped defeat his bid for election as governor of Massachusetts.

With Mary's support, he accepted the presidency of little Antioch College in Ohio, but unfortunately it was underfinanced and went bankrupt. But zealots never quit. Horace and Mary raced around the state raising money, and in two years the college was back in business. (Today it remains one of the nation's better liberal-arts colleges.)

The last battle took its toll. Weak and exhausted, Mann made one more speech at the college's baccalaureate services in July 1859. He ended it by saying, "Be ashamed to die until you have won some victory for humanity."

Less than three weeks later, having nothing to be ashamed of, Horace Mann died. Humanity honors him to this very day as "The Father of the Common School."

JOHN WESLEY POWELL

(1834-1902): Geologist, Ethnologist, Pioneer Environmentalist

"Go West, young man, and grow up with the country," wrote Horace Greeley in his *New York Tribune.* "If you go," countered John Wesley Powell, "be sure and take your water with you."

Millions heeded Greeley's advice. Lured by the promise of 160 acres of free land under the Homestead Act, bewitched by propaganda from the railroads and land speculators, they headed west like crusaders chasing the Holy Grail. No wonder that by 1890 the director of the census could report, "There can hardly be said to be a frontier any longer." The frontier as the inspiration for America's greatness was the theme of a speech given to the American Historical Association by Frederick Jackson Turner, a young history professor at the University of Wisconsin in 1893. Turner maintained that the West not only acted as a "safety valve whenever social conditions . . . tended to press on labor," but it also offered men unlimited opportunity for advancement and helped them develop a vibrant alliance of rugged individualism and nationalism.

John Wesley Powell agreed that the frontier had a profound influence on America. But he believed that, in the race to overtake it, too many wounds were inflicted. He insisted that eastern politicians neither understood nor cared that the West's arid landscape presented problems unknown in the East, and he railed against the nation's ruthless treatment of the native peoples.

John Wesley Powell was born on March 24, 1834, near Rochester, New York. His father was a circuit-riding preacher, an outspoken abolitionist, and a firebrand who frequently ignited opposition. Things got so hot that the family moved to Ohio, but the unpopularity of their abolitionist views forced young John to drop out of the local school and be educated by an eccentric fellow named George Crookham. Crookham had a houseful of natural history and ethnological specimens, and not only did he teach young Powell the classics, but the two also spent many hours on field trips collecting specimens.

Through the years the family continued to move, first to Wisconsin, then Illinois. In between helping to run the family farm, John Wesley pursued his studies, attending several colleges over a period of eight years while teaching at various elementary schools.

All the while, he made long trips into the wilderness, collecting specimens of plants, animals, and fossils. One spring he traveled the length of the Mississippi; a year later he went down the Ohio River. He began to attract attention as a naturalist, was sought out as a lecturer, and became secretary of the Illinois Natural Historical Society.

His own abolitionism undimmed, he volunteered at the outbreak of the Civil War. Seriously wounded at the battle of Shiloh, he suffered the amputation of his right arm above the elbow. Undaunted, he continued to fight in a dozen more bitter campaigns and attained the rank of major. After the war he returned to Illinois, taught at several colleges, and led expeditions to the Rocky Mountains to study the region's geology and collect specimens of flora and fauna.

An eastern journalist described him as "well-educated, enthusiastic, brilliant, resolute, a gallant leader." But those who have knowledge of Powell believe he is a historic figure because of his remarkable feat of traveling the entire length of the Colorado River from its headwaters through the Grand Canyon, a spectacular trip of 1,037 miles. The 1869 trip took 100 days, and Powell and his party of nine survived near-disaster many times. But all the adventurers agreed that "no matter how close we were to the heavenly gates, the Major made us beach our boats so he could climb up the canyon walls to take geological samples."

Intrepid explorer and visionary conservationist, John Wesley Powell was the first to truly focus on the needs of the West.

– photo courtesy U.S. Geological Survey

Powell was famous. He continued his western explorations, and in 1875 he was made director of the U.S. Geological and Geographical Survey, a mammoth project charged with surveying a huge area of the West and reporting on the natural resources. Powell's survey reached very different conclusions from those financed by the railroads and mining companies. He warned that, while the free 160 acres might be a profitable plantation in the well-watered East, out on the high plains, especially west of the 100th meridian, it could not even support a family, let alone produce a cash crop. Too little rain — only eight inches in good years — was the problem, and in drought years irrigation was absolutely necessary. And, wrote Powell in his famous "Report on the Lands of the Arid Region of the United States," under existing homestead laws, an upstream landowner could divert a waterway to irrigate his fields and leave nothing for his downstream neighbor. Powell warned that, without action, the best land could be taken by the railroad and mining companies, timber interests, and land speculators, leaving nothing for the small farmer for whom the Homestead Act had been designed. He predicted that unless the nation took extraordinary efforts to protect the High Plains, disaster was inevitable.

Congress did little but establish a new department, the National Bureau of Ethnology, and Powell accepted the directorship, hoping for a more propitious era. It came when Theodore Roosevelt became president. With Roosevelt and Gifford Pinchot, the new chief of the Forest Service, on his side, Powell renewed his efforts. Legislation was enacted protecting the small farmer's water rights, forcing the removal of barbed wire from government land, and taking back millions of acres from the speculators. Some tentative efforts were made

to improve the lot of native Americans.

Beset by ill health and in constant pain from his amputated arm, Powell died in 1902 at his summer home in Maine. By then over a million homesteaders were on farms in the West, but almost that many had returned east, broken by the droughts, winds, locusts, and bleak, frozen isolation. Many of the land reform measures became eroded over the years, resulting in the dust storms of the Great Depression, the fouling of the streams, and the scarring from open-pit mining.

The battle continues, but John Wesley Powell will be remembered as one who sought to preserve and protect the uniqueness and fragility of the western lands and to remind the nation of its role as guardian.

NIKOLA TESLA
(1856-1943): Unheralded Inventor

On a warm evening in May of 1917, a distinguished gathering of scientists, tycoons, and politicians assembled in the Engineers Club, New York City, to honor a world-famous inventor. Just before the awards ceremony, a slight hitch developed: The honoree had vanished. The chairman, long aware of the inventor's eccentricities, hastened to a nearby park and found him feeding the pigeons. The two men returned, and in his speech the chairman declared, "Were we to eliminate from our industrial world the results of our noble guest's work, the wheels of industry would cease to turn, our cities would be dark, our mills idle. . . ." It wasn't Thomas Alva Edison who was being honored, but his bitter rival, Nikola Tesla, and the award was the renowned Edison medal.

Tesla was born in a small village in Croatia and was given a fine education by his parents. At four he was writing poetry; by the age of eight he was a seasoned inventor. He graduated from the famous Austrian Polytechnic School at Graz where he was outstanding in two respects: He achieved the highest grades in physics and math, and at six feet six inches, weighing 148 pounds, he towered above his classmates like a beanpole.

Hired by the Budapest Telegraph Company as an electrical engineer, he made so many improvements that he was offered a position at Edison's telephone subsidiary in Paris. Tesla accepted, mainly because he had conceived of a rotating magnetic field, the basis of alternating current (AC), and was eager to present his findings to the company, which was using Edison's direct current (DC) system. While the executives were loath to incur Edison's wrath, they did give Tesla a favorable letter of recommendation when he announced his departure for America.

He arrived in June 1884 at a propitious moment. Edison's DC generating station was providing illumination to the Wall Street area and to several Fifth Avenue mansions. But Mrs. Vanderbilt was complaining of sparks flying from the chandelier, and J. P. Morgan was irate over the flickering lights in his library. Worst of all, the steam-driven dynamos on the SS *Oregon* had broken down. When Tesla arrived and launched into a fervent speech on the superiority of AC over DC, Edison cut him short and dispatched him to fix the ship's lighting plant.

– photo courtesy Westinghouse Electric Corporation

The ship sailed on time and Edison hired Tesla, giving him supervision of many research projects. But the match between Tesla, a cultured, educated genius, and Edison, an uncouth, rumpled genius with almost no formal education, was doomed from the start. Tesla could not convince Edison that alternating current, and not Edison's direct current, was the wave of the future. Under AC, high voltage could be transmitted hundreds of miles, then reduced using transformers. Direct current required generating stations every few blocks, an enormously expensive operation.

Finally, after Edison reneged on a promised bonus for the solution to a particularly difficult problem, Tesla left in a huff. But a group of Wall Street investors, alerted to the extraordinary po-

Child prodigy and inventive genius, Nikola Tesla became Edison's rival in the race to electrify the world.

tential of alternating-current electricity, offered to back him, and the Tesla Electric Company was formed. The battle between AC and DC was joined.

Meantime, another inventor in Pittsburgh, George Westinghouse, was building transformers that used AC, but he was unable to adapt motors to the system. Westinghouse persuaded Tesla to come to Pittsburgh and solve the problem. Though he came reluctantly (by now he had become a celebrity in New York), in ten months he had found the solution. Overwhelmed, Westinghouse dashed off a handwritten agreement guaranteeing Tesla $2.50 per horsepower of all future AC sold.

Back in New York, Tesla's celebrity status expanded. He plunged into a whirlwind of invention, dashed around addressing engineering societies, and found time to rush around the city, gathering up wounded pigeons, which he nursed back to health in his suite at the Waldorf Astoria. Had he wanted to keep elephants, the management would have consented. People were in awe of him, women swooned over him, and newspapers carried glowing copy about him.

Edison, furious at the attention being given Tesla, launched an all-out war. He hired a publicity firm to bombard the media with frightening statements about the dangers of AC, but Westinghouse intervened, explaining it was far less hazardous and far more efficient than DC.

Tesla's big chance came at the 1893 World's Columbian Exposition in Chicago. Westinghouse had got the contract to provide illumination, and he gave Tesla full authority to design and install all the equipment. When President Cleveland pressed the switch and the grounds were bathed in light, strong men cried. In the Electricity Building, Nikola Tesla, regal in tails, gave nightly exhibitions, closing the performance by standing calm as one million volts of electricity coursed through his gaunt frame.

Tesla and Westinghouse next harnessed Niagara Falls, converting the hydraulic power to electricity. That finished DC. By 1905 all generating stations were operating on AC.

Over the next decades, Tesla was a human dynamo, pursuing new schemes (some successful, some failures), envisaging dozens of revolutionary ideas — radio, solar power, and others. He was granted 800 patents, but while unscrupulous men made millions from them, he was too busy to sue. When he found that Westinghouse was denied financing because of his agreement to pay Tesla per horsepower of electricity, Tesla tore up the agreement.

His last years were sad. Royalties dried up and his reputation declined. Tesla died broke in his hotel room in 1943 at the age of 86. A bellboy, hearing the cooing of pigeons, found him.

Eight months after his death, the United States Supreme Court ruled that Nikola Tesla was the inventor of radio, just one of his extraordinary accomplishments. In 1993 a number of newspaper articles appeared commemorating the 100th anniversary of Chicago's Columbian Exposition. All told of the dazzling effect of the "new-fangled" electricity, but not one article mentioned Tesla's name.

SAMUEL GOLDWYN
(1882-1974): Pioneer Movie Producer

Sigmund Freud would have understood Schmuel Gelbfisz of Warsaw, Poland. But when Schmuel Gelbfisz became Sam Goldwyn, Freud would have diagnosed him as suffering from a combination of denial syndrome and an obsessive-compulsive personality, an attempt to obliterate all traces of Schmuel Gelbfisz while embracing all

– photo courtesy of the Academy of Motion Picture Arts and Sciences

Samuel Goldwyn, a born salesman, convinced the world that it needed movies.

England when he was 11, eventually reaching New York via steerage at the age of 13 (an immigration official named him Goldfish). He walked to Gloversville, New York, a town named for its product — gloves — and got a job in one of the factories. Eight years later he was the company's highest-paid salesman, and when a rival company offered him a job managing its New York office, he continued his meteoric career in gloves. He also acquired a wife.

Blanche Lasky and her brother Jesse were successful vaudeville producers. Blanche, a lawyer, was beautiful, and Sam, enthralled, mounted a furious campaign to win her. Blanche finally gave in and they were married in May 1910.

On a hot August afternoon in 1913, Sam happened to be passing one of the many nickelodeons that had sprung up to show the "flickers" (named because of the way the film frames jumped). He went in. Fifteen minutes later, he emerged transfixed. He had discovered a gold mine. By 1913 thousands of nickelodeons were operating in the country, showing one- and two-reel movies made by Edison and other early producers. Originally unbelievably crude, the flickers improved, and small buildings were thrown up to house them. These became the nickelodeons where the price of admission soon escalated to a dime, even 15 cents.

Sam hastened to tell Blanche that he was going into the movie business, but Blanche told him he was crazy. Similarly,

the accoutrements of the cultured rich.

It is too bad that Sam never consulted Freud. For though one of his famous aphorisms was, "Anybody who goes to a psychiatrist ought to have his head examined," he himself underwent years of therapy. The man who would be officially designated Samuel Goldwyn in 1918 by the Superior Court of New York State could never escape his earlier self. Time after time the laboriously acquired elegance, the well-honed urbanity fell victim to the illiterate, distrustful Gelbfisz.

Schmuel Gelbfisz was born in the Warsaw ghetto in 1882, but ran away to his impassioned story fell on Jesse's deaf ears, but it was hard to escape Sam's frenzied logorrhea, and Jesse, who had the money, finally gave in. The Lasky Feature Play Company was formed with a fourth partner, Arthur Friend.

None of the four partners knew a thing about making movies, so their first employee was an unemployed Broadway director named Cecil B. De Mille, also ignorant about movies. To learn the secrets of the business, De Mille was dispatched to spy on an Edison film crew, and after one day he reported back, saying, "If that's how they do it, I'll be knighted in a year's time."

Woefully undercapitalized at $15,000, it behooved the fledgling company to make a success of its first film. Goldfish, a functional illiterate, held out for quality, and it was agreed that *The Squaw Man*, a hit play several years old, would be ideal since it was a Western and could be filmed outdoors — appealing to a company that had no studio. De Mille and a small crew were dispatched to Arizona, but one look at Flagstaff and De Mille got back on the train and continued on to Los Angeles, where several movie companies were at work. They found Eden. De Mille rented a barn in a small community called Hollywood and set to work, and in 1914 Hollywood's first full-length movie opened in New York. *The Squaw Man* was a hit.

Sam was jubilant. He resigned from the glove company and wheedled 21 more stage plays from their owners. Jesse sold his and Blanche's interests in the vaudeville company and went west to run things there while Blanche, Sam, and Arthur handled business in New York. In one year the company had produced 21 movies and had run out of plays. Writers were hired, the payroll burgeoned, and by 1915, 80 actors were on the payroll.

But turmoil was Sam's middle name.

His ego demanded that he have the last word on everything, and in his frequent visits to Hollywood, he managed to antagonize everyone in the studio. He also made life hell for his partners. By 1916 they had had enough, voted him out, stripped him of all authority, and barred him from the movie lot. (Blanche divorced him soon after.)

Anyone but Sam Goldfish would have been crushed. Instead, adversity inspired him. He met with Adolph Zukor, an ex-fur salesman, whose Famous Players Company (including Mary Pickford, Douglas Fairbanks, and Charlie Chaplin) was, like the Lasky Company, concerned with the growing clout of the theater owners. He persuaded Zukor to a merger of the two companies and called together his three partners. "The physics has rose from the ashes!" he is reputed to have said. They reluctantly agreed that the phoenix had indeed risen.

Sam was given the figurehead title of chairman of the board, but he so antagonized Mary Pickford that she ordered the "bald-headed slob" removed. He was bought out for $900,000 and immediately formed another company with Edgar Selwyn which they called the Goldwyn Company. It would later become Metro-Goldwyn-Mayer — with Sam once more voted out.

By 1918 he had changed his name and was back in business in 1923 as Samuel Goldwyn Productions, Hollywood's only independent producer. For 50 years he made dozens of movies, some awful, some mediocre, some great. His greatest was the Academy Award-winning *The Best Years of Our Lives*.

Sam Goldwyn died in 1974 at the age of 91. He created a make-believe land and helped millions forget for a few hours what Freud called "the vile realities of life." Perhaps, in his own crazy way, Sam Goldwyn did as much good for humanity as Sigmund Freud did.

NELLIE BLY:

The World's Reporter (1867-1922)

Horatio Alger wrote a mountain of "rags to riches" books wherein unschooled guttersnipes zoomed to the top of the ladder and ended up with at least a junior partnership in the soap and tallow firm and the right to woo the owner's daughter. All the heroes were boys, but it wasn't all Alger's fault. The female of the species had little standing in the latter part of the 19th century, and women attempting to encroach on a man's world were subjected to harassment.

On a cold, dreary day in December 1884, in smoke-shrouded Pittsburgh, the quintessential Alger protagonist appeared at the office of the *Pittsburgh Dispatch*. Nearly penniless, with a widowed mother to support, and on the verge of eviction, this skinny waif had all the hallmarks of an Alger hero, except one — she was female. But Elizabeth Jane Cochrane, with a nimble mind and a good education, had ten times the moxie of Alger's fictional heroes.

Elizabeth Jane was born in Cochran's Mills, Pennsylvania, into a large family that lived well, even though her father died when Elizabeth was six. But over the years, the older children left, the money dribbled away, and finally she and her mother were reduced to working in Pittsburgh's factories for star-

vation wages. It was here that Elizabeth gained first-hand knowledge of the dismal plight of the working class, particularly children, girls, and women. She and her mother hit bottom in December 1884. There had been no work for weeks and the prospect looked hopeless.

But Elizabeth's lucky break came in the form of a column in the *Pittsburgh Dispatch*. The paper's resident curmudgeon, Erasmus Wilson, wrote that he was "sick of shameless women who seek to wrest from men those sacred prerogatives bequeathed to men from heaven." Furious, Elizabeth fired off a blazing letter to the editor, branding Wilson as a

Nellie Bly, satchel in hand, headed off around the world, November 14, 1889.

heartless misogynist, totally ignorant of the difficulties women faced in making a living. Signing it "Lonely Orphan Girl," she mailed it without a return address, but George Madden, the editor, was so impressed that he put an item in the paper requesting the "Orphan Girl" to come to the office for a discussion.

Elizabeth was there the next day, pulling out all the stops, overwhelming Madden with her impassioned tales of Pittsburgh's underclass and her qualifications to tell their stories. Impressed, Madden hired her at $5 a week, and since the few women reporters had to disguise their names, he christened her after the Stephen Foster tune, "Nelly Bly." The printer misspelled her name, and Elizabeth Jane Cochrane became Nellie Bly.

She was on her way. Her first article was on a seldom-discussed topic, divorce. The column set tongues wagging, but, pleased with Nellie's initial efforts, Madden allowed her to choose her own subjects.

In her next series of articles, Nellie followed factory girls from the time they entered the mills in "the bleak, gray dawn" until they collapsed into bed, "after midnight." What were they doing up after midnight? In Nellie's uninhibited, gossipy style, they were "catching a mash" — an encounter with an unattached male. Nellie defended the women, insisting that poverty and loneliness "drove the pathetic creatures to seek a moment's bliss."

Slippery politicians next felt Nellie's scorn, as did some factory owners for their inhumane treatment of employees. The Pittsburgh establishment became quite irritated with "meddlesome Nellie Bly," and the word was passed that she'd better be muzzled. Reluctantly, Madden assigned her to the opera, art exhibition, flower-show circuit. Nellie put up with it for nine months, then wheedled an assignment to Mexico as a foreign correspondent, covering the story of the "oppressed peasants who were once more trying to overthrow the brutal landowners." It took the furious Mexican authorities six months to discover who was sending those inflammatory dispatches to the U.S. Wisely, Nellie took the next train for El Paso.

Her Mexican dispatches had been featured in many city newspapers, and Nellie, flushed with triumph, was all primed to plunge right back into controversy. But this time she was kept under tight leash, assigned innocuous stories. Dreaming bigger dreams, Nellie accumulated a nest egg and then resigned, telling Madden she was "off to crash a New York newspaper, reform the world, fall in love, and marry a millionaire."

Nellie headed for New York and the most successful of the city's 12 newspapers, *The World*. In order to get an interview with the reclusive publisher, Joseph Pulitzer, Nellie had herself rowed out to his yacht, armed with dozens of her clippings. Pulitzer agreed to hire her at $20 a week, provided she could accept an assignment to cover the Women's Lunatic Asylum on Blackwell's Island by pretending insanity.

Nellie could and did. Posing as a deranged woman in a rundown lodging house, she managed to get herself committed, and through an intricate arrangement with confederates, sneaked out hair-raising stories about the deplorable conditions inside the madhouse. After ten days, near lunacy herself, she was rescued by the newspaper, which then ran the lurid headlines, front-page columns, and realistic drawings. New York was outraged. Politicians sprang into action, heads rolled, committees were appointed, and reforms were made. The paper's circulation soared, and Nellie was the talk of the town. She had herself arrested for shoplifting in order to describe conditions in the city's jails; she exposed "slimy mashers preying on innocent young girls," crooked employment agencies, illegal child-adoption schemes. She earned more and more money, but competition from copycat columnists soon exhausted the supply of scalawags.

So Nellie came up with the idea of racing around the world in an attempt to beat the record of Jules Verne's fictional Phileas Fogg in *Around the World in Eighty Days*. Pulitzer agreed, urging her to hurry because *Cosmopolitan* magazine was about to send its society editor, Elizabeth Bisland, on the same journey.

A single satchel in hand, Nellie sailed from New Jersey on November 14, 1889, on the White Star steamer *Augusta Victoria*. *The World* marked her progress in screaming headlines. She returned January 25, 1890, having circumnavigated the globe in 72 days via donkey, elephant, rickshaw, steamship, and dozens of other conveyances. New York went wild. (The Cosmo Girl came in three days later.)

Nellie wrote a book about her trip, then spent some years writing features for *The World*. Two of her goals accomplished, she then married a 72-year-old millionaire. She had reached the top. But a few years later her husband died, the business fell into bankruptcy, and Nellie fled to Europe. World War I broke out, and she became a war correspondent for the *New York Evening Journal*.

After the war, she returned to New York, worked as a columnist, and devoted time to the welfare of homeless children. Nellie died of pneumonia in 1922 at the age of 55, and her obituary appeared in newspapers across the country.

Her efforts to reform the world may have fallen a bit short, but Nellie Bly proved that a woman could indeed go outside her sphere and "wrest from men those sacred prerogatives bequeathed to men from heaven." □□

This year's nominees to The Old Farmer's Almanac Great Americans Hall of Fame join this illustrious company:

Jane Addams
William F. Allen
Johnny Appleseed
Francis Asbury
Benjamin Banneker
Irving Berlin
Mary McLeod Bethune
Clarence Birdseye
Nathaniel Bowditch
Mathew Brady
Luther Burbank
Rachel Carson
Emily Dickinson
Duke Ellington
Fannie Farmer
Stephen Collins Foster
Albert Gallatin
Joseph Glidden
Mother Jones
Chief Joseph
Mary Lyon
Barbara McClintock
Donald McKay
George Mowbray
Gifford Pinchot
Emily Post
Henry Martyn Robert
Knute Rockne
Margaret Sanger
Samuel Slater
Noah Webster
Paul Dudley White
John Greenleaf Whittier

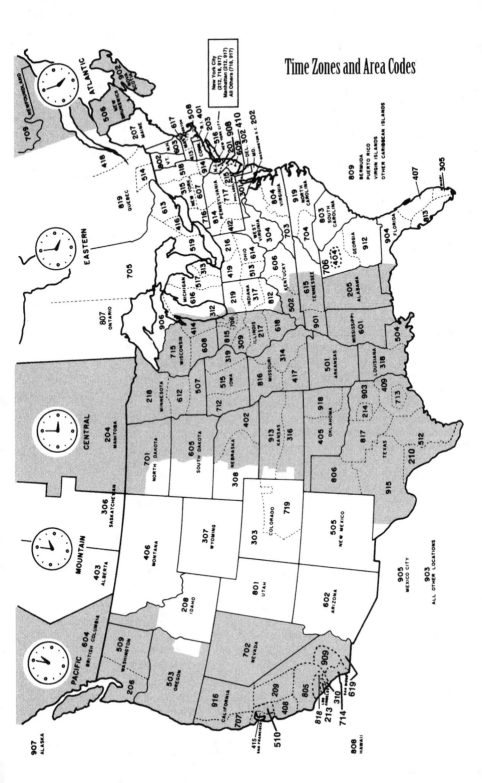

Time Zones and Area Codes

Abbreviations approved by the U.S. Postal Service to be used in addressing mail.

Alley	Aly.
Arcade	Arc.
Avenue	Ave.
Boulevard	Blvd.
Branch	Br.
Bridge	Brg.
Bypass	Byp.
Canyon	Cyn.
Cape	Cpe.
Causeway	Cswy.
Center	Ctr.
Circle	Cir.
Corner	Cor.
Court	Ct.
Courts	Cts.
Crescent	Cres.
Drive	Dr.
Estates	Est.
Expressway	Expy.
Extension	Ext.
Freeway	Fwy.
Gardens	Gdns.
Grove	Grv.
Heights	Hts.
Highway	Hwy.
Lane	Ln.
Manor	Mnr.
Place	Pl.
Plaza	Plz.
Point	Pt.
Road	Rd.
Rural	R.
Square	Sq.
Street	St.
Terrace	Ter.
Trail	Trl.
Turnpike	Tpke.
Viaduct	Via.
Vista	Vis.

Glossary of Almanac Oddities

Many readers have expressed puzzlement over the rather obscure notations that appear on our Right-Hand Calendar Pages (pages 53-79). These "oddities" have long been fixtures in the Almanac, and we are pleased to provide some definitions. (Once explained, it would seem that they are not so odd after all!)

Beware the Pogonip (December): The word *pogonip* is a meteorological term used to describe an uncommon occurrence — frozen fog. The word was coined by American Indians to describe the frozen fogs of fine ice needles that occur in the mountain valleys of the western United States. According to Indian tradition, breathing the fog is injurious to the lungs.

Cat Nights Begin (August): The term harks back to the days when people believed in witches. An old Irish legend has it that a witch could turn herself into a cat eight times and then regain herself, but on the ninth time — August 17 — she couldn't change back. Hence the saying, "A cat has nine lives." Since August is a "yowly" time for cats, this may have prompted the speculation about witches on the prowl in the first place.

Cornscateous Air (July): A term first used by the old almanac makers signifying humid, warm, damp air. While it signals ideal climatic conditions for growing corn, it also poses a danger to those affected by asthma, pneumonia, and other respiratory problems.

Dog Days (July-August): The hottest and most unhealthy days of the year. Also known as "Canicular Days," the name derives from the Dog Star, Sirius. In current almanacs, they are said to begin July 3 and end August 11 — the 40 days preceding the cosmical (at sunrise) rising of Sirius.

Ember Days (and Ember Weeks): The four periods set apart by the Roman Catholic and Anglican churches for special prayer and fasting and the ordination of clergy. The Ember Weeks are the complete weeks following 1) the First Sunday in Lent; 2) Pentecost (Whit Sunday); 3) the Feast of the Holy Cross (September 14); and 4) the Feast of St. Lucy (December 13). The Wednesdays, Fridays, and Saturdays of these weeks are the Ember Days — days marked for fasting. (The word *ember* is thought to derive from an old English term that refers to the revolution of time.)

Folklore has it that the weather on each of the three days foretells weather for three successive months — that is, in September Ember Days, Wednesday forecasts weather for October, Friday for November, and Saturday for December.

Halcyon Days (December): A period (about 14 days) of calm weather, following the blustery winds of autumn's end. The ancient Greeks and Romans believed them to occur around the time of the winter solstice when the halcyon, or kingfisher, was brooding. In a nest floating on the sea, the bird was said to have charmed the wind and waves so the waters were especially calm during this period.

Harvest Home (September): In both Europe and Britain, the conclusion of the harvest each autumn was once marked by great festivals of fun, feasting, and thanksgiving known as "Harvest Home." It was also a time to hold elections, pay workers, and collect rents. These festivals usually took place around the time of the autumnal equinox. Certain ethnic groups in this country, particularly the Pennsylvania Dutch, have kept the tradition alive.

Indian Summer (November): A period of warm weather following a cold spell or a hard frost. While there are differing dates for the time of occurrence, for 203 years the Almanac has adhered to the saying, "If All Saints brings out winter, St. Martin's brings out Indian Summer." Accordingly, Indian Summer can occur between St. Martin's Day, November 11, and November 20. As for the origin of the term, some say it comes from the early Indians who believed the condition was caused by a warm wind sent from the court of their southwestern God, Cautantowwit.

Midsummer Day (June 24): While it occurs near the summer solstice, to the farmer it is the midpoint of the growing season, halfway between planting and harvest, and an occasion for festivity. The English church considered it a "Quarter Day," one of the four major divisions of the liturgical year. It also marks the feast day of St. John the Baptist.

Plough Monday (January): The first Monday after the Epiphany (January 6); so called because it was the end of the Christmas holidays when men returned to their plough — or daily work. It was customary for farm laborers to draw a plough through the village, soliciting money for a "plough-light," which was kept burning in the parish church all year. In some areas, the custom of blessing the plough is maintained.

St. Luke's Little Summer (October): A spell of warm weather occurring about the time of the saint's feast day, October 18. This period is sometimes referred to as "Indian Summer."

Three Chilly Saints (May): Pancratius, Mammertius, and Gervatius, three early Christian saints, whose feast days occur on May 11, 12, and 13, respectively. Because these days are traditionally cold (an old French saying goes: "St. Mammertius, St. Pancras, and St. Gervais do not pass without a frost"), they have come to be known as the Three Chilly Saints.

Table of Measures

Apothecaries'

1 scruple = 20 grains
1 dram = 3 scruples
1 ounce = 8 drams
1 pound = 12 ounces

Avoirdupois

1 ounce = 16 drams
1 pound = 16 ounces
1 hundredweight = 100 pounds
1 ton = 2,000 pounds
1 long ton = 2,240 pounds

Cubic Measure

1 cubic foot = 1,728 cubic
   inches
1 cubic yard = 27 cubic feet
1 cord = 128 cubic feet
1 U.S. liquid gallon = 4
   quarts = 231 cubic inches
1 Imperial gallon = 1.20 U.S.
   gallons = 277.420 cubic
   inches
1 board foot = 144 cubic
   inches

Dry Measure

2 pints = 1 quart
4 quarts = 1 gallon
2 gallons = 1 peck
4 pecks = 1 bushel

Liquid Measure

4 gills = 1 pint
2 pints = 1 quart
4 quarts = 1 gallon
63 gallons = 1 hogshead
2 hogsheads = 1 pipe or butt
2 pipes = 1 tun

Linear Measure

1 foot = 12 inches
1 yard = 3 feet
1 rod = 5½ yards
1 mile = 320 rods = 1,760
   yards = 5,280 feet
1 nautical mile =
   6,076.1155 feet
1 knot = 1 nautical mile
   per hour
1 furlong = ⅛ mile = 660 feet
   = 220 yards
1 league = 3 miles =
   24 furlongs

1 fathom = 2 yards = 6 feet
1 chain = 100 links = 22 yards
1 link = 7.92 inches
1 hand = 4 inches
1 span = 9 inches

Square Measure

1 square foot = 144 square
   inches
1 square yard = 9 square feet
1 square rod = 30¼ square
   yards = 272¼ square feet
1 acre = 160 square rods =
   43,560 square feet
1 square mile = 640 acres
   = 102,400 square rods
1 square rod = 625 square
   links
1 square chain = 16 square
   rods
1 acre = 10 square chains

Household Measures

120 drops of water
   = 1 teaspoon
60 drops thick fluid
   = 1 teaspoon
2 teaspoons = 1 dessertspoon
3 teaspoons = 1 tablespoon
16 tablespoons = 1 cup
2 cups = 1 pint
2 pints = 1 quart
4 quarts = 1 gallon
3 tablespoons flour = 1 ounce
2 tablespoons butter = 1 ounce
2 cups granulated sugar
   = 1 pound
3¾ cups confectioners' sugar
   = 1 pound
2¾ cups brown sugar
   = 1 pound
3½ cups wheat flour = 1 pound
5⅓ cups dry coffee = 1 pound
4 cups cocoa = 1 pound
6½ cups dry tea = 1 pound
2 cups shortening = 1 pound
1 stick butter = ½ cup
3 cups cornmeal = 1 pound
2 tablespoons sugar = 1 ounce
2⅜ cups raisins = 1 pound
3½ cups walnuts (chopped)
   = 1 pound
9 eggs = 1 pound

8 egg whites = 1 cup
16 egg yolks = 1 cup
1 ounce yeast = 1 scant
   tablespoon
3 cups fresh, sliced peaches
   = 1 pound
60 pounds potatoes = 1 bushel
52 pounds onions = 1 bushel
24 pounds string beans
   = 1 bushel
56 pounds tomatoes = 1 bushel
55 pounds turnips = 1 bushel
54 pounds sweet potatoes
   = 1 bushel
45 pounds parsnips = 1 bushel
50 pounds carrots = 1 bushel
60 pounds beets = 1 bushel
60 pounds beans = 1 bushel
48 pounds apples = 1 bushel
196 pounds flour = 1 barrel

Metric

1 inch = 2.54 centimeters
1 centimeter = 0.39 inch
1 meter = 39.37 inches
1 yard = 0.914 meters
1 mile = 1,609.344 meters
   = 1.61 kilometers
1 kilometer = .62 mile
1 square inch = 6.45 square
   centimeters
1 square yard = 0.84 square
   meter
1 square mile = 2.59 square
   kilometers
1 square kilometer = 0.386
   square mile
1 acre = 0.40 hectare
1 hectare = 2.47 acres
1 cubic yard = 0.76 cubic meter
1 cubic meter = 1.31 cubic
   yards
1 liter = 1.057 U.S. liquid
   quarts
1 U.S. liquid quart = 0.946
   liter
1 U.S. liquid gallon = 3.78
   liters
1 gram = 0.035 ounce
1 ounce = 28.349 grams
1 kilogram = 2.2 pounds
1 pound avoirdupois = 0.45
   kilogram

Average Monthly Temperatures for Selected U.S. Cities

Daily maximum (**bold numbers**) and minimum averages in ° F.

	JAN.	FEB.	MAR.	APR.	MAY	JUNE	JULY	AUG.	SEPT.	OCT.	NOV.	DEC.
Mobile,	**59.7**	**63.6**	**70.9**	**78.5**	**84.6**	**90.0**	**91.3**	**90.5**	**86.9**	**79.5**	**70.3**	**62.9**
Alabama	40.0	42.7	50.1	57.1	64.4	70.7	73.2	72.9	68.7	57.3	49.1	43.1
Anchorage,	**21.4**	**25.8**	**33.1**	**42.8**	**54.4**	**61.6**	**65.2**	**63.0**	**55.2**	**40.5**	**27.2**	**22.5**
Alaska	8.4	11.5	18.1	28.6	38.8	47.2	51.7	49.5	41.6	28.7	15.1	10.0
Phoenix,	**65.9**	**70.7**	**75.5**	**84.5**	**93.6**	**103.5**	**105.9**	**103.7**	**98.3**	**88.1**	**74.9**	**66.2**
Arizona	41.2	44.7	48.8	55.3	63.9	72.9	81.0	79.2	72.8	60.8	48.9	41.8
Little Rock,	**49.0**	**53.9**	**64.0**	**73.4**	**81.3**	**89.3**	**92.4**	**91.4**	**84.6**	**75.1**	**62.7**	**52.5**
Arkansas	29.1	33.2	42.2	50.7	59.0	67.4	71.5	69.8	63.5	50.9	41.5	33.1
San Francisco,	**55.6**	**59.4**	**60.8**	**63.9**	**66.5**	**70.3**	**71.6**	**72.3**	**73.6**	**70.1**	**62.4**	**56.1**
California	41.8	45.0	45.8	47.2	49.7	52.6	53.9	55.0	55.2	51.8	47.1	42.7
Denver,	**43.2**	**46.6**	**52.2**	**61.8**	**70.8**	**81.4**	**88.2**	**85.8**	**76.9**	**66.3**	**52.5**	**44.5**
Colorado	16.1	20.2	25.8	34.5	43.6	52.4	58.6	56.9	47.6	36.4	25.4	17.4
Hartford,	**33.2**	**36.4**	**46.8**	**59.9**	**71.6**	**80.0**	**85.0**	**82.7**	**74.8**	**63.7**	**51.0**	**37.5**
Connecticut	15.8	18.6	28.1	37.5	47.6	56.9	62.2	60.4	51.8	40.7	32.8	21.3
Washington,	**42.3**	**45.9**	**56.5**	**66.7**	**76.2**	**84.7**	**88.5**	**86.9**	**80.1**	**69.1**	**58.3**	**47.0**
D.C.	26.8	29.1	37.7	46.4	56.6	66.5	71.4	70.0	62.5	50.3	41.1	31.7
Miami,	**75.2**	**76.5**	**79.1**	**82.4**	**85.3**	**87.6**	**89.0**	**89.0**	**87.8**	**84.5**	**80.4**	**76.7**
Florida	59.2	60.4	64.2	67.8	72.1	75.1	76.2	76.7	75.9	72.1	66.7	61.5
Atlanta,	**50.4**	**55.0**	**64.3**	**72.7**	**79.6**	**85.8**	**88.0**	**87.1**	**81.8**	**72.7**	**63.4**	**54.0**
Georgia	31.5	34.5	42.5	50.2	58.7	66.2	69.5	69.0	63.5	51.9	42.8	35.0
Honolulu,	**80.1**	**80.5**	**81.6**	**82.8**	**84.7**	**86.5**	**87.5**	**88.7**	**88.5**	**86.9**	**84.1**	**81.2**
Hawaii	65.6	65.4	67.2	68.7	70.3	72.2	73.5	74.2	73.5	72.3	70.3	67.0
Boise,	**36.4**	**44.2**	**52.9**	**61.4**	**71.0**	**80.9**	**90.2**	**88.1**	**77.0**	**64.6**	**48.7**	**37.7**
Idaho	21.6	27.5	31.9	36.7	43.9	52.1	57.7	56.7	48.2	39.0	31.1	22.5
Chicago,	**29.0**	**33.5**	**45.8**	**58.6**	**70.1**	**79.6**	**83.7**	**81.8**	**74.8**	**63.3**	**48.4**	**34.0**
Illinois	12.9	17.2	28.5	38.6	47.7	57.5	62.6	61.6	53.9	42.2	31.6	19.1
Indianapolis,	**33.9**	**38.2**	**50.0**	**62.4**	**73.2**	**82.3**	**85.6**	**83.8**	**78.0**	**65.8**	**52.2**	**39.2**
Indiana	17.2	20.3	30.9	41.2	51.6	61.1	65.4	62.9	55.8	43.4	34.4	23.1
Des Moines,	**28.1**	**33.7**	**46.9**	**61.8**	**73.0**	**82.2**	**86.7**	**84.2**	**75.6**	**64.3**	**48.0**	**32.6**
Iowa	10.7	15.6	27.6	40.0	51.5	61.2	66.5	63.6	54.5	42.7	29.9	16.1
Wichita,	**39.8**	**45.9**	**57.2**	**68.3**	**76.9**	**86.8**	**92.8**	**90.7**	**81.4**	**70.6**	**55.3**	**43.0**
Kansas	19.2	23.7	33.6	44.5	54.3	64.6	69.9	67.9	81.4	46.6	33.9	23.0
Louisville,	**40.3**	**44.8**	**56.3**	**67.3**	**76.0**	**83.5**	**87.0**	**85.7**	**80.3**	**69.2**	**56.8**	**45.1**
Kentucky	23.2	26.5	36.2	45.4	54.7	62.9	67.3	65.8	58.7	45.8	37.3	28.6
New Orleans,	**61.3**	**64.5**	**71.8**	**78.7**	**84.5**	**89.4**	**90.8**	**90.5**	**87.1**	**80.0**	**71.5**	**64.8**
Louisiana	44.1	47.1	54.2	60.9	67.5	73.0	74.9	74.8	71.7	61.8	54.1	47.6
Portland,	**30.3**	**33.1**	**41.4**	**52.3**	**63.2**	**72.7**	**78.8**	**77.4**	**69.3**	**58.7**	**47.0**	**35.1**
Maine	11.4	13.5	24.5	34.1	43.4	52.1	58.3	57.1	48.9	38.3	30.4	17.8
Boston,	**35.7**	**37.5**	**45.8**	**55.9**	**66.6**	**76.3**	**81.8**	**79.8**	**72.8**	**62.7**	**52.2**	**40.4**
Massachusetts	21.6	23.0	31.3	40.2	49.8	59.1	65.1	64.0	56.8	46.9	38.3	26.7
Detroit,	**30.3**	**33.3**	**44.4**	**57.7**	**69.6**	**78.9**	**83.3**	**81.3**	**73.9**	**61.5**	**48.1**	**35.2**
Michigan	15.6	17.6	27.0	36.8	47.1	56.3	61.3	59.6	52.5	40.9	32.2	21.4
Minneapolis-	**20.7**	**26.6**	**39.2**	**56.5**	**69.4**	**78.8**	**84.0**	**80.7**	**70.7**	**58.8**	**41.0**	**25.5**
St. Paul, Minnesota	2.8	9.2	22.7	36.2	47.6	57.6	63.1	60.3	50.3	38.8	25.2	10.2

	JAN.	FEB.	MAR.	APR.	MAY	JUNE	JULY	AUG.	SEPT.	OCT.	NOV.	DEC.
Jackson,	55.6	60.1	69.3	77.4	84.0	90.6	92.4	92.0	88.0	79.1	69.2	59.5
Mississippi	32.7	35.7	44.1	51.9	60.0	67.1	70.5	69.7	63.7	50.3	42.3	36.1
St. Louis,	37.7	42.6	54.6	66.9	76.1	85.2	89.3	87.3	79.9	68.5	54.7	41.7
Missouri	20.8	25.1	35.5	46.4	56.0	65.7	70.4	69.7	60.5	48.3	37.7	26.0
Butte,	28.5	33.9	39.9	50.4	60.3	70.2	80.1	78.4	66.4	55.5	39.3	29.4
Montana	5.0	10.0	16.7	25.9	34.0	41.7	45.7	44.0	35.1	26.4	16.0	5.5
Omaha,	29.7	35.0	47.6	62.4	72.8	82.4	86.5	84.0	74.9	64.0	47.7	32.9
Nebraska	11.2	16.6	27.8	40.3	51.8	61.4	66.5	63.8	54.7	43.0	29.7	15.9
Reno,	45.1	51.7	56.3	63.7	72.9	83.1	91.9	89.6	79.5	68.6	53.8	45.5
Nevada	20.7	24.2	29.2	33.3	40.1	46.9	51.3	49.6	41.3	32.9	26.7	19.9
Albuquerque,	46.8	53.5	61.4	70.8	79.7	90.0	92.5	89.0	81.9	71.0	57.3	47.5
New Mexico	21.7	26.4	32.2	39.6	48.6	58.3	64.4	62.6	55.2	43.0	31.2	23.1
Buffalo,	30.2	31.6	41.7	54.2	66.1	75.3	80.2	77.9	70.8	59.4	47.1	35.3
New York	17.0	17.4	25.9	36.2	47.0	56.5	61.9	60.1	53.0	42.7	33.9	22.9
Charlotte,	49.0	53.0	62.3	71.2	78.3	85.8	88.9	87.7	81.9	72.0	62.6	52.3
North Carolina	29.6	31.9	39.4	47.5	56.4	65.6	69.6	68.9	62.9	50.6	41.5	32.8
Bismarck,	20.2	26.4	38.5	54.9	67.8	77.1	84.4	82.7	70.8	58.7	39.3	24.5
North Dakota	-1.7	5.1	17.8	31.0	42.2	51.6	56.4	53.9	43.1	32.5	17.8	3.3
Columbus,	34.1	38.0	50.5	62.0	72.3	80.4	83.7	82.1	76.2	64.5	51.4	39.2
Ohio	18.5	21.2	31.2	40.0	50.1	58.0	62.7	60.8	54.8	42.9	34.3	24.6
Tulsa,	45.4	51.0	62.1	73.0	79.7	87.7	93.7	92.5	83.6	73.8	60.3	48.8
Oklahoma	24.9	29.5	39.1	49.9	58.8	67.7	72.8	70.6	63.0	50.7	39.5	28.9
Portland,	45.4	51.0	56.0	60.6	67.1	74.0	79.9	80.3	74.6	64.0	52.6	45.6
Oregon	33.7	36.1	38.6	41.3	47.0	52.9	56.5	56.9	52.0	44.9	39.5	34.8
Philadelphia,	37.9	41.0	51.6	62.6	73.1	81.7	86.1	84.6	77.6	66.3	55.1	43.4
Pennsylvania	22.8	24.8	33.2	42.1	52.7	61.8	67.2	66.3	58.7	46.4	37.6	28.1
Charleston,	57.8	61.0	68.6	75.8	82.7	87.6	90.2	89.0	84.9	77.2	69.5	61.6
South Carolina	37.7	40.0	47.5	53.9	62.9	69.1	72.7	72.2	67.9	56.3	47.2	40.7
Huron,	24.1	29.7	42.1	58.6	70.4	80.3	87.1	84.8	74.2	61.5	43.0	28.3
South Dakota	2.3	9.1	21.7	34.0	44.8	55.5	61.7	58.8	47.3	35.4	21.8	7.8
Nashville,	45.9	50.8	61.2	70.8	78.8	86.5	89.5	88.4	82.5	72.5	60.4	50.2
Tennessee	26.5	29.9	39.1	47.5	56.6	64.7	68.9	67.7	61.1	48.3	39.6	30.9
Houston,	61.0	65.3	71.1	78.4	84.6	90.1	92.7	92.5	88.4	81.6	72.4	64.7
Texas	39.7	42.6	50.0	58.1	64.4	70.6	72.4	72.0	67.9	57.6	49.6	42.2
Salt Lake City,	36.4	43.6	52.2	61.3	71.9	82.8	92.2	89.4	79.2	66.1	50.8	37.8
Utah	19.3	24.6	31.4	37.9	45.6	55.4	63.7	61.8	51.0	40.2	30.9	21.6
Burlington,	25.1	27.5	39.3	53.6	67.2	75.8	81.2	77.9	69.0	57.0	44.0	30.4
Vermont	7.5	8.9	22.0	34.2	45.4	54.6	59.7	57.9	48.8	38.6	29.6	15.5
Richmond,	45.7	49.2	59.5	70.0	77.8	85.1	88.4	87.1	80.9	70.7	61.3	50.2
Virginia	25.7	28.1	36.3	44.6	54.2	62.7	67.5	66.4	59.0	46.5	37.9	29.9
Seattle-Tacoma,	45.0	49.5	52.7	57.2	63.9	69.9	75.2	75.2	69.3	59.7	50.5	45.1
Washington	35.2	37.4	38.5	41.2	46.3	51.9	55.2	55.7	51.9	45.8	40.1	35.8
Charleston,	41.2	45.3	56.7	66.8	75.5	83.1	85.7	84.4	78.8	68.2	57.3	46.0
West Virginia	23.0	25.7	35.0	42.8	51.5	59.8	64.4	63.4	56.5	44.2	36.3	28.0
Madison,	24.8	30.1	41.5	56.7	68.9	78.2	82.4	79.6	71.5	59.9	44.0	29.8
Wisconsin	7.2	11.1	23.0	34.1	44.2	54.2	59.5	56.9	48.2	37.7	26.7	13.5
Cheyenne,	37.7	40.5	44.9	54.7	64.6	74.4	82.2	80.0	71.1	60.0	46.8	38.8
Wyoming	15.2	18.1	22.1	30.1	39.4	48.3	54.6	52.3	43.7	33.9	23.7	16.7

(courtesy Dr. Richard Head and National Climatic Data Center)

Beaufort's Scale of Wind Speeds

"Used Mostly at Sea but of Help to all who are interested in the Weather"

A scale of wind velocity was devised by Admiral Sir Francis Beaufort of the British Navy in 1806. The numbers 0 to 12 were arranged by Beaufort to indicate the strength of the wind from a calm, force 0, to a hurricane, force 12. This adaptation of Beaufort's scale is used by the U.S. National Weather Service.

Force	Description	Statute Miles Per Hour
0	Calm	less than 1
1	Light air	1 to 3
2	Light breeze	4 to 7
3	Gentle breeze	8 to 12
4	Moderate breeze	13 to 18
5	Fresh breeze	19 to 24
6	Strong breeze	25 to 31
7	Moderate gale	32 to 38
8	Fresh gale	39 to 46
9	Strong gale	47 to 54
10	Whole gale	55 to 63
11	Storm	64 to 72
12	Hurricane	73 or more

A Table Foretelling the Weather Through All the Lunations of Each Year (Forever)

This table is the result of many years' actual observation and shows what sort of weather will probably follow the Moon's entrance into any of its quarters. For example, the weather for the week following April 15, 1995, would be windy and rainy because the Moon becomes full that day at 7:09 A.M., EST.

Editor's note: *While the data in this table are taken into consideration in the yearlong process of compiling the annual long-range weather forecasts for* The Old Farmer's Almanac, *we rely far more on our projections of solar activity.*

Time of Change	Summer	Winter
Midnight to 2 A.M.	Fair	Hard frost, unless wind is south or west
2 A.M. to 4 A.M.	Cold, with frequent showers	Snow and stormy
4 A.M. to 6 A.M.	Rain	Rain
6 A.M. to 8 A.M.	Wind and rain	Stormy
8 A.M. to 10 A.M.	Changeable	Cold rain if wind is west; snow if east
10 A.M. to noon	Frequent showers	Cold with high winds
Noon to 2 P.M.	Very rainy	Snow or rain
2 P.M. to 4 P.M.	Changeable	Fair and mild
4 P.M. to 6 P.M.	Fair	Fair
6 P.M. to 10 P.M.	Fair if wind is northwest; rain if south or southwest	Fair and frosty if wind is north or northeast; rain or snow if wind is south or southwest
10 P.M. to midnight	Fair	Fair and frosty

This table was created more than 160 years ago by Dr. Herschell for the Boston Courier; *it first appeared in* The Old Farmer's Almanac *in 1834.*

Atlantic Hurricane Names for 1995

Allison	Felix	Karen	Pablo	Wendy
Barry	Gabrielle	Luis	Roxanne	
Chantal	Humberto	Marilyn	Sebastien	
Dean	Iris	Noel	Tanya	
Erin	Jerry	Opal	Van	

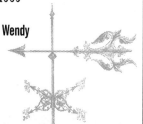

Wind/Barometer Table

Barometer (Reduced to Sea Level)	Wind Direction	Character of Weather Indicated
30.00 to 30.20, and steady	westerly	Fair, with slight changes in temperature, for one to two days.
30.00 to 30.20, and rising rapidly	westerly	Fair, followed within two days by warmer and rain.
30.00 to 30.20, and falling rapidly	south to east	Warmer, and rain within 24 hours.
30.20 or above, and falling rapidly	south to east	Warmer, and rain within 36 hours.
30.20 or above, and falling rapidly	west to north	Cold and clear, quickly followed by warmer and rain.
30.20 or above, and steady	variable	No early change.
30.00 or below, and falling slowly	south to east	Rain within 18 hours that will continue a day or two.
30.00 or below, and falling rapidly	southeast to northeast	Rain, with high wind, followed within two days by clearing, colder.
30.00 or below, and rising	south to west	Clearing and colder within 12 hours.
29.80 or below, and falling rapidly	southeast to northeast	Severe storm of wind and rain imminent. In winter, snow or cold wave within 24 hours.
29.80 or below, and falling rapidly	east to north	Severe northeast gales and heavy rain or snow, followed in winter by cold wave.
29.80 or below, and rising rapidly	going to west	Clearing and colder.

Note: *A barometer should be adjusted to show equivalent sea-level pressure for the altitude at which it is to be used. A change of 100 feet in elevation will cause a decrease of 1/10 inch in the reading.*

Is It Raining, Drizzling, or Misting?

	Drops (per sq. ft. per second)	Diameter of Drops (mm)	Intensity (in. per hr.)
Cloudburst	113	2.85	4.00
Excessive Rain	76	2.40	1.60
Heavy Rain	46	2.05	.60
Moderate Rain	46	1.60	.15
Light Rain	26	1.24	.04
Drizzle	14	.96	.01
Mist	2,510	.10	.002
Fog	6,264,000	.01	.005

States of the United States

State		State Nickname	Capital	Entered Union
Alabama	(AL)	Heart of Dixie State; Camellia State	Montgomery	Dec. 14, 1819
Alaska	(AK)	The Last Frontier State	Juneau	Jan. 3, 1959
Arizona	(AZ)	Grand Canyon State	Phoenix	Feb. 14, 1912
Arkansas	(AR)	Natural State; Land of Opportunity State	Little Rock	June 15, 1836
California	(CA)	Golden State	Sacramento	Sept. 9, 1850
Colorado	(CO)	Centennial State	Denver	Aug. 1, 1876
Connecticut	(CT)	Nutmeg State; Constitution State	Hartford	Jan. 9, 1788
Delaware	(DE)	First State; Diamond State	Dover	Dec. 7, 1787
Florida	(FL)	Sunshine State	Tallahassee	Mar. 3, 1845
Georgia	(GA)	Peach State; Empire State of the South	Atlanta	Jan. 2, 1788
Hawaii	(HI)	Aloha State	Honolulu	Aug. 21, 1959
Idaho	(ID)	Gem State; Spud State	Boise	July 3, 1890
Illinois	(IL)	Prairie State	Springfield	Dec. 3, 1818
Indiana	(IN)	Hoosier State	Indianapolis	Dec. 11, 1816
Iowa	(IA)	Hawkeye State	Des Moines	Dec. 28, 1846
Kansas	(KS)	Sunflower State; Jayhawk State	Topeka	Jan. 29, 1861
Kentucky	(KY)	Bluegrass State	Frankfort	June 1, 1792
Louisiana	(LA)	Pelican State; Creole State	Baton Rouge	Apr. 30, 1812
Maine	(ME)	Pine Tree State	Augusta	Mar. 15, 1820
Maryland	(MD)	Old Line State; Free State	Annapolis	Apr. 28, 1788
Massachusetts	(MA)	Bay State; Old Colony	Boston	Feb. 6, 1788
Michigan	(MI)	Great Lake State; Wolverine State	Lansing	Jan. 26, 1837
Minnesota	(MN)	North Star State; Gopher State	St. Paul	May 11, 1858
Mississippi	(MS)	Magnolia State	Jackson	Dec. 10, 1817
Missouri	(MO)	Show-Me State	Jefferson City	Aug. 10, 1821
Montana	(MT)	Treasure State	Helena	Nov. 8, 1889
Nebraska	(NE)	Cornhusker State; Beef State	Lincoln	Mar. 1, 1867
Nevada	(NV)	Sagebrush State; Battle-Born State	Carson City	Oct. 31, 1864
New Hampshire	(NH)	Granite State	Concord	June 21, 1788
New Jersey	(NJ)	Garden State	Trenton	Dec. 18, 1787
New Mexico	(NM)	Land of Enchantment; Sunshine State	Santa Fe	Jan. 6, 1912
New York	(NY)	Empire State	Albany	July 26, 1788
North Carolina	(NC)	Tar Heel State; Old North State	Raleigh	Nov. 21, 1789
North Dakota	(ND)	Peace Garden State	Bismarck	Nov. 2, 1889
Ohio	(OH)	Buckeye State	Columbus	Mar. 1, 1803
Oklahoma	(OK)	Sooner State	Oklahoma City	Nov. 16, 1907
Oregon	(OR)	Beaver State	Salem	Feb. 14, 1859
Pennsylvania	(PA)	Keystone State	Harrisburg	Dec. 12, 1787
Rhode Island	(RI)	Ocean State; Little Rhody	Providence	May 29, 1790
South Carolina	(SC)	Palmetto State	Columbia	May 23, 1788
South Dakota	(SD)	Coyote State; Rushmore State	Pierre	Nov. 2, 1889

States of the United States

State		State Nickname	Capital	Entered Union
Tennessee	(TN)	Volunteer State	Nashville	June 1, 1796
Texas	(TX)	Lone Star State	Austin	Dec. 29, 1845
Utah	(UT)	Beehive State	Salt Lake City	Jan. 4, 1896
Vermont	(VT)	Green Mountain State	Montpelier	Mar. 4, 1791
Virginia	(VA)	Old Dominion	Richmond	June 25, 1788
Washington	(WA)	Evergreen State	Olympia	Nov. 11, 1889
West Virginia	(WV)	Mountain State	Charleston	June 20, 1863
Wisconsin	(WI)	Badger State	Madison	May 29, 1848
Wyoming	(WY)	Equality State	Cheyenne	July 10, 1890

The Sequence of Presidential Succession

1. Vice President
2. Speaker of the House
3. President Pro Tempore of the Senate
4. Secretary of State
5. Secretary of the Treasury
6. Secretary of Defense
7. Attorney General
8. Secretary of the Interior
9. Secretary of Agriculture
10. Secretary of Commerce
11. Secretary of Labor
12. Secretary of Health and Human Services
13. Secretary of Housing and Urban Development
14. Secretary of Transportation
15. Secretary of Energy
16. Secretary of Education

The Golden Rule *(It's True in All Faiths)*

BRAHMANISM:
This is the sum of duty:
Do naught unto others
which would cause you pain
if done to you.
Mahabharata 5:1517

BUDDHISM:
Hurt not others in ways that
you yourself would find
hurtful.
Udana-Varga 5:18

CONFUCIANISM:
Surely it is the maxim
of loving-kindness: Do
not unto others what you
would not have them
do unto you.
Analects 15:23

TAOISM:
Regard your neighbor's
gain as your own gain and
your neighbor's loss as
your own loss.
T'ai Shang Kan Ying P'ien

ZOROASTRIANISM:
That nature alone is good
which refrains from doing
unto another whatsoever is
not good for itself.
Dadistan-i-dinik 94:5

JUDAISM:
What is hateful to you, do
not to your fellowman. That
is the entire Law; all the rest
is commentary.
Talmud, Shabbat 31a

CHRISTIANITY:
All things whatsoever ye
would that men should do to
you, do ye even so to them;
for this is the law and the
prophets.
Matthew 7:12

ISLAM:
No one of you is a believer
until he desires for his
brother that which he
desires for himself.
Sunnah

– courtesy of
Elizabeth Pool

Gestation and Mating Table

	Proper age for first mating	Period of fertility, in years	No. of females for one male	Period of gestation in days Range	Average
Ewe	90 lbs. or 1 yr.	6		142-154	147 / 151[8]
Ram	12-14 mos., well matured	7	50-75[2] / 35-40[3]		
Mare	3 yrs.	10-12		310-370	336
Stallion	3 yrs.	12-15	40-45[4] / Record 252[5]		
Cow	15-18 mos.[1]	10-14		279-290[6] 262-300[7]	283
Bull	1 yr., well matured	10-12	50[4] / Thousands[5]		
Sow	5-6 mos. or 250 lbs.	6		110-120	115
Boar	250-300 lbs.	6	50[2] / 35-40[3]		
Doe goat	10 mos. or 85-90 lbs.	6		145-155	150
Buck goat	Well matured	5	30		
Bitch	16-18 mos.	8		58-67	63
Male dog	12-16 mos.	8			
She cat	12 mos.	6		60-68	63
Doe rabbit	6 mos.	5-6		30-32	31
Buck rabbit	6 mos.	5-6	30		

[1]Holstein & Beef: 750 lbs.; Jersey: 500 lbs. [2]Handmated. [3]Pasture. [4]Natural. [5]Artificial. [6]Beef; 8-10 days shorter for Angus. [7]Dairy. [8]For fine wool breeds.

Bird and Poultry Incubation Periods, in Days

Chicken......21	Goose......30-34	Guinea........26-28
Turkey.......28	Swan.............42	Canary.......14-15
Duck 26-32	Pheasant ..22-24	Parakeet 18-20

Gestation Periods, Wild Animals, in Days

Black bear...................210	Seal............................330
Hippo 225-250	Squirrel, gray............44
Moose 240-250	Whale, sperm 480
Otter.....................270-300	Wolf 60-63
Reindeer..............210-240	

Maximum Life Spans of Animals in Capitivity, in Years

Box Turtle	Elephant 84	Oyster
(Eastern) 138	Giant Tortoise 190	(Freshwater) 80
Bullfrog 16	Giraffe....................28	Pig 10
Camel 25	Goat 17	Polar Bear 41
Cat (Domestic) 23	Gorilla....................33	Rabbit......................13
Cheetah..................16	Grizzly Bear 31	Rattlesnake............20
Chicken 14	Horse	Reindeer...............15
Chimpanzee...........37	(Domestic) 50	Sea Lion 28
Cow........................20	Kangaroo...............16	Sheep......................20
Dog (Domestic) 22	Lion 30	Tiger.......................25
Dolphin 30	Moose 20	Timber Wolf 15
Eagle......................55	Owl.........................68	Toad........................36
		Zebra 25

	Recurs if not bred	Estrual cycle incl. heat period (days)		In heat for		Usual time of ovulation
	Days	Ave.	Range	Ave.	Range	
Mare	21	21	10-37	5-6 days	2-11 days	24-48 hours before end of estrus
Sow	21	21	18-24	2-3 days	1-5 days	30-36 hours after start of estrus
Ewe	16½	16½	14-19	30 hours	24-32 hours	12-24 hours before end of estrus
Goat	21	21	18-24	2-3 days	1-4 days	Near end of estrus
Cow	21	21	18-24	18 hours	10-24 hours	10-12 hours after end of estrus
Bitch	pseudo-pregnancy	24		7 days	5-9 days	1-3 days after first acceptance
Cat	pseudo-pregnancy		15-21	3-4 if mated	9-10 days in absence of male	24-56 hours after coitus

Manure Guide

Type of Manure	Water Content	Primary Nutrients (pounds per ton)		
		Nitrogen	Phosphate	Potash
Cow, horse	60%-80%	12-14	5-9	9-12
Sheep, pig, goat	65%-75%	10-21	7	13-19
Chicken: Wet, sticky, and caked	75%	30	20	10
Moist, crumbly to sticky	50%	40	40	20
Crumbly	30%	60	55	30
Dry	15%	90	70	40
Ashed	none		135	100

Type of Garden	Best Type of Manure	Best Time to Apply
Flower	cow, horse	early spring
Vegetable	chicken, cow, horse	fall, spring
Potato or root crop	cow, horse	fall
Acid-loving plants (blueberries, azaleas, mountain laurel, rhododendrons)	cow, horse	early fall or not at all

Plants That Attract Butterflies

Aster	Aster
Bee Balm	Monarda
Butterfly Bush	Buddleia
Daylily	Hemerocallis
False Indigo	Baptisia
Floss Flower	Ageratum
Goldenrod	Solidago
Hollyhock	Alcea
Honeysuckle	Lonicera
Lilac	Syringa
Lupine	Lupinus
Mallow	Malva
Milkweed	Asclepias
Mint	Mentha
Pansy	Viola
Phlox	Phlox
Privet	Ligustrum
Purple Coneflower	Echinacea
Rock Cress	Arabis
Sage	Salvia
Shasta Daisy	Chrysanthemum
Snapdragon	Antirrhinum
Sweet Alyssum	Lobularia
Tickseed	Coreopsis
Zinnia	Zinnia

How Long Household Items Last

Item	Years (Approx. Averages)	Item	Years (Approx. Averages)
Electric Shavers	4	Blenders	8
Personal Computers	6	Room Air-Conditioners	9
Lawn Mowers	6	Vacuum Cleaners	10
Automatic Coffee Makers	6	Microwave Ovens	10
VCRs	6	Dishwashers	11
Food Processors	7	Dehumidifiers	12
Electric Can Openers	7	Washing Machines	13
CD Players	7	Electric Dryers	13
Camcorders	7	Refrigerators	14
Toasters	8	Gas Dryers	14
Stereo Receivers	8	Electric Ranges	15
Color TV sets	8	Gas Ranges	18

The life span of a product doesn't depend only on its actual durability but also on your desire for some new convenience found only on a new model.

— courtesy Consumer Reports

Full Moon Names

The native Indians of what are now the northern and eastern United States kept track of the seasons by distinctive names given to each recurring full Moon, these names being applied to the entire month in which it occurred. With some variations, the same Moon names were used throughout the Algonquin tribes from New England to Lake Superior.

Name	Month	Other Names Used
Full Wolf Moon	January	Full Old Moon
Full Snow Moon	February	Full Hunger Moon
Full Worm Moon	March	Full Crow Moon, Full Crust Moon, Full Sugar Moon, Full Sap Moon
Full Pink Moon	April	Full Sprouting Grass Moon, Full Egg Moon, Full Fish Moon
Full Flower Moon	May	Full Corn Planting Moon, Full Milk Moon
Full Strawberry Moon	June	Full Rose Moon, Full Hot Moon
Full Buck Moon	July	Full Thunder Moon, Full Hay Moon
Full Sturgeon Moon	August	Full Red Moon, Full Green Corn Moon
Full Harvest Moon*	September	Full Corn Moon
Full Hunter's Moon	October	Full Travel Moon, Full Dying Grass Moon
Full Beaver Moon	November	Full Frost Moon
Full Cold Moon	December	Full Long Nights Moon

* The Harvest Moon is always the full Moon closest to the autumnal equinox. If it occurs in October, the September full Moon is usually called the Corn Moon.

Phases of the Moon

NEW   FIRST   FULL   LAST   NEW

W a x i n g   W a n i n g

Composition of the Moon and Earth

	Oxide	Moon (Estimated)	Earth's Crust
Silicon	SiO_2	43.3 - 48.7 %	45.0%
Magnesium	MgO	25.3 - 33.4	6.8
Iron	FeO	11.3 - 13.9	6.6
Aluminum	Al_2O_3	3.7 - 7.6	24.6
Calcium	CaO	3.4 - 6.1	15.8
Chromium	Cr_2O_3	0.3 - 0.4	0.1
Titanium	TiO_2	0.2 - 0.4	0.6
Sodium	Na_2O	0.005 - 0.15	0.5
Potassium	K_2O	0.01	0.1

Source: *The Geology of the Terrestrial Planets*, NASA, 1984

Safe Ice Thickness *

Ice Thickness	Permissible load
2 inches	one person on foot
3 inches	group in single file
7½ inches	passenger car (2-ton gross)
8 inches	light truck (2½-ton gross)
10 inches	medium truck (3½-ton gross)
12 inches	heavy truck (8-ton gross)
15 inches	10 tons
20 inches	25 tons
30 inches	70 tons
36 inches	110 tons

* Solid clear blue/black pond and lake ice

☞ Slush ice has only one-half the strength of blue ice.

☞ Strength value of river ice is 15 percent less.

Source: *American Pulpwood Association*

The Greek Alphabet

α	alpha	ν	nu
β	beta	ξ	xi
γ	gamma	ο	omicron
δ	delta	π	pi
ε	epsilon	ρ	rho
ζ	zeta	σ	sigma
η	eta	τ	tau
θ	theta	υ	upsilon
ι	iota	φ	phi
κ	kappa	χ	chi
λ	lambda	ψ	psi
μ	mu	ω	omega

How to Find the Day of the Week for Any Given Date

To compute the day of the week for any given date as far back as the mid-18th century, proceed as follows:

Add the last two digits of the year to one-quarter of the last two digits (discard any remainder if it doesn't come out even), the given date, and the month key from the key-box below. Divide the sum by seven; the number left over is the day of the week (one is Sunday, two is Monday, and so on). If it comes out even, the day is Saturday. If you go back before 1900, add two to the sum before dividing; before 1800, add four; and so on. Don't go back before 1753.

Example: **The Dayton Flood was on Tuesday, March 25, 1913.**

Last two digits of year:	13
One-quarter of these two digits:	3
Given day of month:	25
Key number for March:	4
Sum:	45

45/7 = 6, with a remainder of 3. The flood took place on Tuesday, the third day of the week.

KEY

Jan.	1
leap yr.	0
Feb.	4
leap yr.	3
Mar.	4
Apr.	0
May	2
June	5
July	0
Aug.	3
Sept.	6
Oct.	1
Nov.	4
Dec.	6

Suggestions for 30 people.
Choose your favorites.

M E N U

Hors d'Oeuvres:

5 bags of chips
3 pounds of cheese
1½ pounds of crackers
3 pounds nuts
5 cups dip
7 pounds mixed raw vegetables
200 finger foods (frankfurters, shrimp, or cocktail sandwiches)

Dinner Suggestions:

5 loaves of bread
1 pound butter or margarine
5 heads of lettuce
8 tomatoes
4 large cucumbers
3 bottles of salad dressing
15 pounds meat (with bone)
7½ pounds boneless meat
15 pounds poultry (with bone)
7½ pounds fish fillets
2 pounds pasta
8 cups rice
8 pounds any vegetable

Desserts:

8 pounds mixed fruit
3 cakes or 5 pies
90 cookies
5 quarts ice cream

Where to Find Vitamins in Your Daily Diet

Vitamin A
Sources: Milk, eggs, liver, cheese, fish oil, yellow fruits, and dark green and yellow vegetables.

Vitamin C
Sources: Citrus fruits and juices, berries, tomatoes, peppers, broccoli, potatoes, kale, cauliflower, cantaloupe, and brussels sprouts.

Vitamin D
Sources: Fish, fish oils, milk, dairy products, and fortified margarine.

Vitamin E
Sources: Vegetable oils, nuts, margarine, soybeans, asparagus, olives, wheat germ, and leafy greens.

Thiamin (B_1)
Sources: Whole grains, brewer's yeast, bran, most vegetables, nuts, beans, liver, and fish.

Riboflavin (B_2)
Sources: Dairy products, liver, meat, poultry, fish, eggs, beans, leafy greens, and enriched grain products.

Niacin (B_3)
Sources: Fish, poultry, peanuts, dairy products, brewer's yeast, and liver.

B_6 (pyridoxine)
Sources: Whole grains, brewer's yeast, wheat germ, bananas, beans, nuts, liver, fish, and poultry.

B_{12} (cyanocobalamin)
Sources: Liver, beef, pork, poultry, shellfish, eggs, milk, cheese, and fortified cereals.

Folacin (folic acid)
Sources: Deep green leafy greens, wheat germ, liver, beans, whole grains, citrus fruits and juices, avocados, and asparagus.

Biotin
Sources: Eggs, liver, brewer's yeast, milk, bananas, and whole grains.

Pantothenic acid (B_5)
Sources: Whole grains, beans, milk, eggs, liver, and nuts.